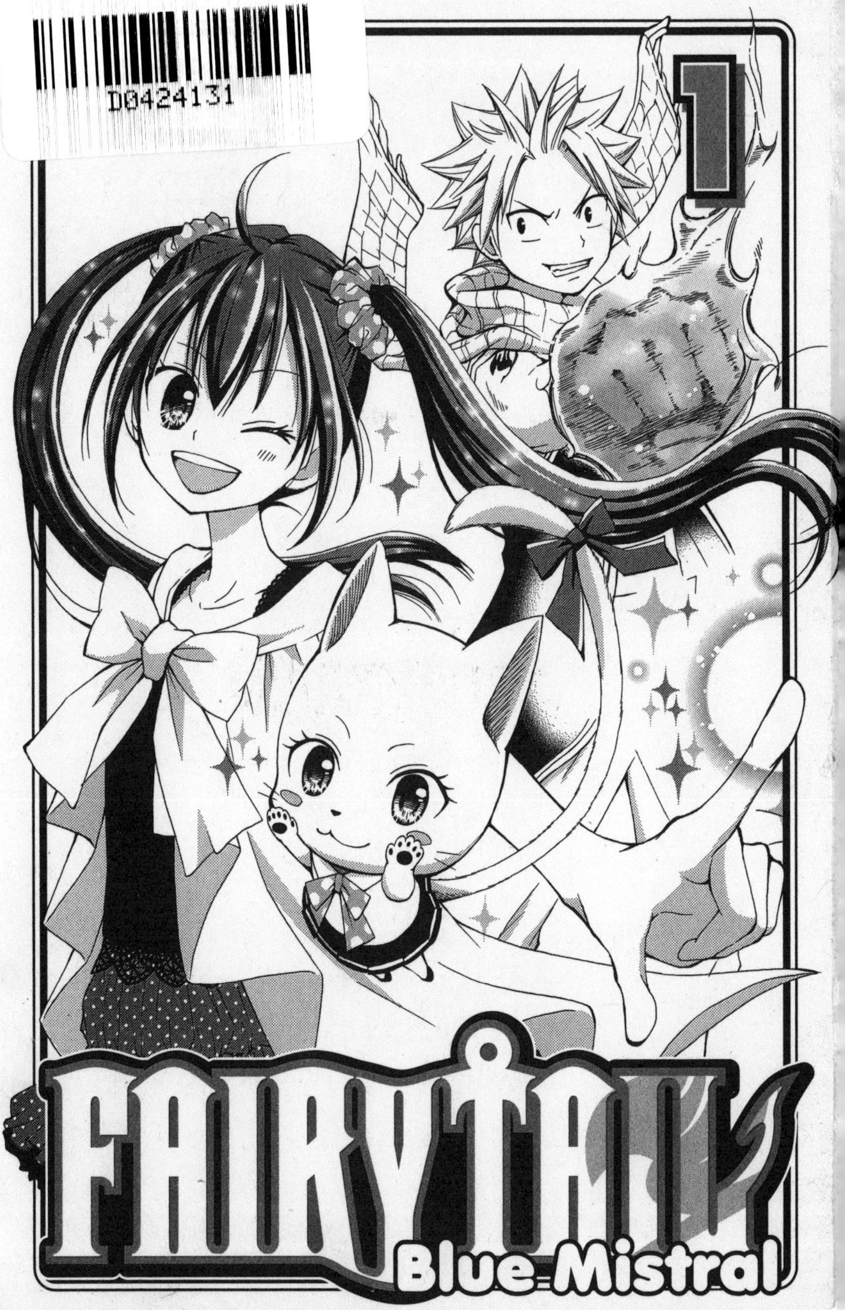
1
FAIRY TAIL
Blue Mistral

FAIRY TAIL Blue Mistral

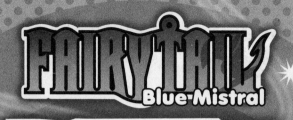

Dragon Slayer Magic...

It is accomplished by allowing your own body to take on aspects of a dragon.

It is an Ancient Spell.

There once appeared a young girl who could perform Dragon Slayer Magic!

And that power could shake the sky and cause the ground to tremble...

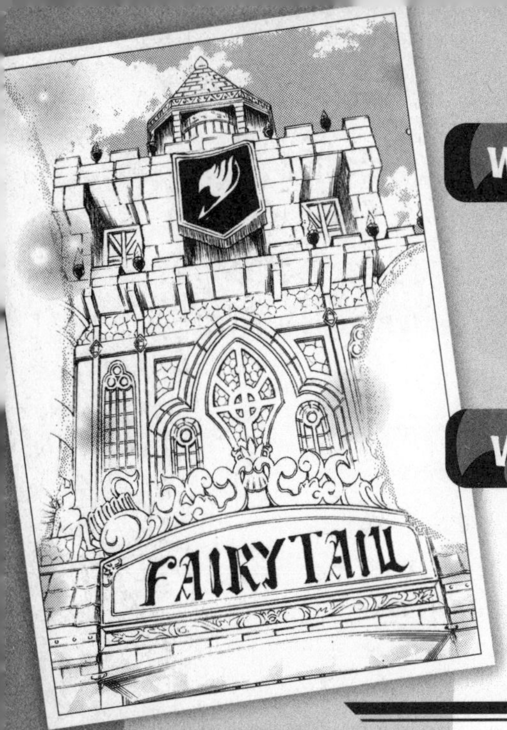
FAIRY TAIL

The World Where This Story Takes Place

What is FAIRY TAIL?

It's the guild that Wendy and Carla are in. They call it the most powerful guild in the Kingdom of Fiore.

What is A GUILD?

It's a place where wizards gather. The guild is where the wizards get information on jobs they can take on.

Main Characters

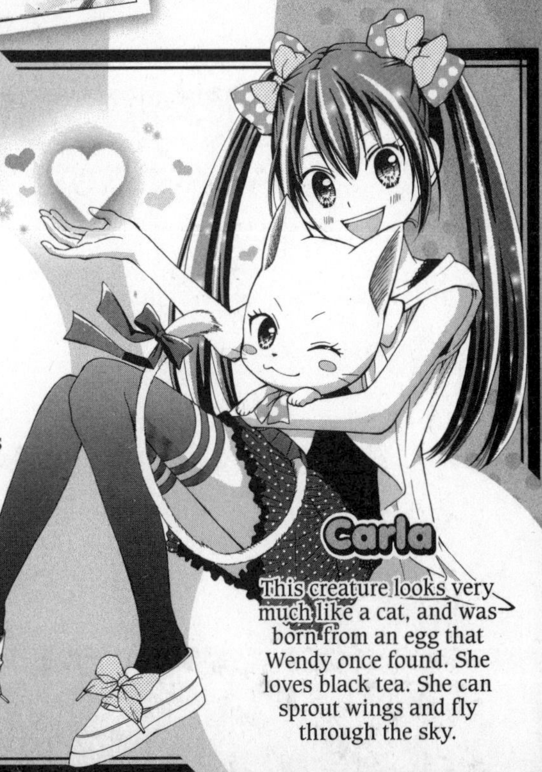

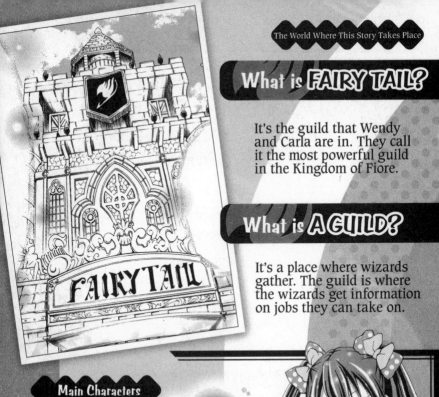

Wendy Marvell

A 12-year-old dragon slayer wizard who specializes in a magic that uses air, Sky Magic. When she was very little, she was raised by a dragon. She loves Carla. She hates pickled plums.

Carla

This creature looks very much like a cat, and was born from an egg that Wendy once found. She loves black tea. She can sprout wings and fly through the sky.

Contents

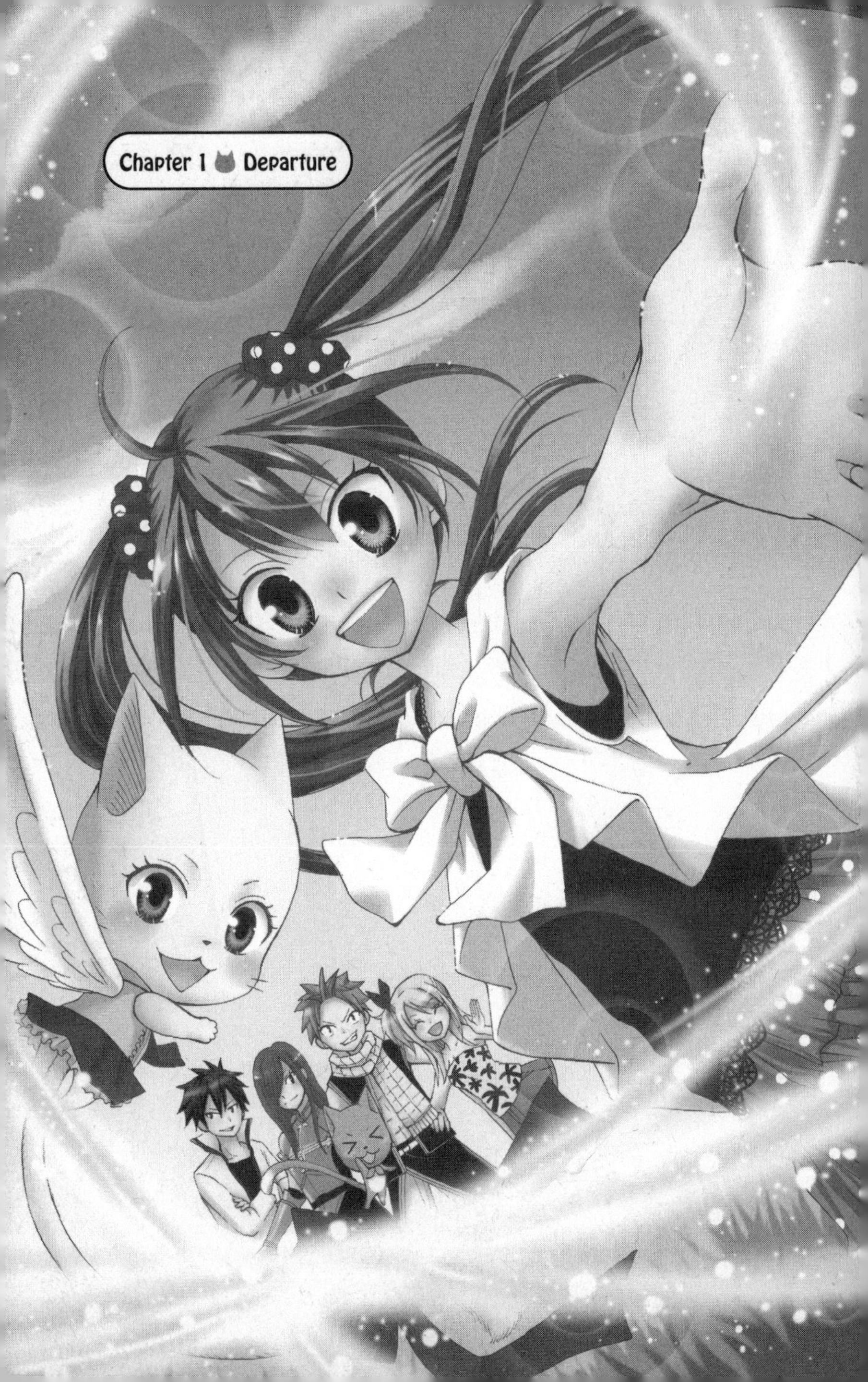
Chapter 1 Departure

FAIRY TAIL 1
BLUE MISTRAL

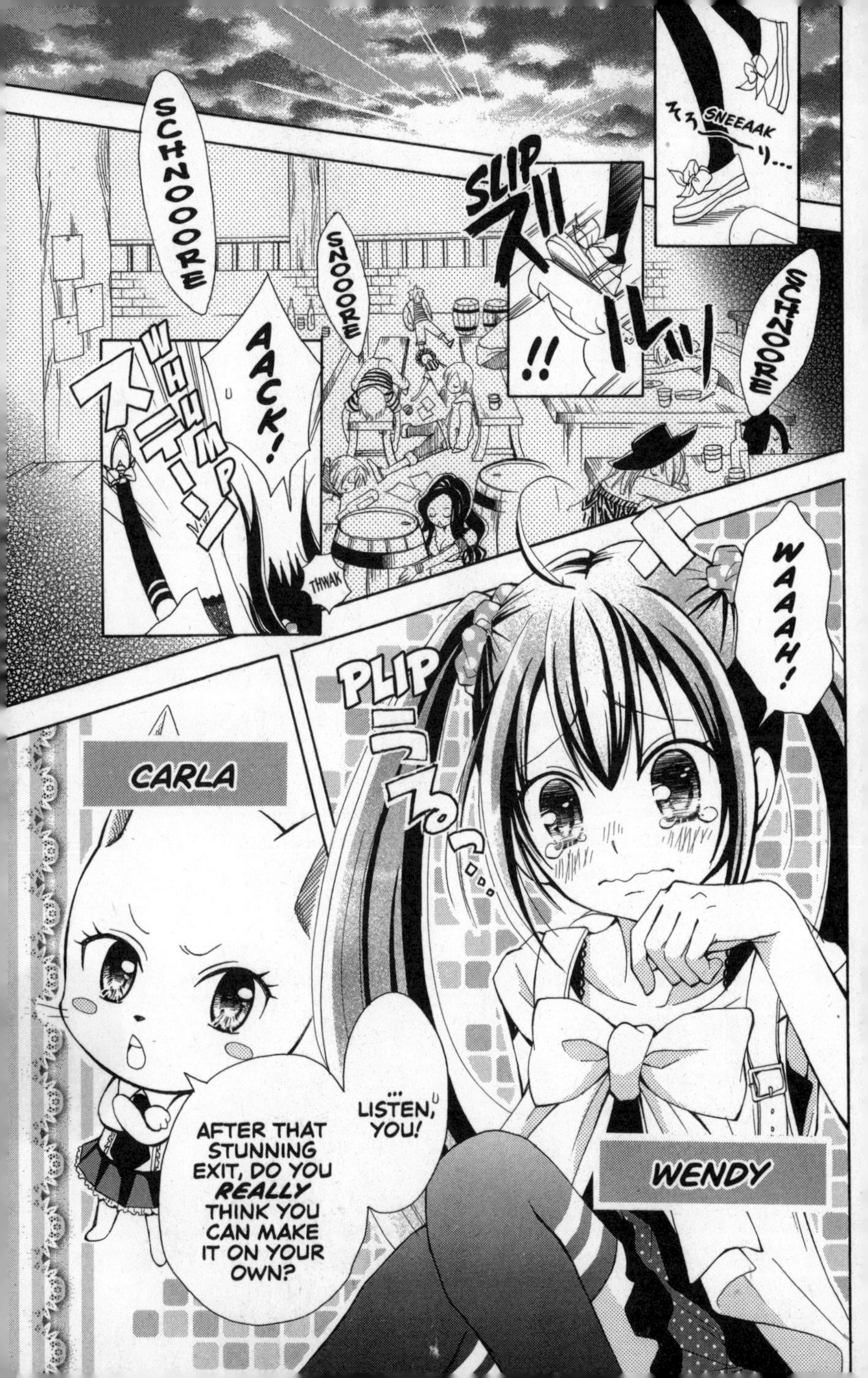
SNEEAAK
SLIP
!!
SCHNOOORE
SNOOORE
SCHNOOOORE
AACK!
WHUMP
THWAK
WAAAAH!
PLIP
WENDY
CARLA
...LISTEN, YOU!
AFTER THAT STUNNING EXIT, DO YOU *REALLY* THINK YOU CAN MAKE IT ON YOUR OWN?

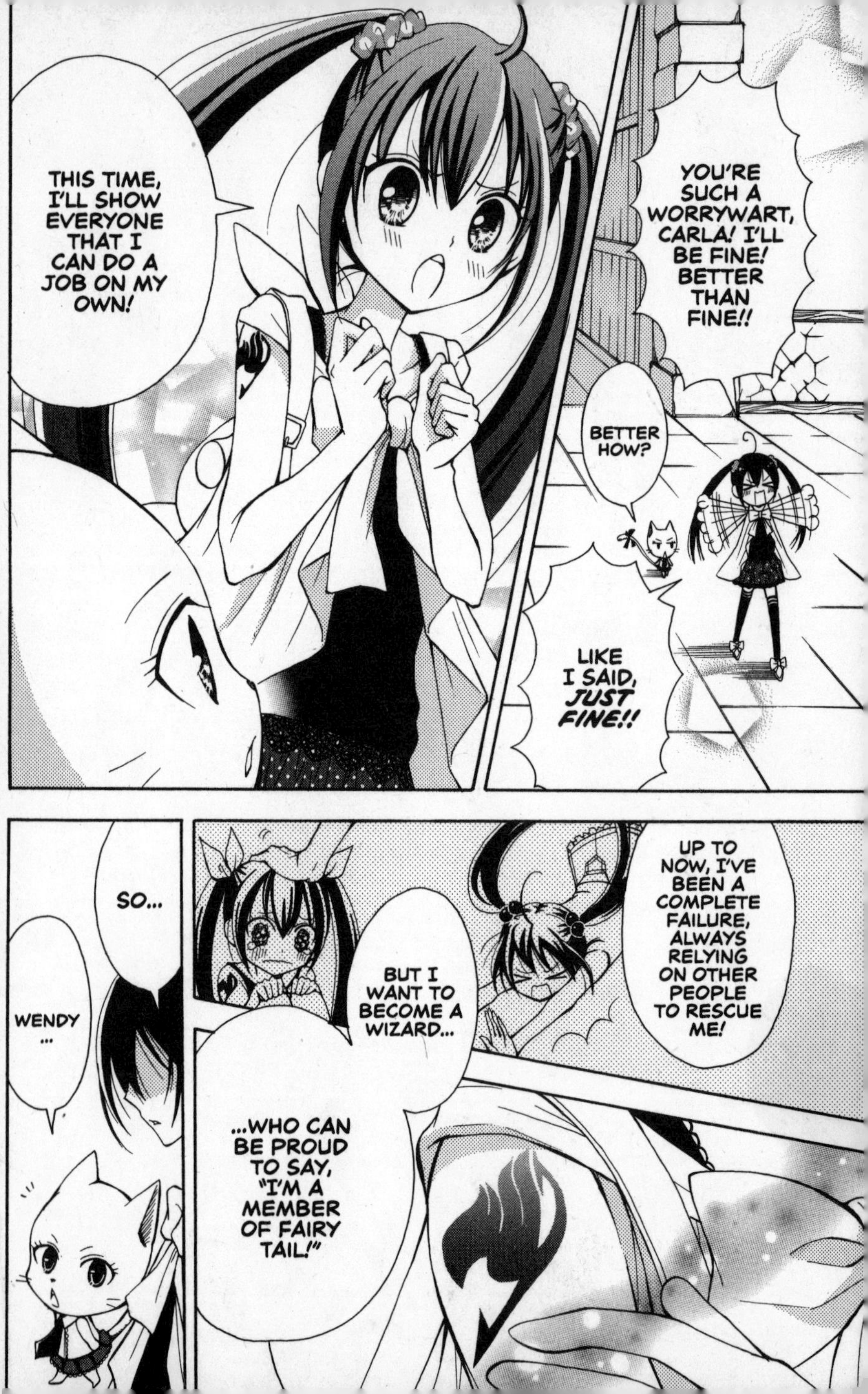
YOU'RE SUCH A WORRYWART, CARLA! I'LL BE FINE! BETTER THAN FINE!!
BETTER HOW?
LIKE I SAID, *JUST FINE!!*
THIS TIME, I'LL SHOW EVERYONE THAT I CAN DO A JOB ON MY OWN!
UP TO NOW, I'VE BEEN A COMPLETE FAILURE, ALWAYS RELYING ON OTHER PEOPLE TO RESCUE ME!
BUT I WANT TO BECOME A WIZARD...
...WHO CAN BE PROUD TO SAY, "I'M A MEMBER OF FAIRY TAIL!"
SO...
WENDY ...

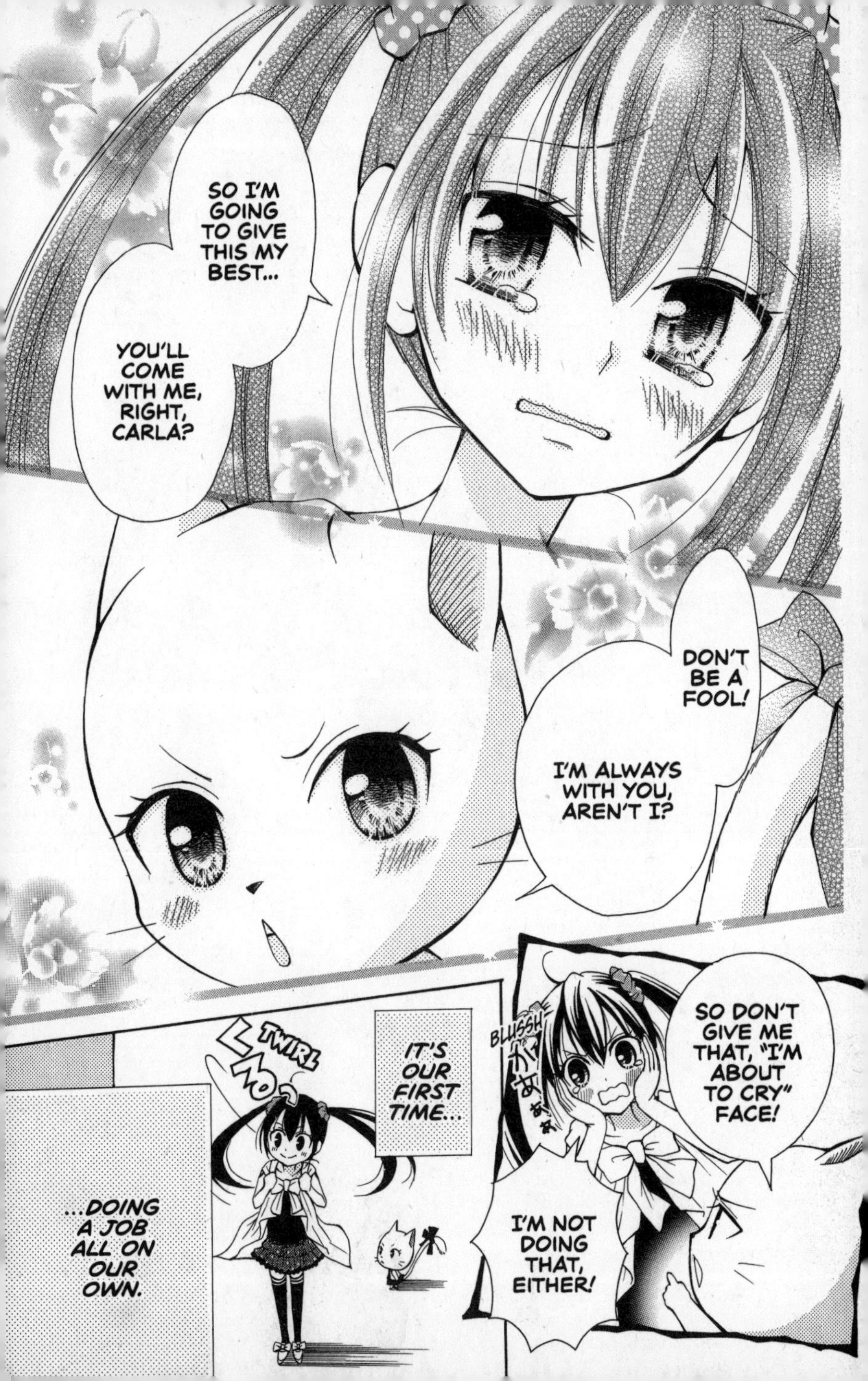
SO I'M GOING TO GIVE THIS MY BEST...
YOU'LL COME WITH ME, RIGHT, CARLA?
DON'T BE A FOOL!
I'M ALWAYS WITH YOU, AREN'T I?
SO DON'T GIVE ME THAT, "I'M ABOUT TO CRY" FACE!
BLUSSH
I'M NOT DOING THAT, EITHER!
TWIRL
IT'S OUR FIRST TIME...
...DOING A JOB ALL ON OUR OWN.

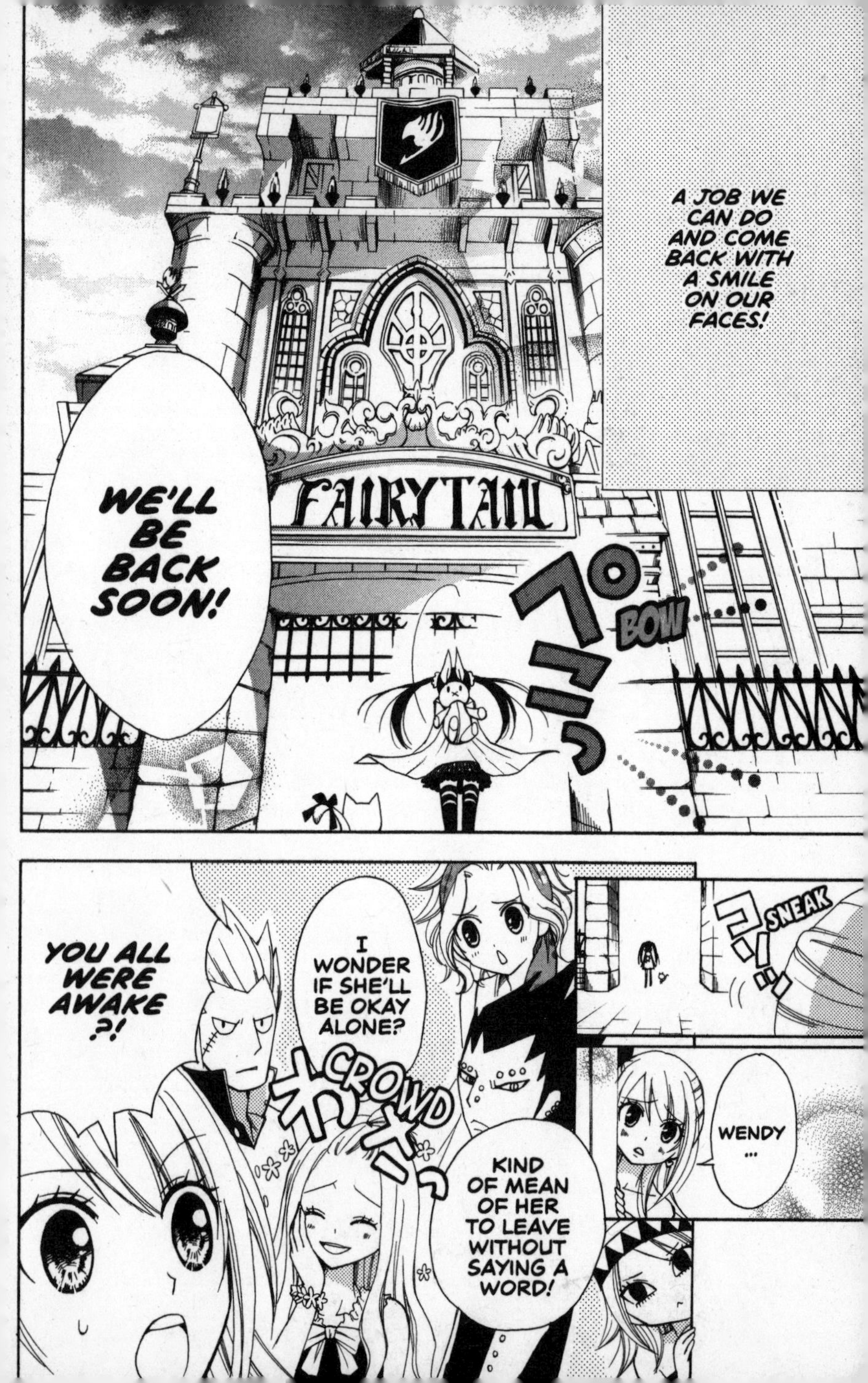
A JOB WE CAN DO AND COME BACK WITH A SMILE ON OUR FACES!
WE'LL BE BACK SOON!
BOW
SNEAK
WENDY ...
I WONDER IF SHE'LL BE OKAY ALONE?
YOU ALL WERE AWAKE ?!
CROWD
KIND OF MEAN OF HER TO LEAVE WITHOUT SAYING A WORD!

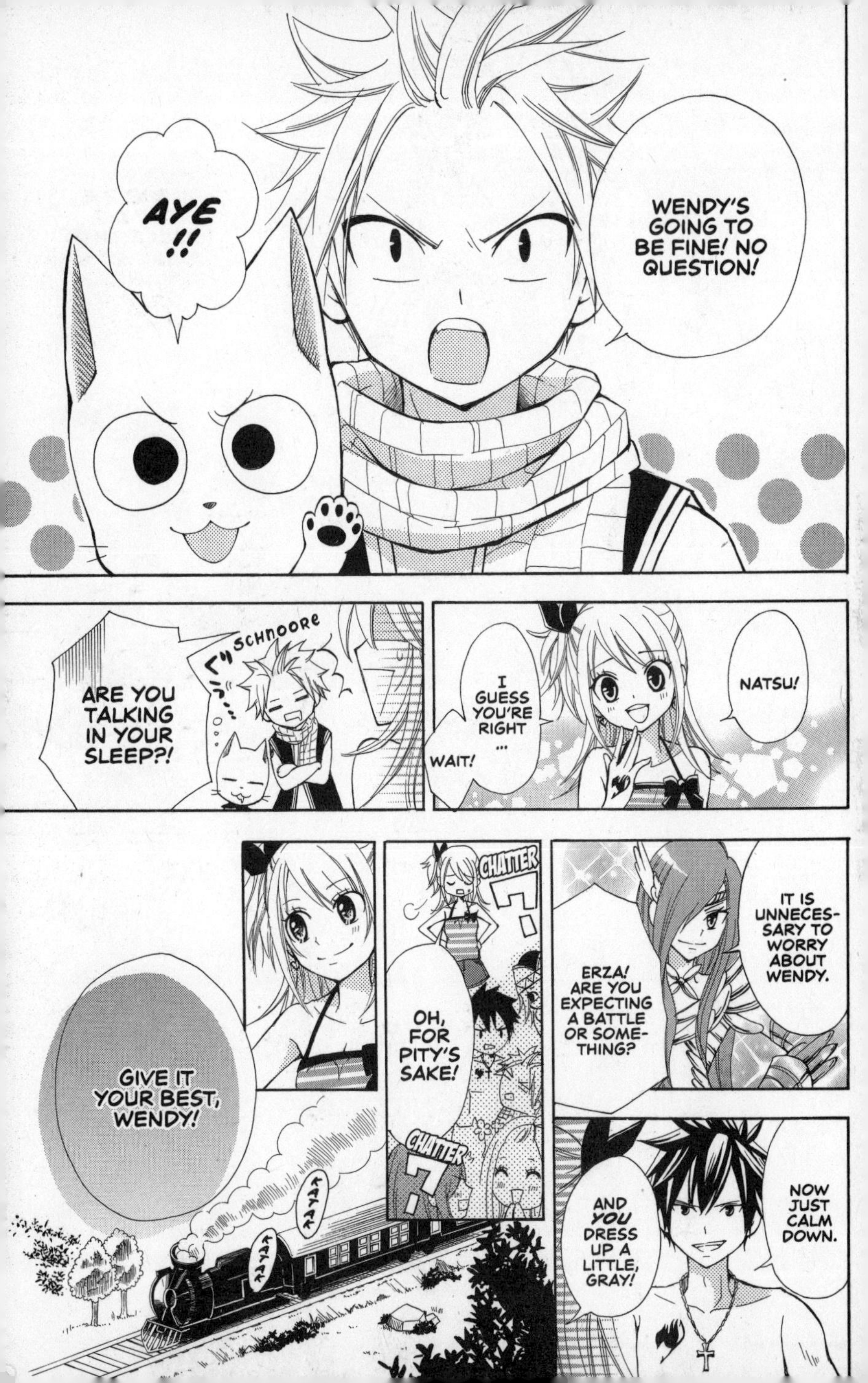
WENDY'S GOING TO BE FINE! NO QUESTION!
AYE !!
NATSU!
I GUESS YOU'RE RIGHT ...
WAIT!
SCHNOORE
ARE YOU TALKING IN YOUR SLEEP?!
IT IS UNNECES-SARY TO WORRY ABOUT WENDY.
ERZA! ARE YOU EXPECTING A BATTLE OR SOME-THING?
NOW JUST CALM DOWN.
AND YOU DRESS UP A LITTLE, GRAY!
CHATTER
OH, FOR PITY'S SAKE!
CHATTER
GIVE IT YOUR BEST, WENDY!

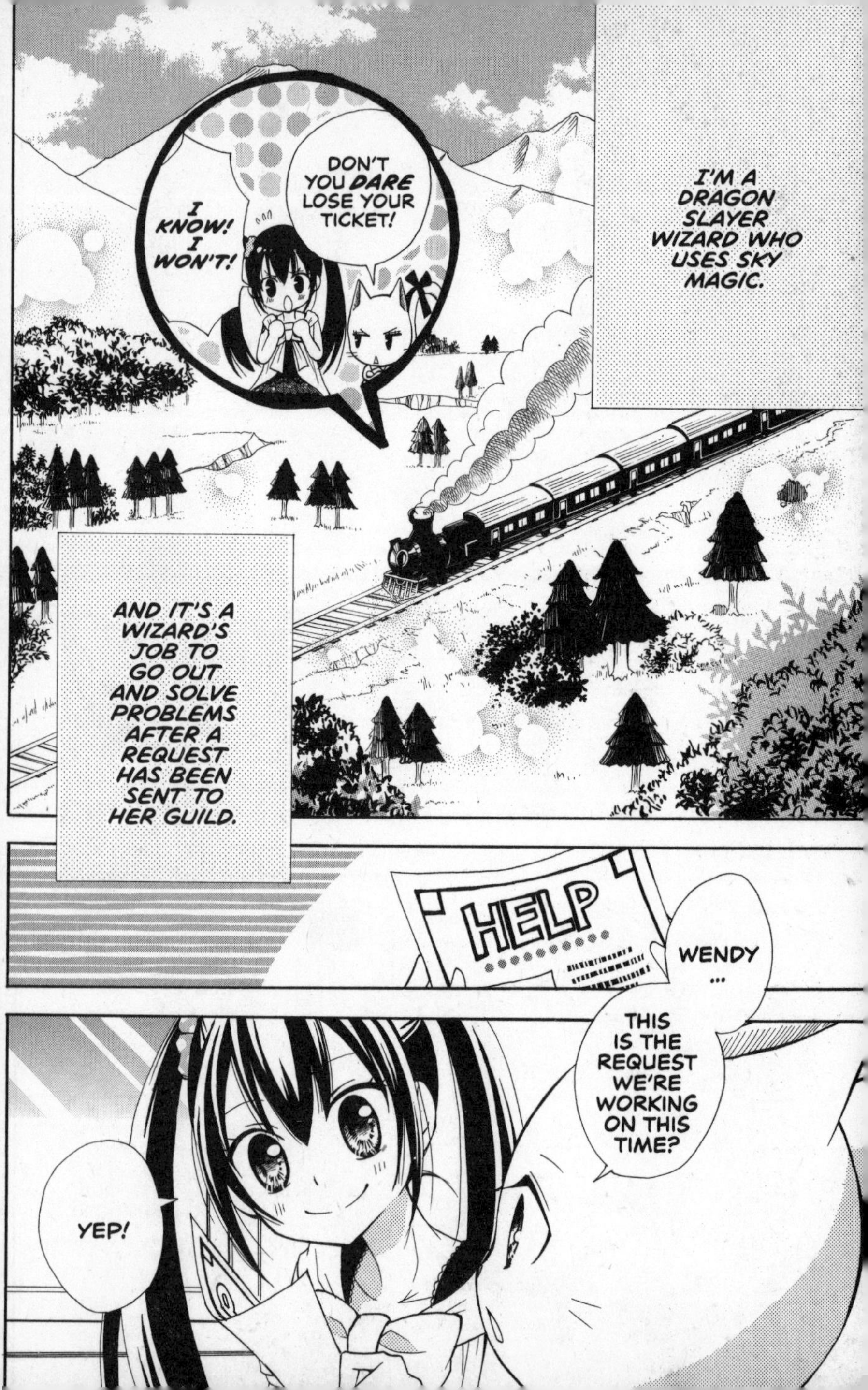
I'M A DRAGON SLAYER WIZARD WHO USES SKY MAGIC.
DON'T YOU DARE LOSE YOUR TICKET!
I KNOW! I WON'T!
AND IT'S A WIZARD'S JOB TO GO OUT AND SOLVE PROBLEMS AFTER A REQUEST HAS BEEN SENT TO HER GUILD.
HELP
WENDY ...
THIS IS THE REQUEST WE'RE WORKING ON THIS TIME?
YEP!

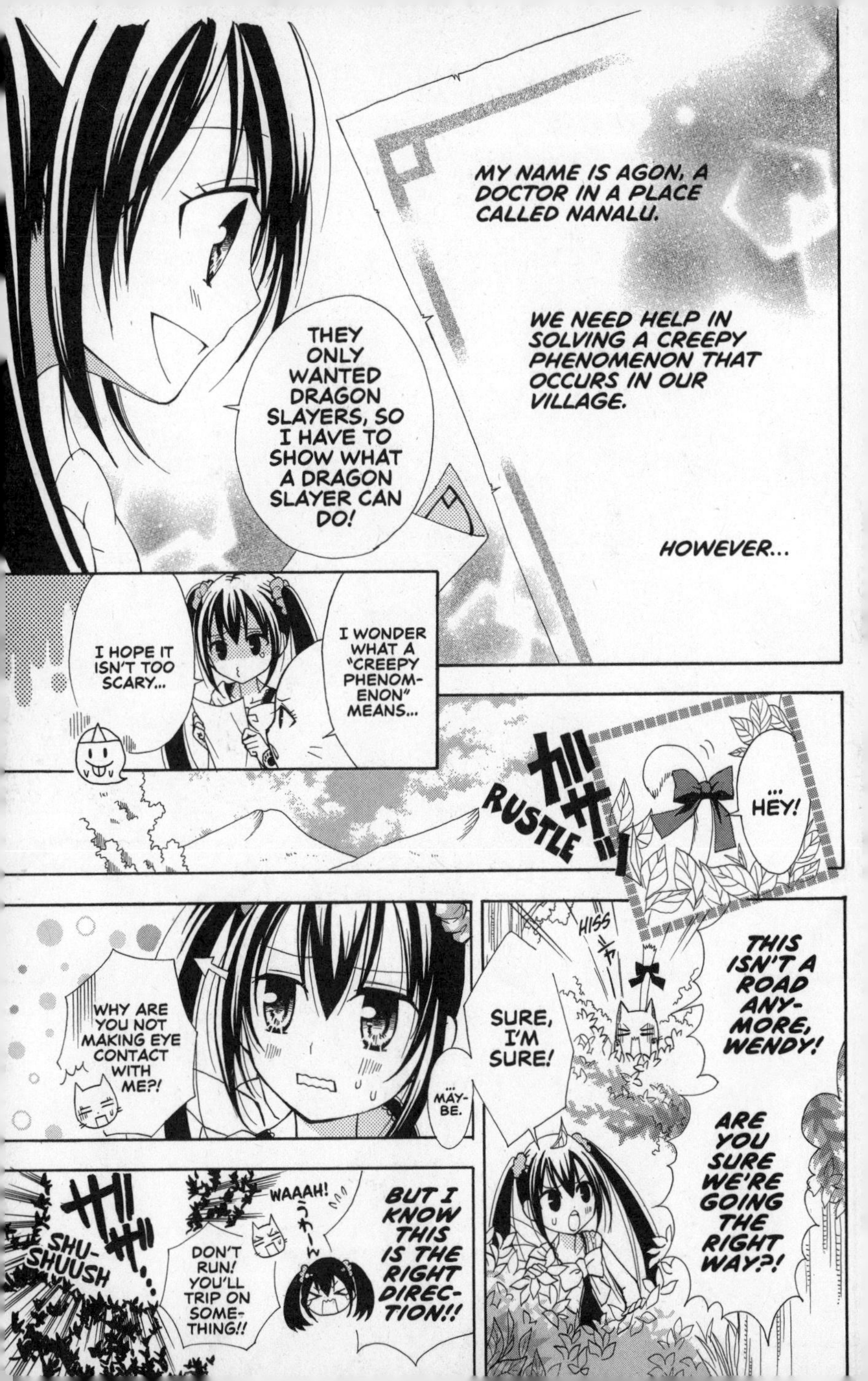
MY NAME IS AGON, A DOCTOR IN A PLACE CALLED NANALU.
WE NEED HELP IN SOLVING A CREEPY PHENOMENON THAT OCCURS IN OUR VILLAGE.
HOWEVER...
THEY ONLY WANTED DRAGON SLAYERS, SO I HAVE TO SHOW WHAT A DRAGON SLAYER CAN DO!
I WONDER WHAT A "CREEPY PHENOMENON" MEANS...
I HOPE IT ISN'T TOO SCARY...
...HEY!
RUSTLE
THIS ISN'T A ROAD ANYMORE, WENDY!
ARE YOU SURE WE'RE GOING THE RIGHT WAY?!
HISS
SURE, I'M SURE!
...MAYBE.
WHY ARE YOU NOT MAKING EYE CONTACT WITH ME?!
BUT I KNOW THIS IS THE RIGHT DIRECTION!!
WAAAH!
DON'T RUN! YOU'LL TRIP ON SOMETHING!!
SHU-SHUUSH

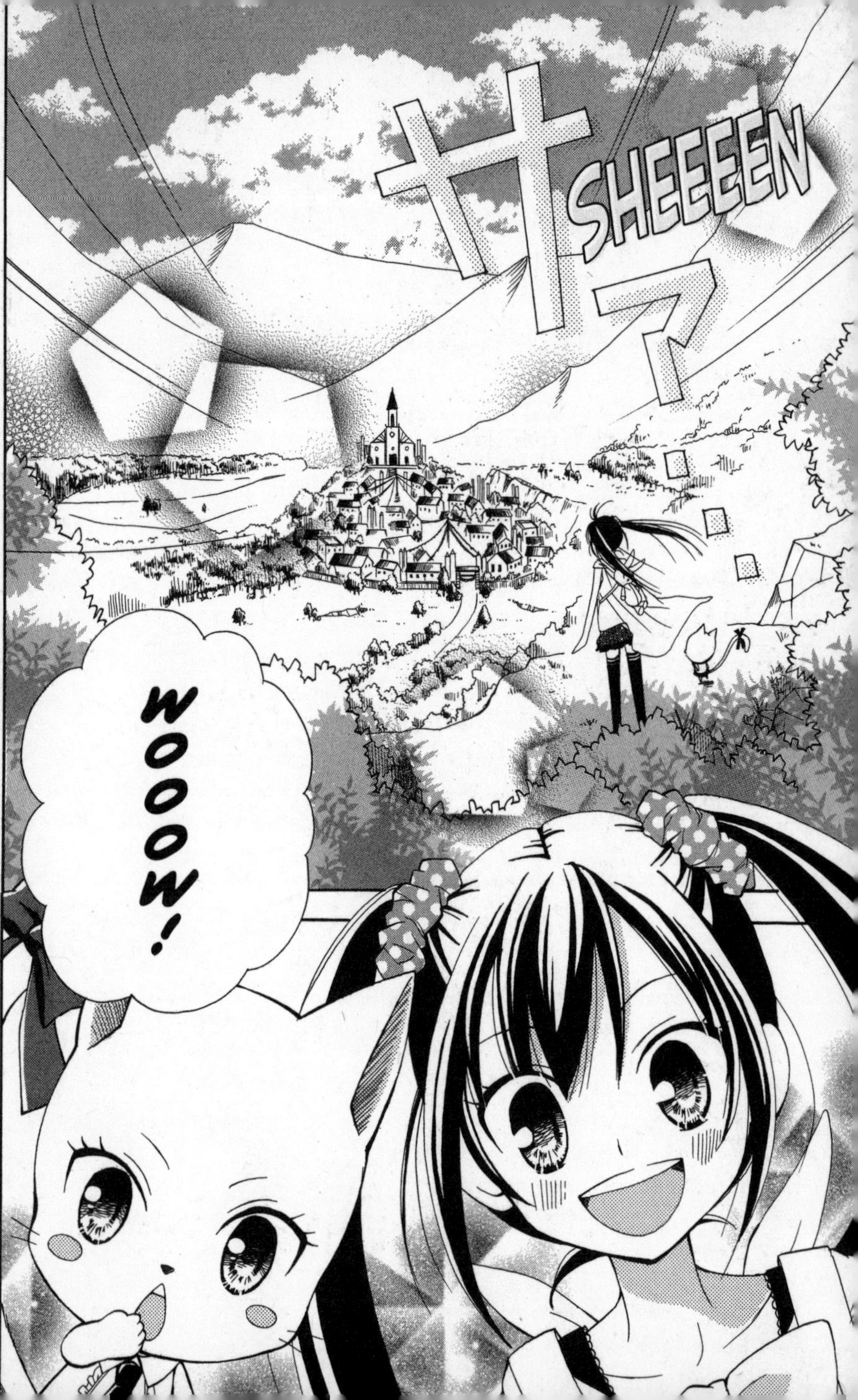
SHEEEEN
WOOOW!

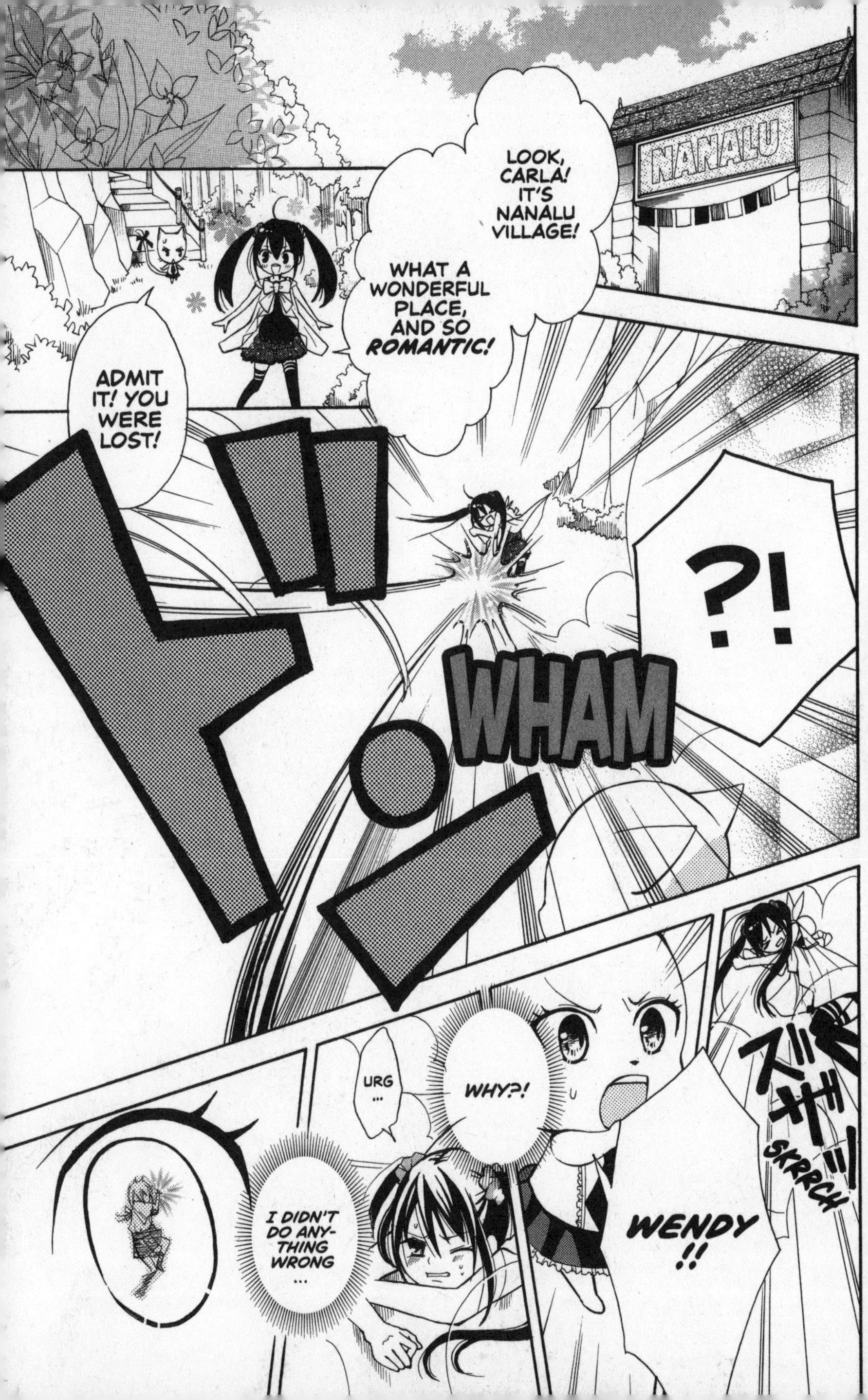
NANALU
LOOK, CARLA! IT'S NANALU VILLAGE!
WHAT A WONDERFUL PLACE, AND SO *ROMANTIC!*
ADMIT IT! YOU WERE LOST!
?!
WHAM
SKRRCH
WENDY !!
WHY?!
URG ...
I DIDN'T DO ANY-THING WRONG ...

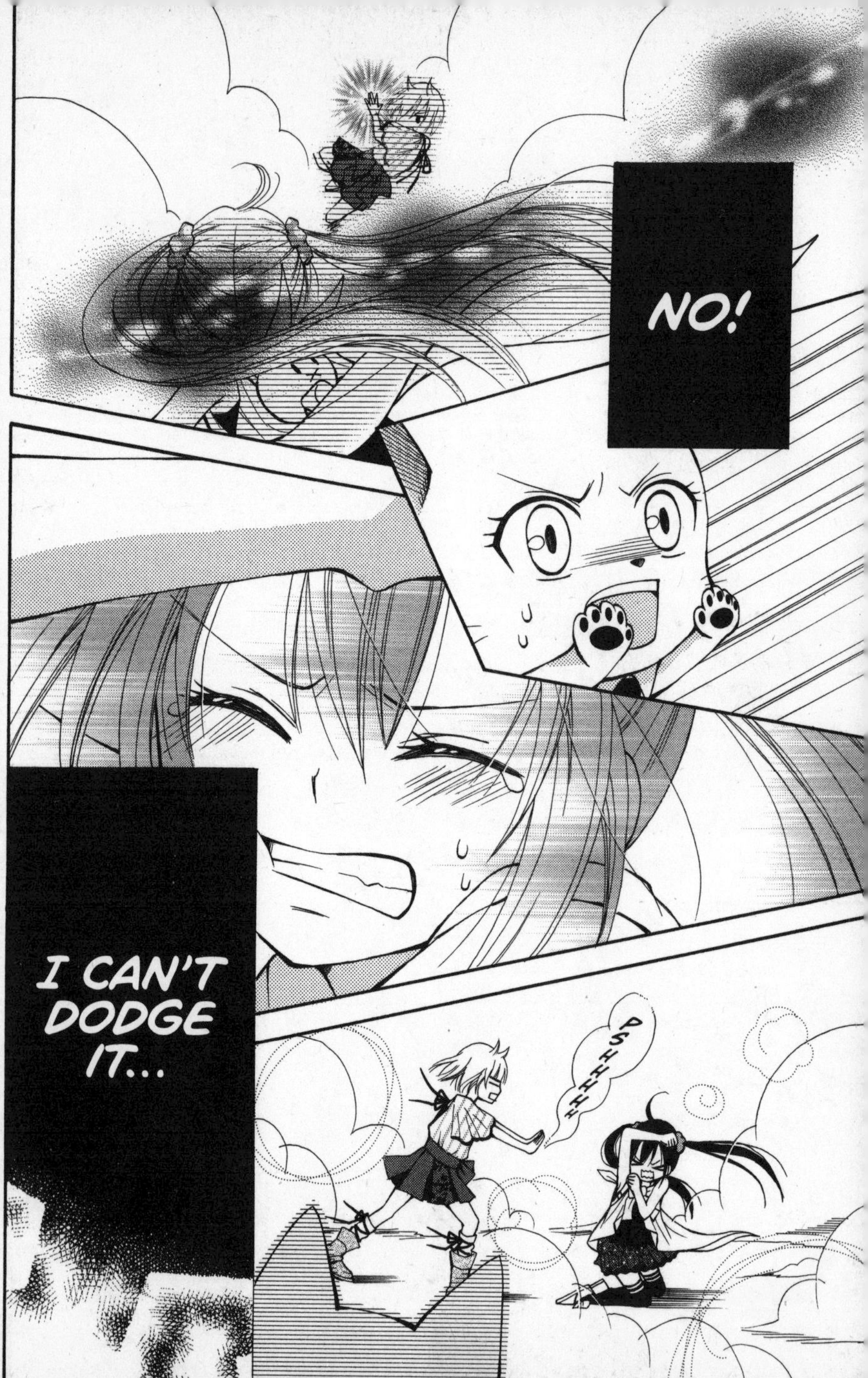
NO!
I CAN'T DODGE IT...
PSHHHHH

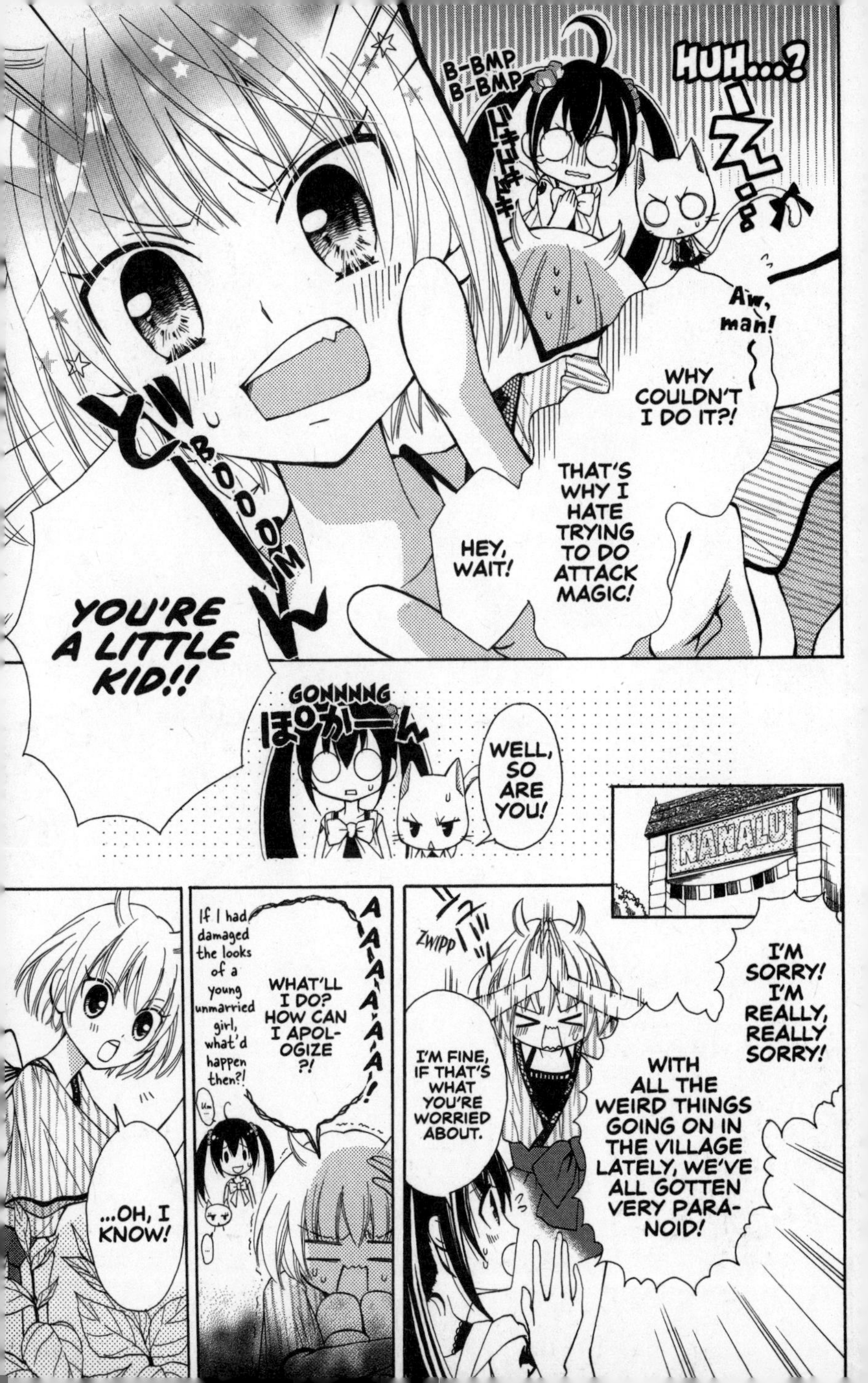
HUH...?
B-BMP
B-BMP
Aw, man!
WHY COULDN'T I DO IT?!
THAT'S WHY I HATE TRYING TO DO ATTACK MAGIC!
HEY, WAIT!
BOOOOM
YOU'RE A LITTLE KID!!
GONNNNG
WELL, SO ARE YOU!
NANALU
ZWIPP
I'M SORRY! I'M REALLY, REALLY SORRY!
WITH ALL THE WEIRD THINGS GOING ON IN THE VILLAGE LATELY, WE'VE ALL GOTTEN VERY PARA-NOID!
I'M FINE, IF THAT'S WHAT YOU'RE WORRIED ABOUT.
AAAAAAA!
WHAT'LL I DO? HOW CAN I APOL-OGIZE ?!
If I had damaged the looks of a young unmarried girl, what'd happen then?!
...OH, I KNOW!

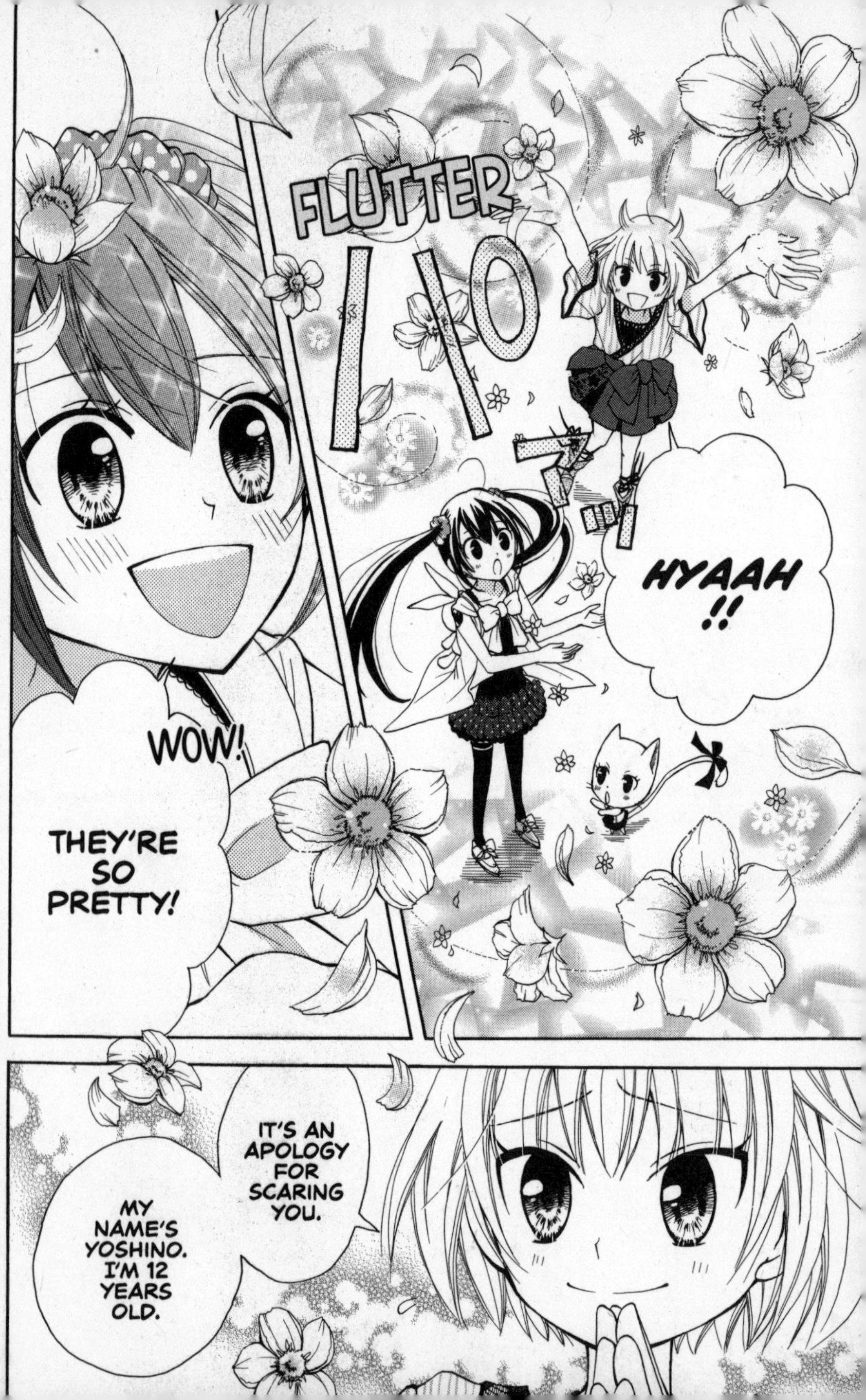
FLUTTER
HYAAH!!
WOW!
THEY'RE SO PRETTY!
IT'S AN APOLOGY FOR SCARING YOU.
MY NAME'S YOSHINO. I'M 12 YEARS OLD.

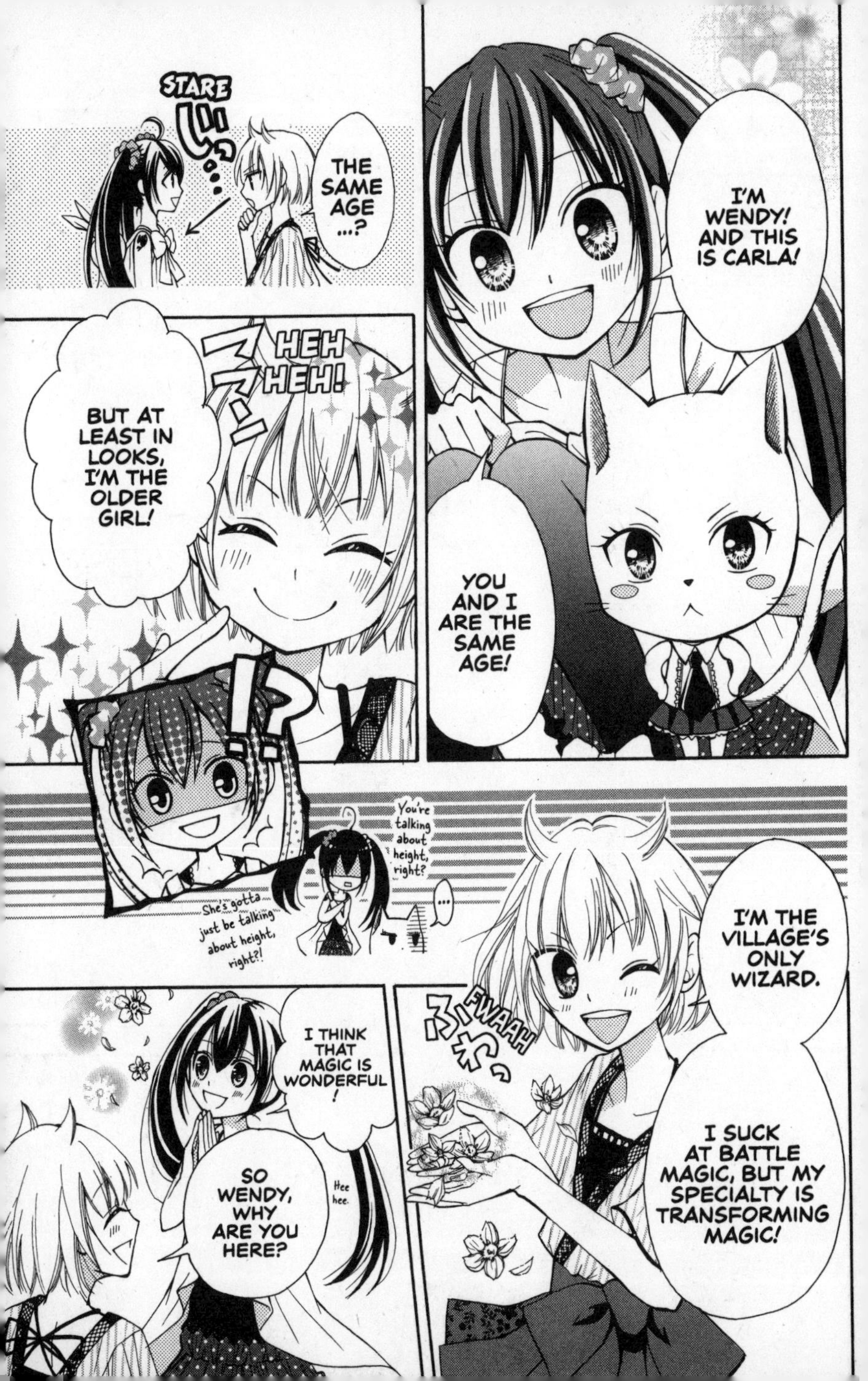
I'M WENDY! AND THIS IS CARLA!
YOU AND I ARE THE SAME AGE!
STARE
THE SAME AGE ...?
HEH HEH!
BUT AT LEAST IN LOOKS, I'M THE OLDER GIRL!
I'M THE VILLAGE'S ONLY WIZARD.
FWAAH
I SUCK AT BATTLE MAGIC, BUT MY SPECIALTY IS TRANSFORMING MAGIC!
You're talking about height, right?
...
She's gotta just be talking about height, right?!
I THINK THAT MAGIC IS WONDERFUL!
Hee hee.
SO WENDY, WHY ARE YOU HERE?

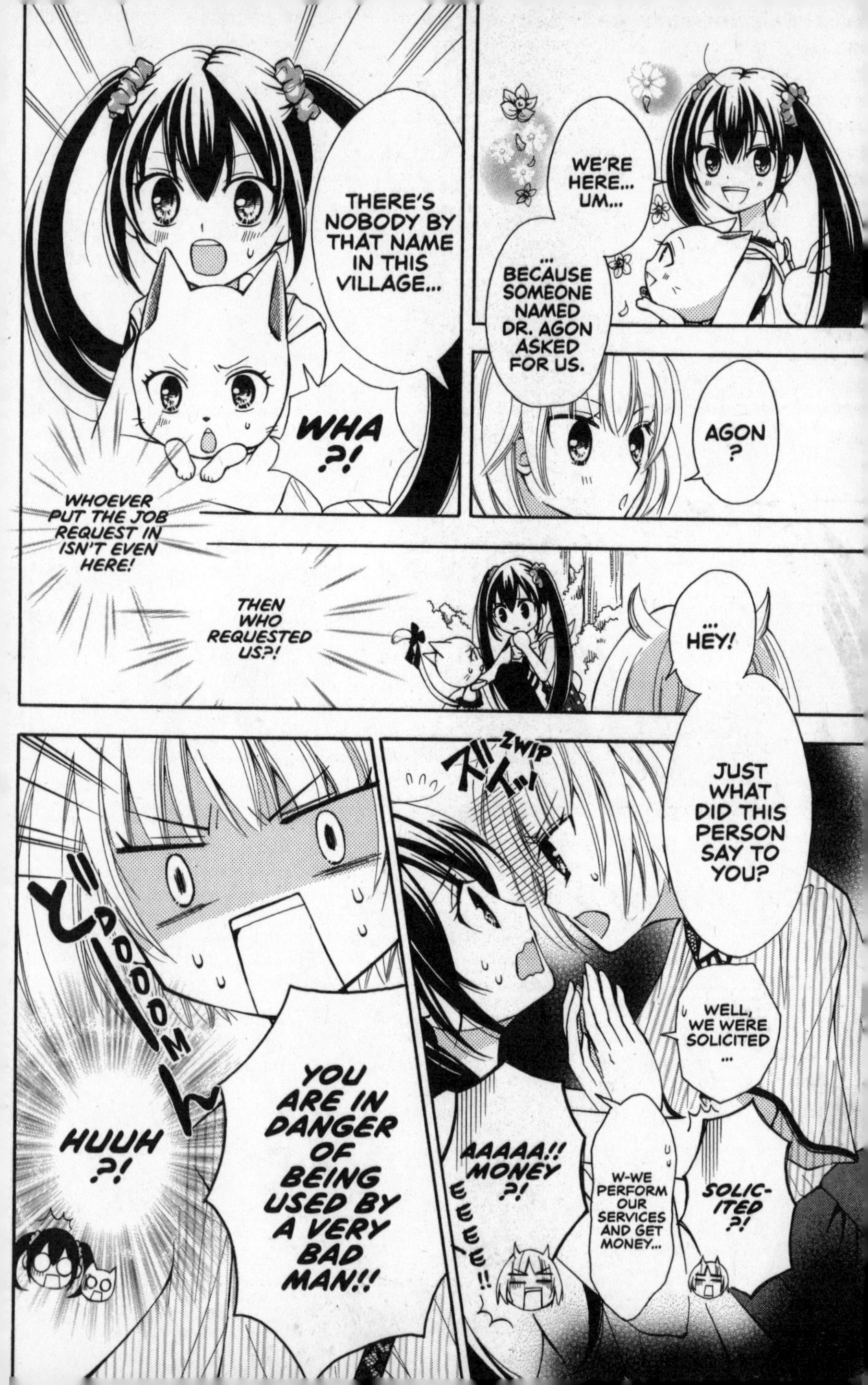
WE'RE HERE... UM...
...BECAUSE SOMEONE NAMED DR. AGON ASKED FOR US.
AGON?
THERE'S NOBODY BY THAT NAME IN THIS VILLAGE...
WHA?!
WHOEVER PUT THE JOB REQUEST IN ISN'T EVEN HERE!
THEN WHO REQUESTED US?!
...HEY!
ZWIP
JUST WHAT DID THIS PERSON SAY TO YOU?
WELL, WE WERE SOLICITED...
SOLICITED?!
W-WE PERFORM OUR SERVICES AND GET MONEY...
AAAAA!! MONEY?!
EEEEE!!
DOOOOM
YOU ARE IN DANGER OF BEING USED BY A VERY BAD MAN!!
HUUH?!

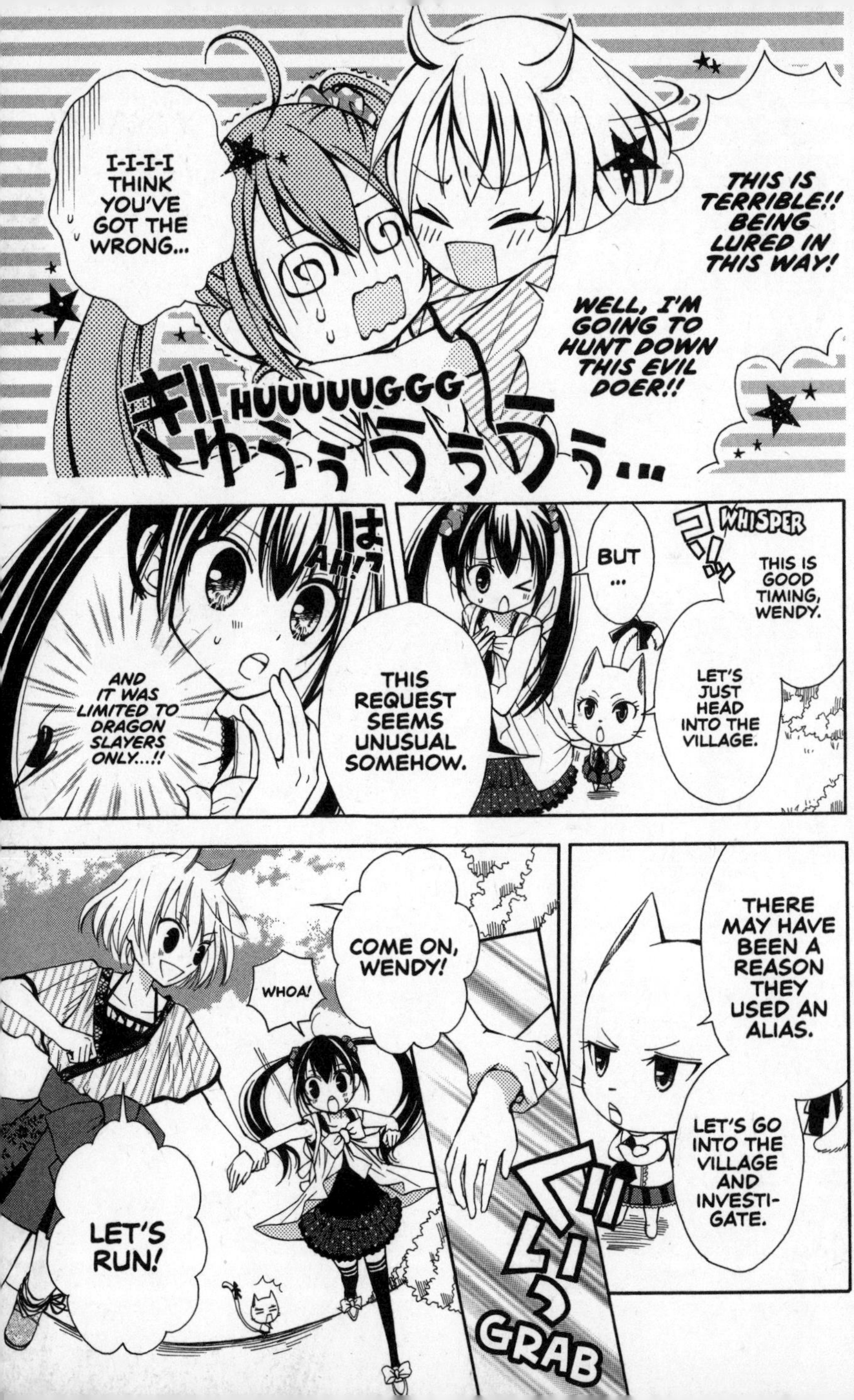
THIS IS TERRIBLE!! BEING LURED IN THIS WAY!
WELL, I'M GOING TO HUNT DOWN THIS EVIL DOER!!
I-I-I-I THINK YOU'VE GOT THE WRONG...
HUUUUUUGGG
WHISPER
THIS IS GOOD TIMING, WENDY.
BUT ...
LET'S JUST HEAD INTO THE VILLAGE.
AH!?
THIS REQUEST SEEMS UNUSUAL SOMEHOW.
AND IT WAS LIMITED TO DRAGON SLAYERS ONLY...!!
THERE MAY HAVE BEEN A REASON THEY USED AN ALIAS.
LET'S GO INTO THE VILLAGE AND INVESTIGATE.
GRAB
COME ON, WENDY!
WHOA!
LET'S RUN!

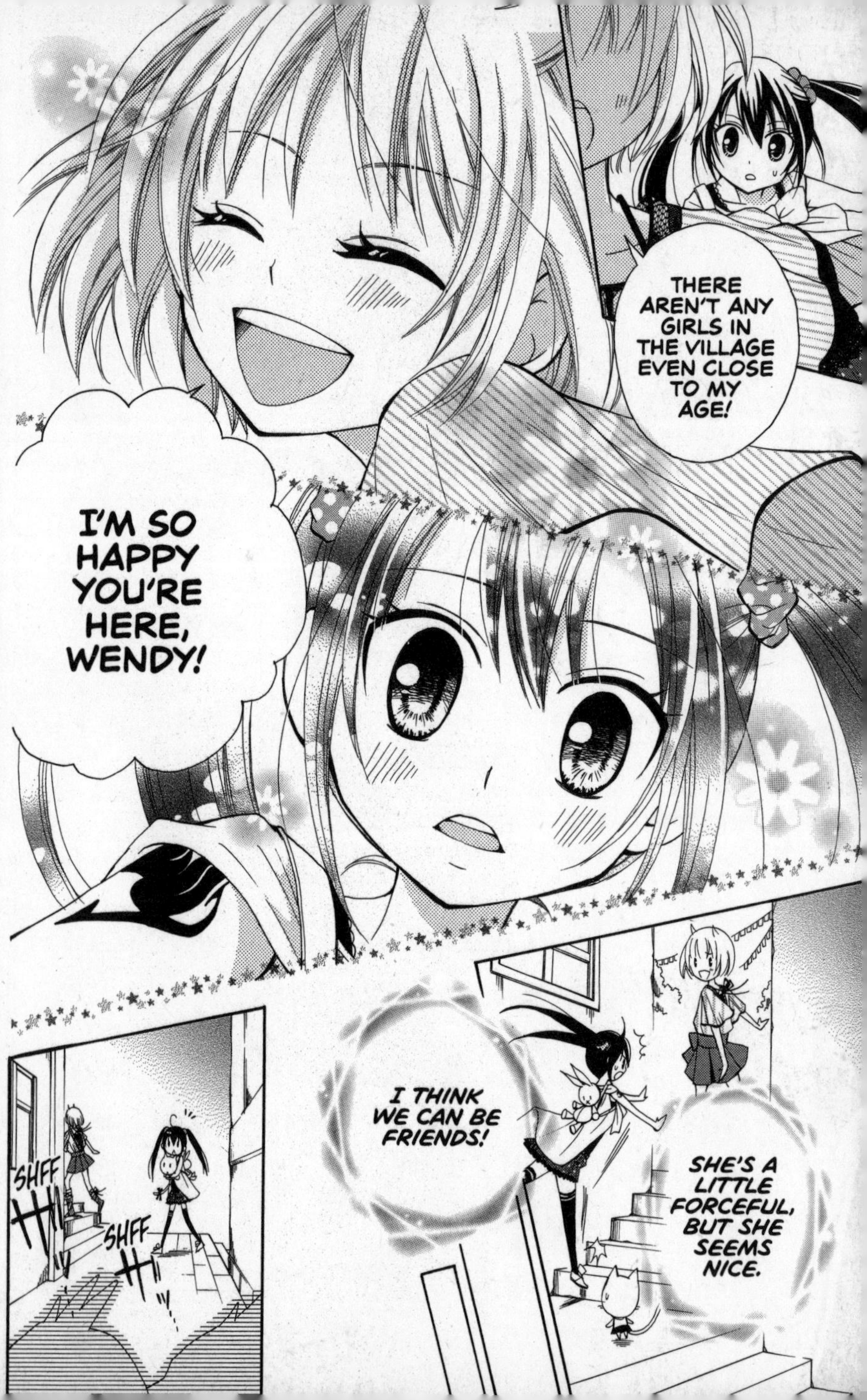
THERE AREN'T ANY GIRLS IN THE VILLAGE EVEN CLOSE TO MY AGE!
I'M SO HAPPY YOU'RE HERE, WENDY!
I THINK WE CAN BE FRIENDS!
SHE'S A LITTLE FORCEFUL, BUT SHE SEEMS NICE.
SHFF
SHFF

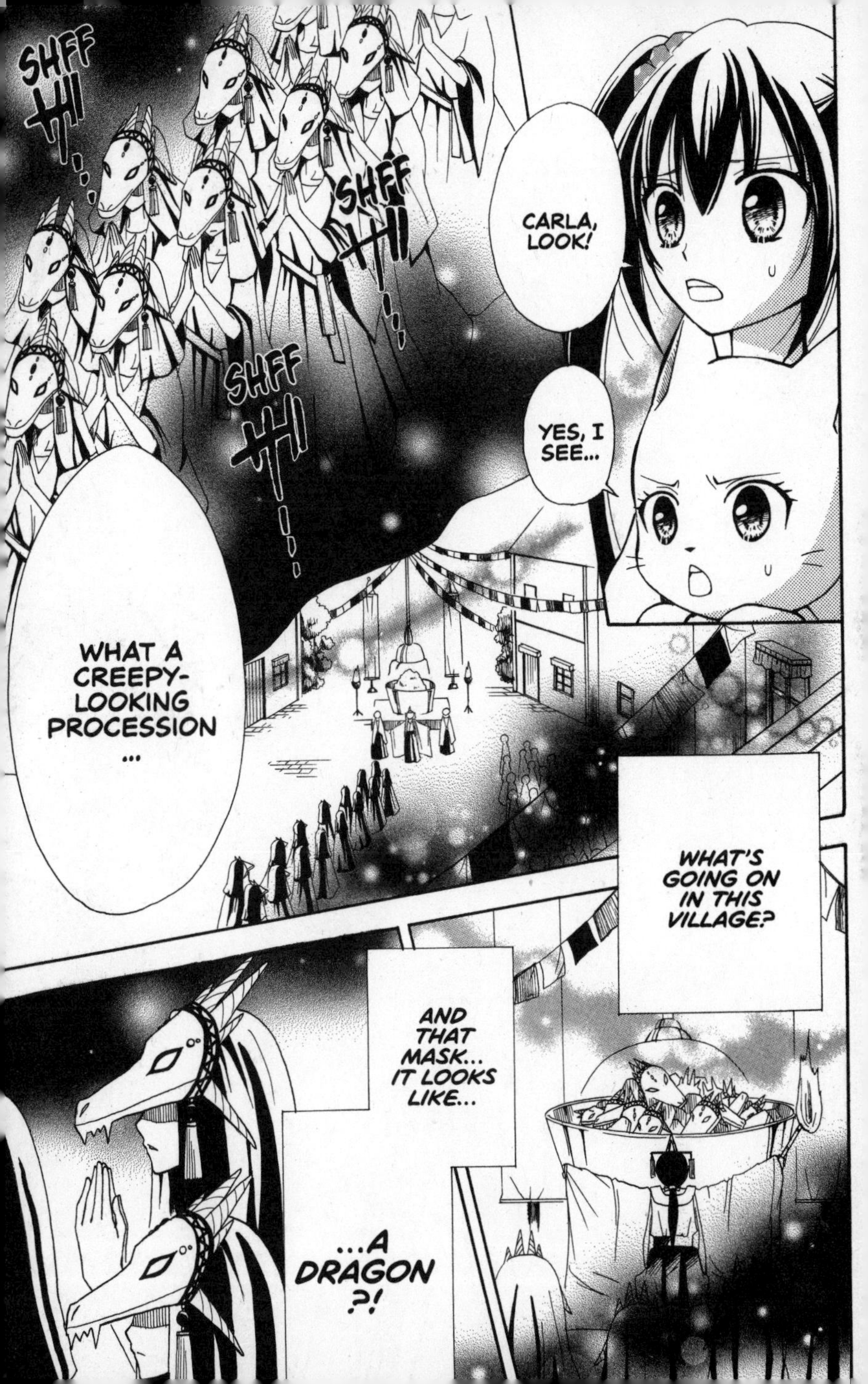
CARLA, LOOK!
YES, I SEE...
SHFF
SHFF
SHFF
WHAT A CREEPY-LOOKING PROCESSION...
WHAT'S GOING ON IN THIS VILLAGE?
AND THAT MASK... IT LOOKS LIKE...
...A DRAGON?!

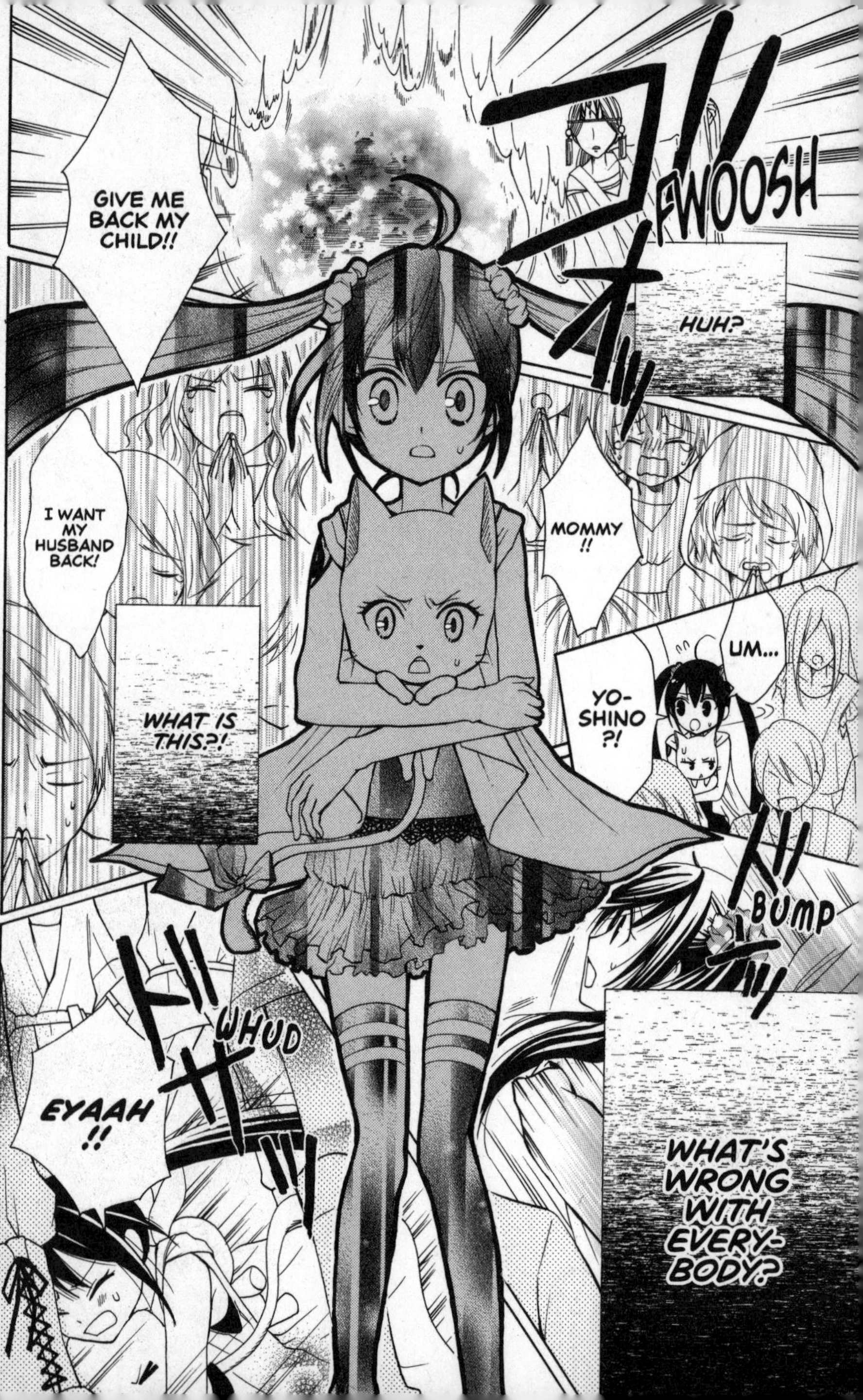
FWOOSH
HUH?
GIVE ME BACK MY CHILD!!
MOMMY!!
I WANT MY HUSBAND BACK!
WHAT IS THIS?!
UM...
YO-SHINO?!
BUMP
WHAT'S WRONG WITH EVERY-BODY?
WHUD
EYAAH!!

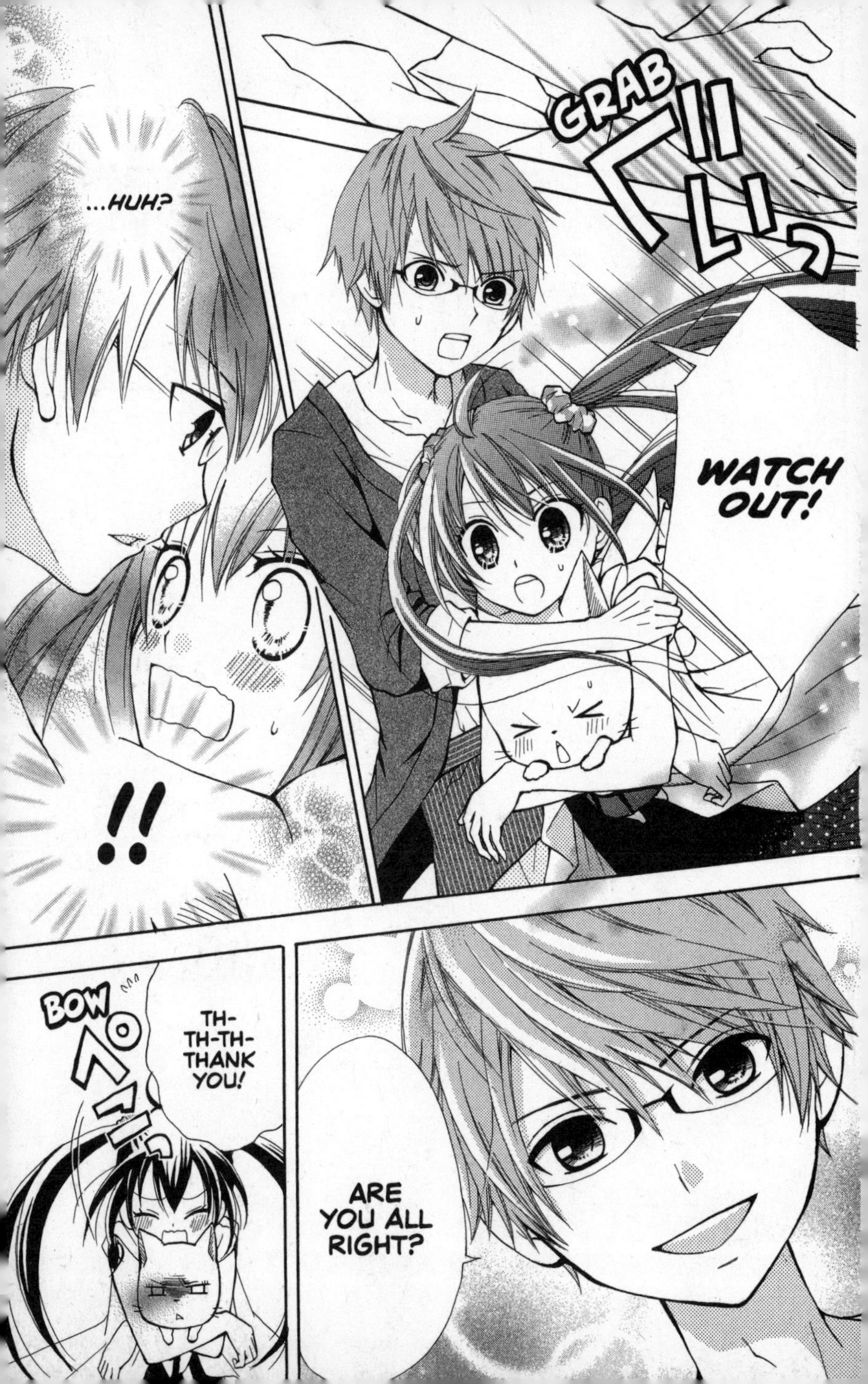
GRAB
WATCH OUT!
...HUH?
!!
ARE YOU ALL RIGHT?
TH-TH-TH-THANK YOU!
BOW

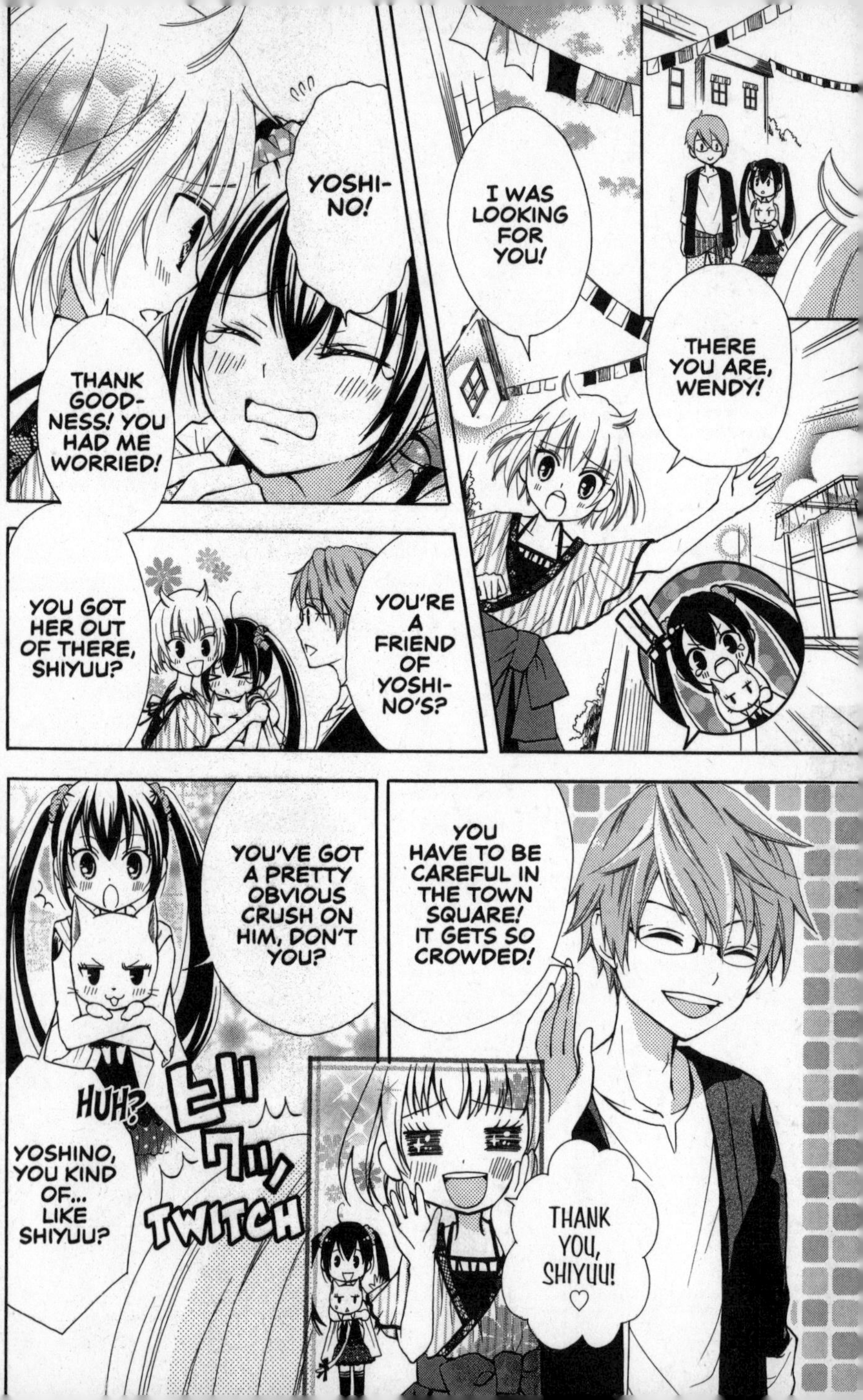
THERE YOU ARE, WENDY!
I WAS LOOKING FOR YOU!
YOSHI-NO!
THANK GOOD-NESS! YOU HAD ME WORRIED!
YOU'RE A FRIEND OF YOSHI-NO'S?
YOU GOT HER OUT OF THERE, SHIYUU?
YOU HAVE TO BE CAREFUL IN THE TOWN SQUARE! IT GETS SO CROWDED!
THANK YOU, SHIYUU! ♡
YOU'VE GOT A PRETTY OBVIOUS CRUSH ON HIM, DON'T YOU?
HUH?
TWITCH
YOSHINO, YOU KIND OF... LIKE SHIYUU?

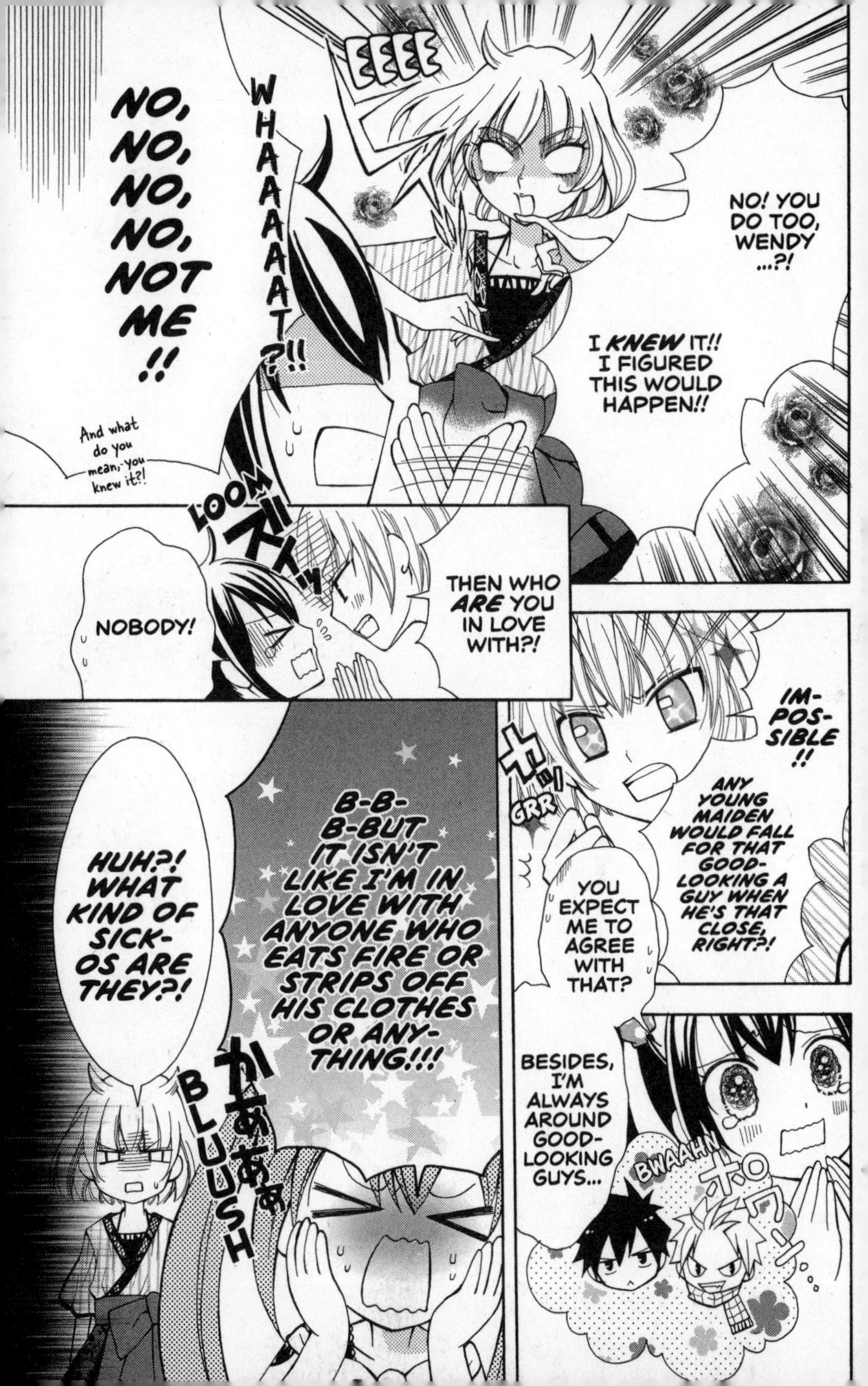
EEEE
NO! YOU DO TOO, WENDY ...?!
I *KNEW* IT!! I FIGURED THIS WOULD HAPPEN!!
WHAAAAAAAT?!!
NO, NO, NO, NO, NOT ME!!
And what do you mean, you knew it?!
LOOM
THEN WHO *ARE* YOU IN LOVE WITH?!
NOBODY!
IM-POS-SIBLE!!
GRR
ANY YOUNG MAIDEN WOULD FALL FOR THAT GOOD-LOOKING A GUY WHEN HE'S THAT CLOSE, RIGHT?!
YOU EXPECT ME TO AGREE WITH THAT?
BESIDES, I'M ALWAYS AROUND GOOD-LOOKING GUYS...
BWAAHN
B-B-B-BUT IT ISN'T LIKE I'M IN LOVE WITH ANYONE WHO EATS FIRE OR STRIPS OFF HIS CLOTHES OR ANY-THING!!!
BLUUSH
HUH?! WHAT KIND OF SICK-OS ARE THEY?!

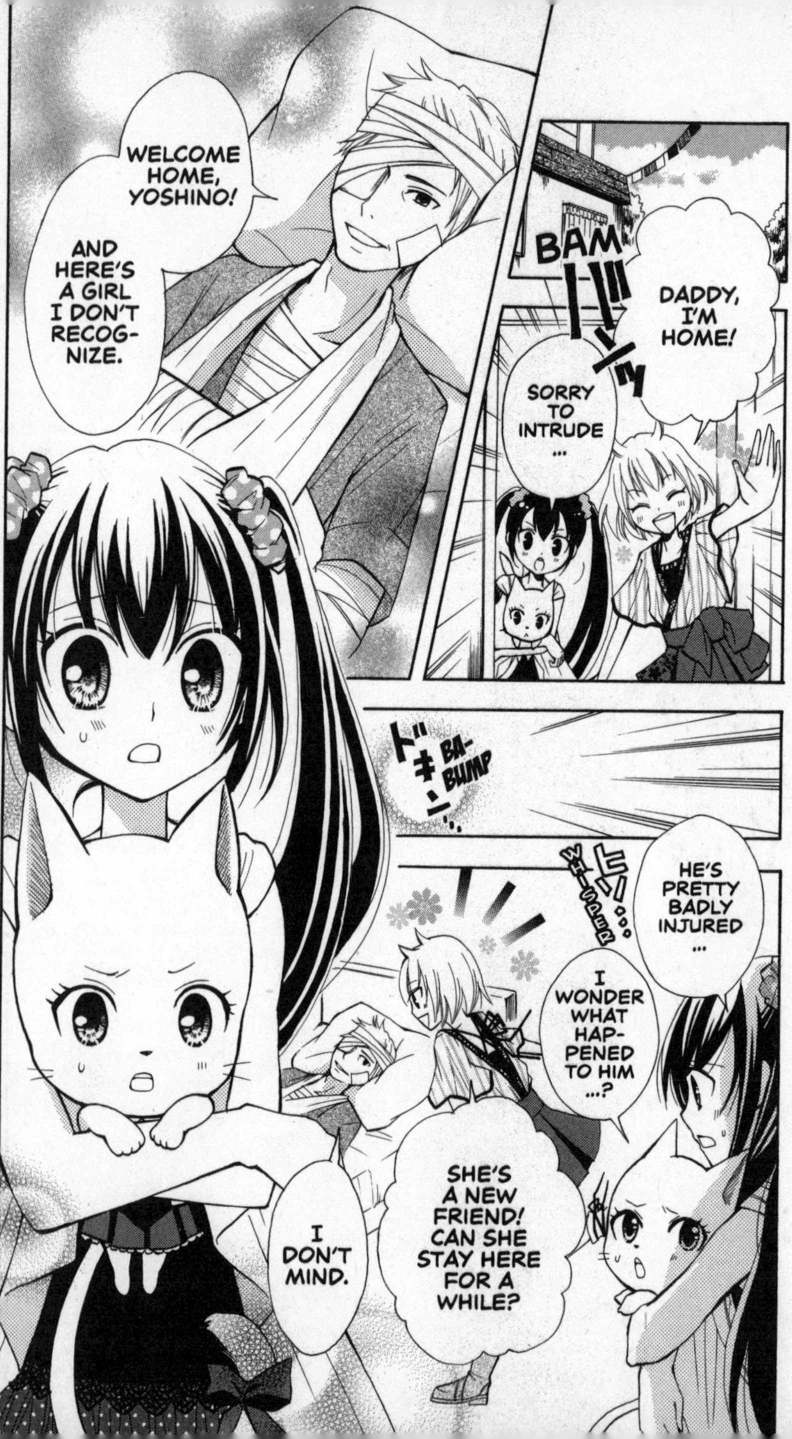
BAM
DADDY, I'M HOME!
SORRY TO INTRUDE ...
WELCOME HOME, YOSHINO!
AND HERE'S A GIRL I DON'T RECOG-NIZE.
BA-BUMP
WHISPER
HE'S PRETTY BADLY INJURED ...
I WONDER WHAT HAP-PENED TO HIM ...?
SHE'S A NEW FRIEND! CAN SHE STAY HERE FOR A WHILE?
I DON'T MIND.

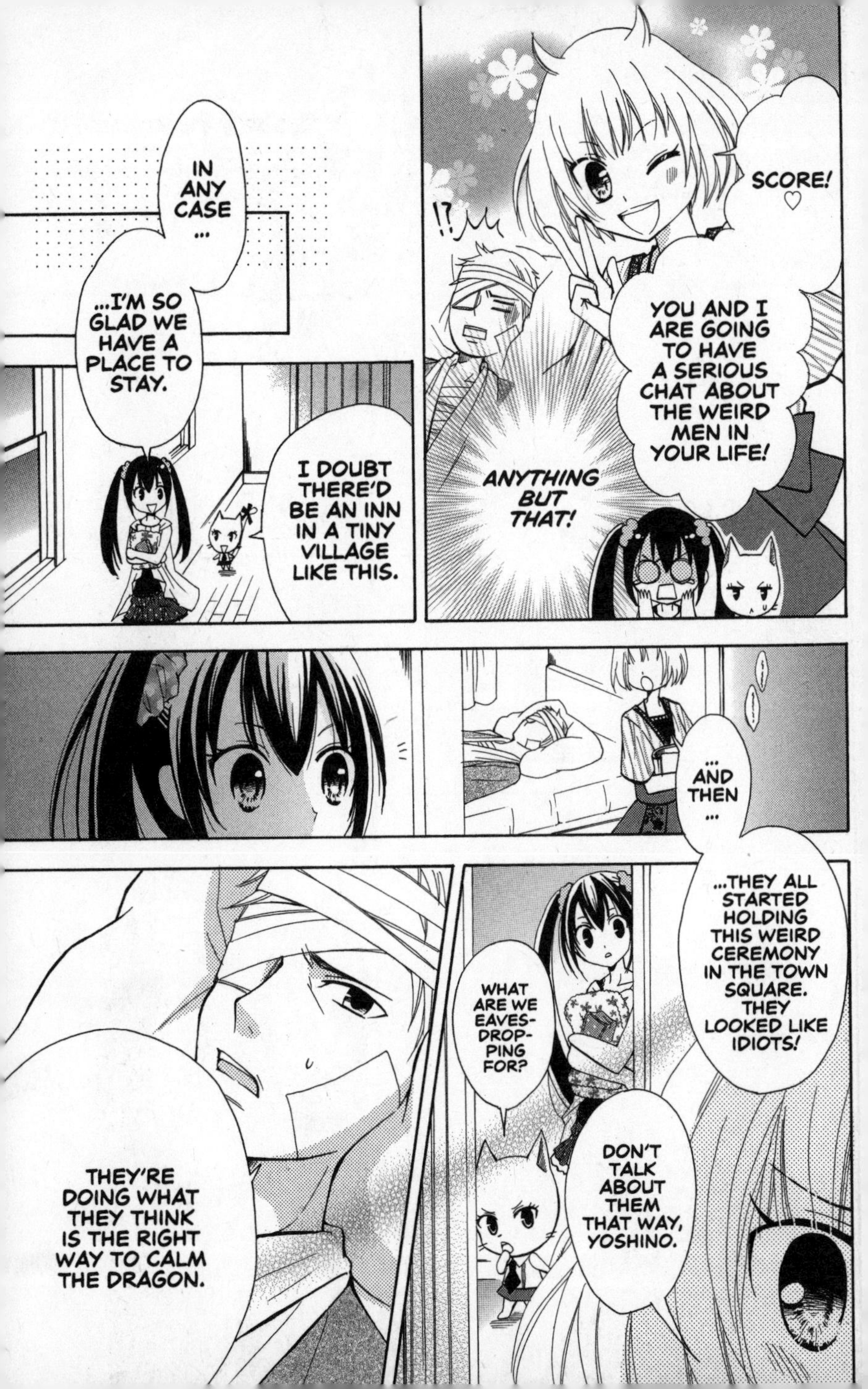
SCORE! ♡
YOU AND I ARE GOING TO HAVE A SERIOUS CHAT ABOUT THE WEIRD MEN IN YOUR LIFE!
!?
ANYTHING BUT THAT!
IN ANY CASE ...
...I'M SO GLAD WE HAVE A PLACE TO STAY.
I DOUBT THERE'D BE AN INN IN A TINY VILLAGE LIKE THIS.
... AND THEN ...
...THEY ALL STARTED HOLDING THIS WEIRD CEREMONY IN THE TOWN SQUARE. THEY LOOKED LIKE IDIOTS!
DON'T TALK ABOUT THEM THAT WAY, YOSHINO.
WHAT ARE WE EAVES-DROP-PING FOR?
THEY'RE DOING WHAT THEY THINK IS THE RIGHT WAY TO CALM THE DRAGON.

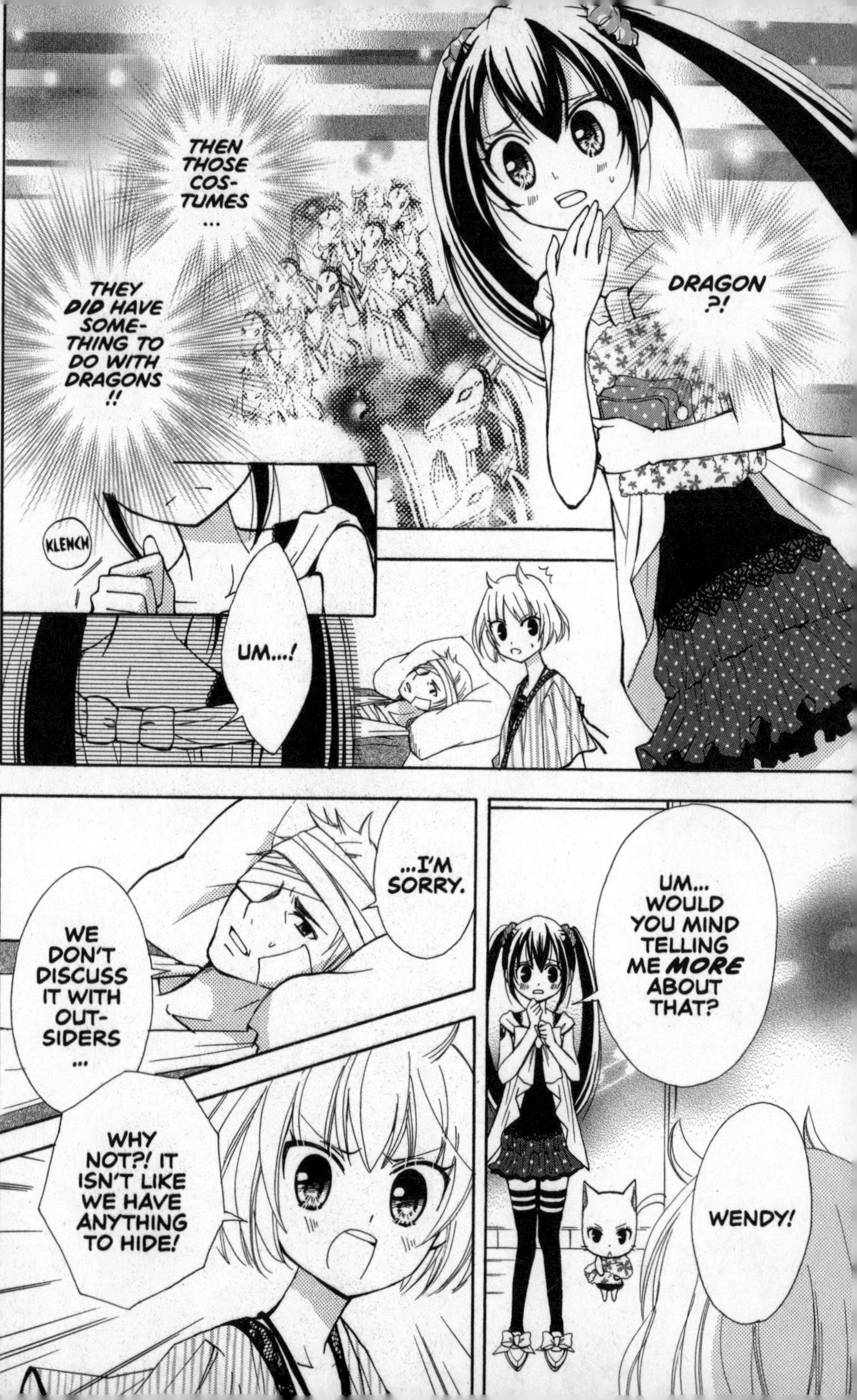
DRAGON ?!
THEN THOSE COS-TUMES ...
THEY *DID* HAVE SOME-THING TO DO WITH DRAGONS !!
KLENCH
UM...!
UM... WOULD YOU MIND TELLING ME *MORE* ABOUT THAT?
WENDY!
...I'M SORRY.
WE DON'T DISCUSS IT WITH OUT-SIDERS ...
WHY NOT?! IT ISN'T LIKE WE HAVE ANYTHING TO HIDE!

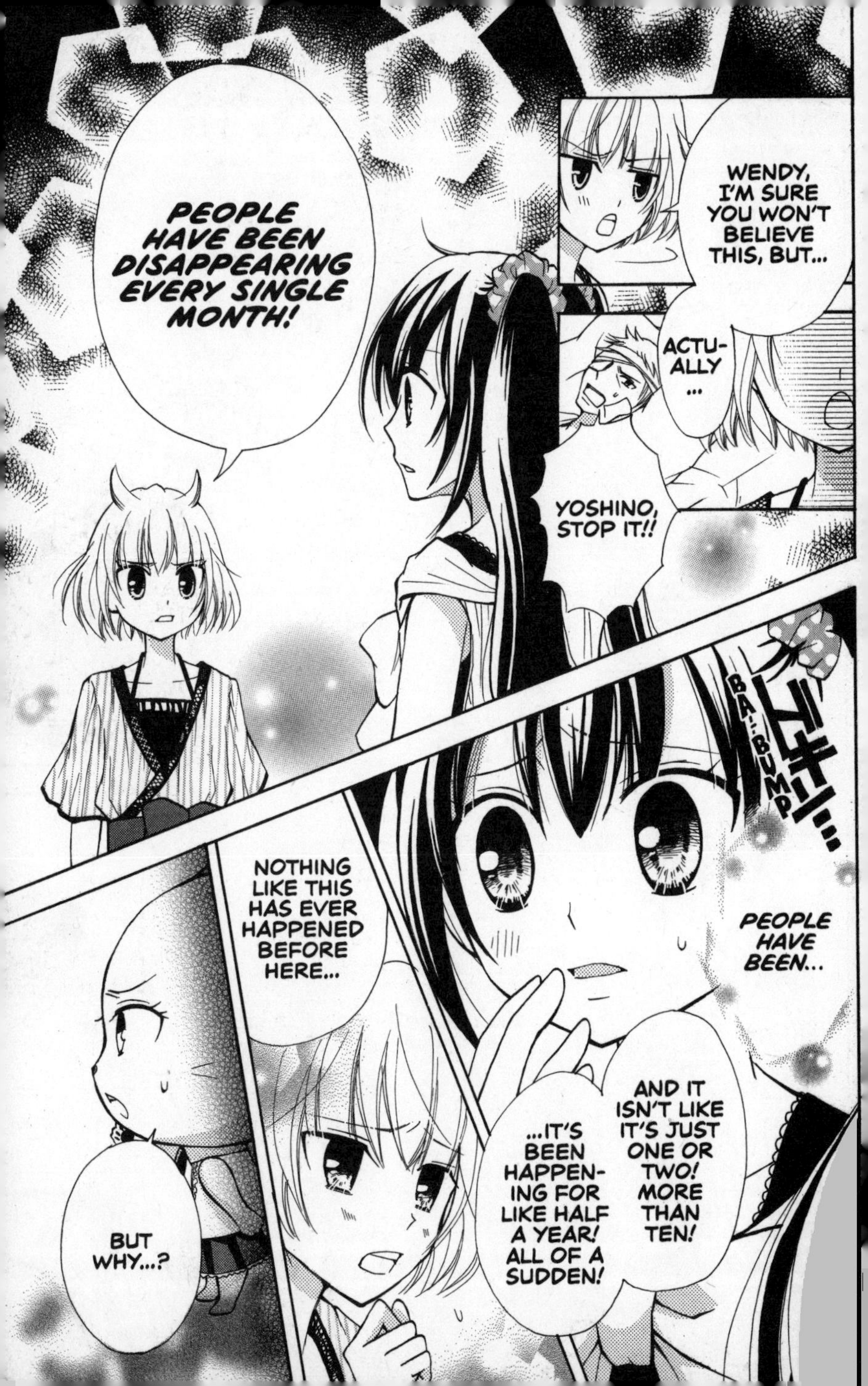
WENDY, I'M SURE YOU WON'T BELIEVE THIS, BUT...
ACTU-ALLY ...
YOSHINO, STOP IT!!
PEOPLE HAVE BEEN DISAPPEARING EVERY SINGLE MONTH!
BA-BUMP
PEOPLE HAVE BEEN...
AND IT ISN'T LIKE IT'S JUST ONE OR TWO! MORE THAN TEN!
...IT'S BEEN HAPPEN-ING FOR LIKE HALF A YEAR! ALL OF A SUDDEN!
NOTHING LIKE THIS HAS EVER HAPPENED BEFORE HERE...
BUT WHY...?

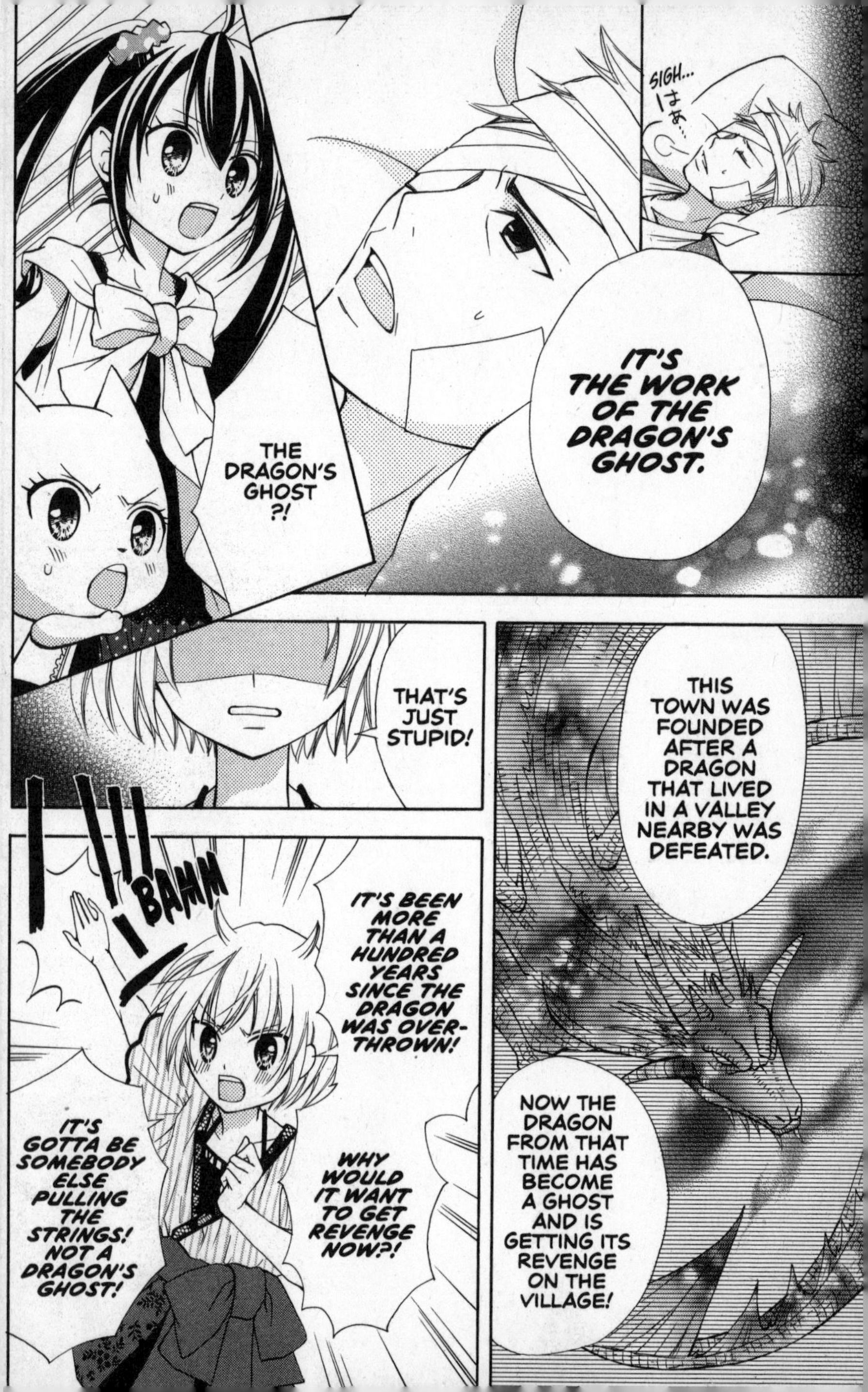
SIGH...
はぁ…
IT'S THE WORK OF THE DRAGON'S GHOST.
THE DRAGON'S GHOST ?!
THIS TOWN WAS FOUNDED AFTER A DRAGON THAT LIVED IN A VALLEY NEARBY WAS DEFEATED.
NOW THE DRAGON FROM THAT TIME HAS BECOME A GHOST AND IS GETTING ITS REVENGE ON THE VILLAGE!
THAT'S JUST STUPID!
BAMM
IT'S BEEN MORE THAN A HUNDRED YEARS SINCE THE DRAGON WAS OVER-THROWN!
WHY WOULD IT WANT TO GET REVENGE NOW?!
IT'S GOTTA BE SOMEBODY ELSE PULLING THE STRINGS! NOT A DRAGON'S GHOST!

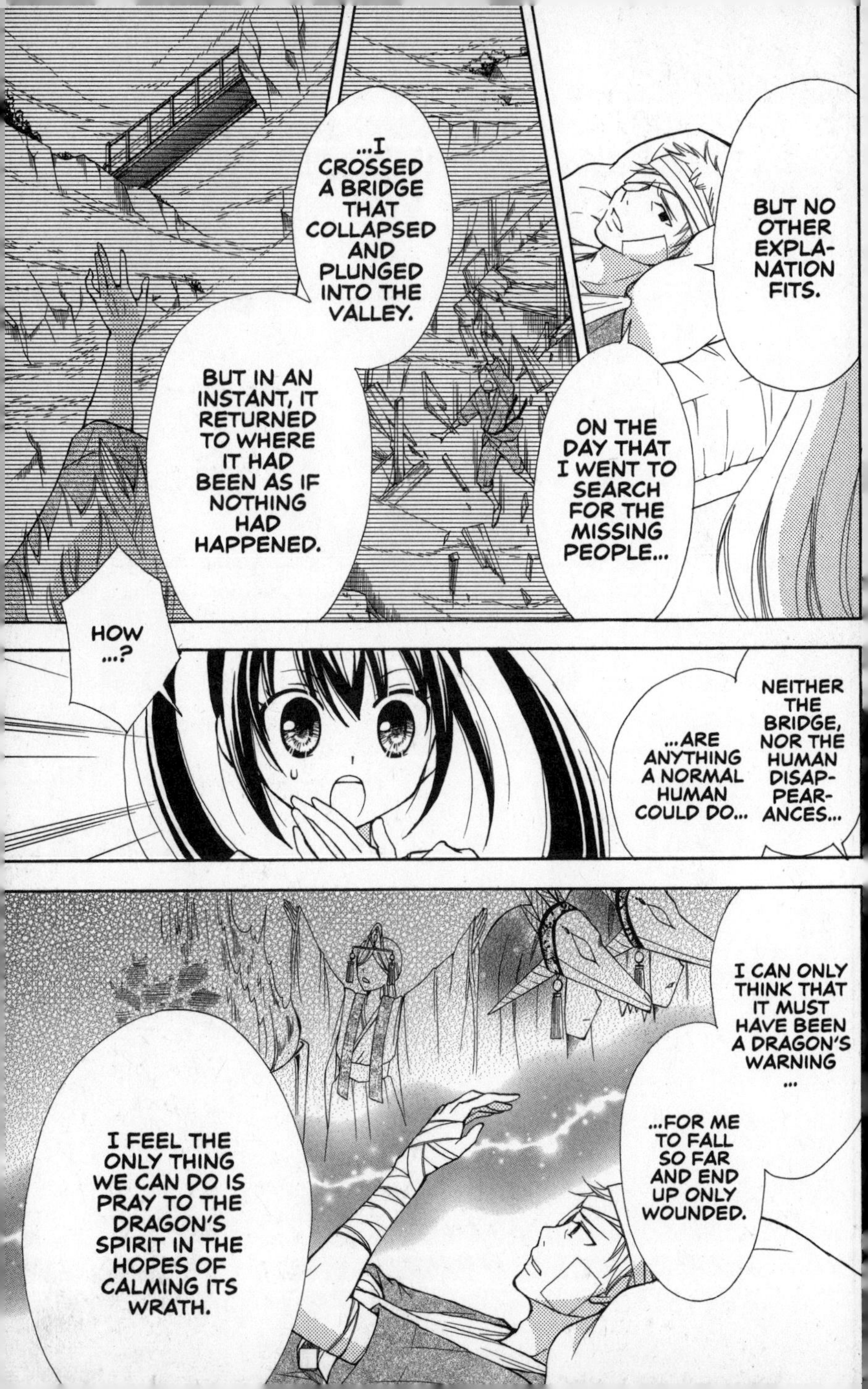
BUT NO OTHER EXPLANATION FITS.
ON THE DAY THAT I WENT TO SEARCH FOR THE MISSING PEOPLE...
...I CROSSED A BRIDGE THAT COLLAPSED AND PLUNGED INTO THE VALLEY.
BUT IN AN INSTANT, IT RETURNED TO WHERE IT HAD BEEN AS IF NOTHING HAD HAPPENED.
NEITHER THE BRIDGE, NOR THE HUMAN DISAPPEARANCES...
...ARE ANYTHING A NORMAL HUMAN COULD DO...
HOW ...?
I CAN ONLY THINK THAT IT MUST HAVE BEEN A DRAGON'S WARNING ...
...FOR ME TO FALL SO FAR AND END UP ONLY WOUNDED.
I FEEL THE ONLY THING WE CAN DO IS PRAY TO THE DRAGON'S SPIRIT IN THE HOPES OF CALMING ITS WRATH.

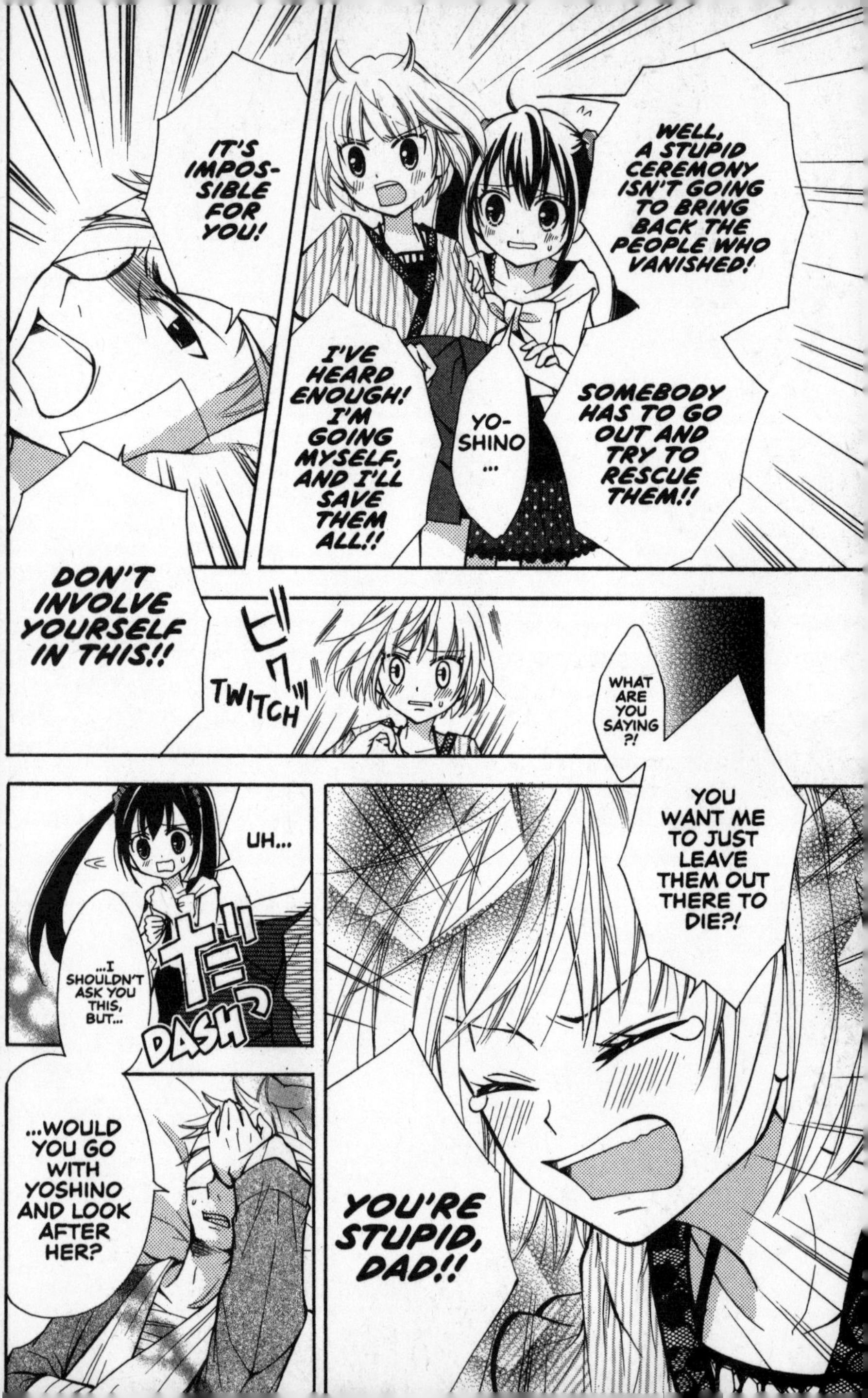
WELL, A STUPID CEREMONY ISN'T GOING TO BRING BACK THE PEOPLE WHO VANISHED!
SOMEBODY HAS TO GO OUT AND TRY TO RESCUE THEM!!
YO-SHINO...
I'VE HEARD ENOUGH! I'M GOING MYSELF, AND I'LL SAVE THEM ALL!!
IT'S IMPOSSIBLE FOR YOU!
DON'T INVOLVE YOURSELF IN THIS!!
WHAT ARE YOU SAYING?!
TWITCH
YOU WANT ME TO JUST LEAVE THEM OUT THERE TO DIE?!
YOU'RE STUPID, DAD!!
UH...
DASH
...I SHOULDN'T ASK YOU THIS, BUT...
...WOULD YOU GO WITH YOSHINO AND LOOK AFTER HER?

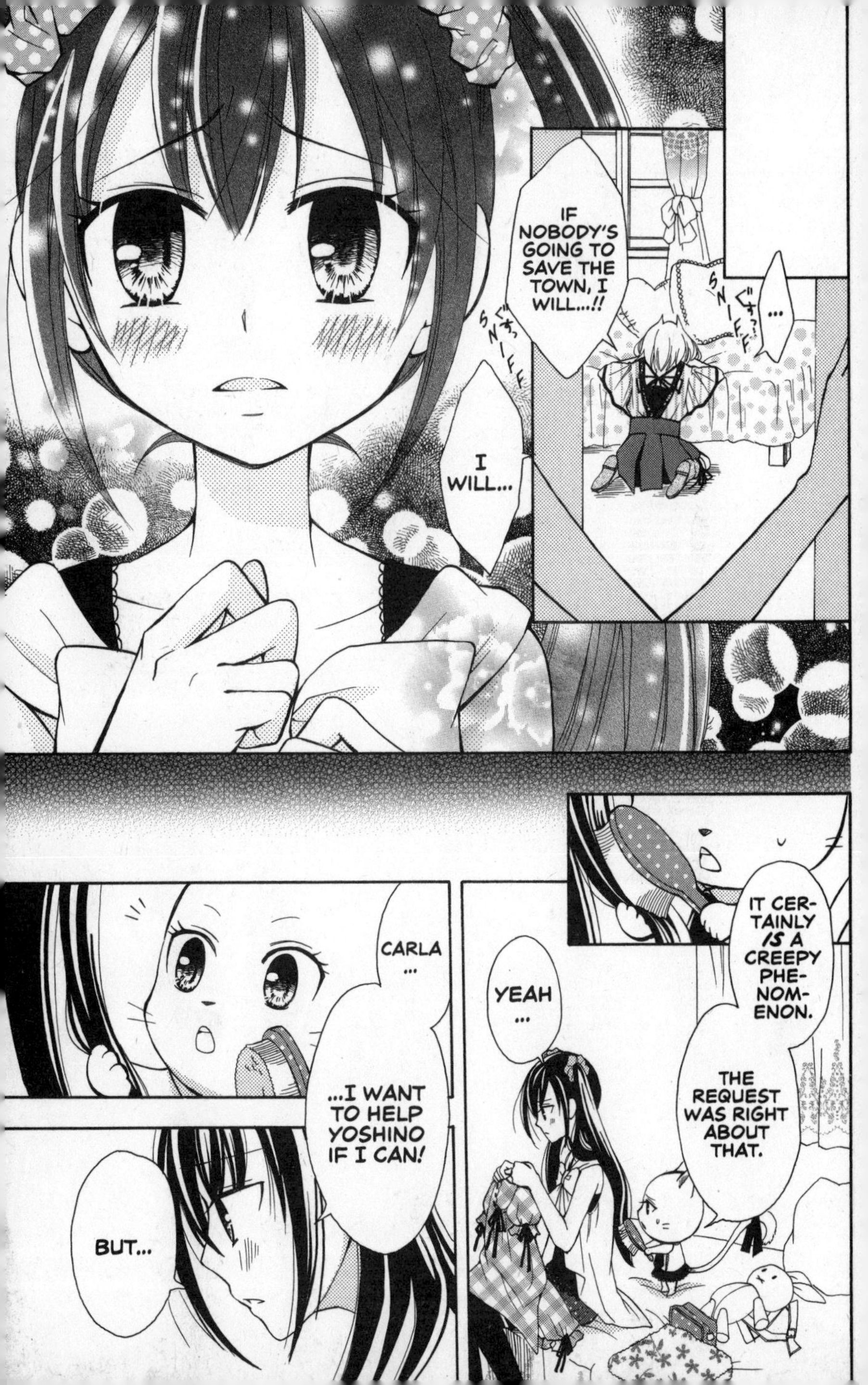
...
ぐすっ SNIFF
IF NOBODY'S GOING TO SAVE THE TOWN, I WILL...!!
ぐすっ SNIFF
I WILL...
IT CERTAINLY *IS* A CREEPY PHENOMENON.
THE REQUEST WAS RIGHT ABOUT THAT.
YEAH...
CARLA...
...I WANT TO HELP YOSHINO IF I CAN!
BUT...

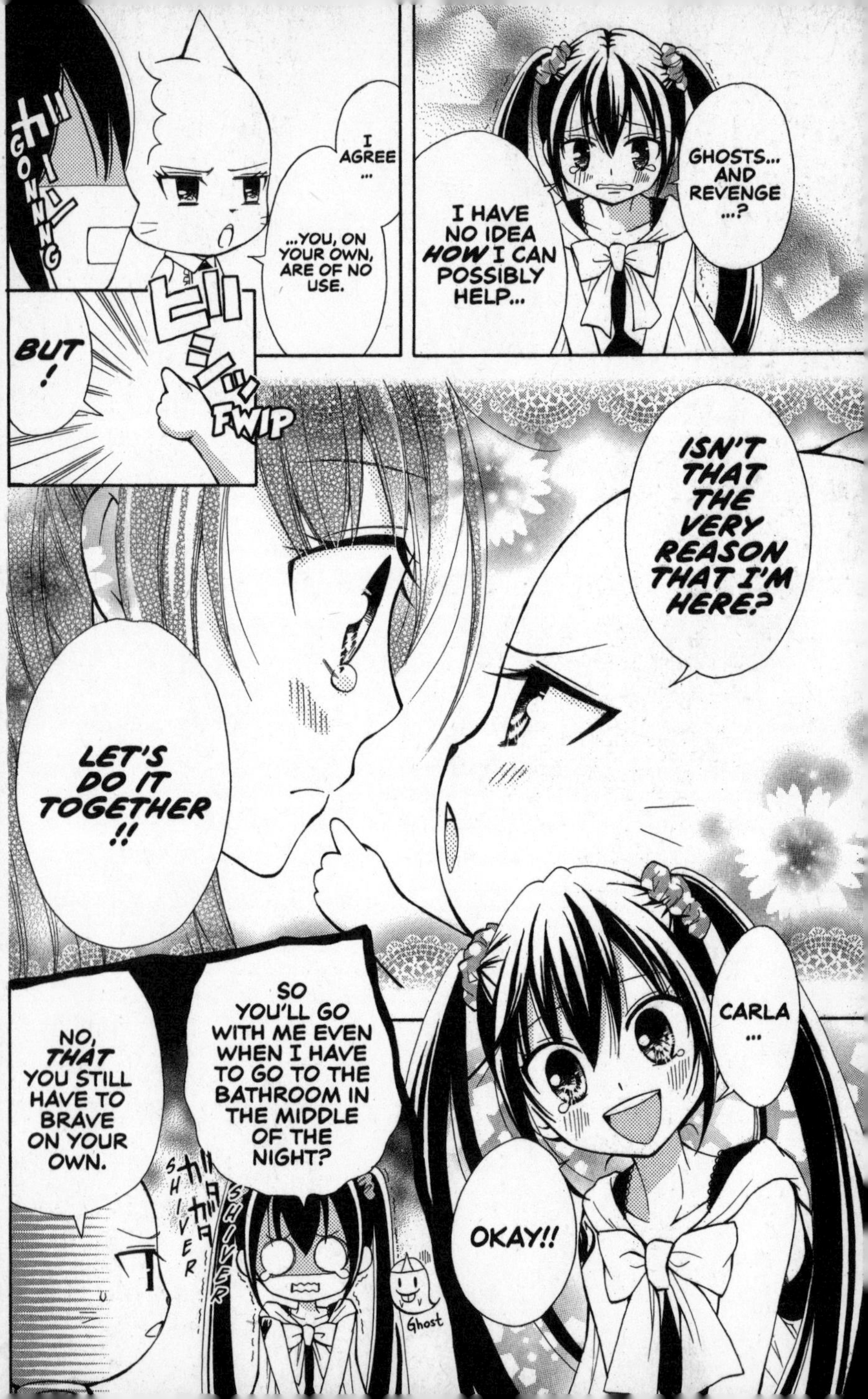
GHOSTS... AND REVENGE ...?
I HAVE NO IDEA *HOW* I CAN POSSIBLY HELP...
I AGREE ...
...YOU, ON YOUR OWN, ARE OF NO USE.
GONNNG
BUT!
FWIP
ISN'T THAT THE VERY REASON THAT I'M HERE?
LET'S DO IT TOGETHER!!
CARLA ...
OKAY!!
SO YOU'LL GO WITH ME EVEN WHEN I HAVE TO GO TO THE BATHROOM IN THE MIDDLE OF THE NIGHT?
NO, *THAT* YOU STILL HAVE TO BRAVE ON YOUR OWN.
SHIVER
SHIVER
Ghost

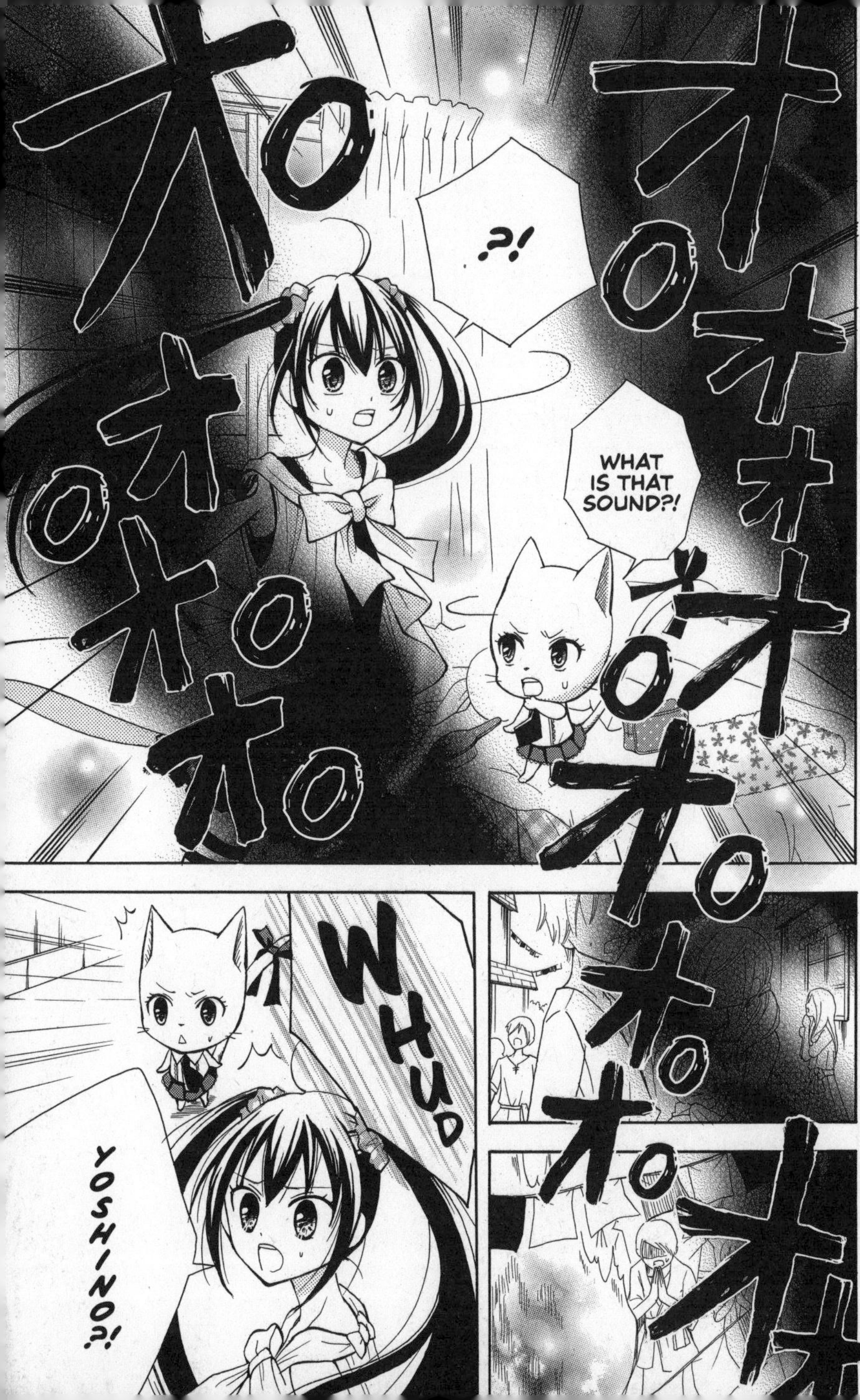
?!
WHAT IS THAT SOUND?!
WHUD
YOSHINO?!

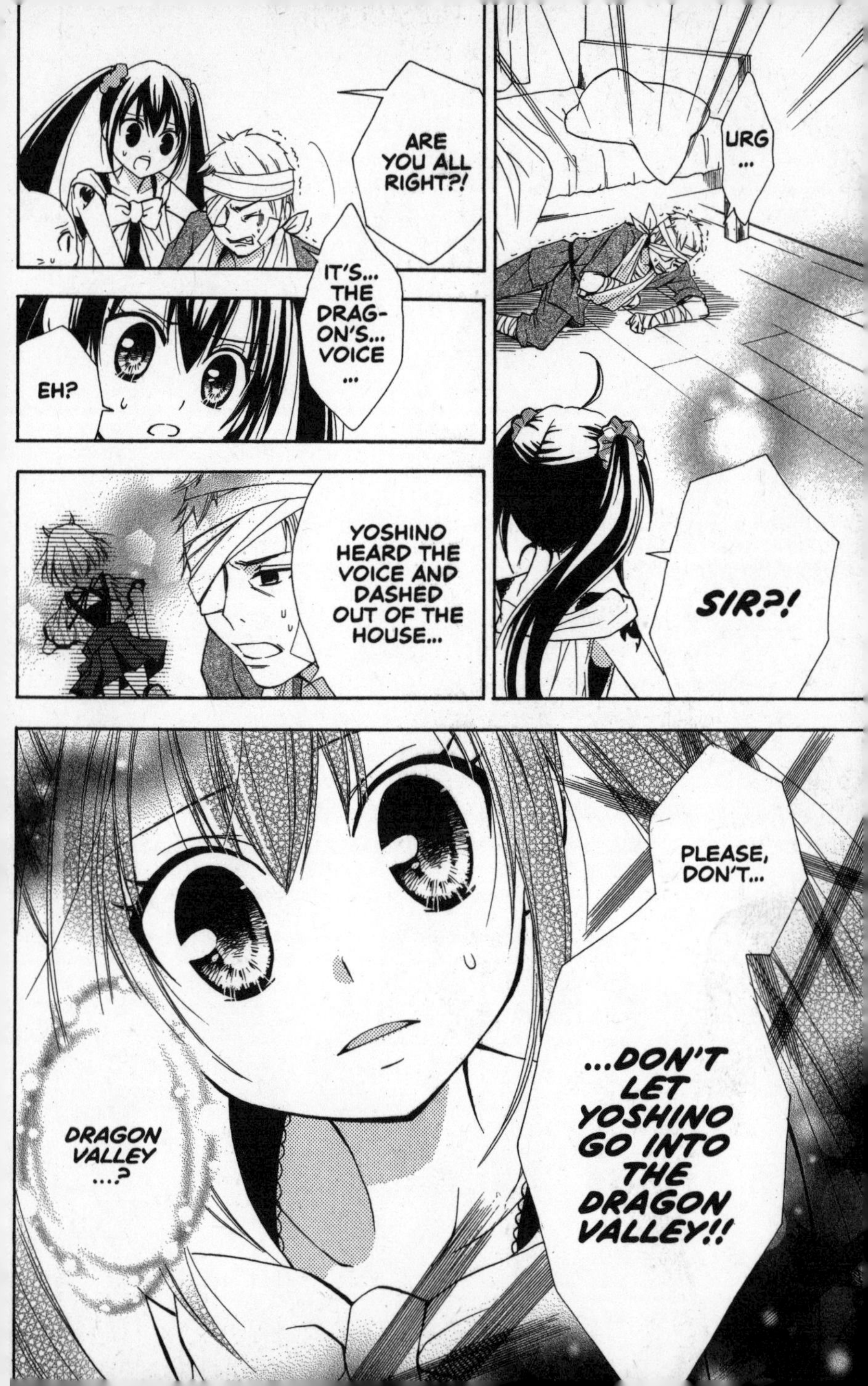
URG ...
SIR?!
ARE YOU ALL RIGHT?!
IT'S... THE DRAG-ON'S... VOICE ...
EH?
YOSHINO HEARD THE VOICE AND DASHED OUT OF THE HOUSE...
PLEASE, DON'T...
...DON'T LET YOSHINO GO INTO THE DRAGON VALLEY!!
DRAGON VALLEY ...?

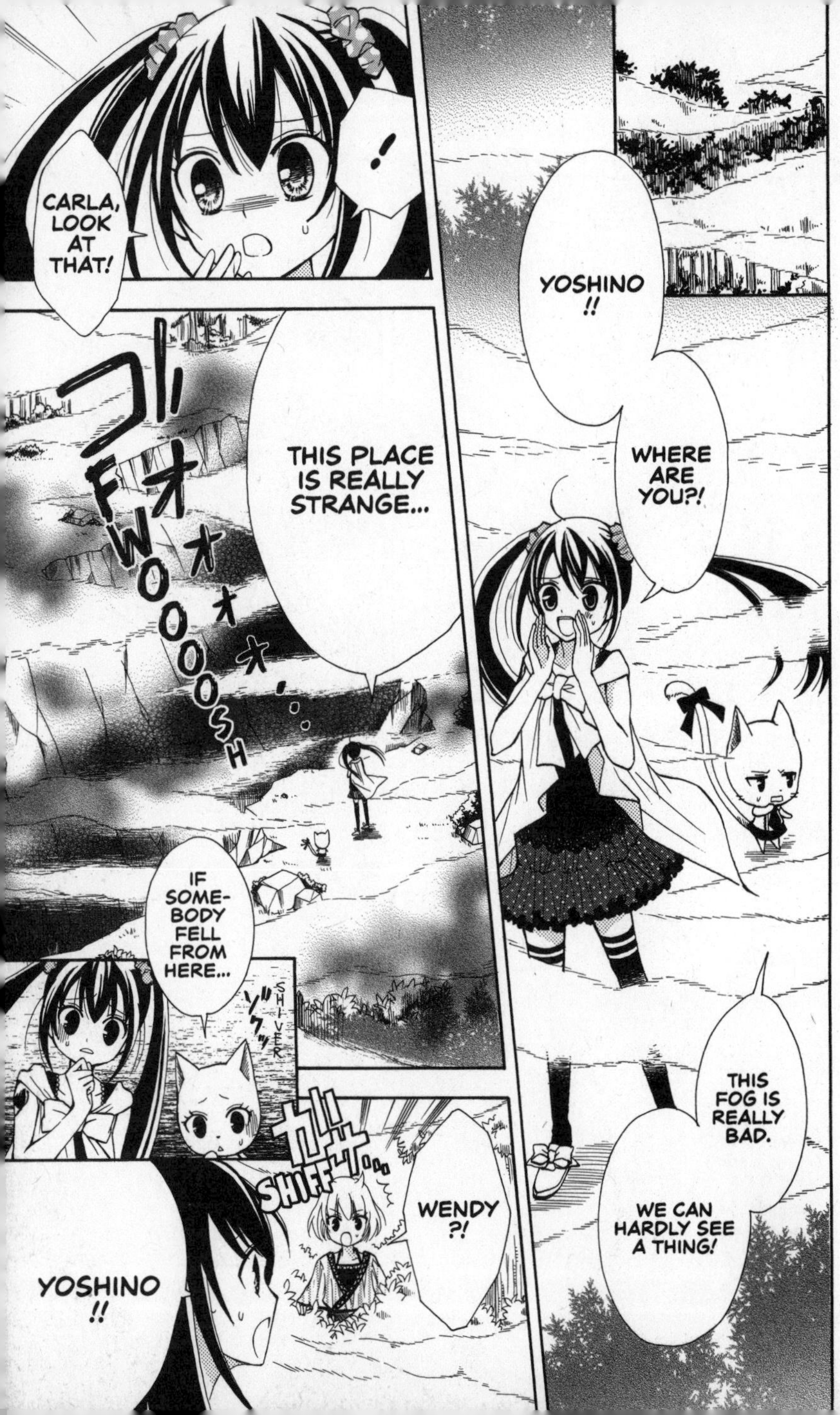

YOSHINO !!
WHERE ARE YOU?!
THIS FOG IS REALLY BAD.
WE CAN HARDLY SEE A THING!
!
CARLA, LOOK AT THAT!
THIS PLACE IS REALLY STRANGE...
FWOOOOSH
IF SOMEBODY FELL FROM HERE...
SHIVER
SHIFF
WENDY ?!
YOSHINO !!

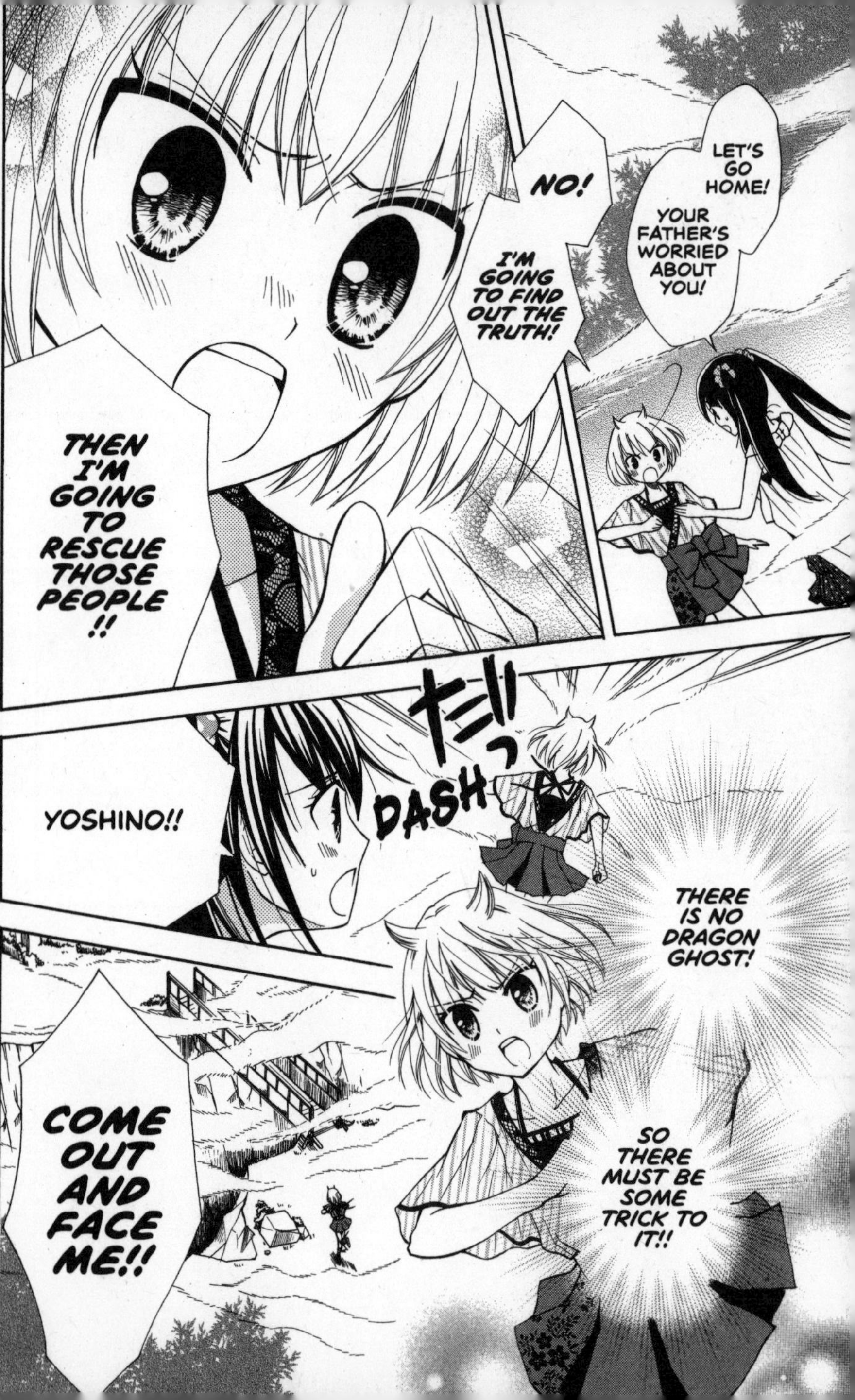
LET'S GO HOME! YOUR FATHER'S WORRIED ABOUT YOU!
NO! I'M GOING TO FIND OUT THE TRUTH!
THEN I'M GOING TO RESCUE THOSE PEOPLE!!
DASH
YOSHINO!!
THERE IS NO DRAGON GHOST!
SO THERE MUST BE SOME TRICK TO IT!!
COME OUT AND FACE ME!!

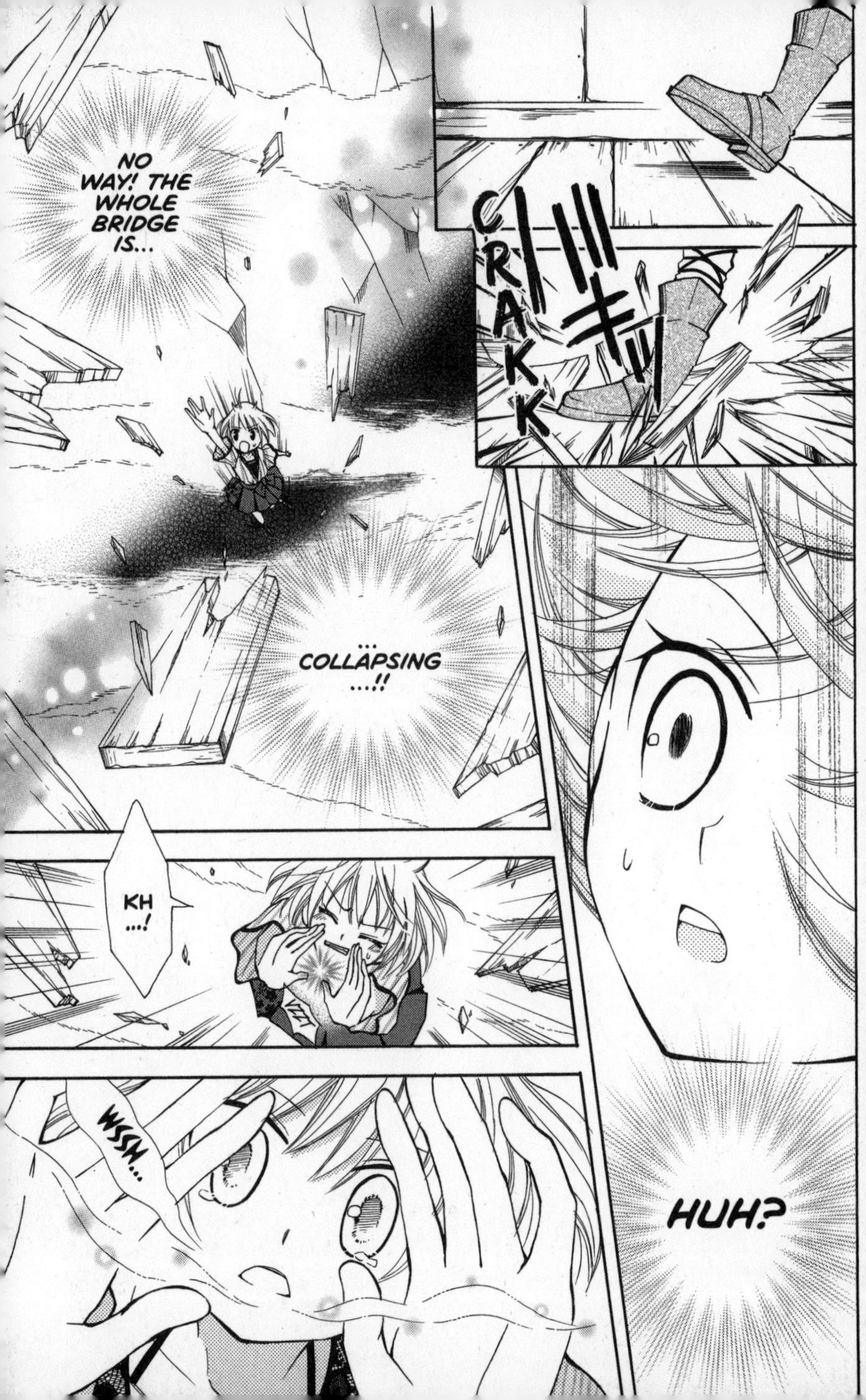
CRAKK
NO WAY! THE WHOLE BRIDGE IS...
...COLLAPSING...!!
HUH?
KH ...!
VZZT
WSSH...

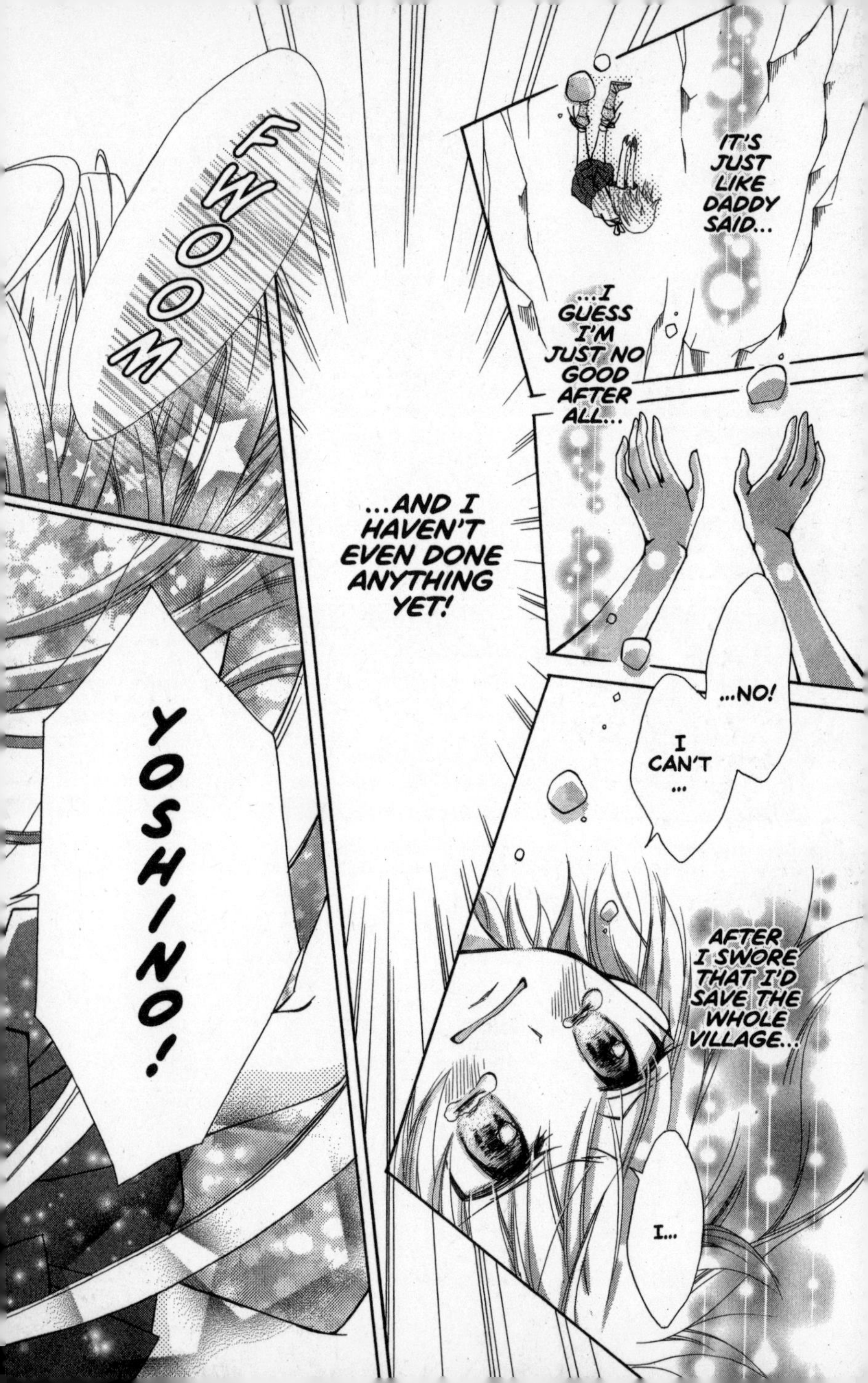
IT'S JUST LIKE DADDY SAID...
...I GUESS I'M JUST NO GOOD AFTER ALL...
...NO!
I CAN'T ...
AFTER I SWORE THAT I'D SAVE THE WHOLE VILLAGE...
I...
...AND I HAVEN'T EVEN DONE ANYTHING YET!
FWOOM
YOSHINO!

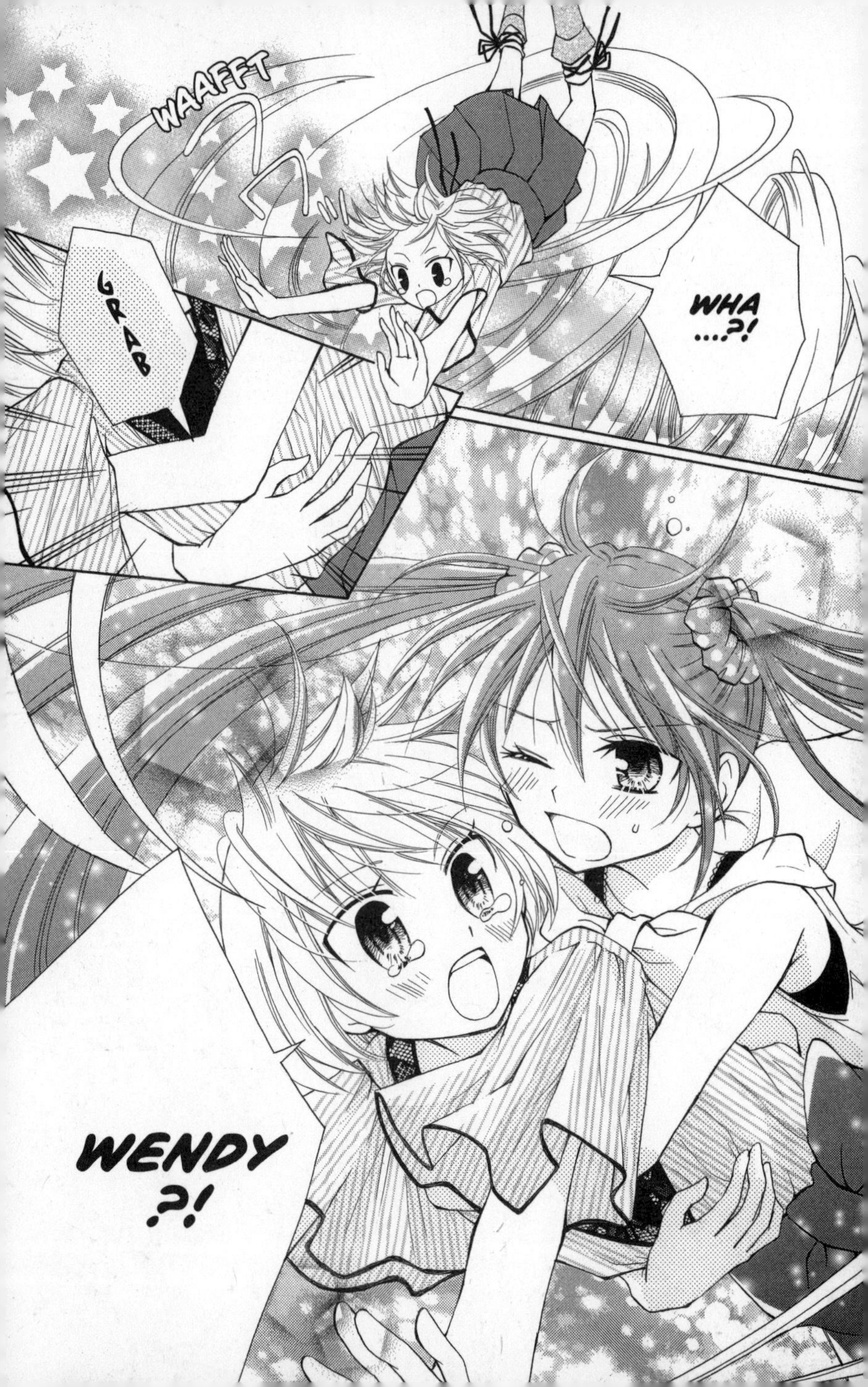
WAAFFT
WHA ...?!
GRAB
WENDY ?!

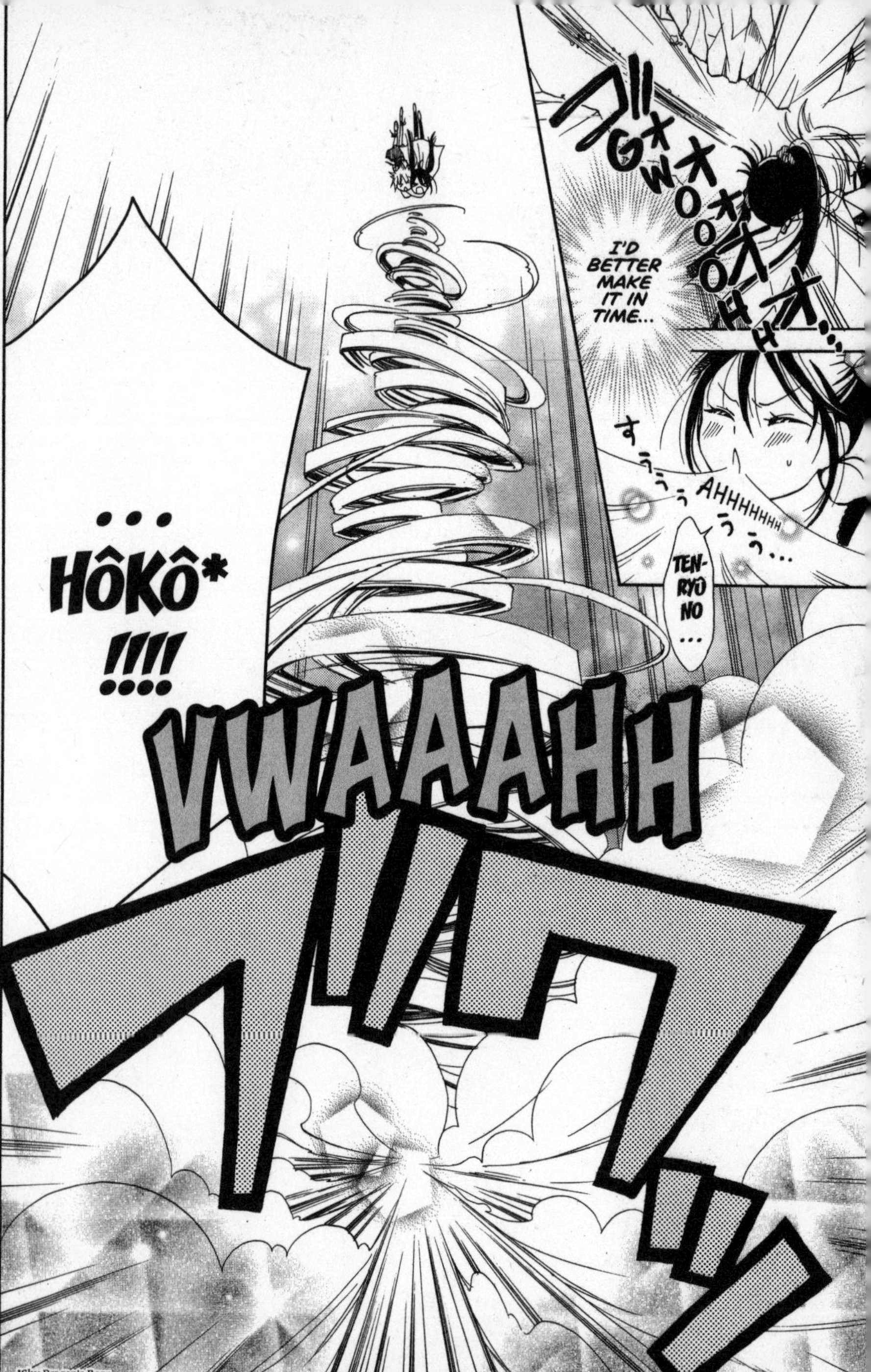
GWOOOHH
I'D BETTER MAKE IT IN TIME...
AHHHHHHH
TEN-RYÛ NO ...
... HÔKÔ* !!!!
VWAAAHH

*Sky Dragon's Roar

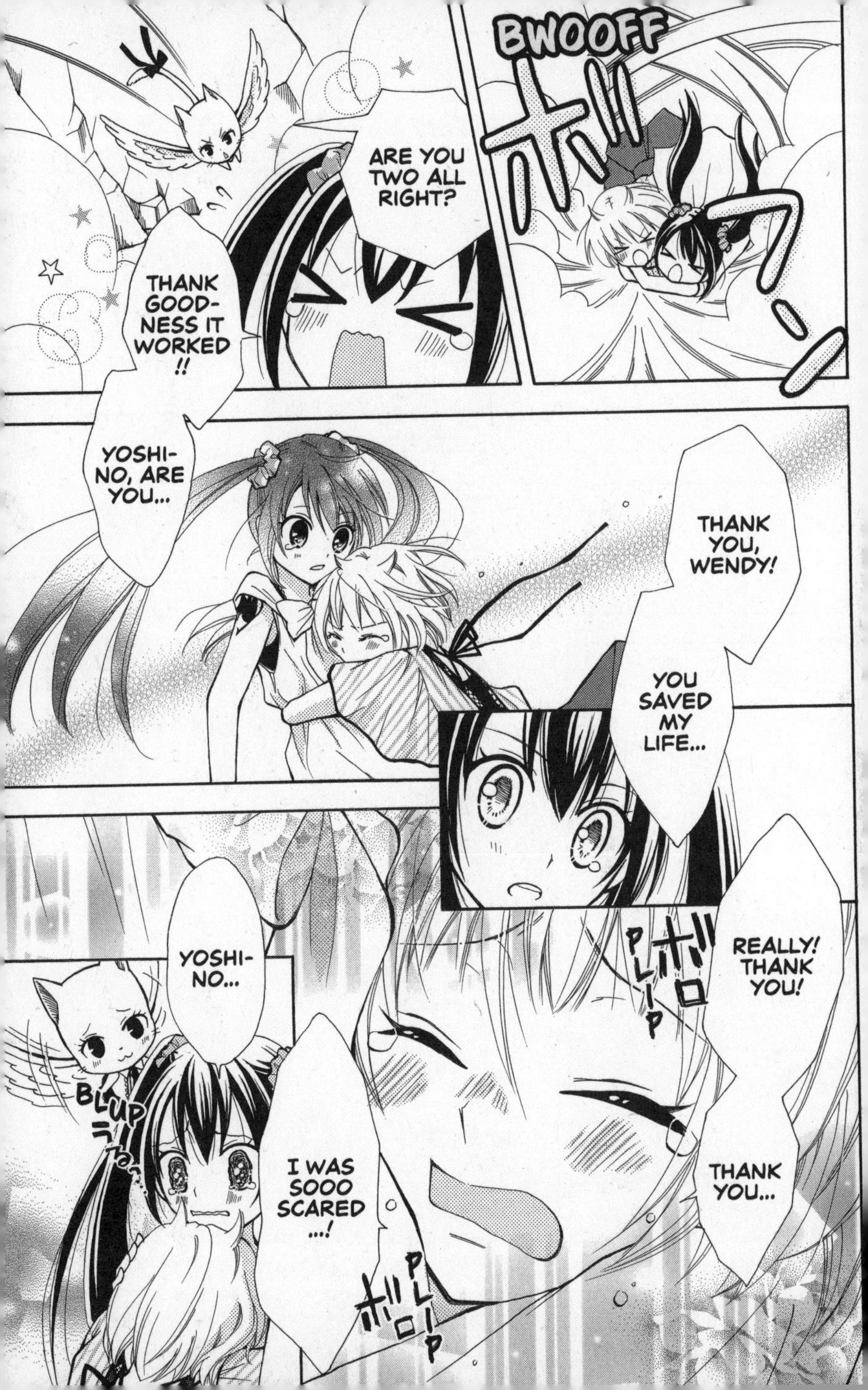
BWOOFF
ARE YOU TWO ALL RIGHT?
THANK GOODNESS IT WORKED!!
YOSHINO, ARE YOU...
THANK YOU, WENDY!
YOU SAVED MY LIFE...
REALLY! THANK YOU!
PLIP
THANK YOU...
YOSHINO...
BLUP
I WAS SOOO SCARED...!
PLIP

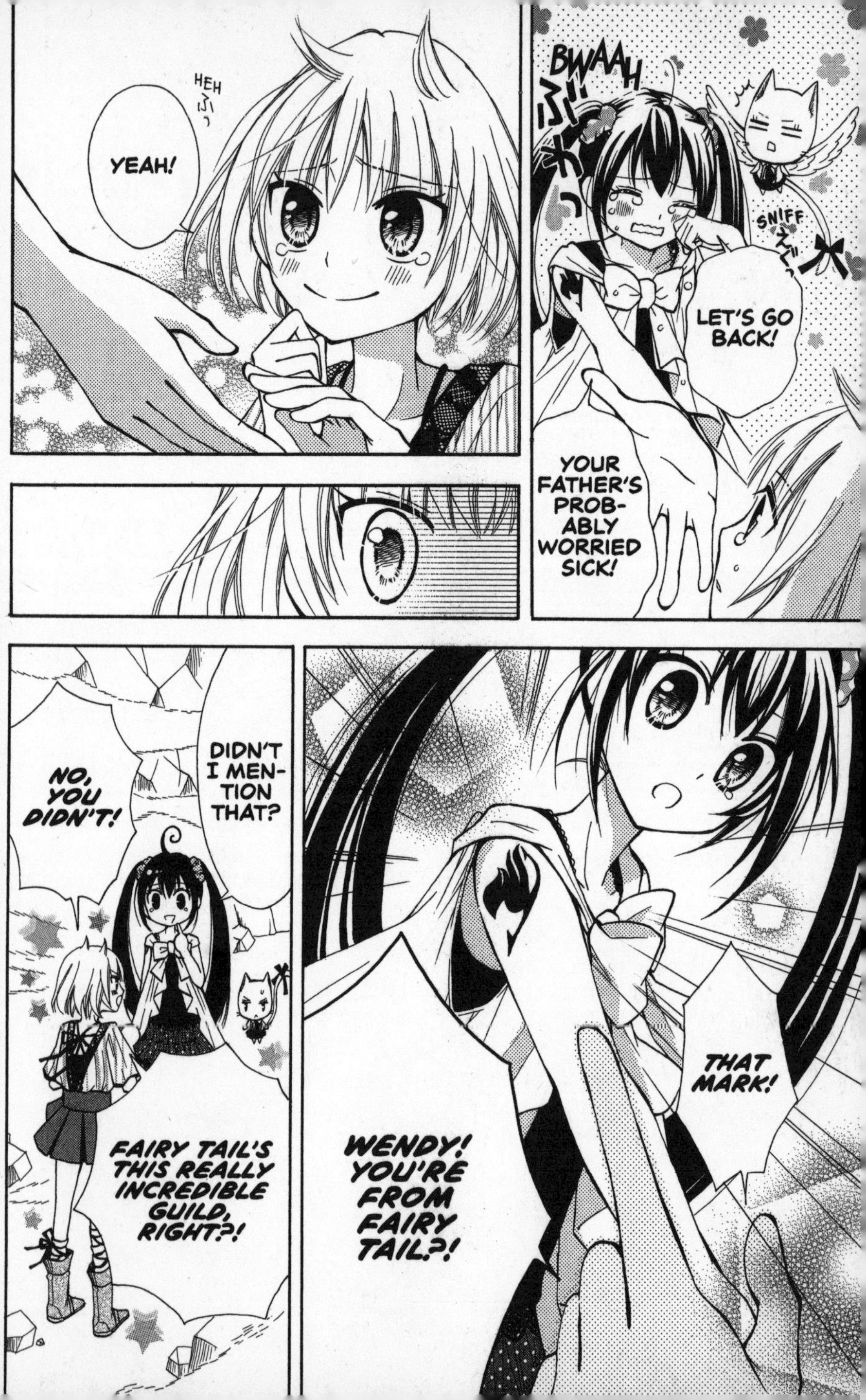
BWAAH
SNIFF
LET'S GO BACK!
YOUR FATHER'S PROB-ABLY WORRIED SICK!
HEH
YEAH!
THAT MARK!
WENDY! YOU'RE FROM FAIRY TAIL?!
DIDN'T I MEN-TION THAT?
NO, YOU DIDN'T!
FAIRY TAIL'S THIS REALLY INCREDIBLE GUILD, RIGHT?!

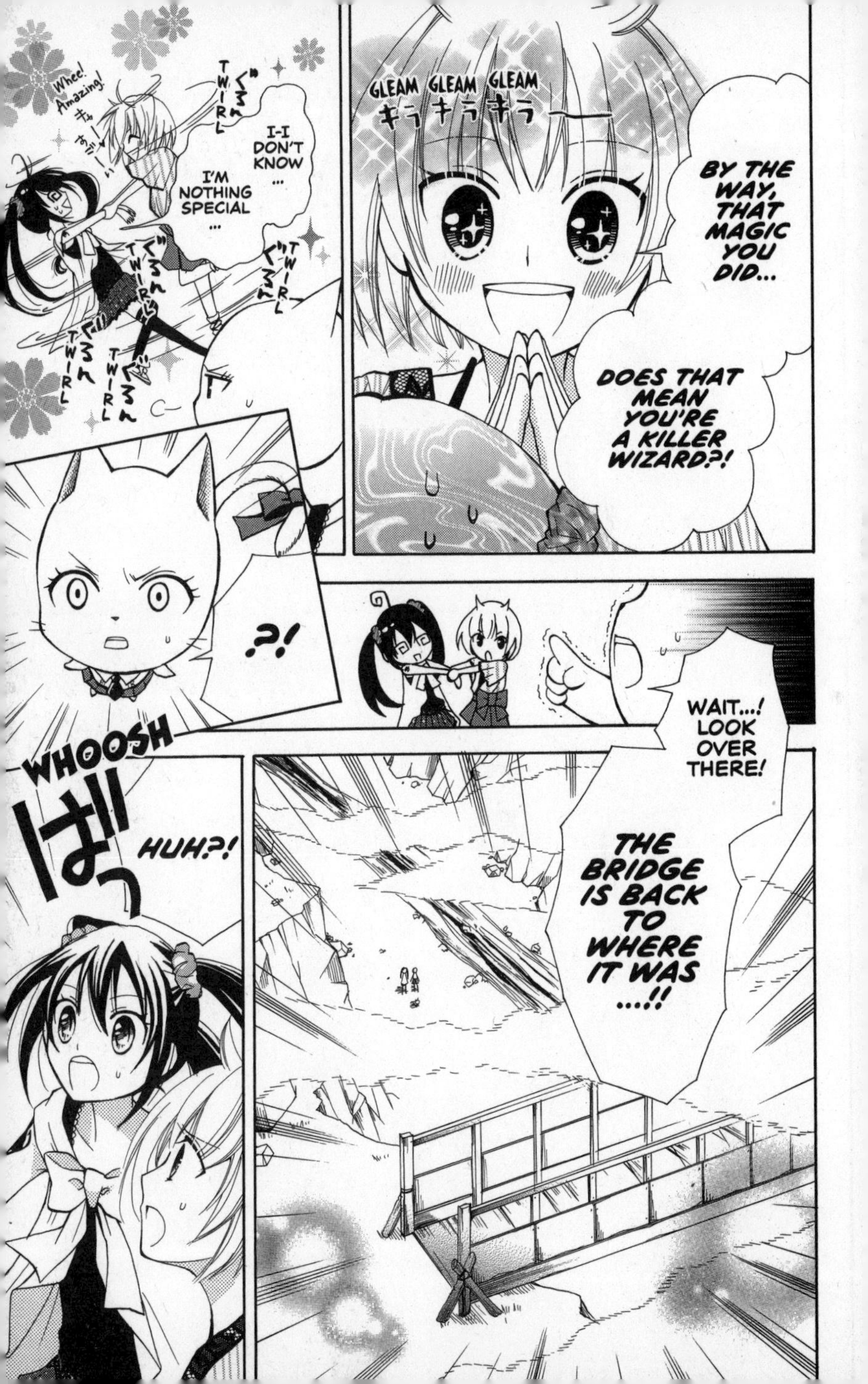
GLEAM GLEAM GLEAM
キラキラキラー
BY THE WAY, THAT MAGIC YOU DID...
DOES THAT MEAN YOU'RE A KILLER WIZARD?!
Whee! Amazing!
きゃ すごーい
TWIRL ぐるん
I-I DON'T KNOW ...
I'M NOTHING SPECIAL ...
TWIRL ぐるん
TWIRL ぐるん
TWIRL ぐるん
TWIRL ぐるん
WAIT...! LOOK OVER THERE!
?!
THE BRIDGE IS BACK TO WHERE IT WAS ...!!
WHOOSH
はっ
HUH?!

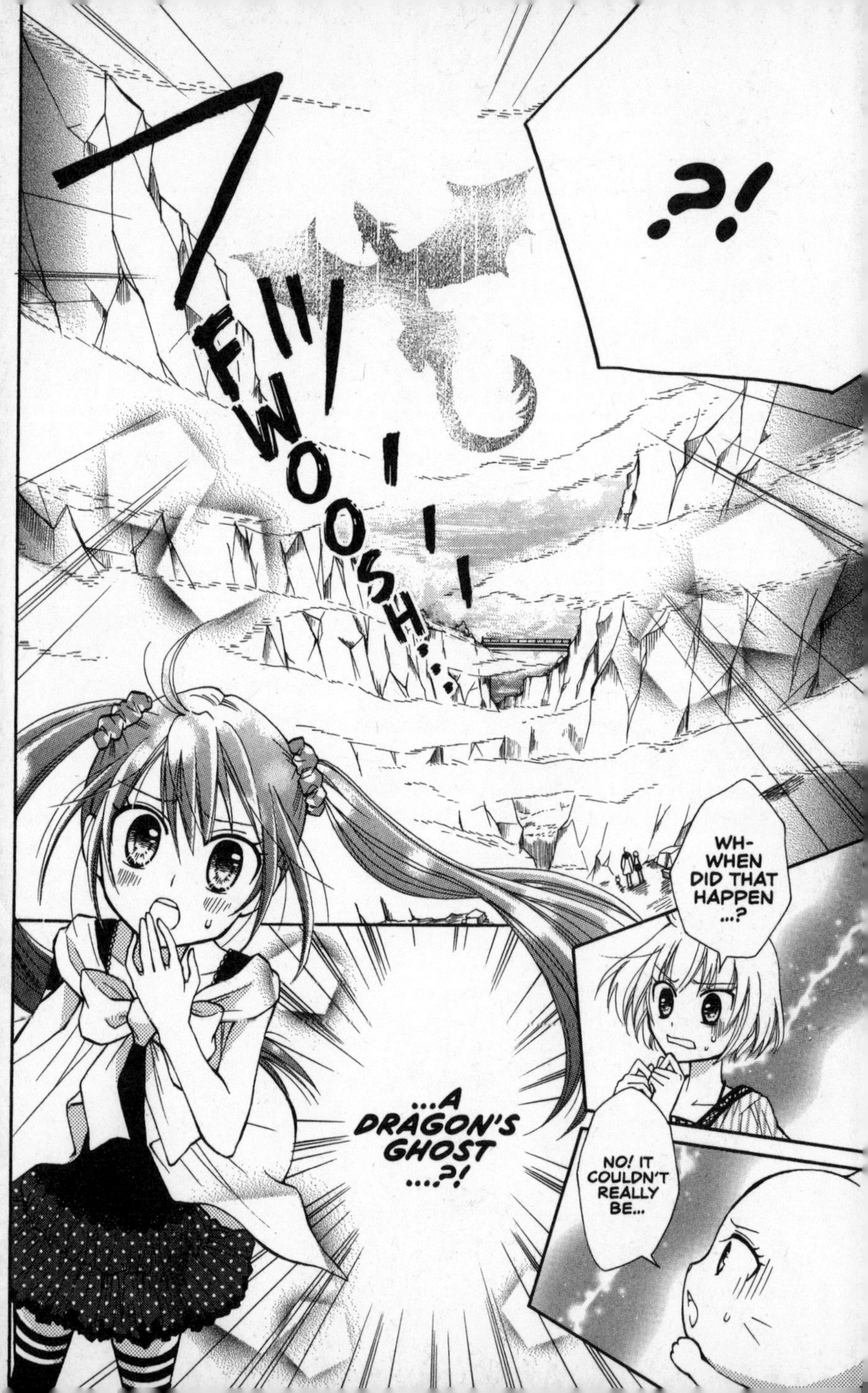
?!
FWOOSH...
WH- WHEN DID THAT HAPPEN ...?
NO! IT COULDN'T REALLY BE...
...A DRAGON'S GHOST ...?!

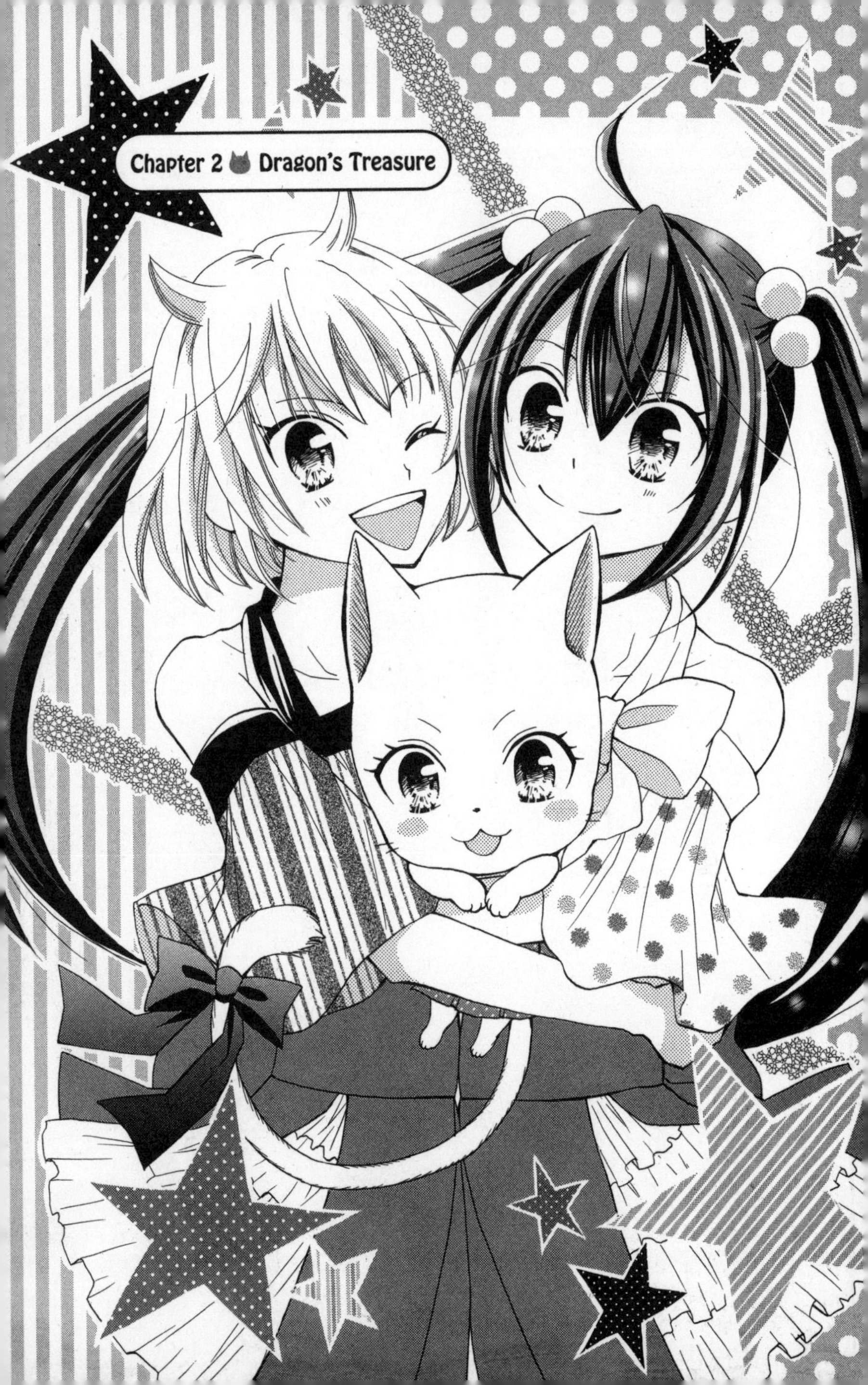
Chapter 2 Dragon's Treasure

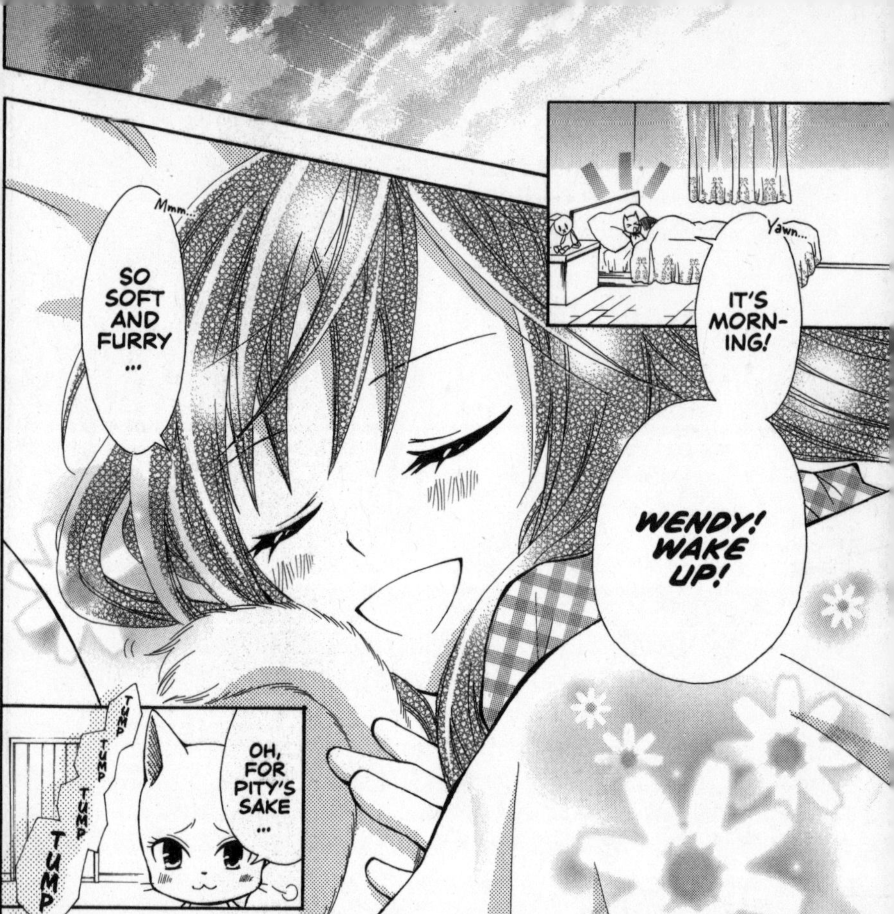
Yawn...
IT'S MORNING!
WENDY! WAKE UP!
Mmm...
SO SOFT AND FURRY...
OH, FOR PITY'S SAKE...
TUMP TUMP TUMP TUMP

Nice to meet you!
I'm Rui Watanabe.
To all the fans of the
original series and for those
of you reading Fairy Tail for
the first time, it'd make me
very happy if you just have
fun with this series!

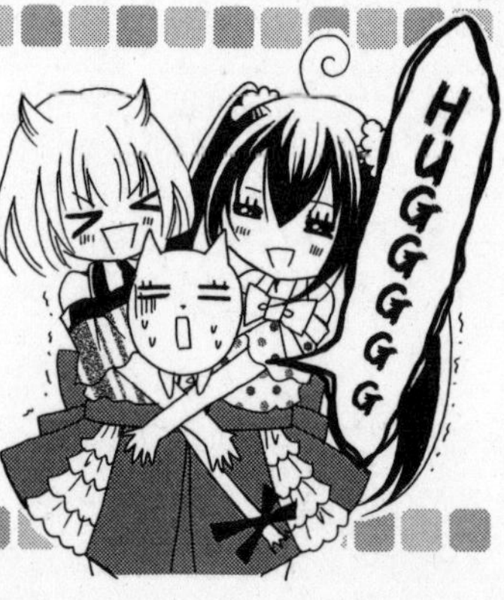
HUGGGGGG

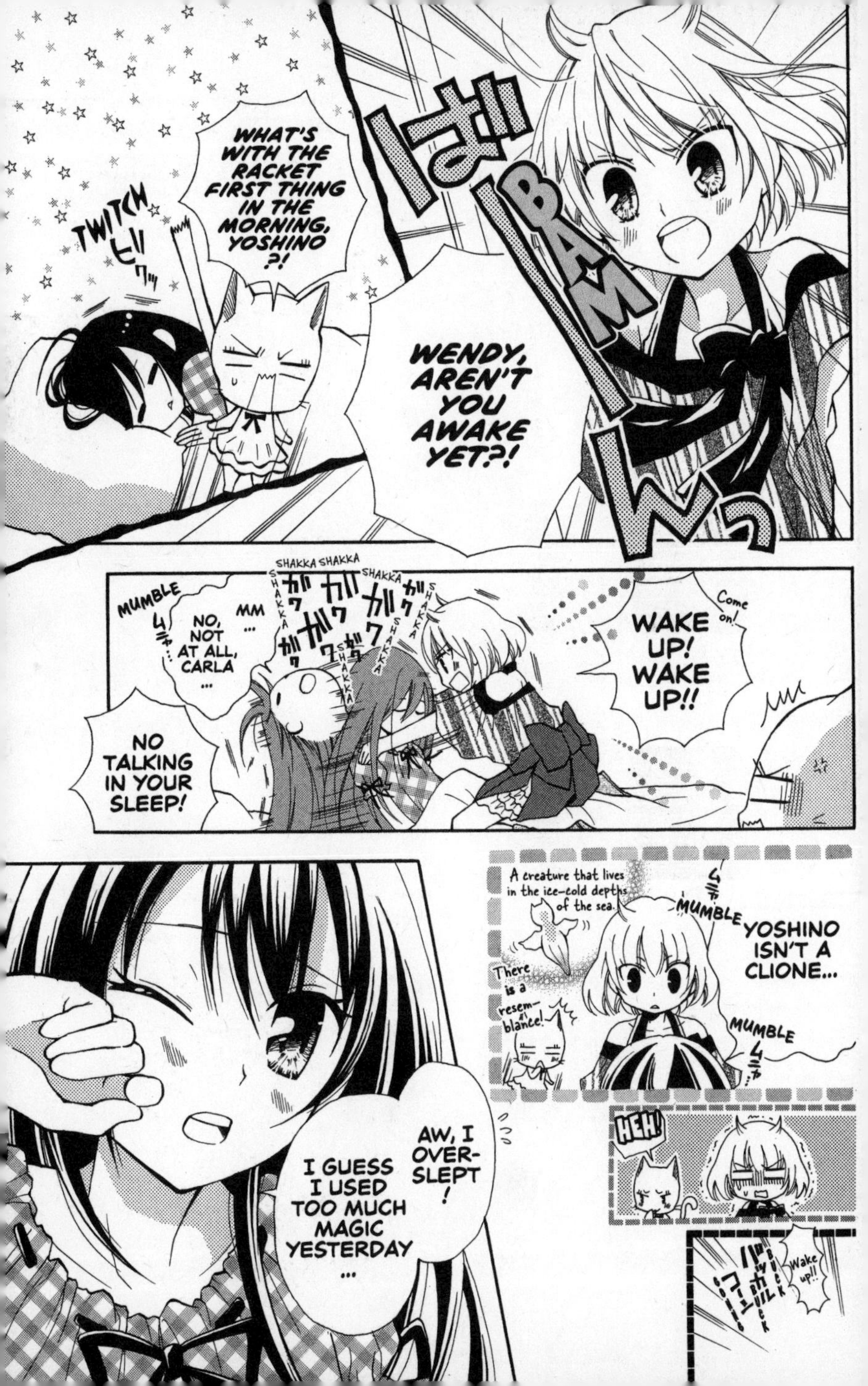
BAM
WENDY, AREN'T YOU AWAKE YET?!
WHAT'S WITH THE RACKET FIRST THING IN THE MORNING, YOSHINO?!
TWITCH
Come on!
WAKE UP! WAKE UP!!
SHAKKA SHAKKA
SHAKKA SHAKKA
MM... NO, NOT AT ALL, CARLA...
MUMBLE
NO TALKING IN YOUR SLEEP!
MUMBLE
YOSHINO ISN'T A CLIONE...
A creature that lives in the ice-cold depths of the sea.
There is a resemblance!
MUMBLE
HEH!
Wake up!!
BUCK BUCK
AW, I OVERSLEPT!
I GUESS I USED TOO MUCH MAGIC YESTERDAY...

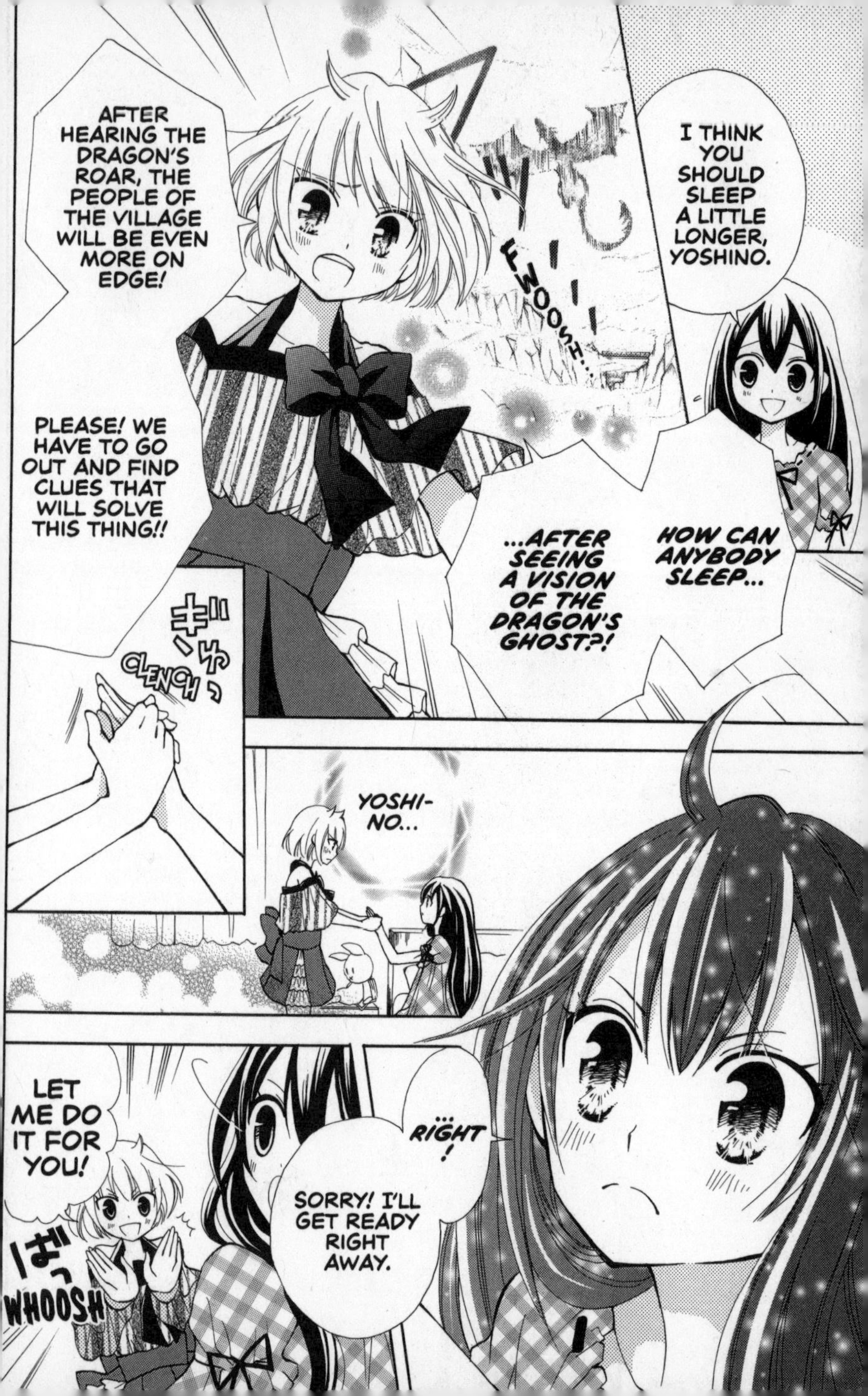
I THINK YOU SHOULD SLEEP A LITTLE LONGER, YOSHINO.
FWOOSH...
HOW CAN ANYBODY SLEEP...
...AFTER SEEING A VISION OF THE DRAGON'S GHOST?!
AFTER HEARING THE DRAGON'S ROAR, THE PEOPLE OF THE VILLAGE WILL BE EVEN MORE ON EDGE!
PLEASE! WE HAVE TO GO OUT AND FIND CLUES THAT WILL SOLVE THIS THING!!
YOSHI-NO...
ぎゅっ
CLENCH
...RIGHT!
SORRY! I'LL GET READY RIGHT AWAY.
LET ME DO IT FOR YOU!
ばっ
WHOOSH

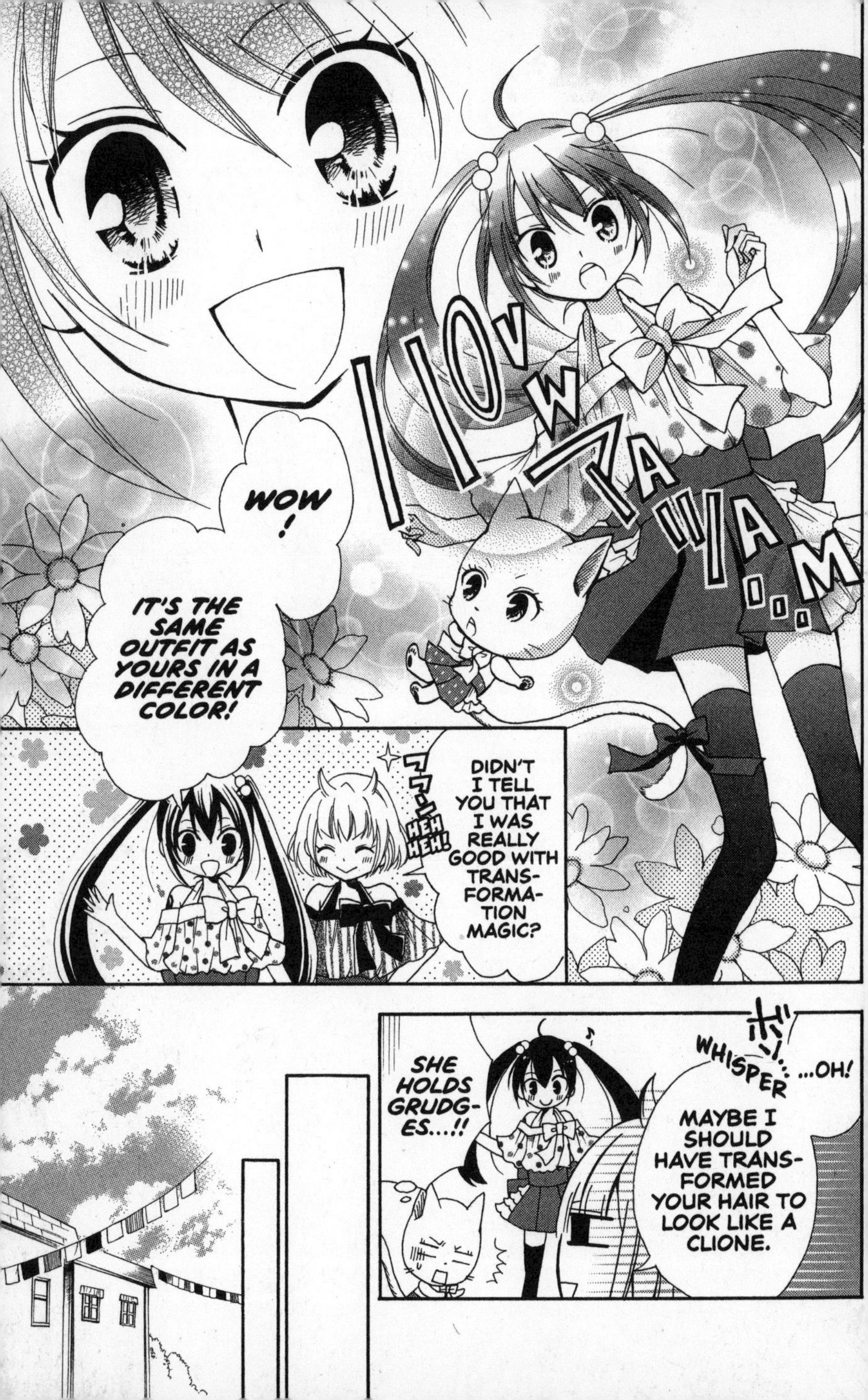
WOW!
IT'S THE SAME OUTFIT AS YOURS IN A DIFFERENT COLOR!
DIDN'T I TELL YOU THAT I WAS REALLY GOOD WITH TRANS-FORMA-TION MAGIC?
HEH HEH!
...OH!
WHISPER
MAYBE I SHOULD HAVE TRANS-FORMED YOUR HAIR TO LOOK LIKE A CLIONE.
SHE HOLDS GRUDG-ES...!!

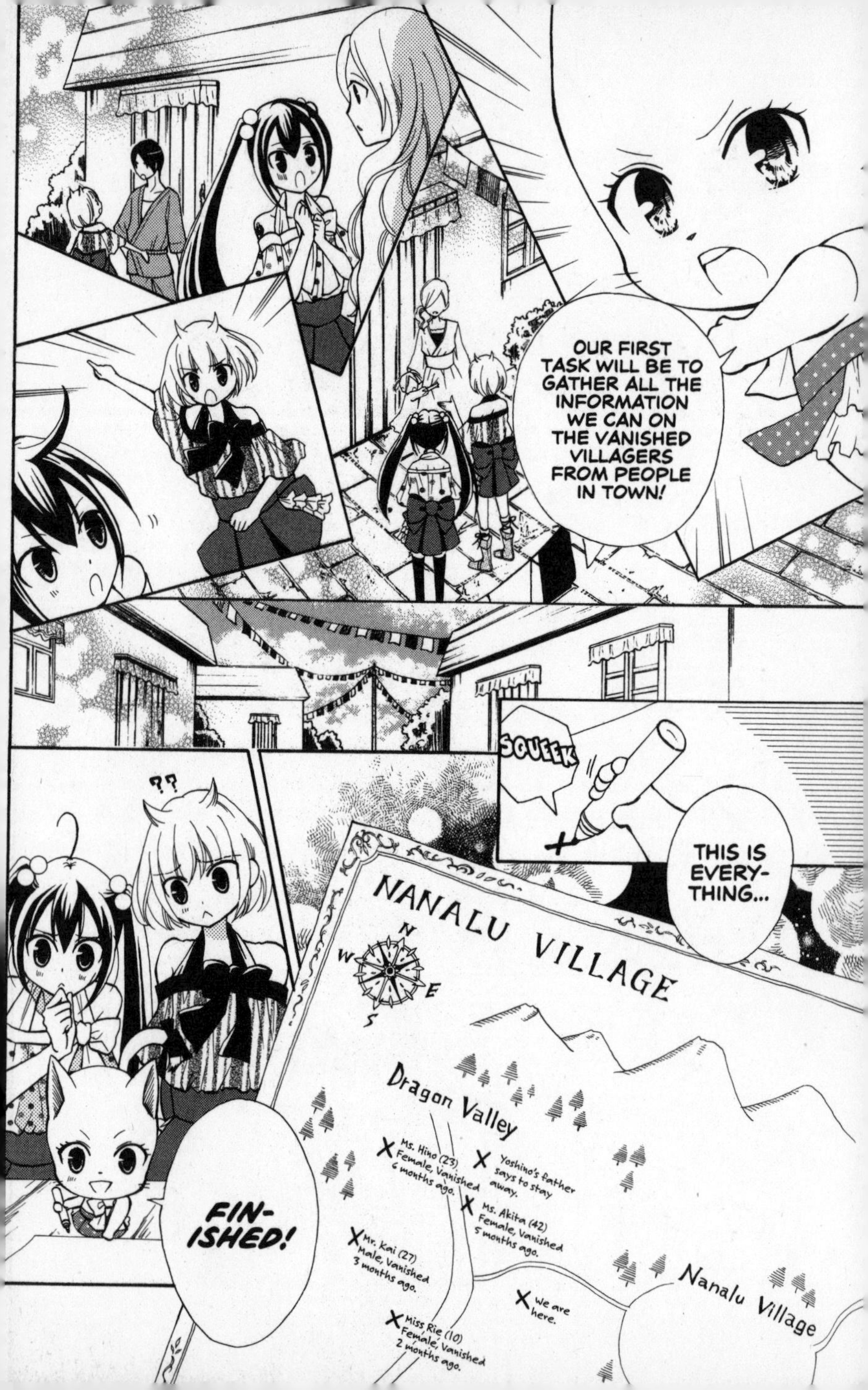
OUR FIRST TASK WILL BE TO GATHER ALL THE INFORMATION WE CAN ON THE VANISHED VILLAGERS FROM PEOPLE IN TOWN!
SQUEEK
THIS IS EVERY-THING...
NANALU VILLAGE
N
W
E
S
Dragon Valley
Ms. Hino (23) Female, Vanished 6 months ago.
Yoshino's father says to stay away.
Ms. Akita (42) Female, Vanished 5 months ago.
Mr. Kai (27) Male, Vanished 3 months ago.
We are here.
Miss Rie (10) Female, Vanished 2 months ago.
Nanalu Village
??
FIN-ISHED!

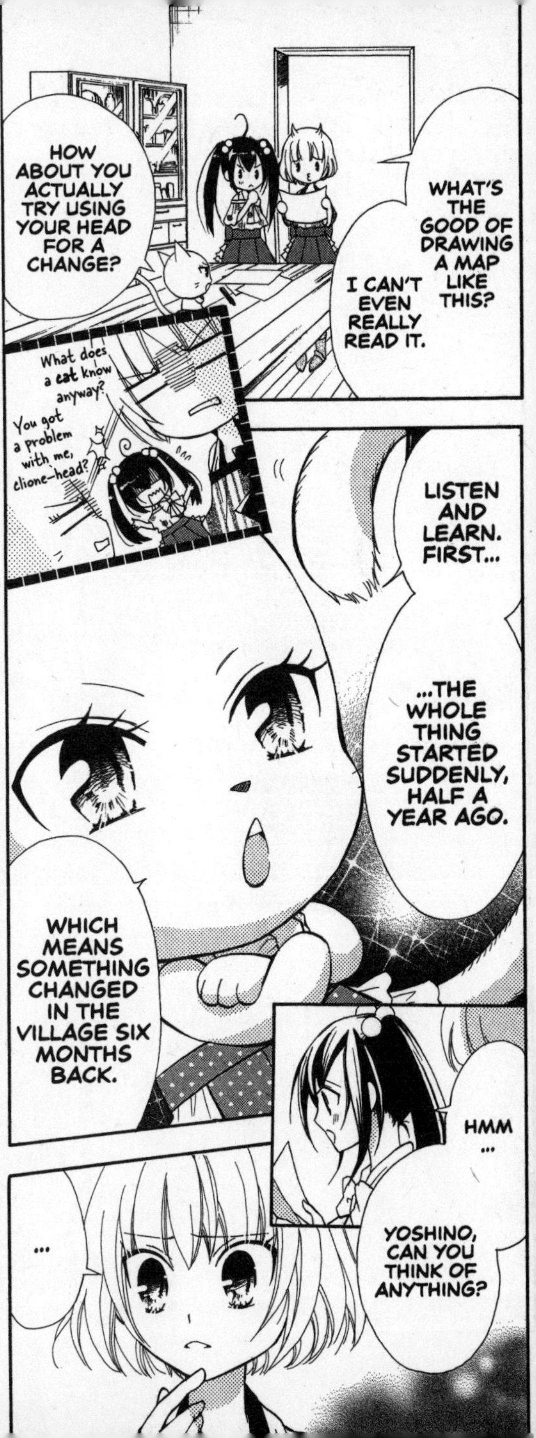
WHAT'S THE GOOD OF DRAWING A MAP LIKE THIS?
I CAN'T EVEN REALLY READ IT.
HOW ABOUT YOU ACTUALLY TRY USING YOUR HEAD FOR A CHANGE?
What does a **cat** know anyway?
You got a problem with me, clione-head?
LISTEN AND LEARN. FIRST...
...THE WHOLE THING STARTED SUDDENLY, HALF A YEAR AGO.
WHICH MEANS SOMETHING CHANGED IN THE VILLAGE SIX MONTHS BACK.
HMM...
YOSHINO, CAN YOU THINK OF ANYTHING?
...

BONUS MANGA 1

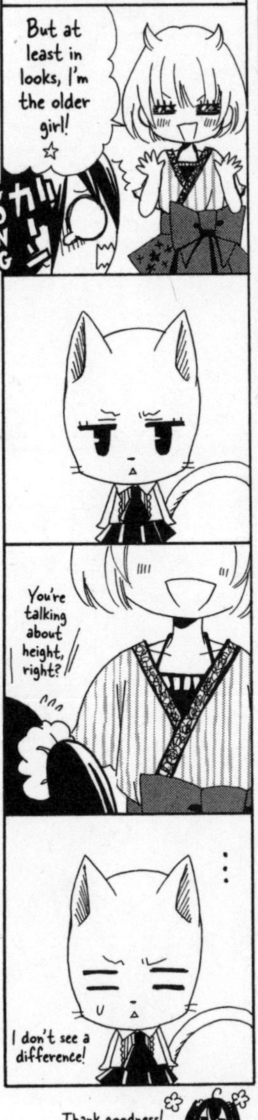
But at least in looks, I'm the older girl! ☆
GONG
You're talking about height, right?
...
I don't see a difference!

Thank goodness!

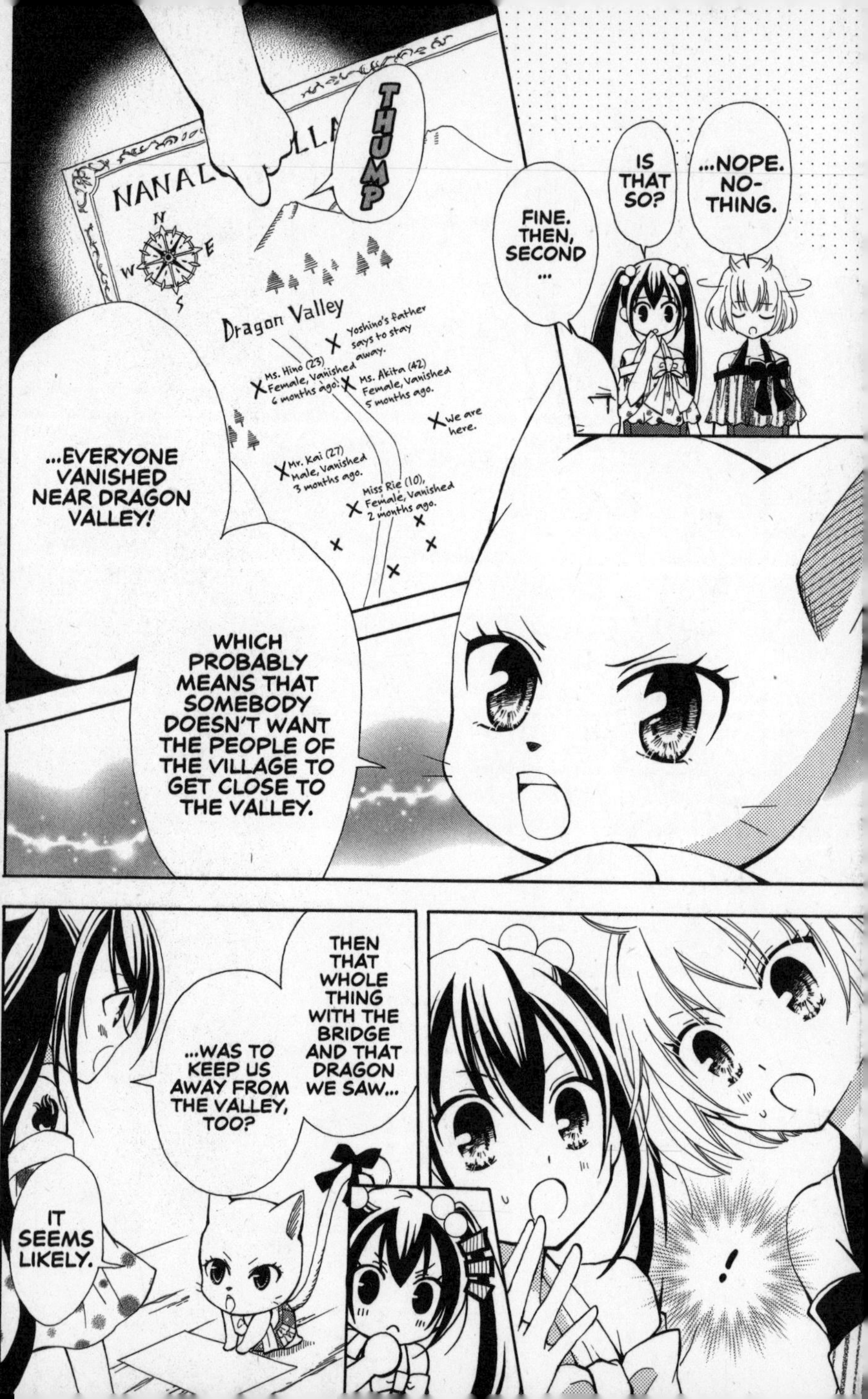
...NOPE. NO-THING.
IS THAT SO?
FINE. THEN, SECOND ...
THUMP
NANAL
N
E
W
S
Dragon Valley
Yoshino's father says to stay away.
Ms. Hino (23) Female, Vanished 6 months ago.
Ms. Akita (42) Female, Vanished 5 months ago.
We are here.
Mr. Kai (27) Male, Vanished 3 months ago.
Miss Rie (10), Female, Vanished 2 months ago.
...EVERYONE VANISHED NEAR DRAGON VALLEY!
WHICH PROBABLY MEANS THAT SOMEBODY DOESN'T WANT THE PEOPLE OF THE VILLAGE TO GET CLOSE TO THE VALLEY.
THEN THAT WHOLE THING WITH THE BRIDGE AND THAT DRAGON WE SAW...
...WAS TO KEEP US AWAY FROM THE VALLEY, TOO?
IT SEEMS LIKELY.

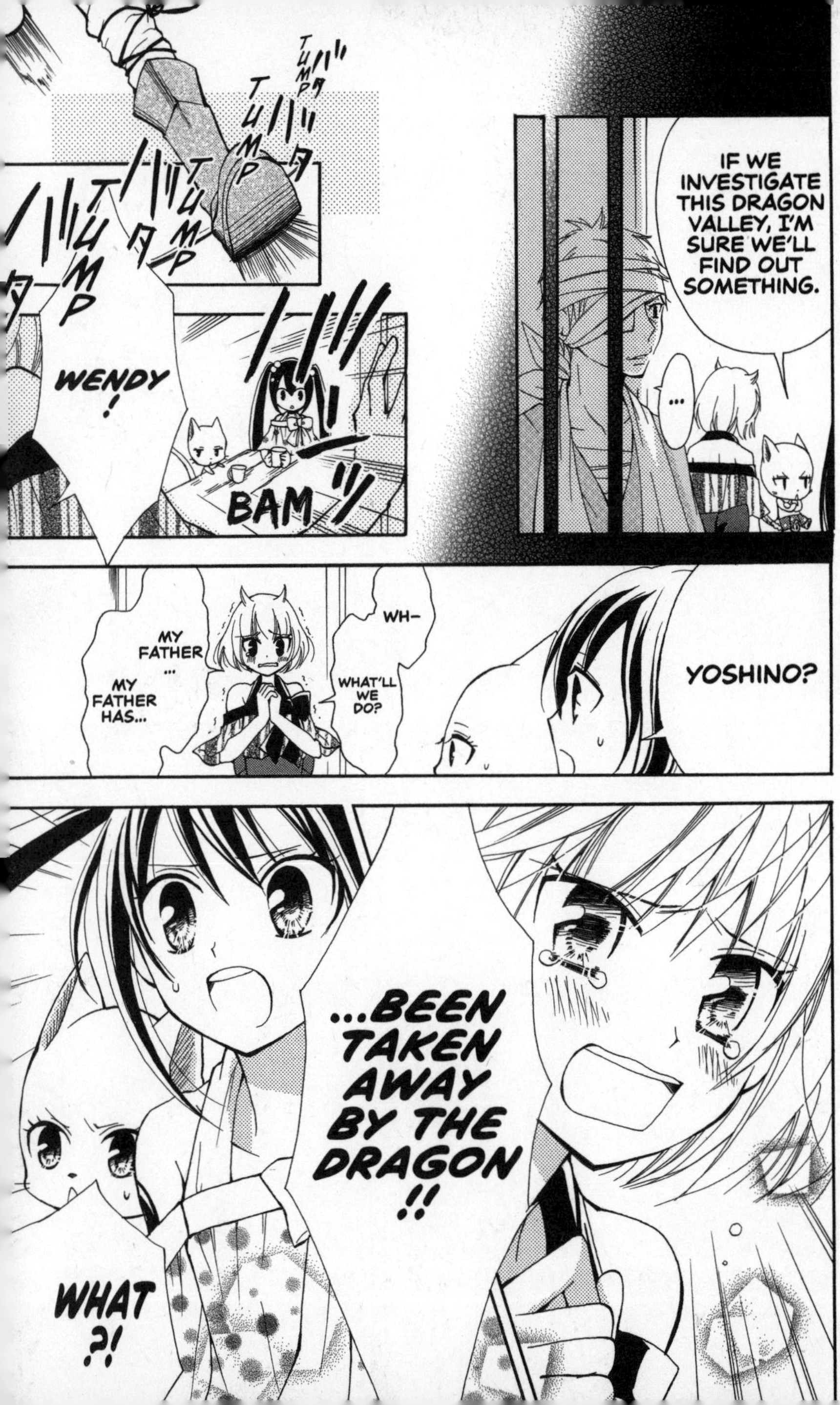
IF WE INVESTIGATE THIS DRAGON VALLEY, I'M SURE WE'LL FIND OUT SOMETHING.
...
TUMP TUMP
TUMP TUMP
WENDY!
BAM
YOSHINO?
WH-
WHAT'LL WE DO?
MY FATHER...
MY FATHER HAS...
...BEEN TAKEN AWAY BY THE DRAGON!!
WHAT?!

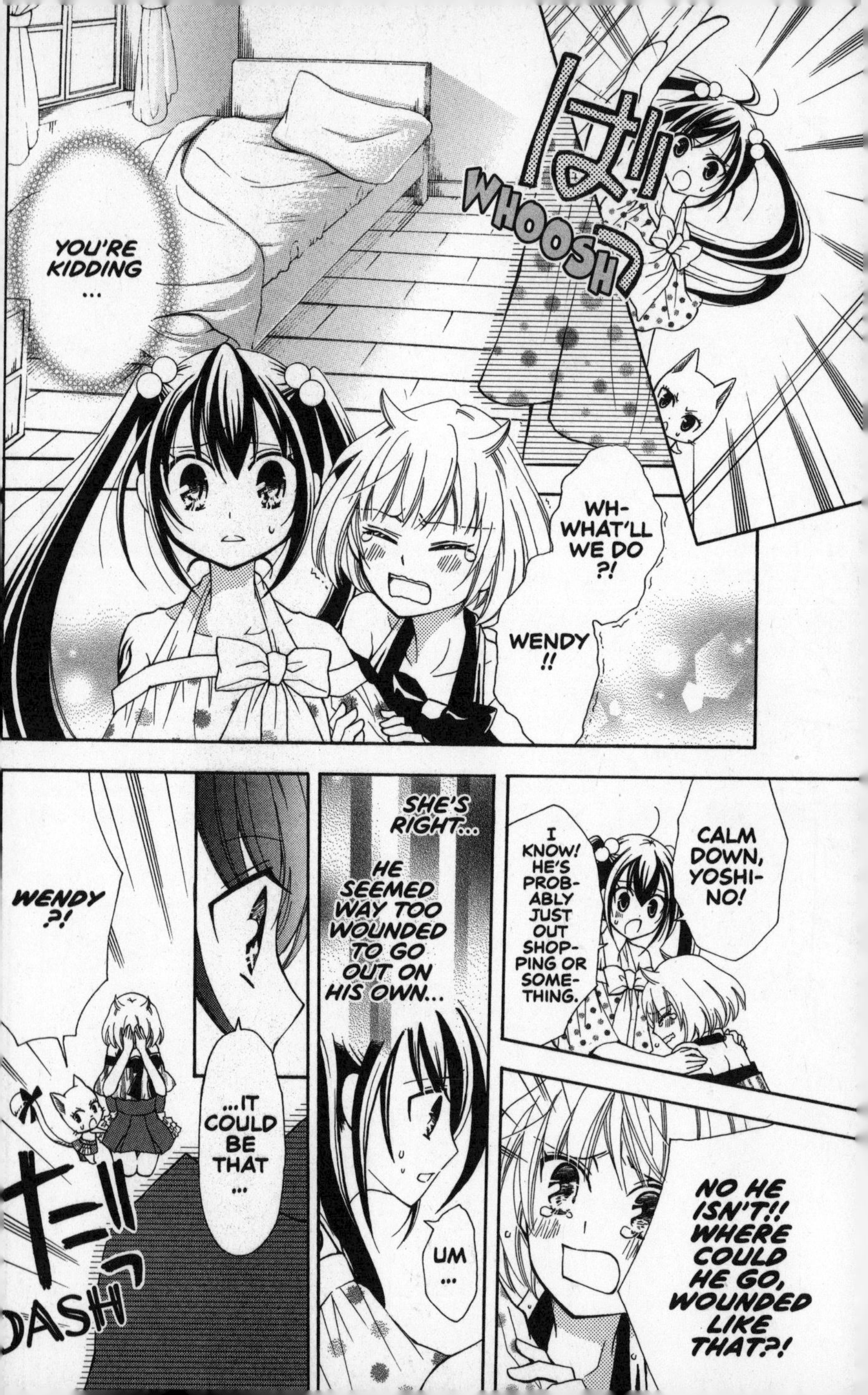
WHOOSH
YOU'RE KIDDING...
WH-WHAT'LL WE DO?!
WENDY!!
CALM DOWN, YOSHINO!
I KNOW! HE'S PROBABLY JUST OUT SHOPPING OR SOMETHING.
NO HE ISN'T!! WHERE COULD HE GO, WOUNDED LIKE THAT?!
SHE'S RIGHT...
HE SEEMED WAY TOO WOUNDED TO GO OUT ON HIS OWN...
UM...
...IT COULD BE THAT...
WENDY?!
DASH

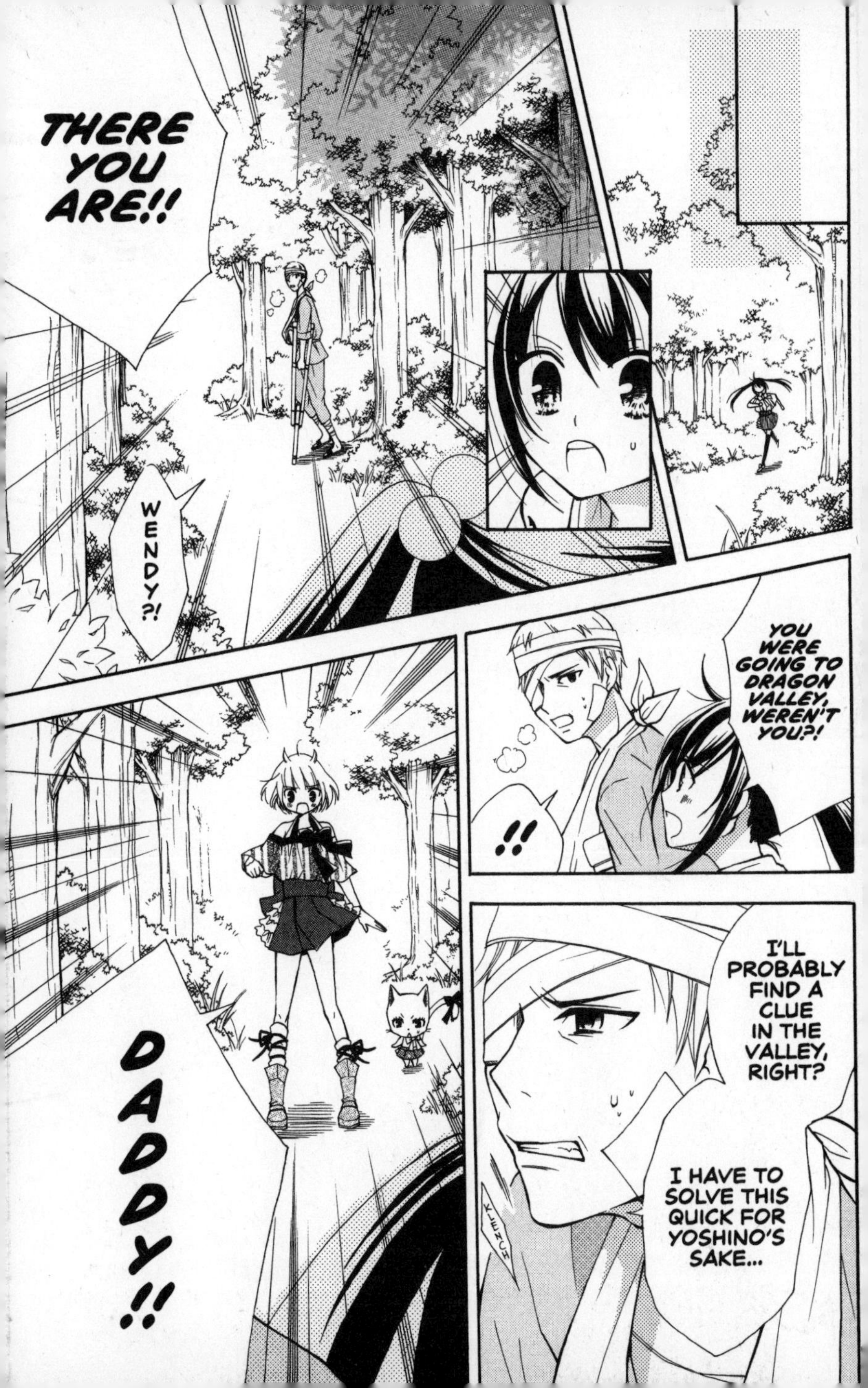
THERE YOU ARE!!
WENDY?!
YOU WERE GOING TO DRAGON VALLEY, WEREN'T YOU?!
!!
I'LL PROBABLY FIND A CLUE IN THE VALLEY, RIGHT?
I HAVE TO SOLVE THIS QUICK FOR YOSHINO'S SAKE...
KLENCH
DADDY!!

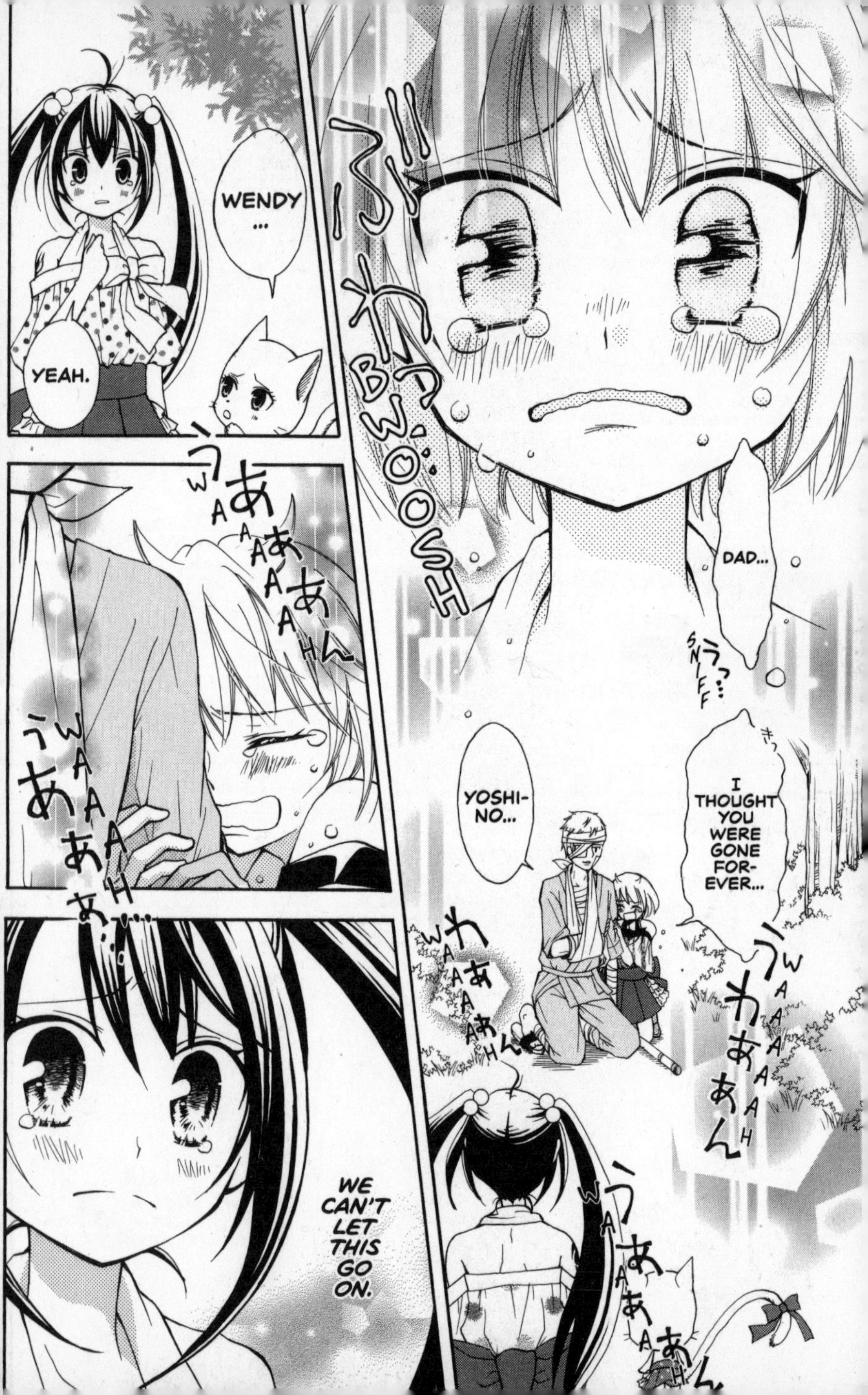
ふわっ
BWOOSH
DAD...
うっ...
SNIFF
I THOUGHT YOU WERE GONE FOREVER...
YOSHINO...
うわああああん
WAAAAAH
わあああん
WAAAAAH
うあああん
WAAAAH
WENDY...
YEAH.
うあああん
WAAAAAH
うあああ...
WAAAH...
WE CAN'T LET THIS GO ON.

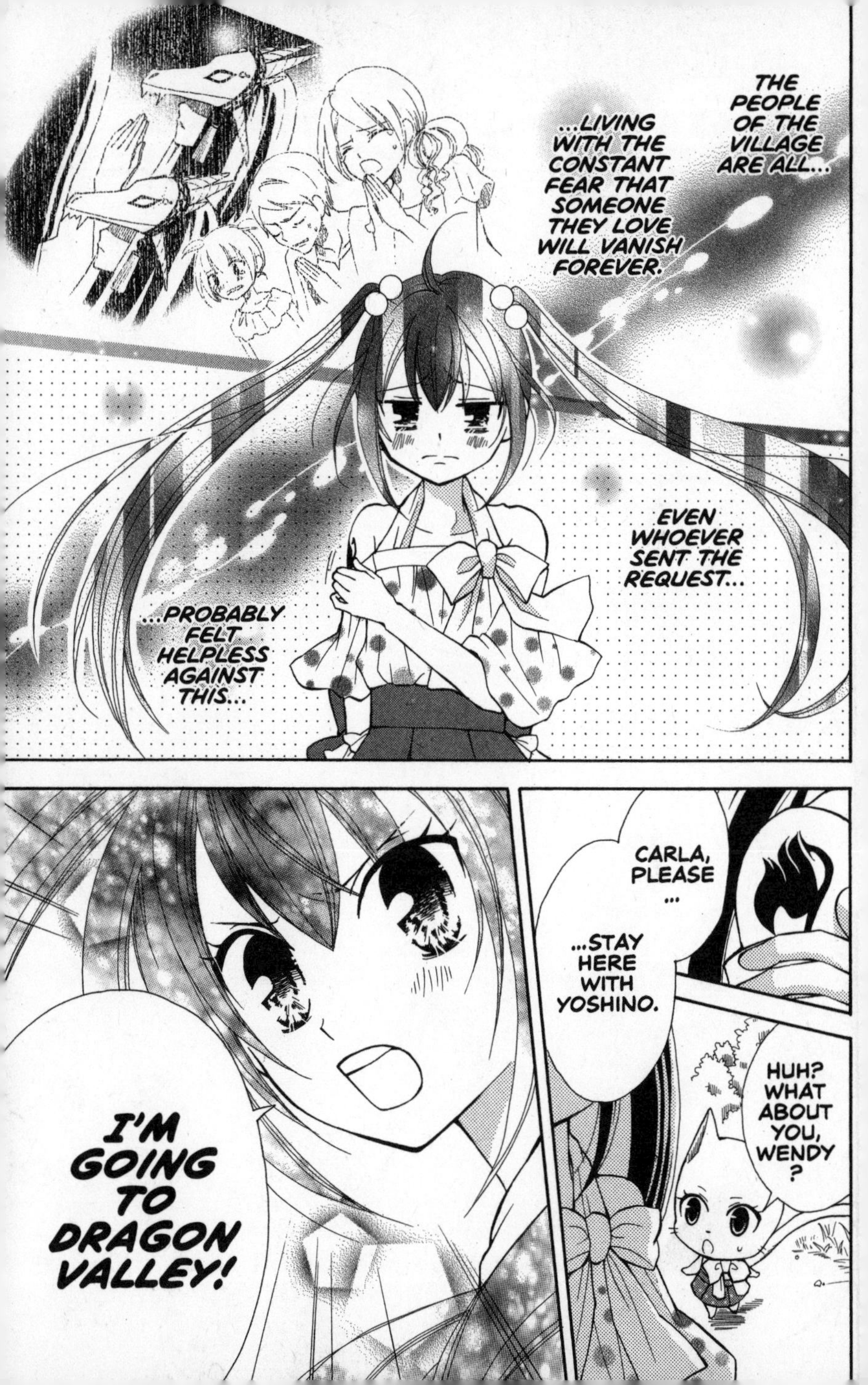
THE PEOPLE OF THE VILLAGE ARE ALL...
...LIVING WITH THE CONSTANT FEAR THAT SOMEONE THEY LOVE WILL VANISH FOREVER.
EVEN WHOEVER SENT THE REQUEST...
...PROBABLY FELT HELPLESS AGAINST THIS...
CARLA, PLEASE ...
...STAY HERE WITH YOSHINO.
HUH? WHAT ABOUT YOU, WENDY?
I'M GOING TO DRAGON VALLEY!

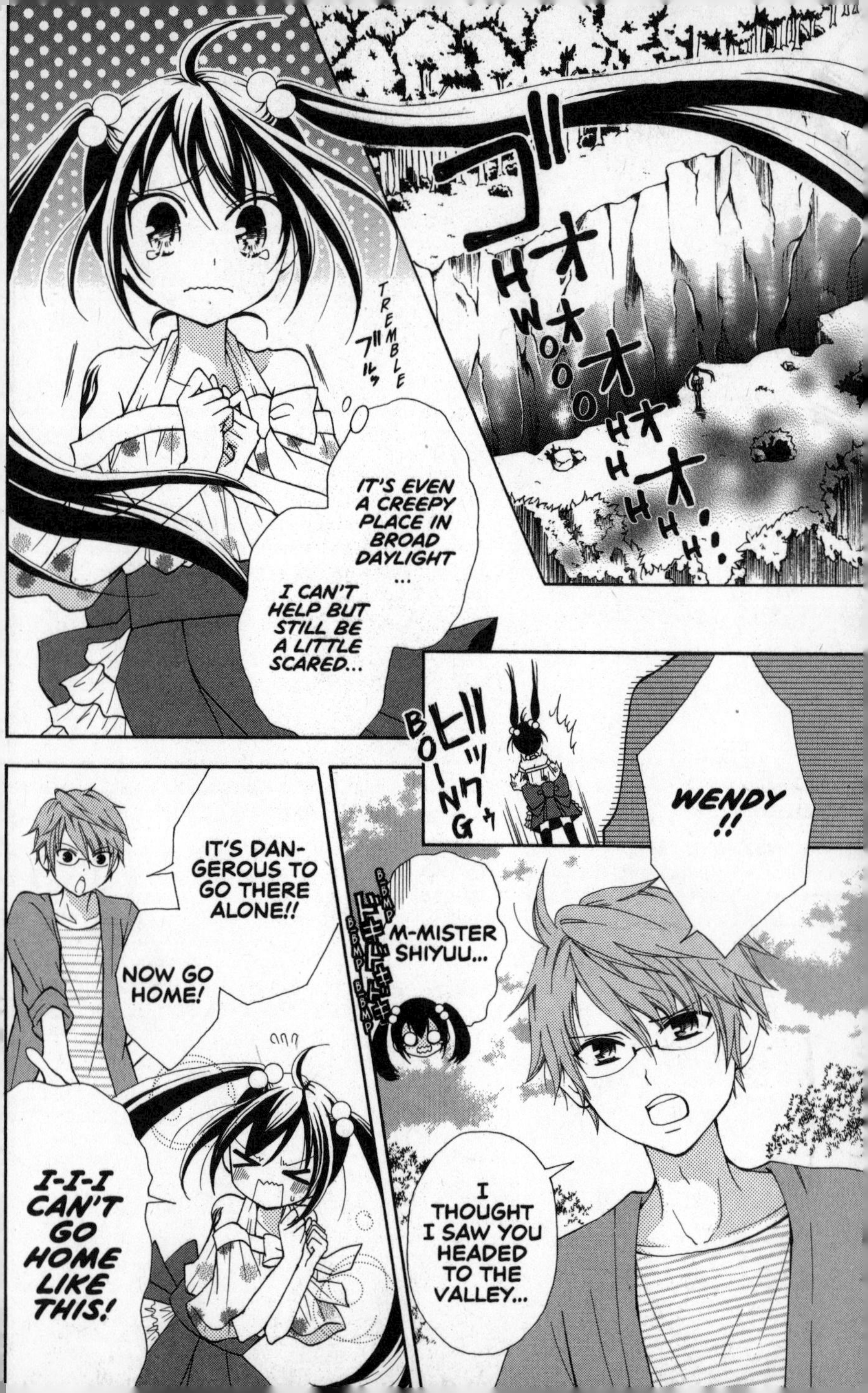
HWOOOOHHHHH!!
TREMBLE
IT'S EVEN A CREEPY PLACE IN BROAD DAYLIGHT ...
I CAN'T HELP BUT STILL BE A LITTLE SCARED...
WENDY!!
BOING
I THOUGHT I SAW YOU HEADED TO THE VALLEY...
M-MISTER SHIYUU...
B-BMP B-BMP B-BMP
IT'S DAN-GEROUS TO GO THERE ALONE!!
NOW GO HOME!
I-I-I CAN'T GO HOME LIKE THIS!

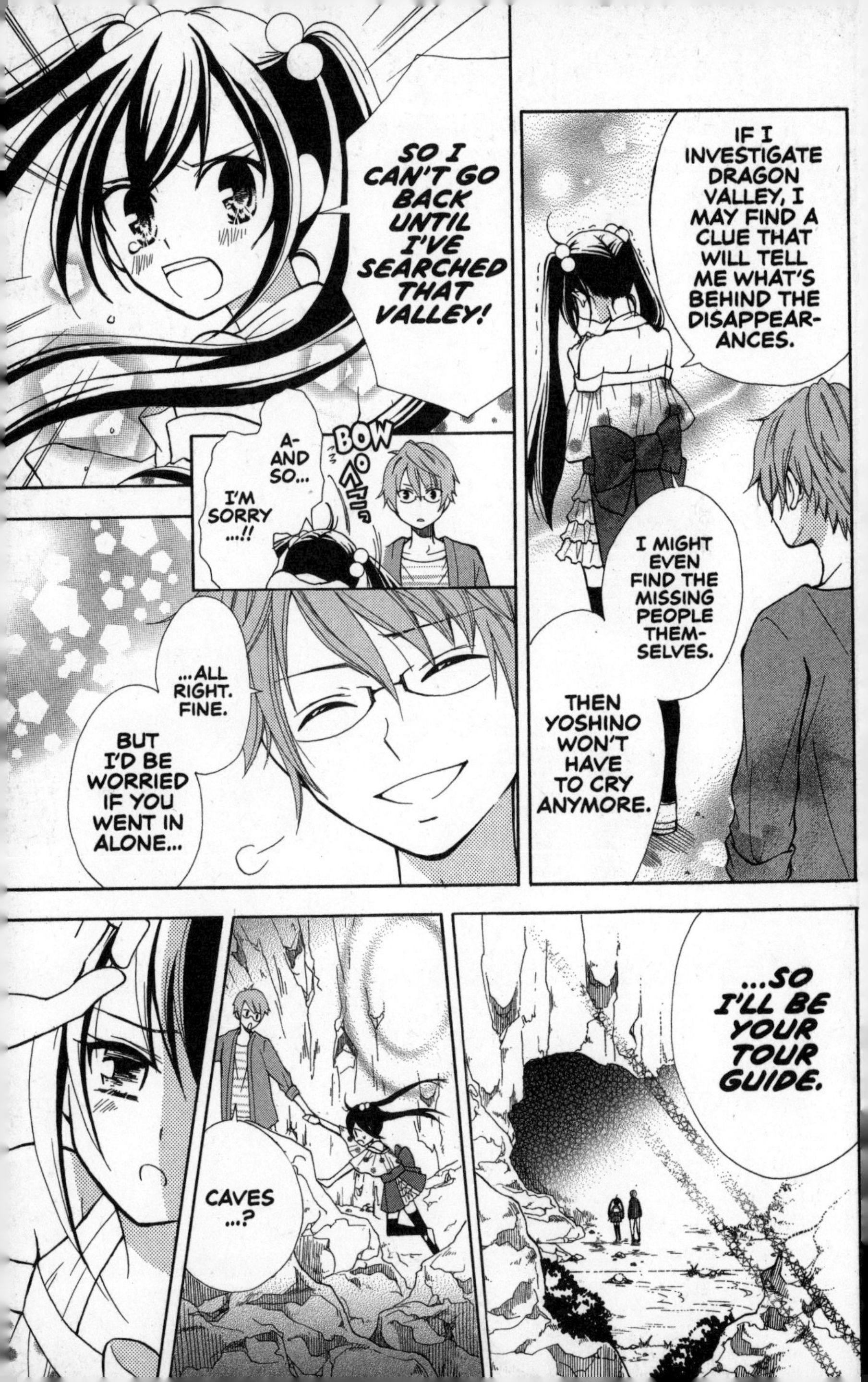
IF I INVESTIGATE DRAGON VALLEY, I MAY FIND A CLUE THAT WILL TELL ME WHAT'S BEHIND THE DISAPPEAR-ANCES.
I MIGHT EVEN FIND THE MISSING PEOPLE THEM-SELVES.
THEN YOSHINO WON'T HAVE TO CRY ANYMORE.
SO I CAN'T GO BACK UNTIL I'VE SEARCHED THAT VALLEY!
A- AND SO...
I'M SORRY ...!!
BOW
...ALL RIGHT. FINE.
BUT I'D BE WORRIED IF YOU WENT IN ALONE...
...SO I'LL BE YOUR TOUR GUIDE.
CAVES ...?

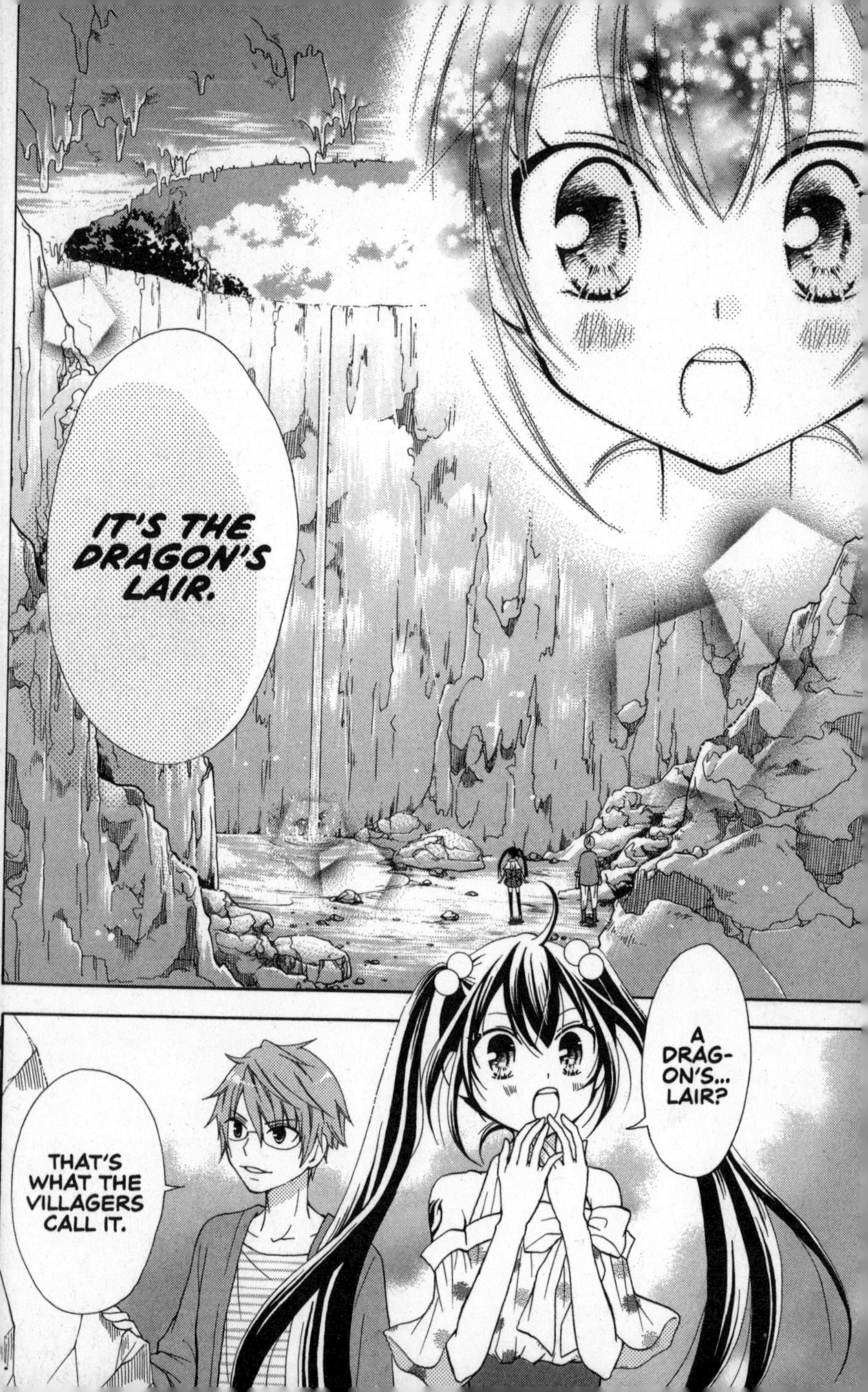
IT'S THE DRAGON'S LAIR.
A DRAG-ON'S... LAIR?
THAT'S WHAT THE VILLAGERS CALL IT.

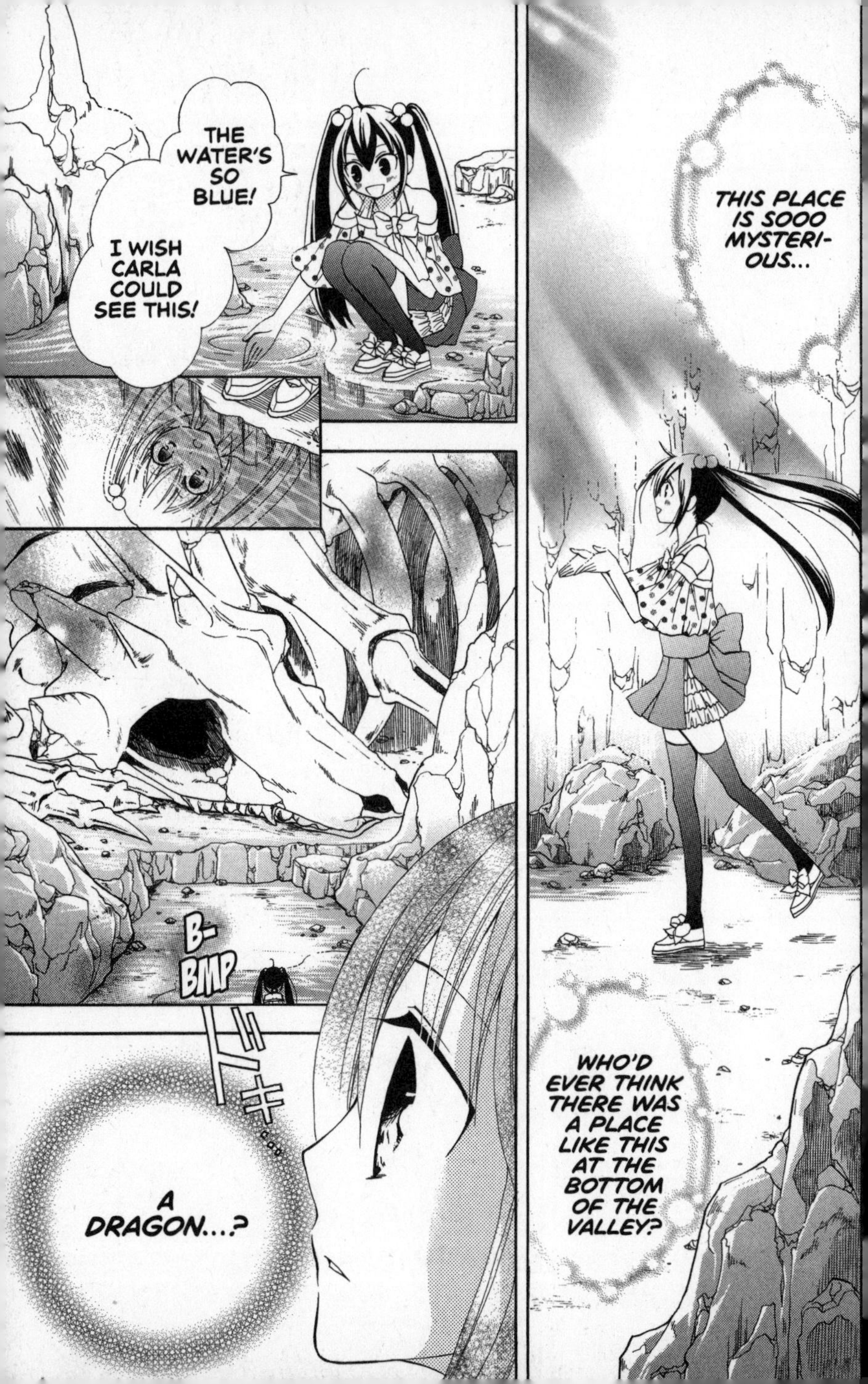
THIS PLACE IS SOOO MYSTERI-OUS...
WHO'D EVER THINK THERE WAS A PLACE LIKE THIS AT THE BOTTOM OF THE VALLEY?
THE WATER'S SO BLUE!
I WISH CARLA COULD SEE THIS!
B-BMP
ドキ…
A DRAGON...?

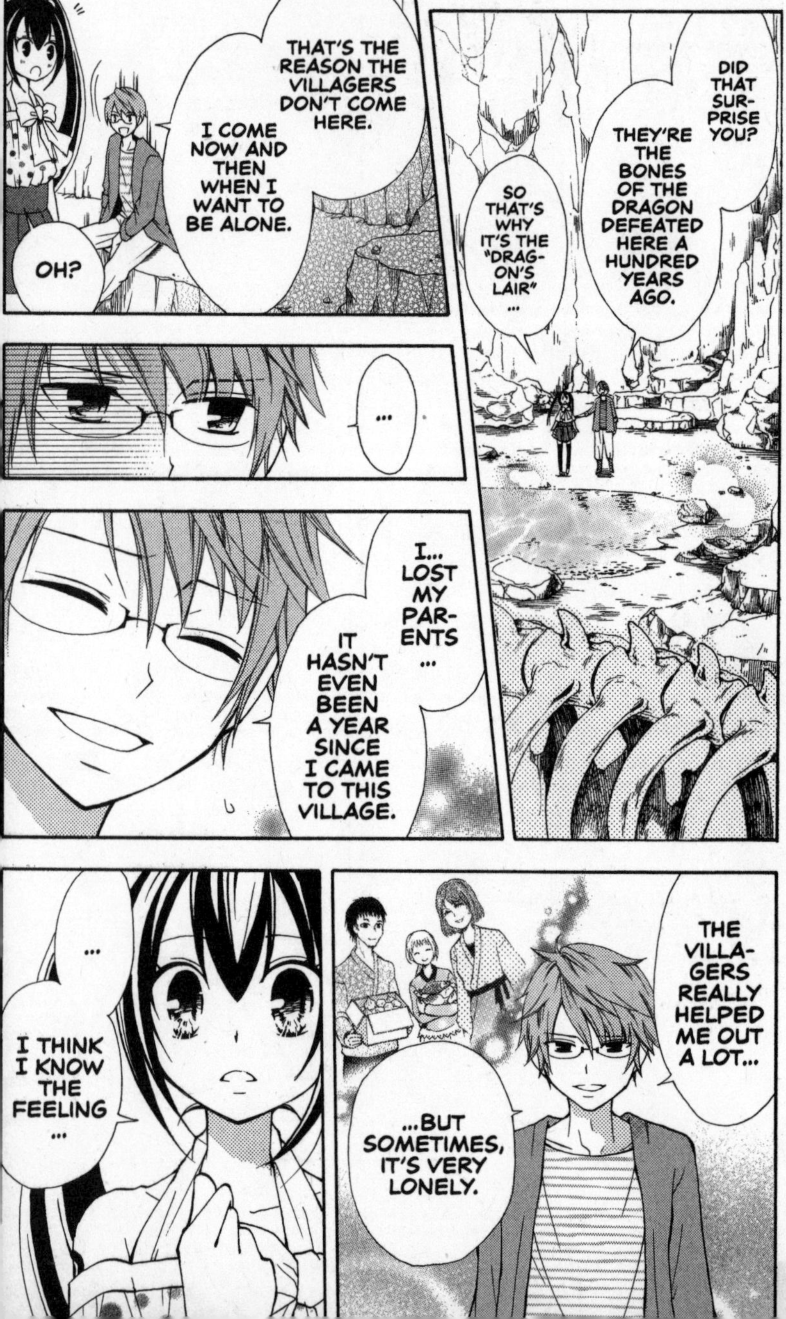
DID THAT SURPRISE YOU?
THEY'RE THE BONES OF THE DRAGON DEFEATED HERE A HUNDRED YEARS AGO.
SO THAT'S WHY IT'S THE "DRAG-ON'S LAIR"...
THAT'S THE REASON THE VILLAGERS DON'T COME HERE.
I COME NOW AND THEN WHEN I WANT TO BE ALONE.
OH?
...
I... LOST MY PAR-ENTS...
IT HASN'T EVEN BEEN A YEAR SINCE I CAME TO THIS VILLAGE.
THE VILLA-GERS REALLY HELPED ME OUT A LOT...
...BUT SOMETIMES, IT'S VERY LONELY.
...
I THINK I KNOW THE FEELING...

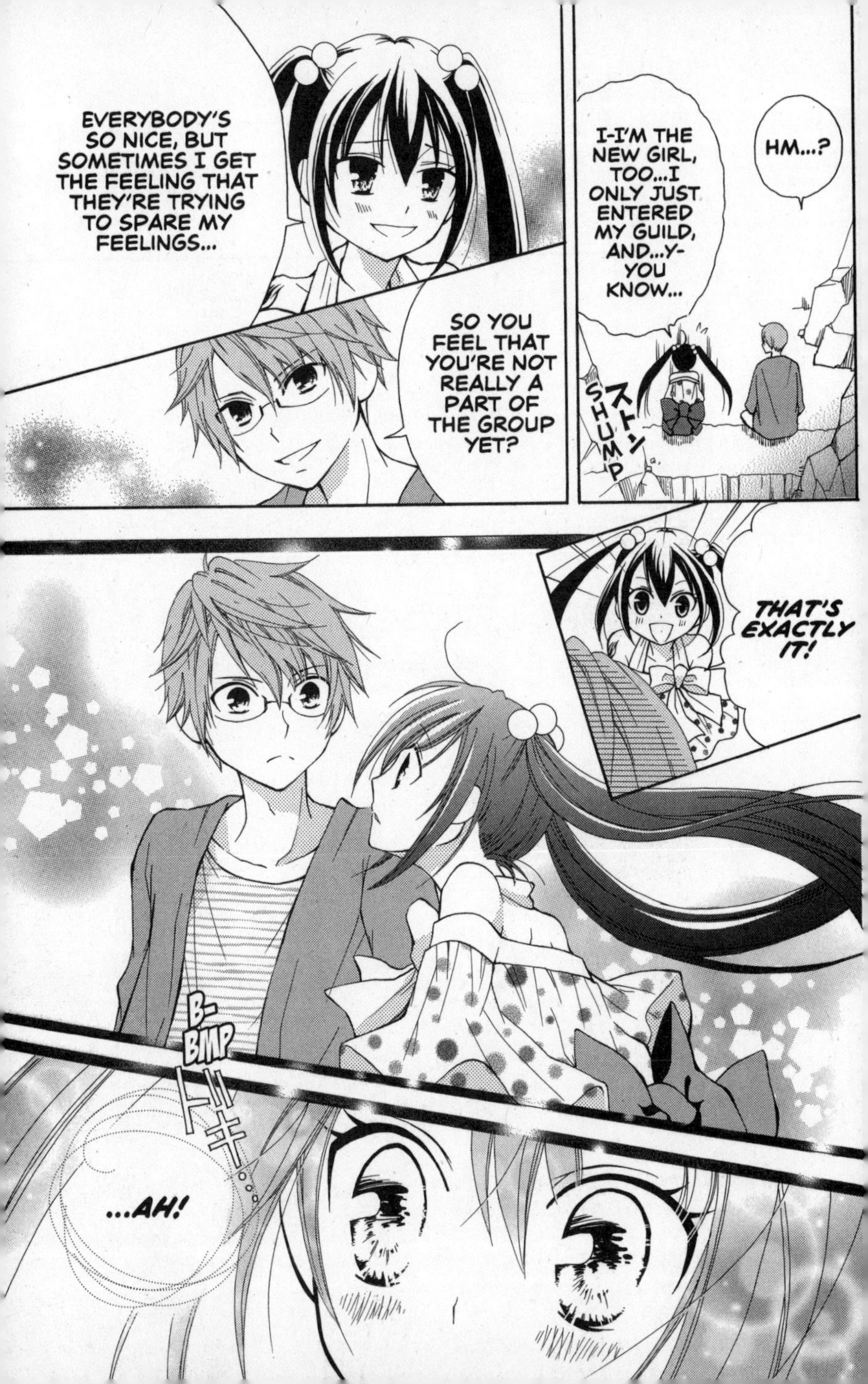
HM...?
I-I'M THE NEW GIRL, TOO...I ONLY JUST ENTERED MY GUILD, AND...Y-YOU KNOW...
ストン
SHUMP
EVERYBODY'S SO NICE, BUT SOMETIMES I GET THE FEELING THAT THEY'RE TRYING TO SPARE MY FEELINGS...
SO YOU FEEL THAT YOU'RE NOT REALLY A PART OF THE GROUP YET?
THAT'S EXACTLY IT!
B-BMP
ドキ
...AH!

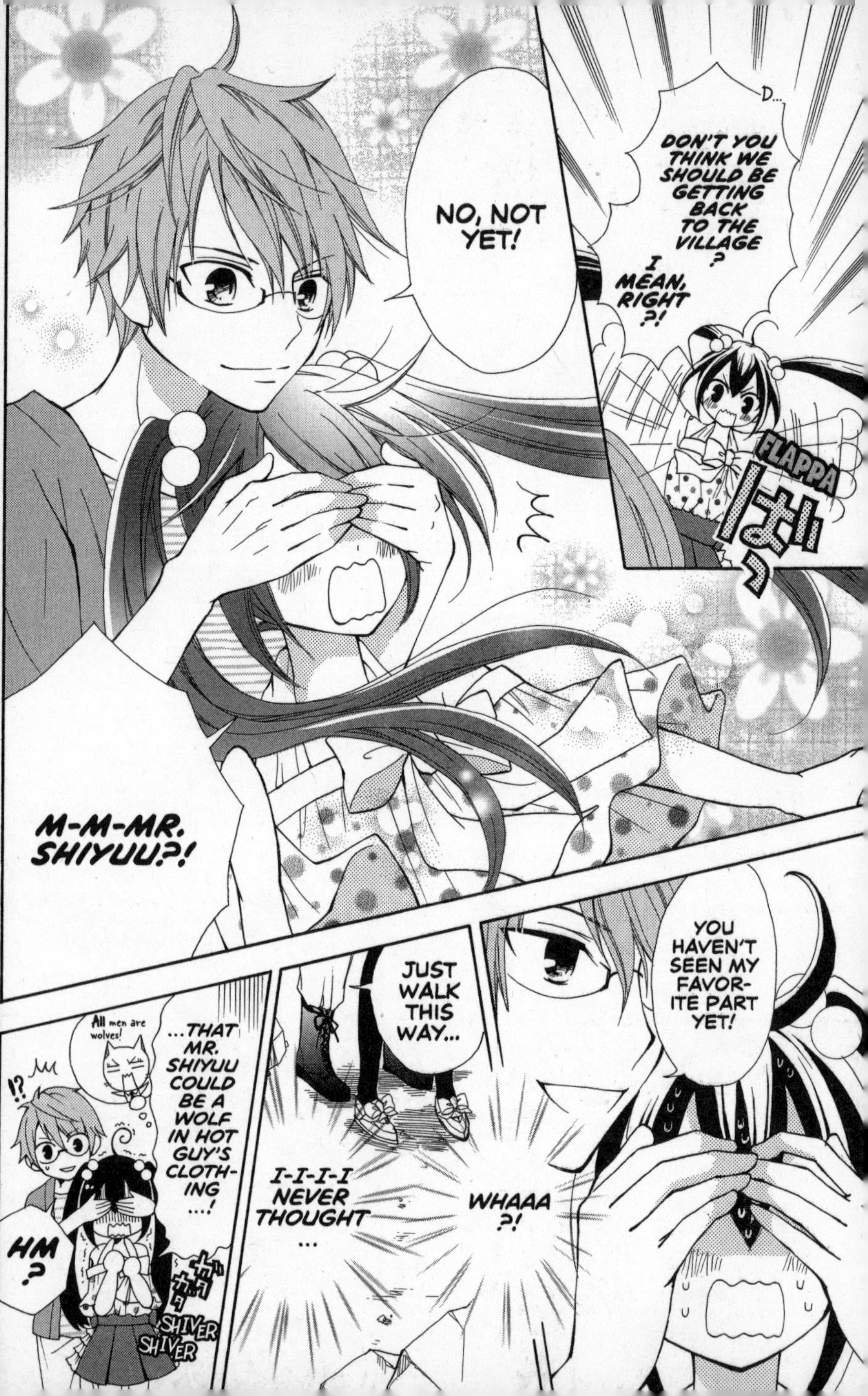
D...
DON'T YOU THINK WE SHOULD BE GETTING BACK TO THE VILLAGE?
I MEAN, RIGHT?!
FLAPPA
ぱっ
NO, NOT YET!
M-M-MR. SHIYUU?!
YOU HAVEN'T SEEN MY FAVOR-ITE PART YET!
WHAAA?!
JUST WALK THIS WAY...
I-I-I-I NEVER THOUGHT...
...THAT MR. SHIYUU COULD BE A WOLF IN HOT GUY'S CLOTH-ING...!
All men are wolves!
!?
HM?
SHIVER SHIVER

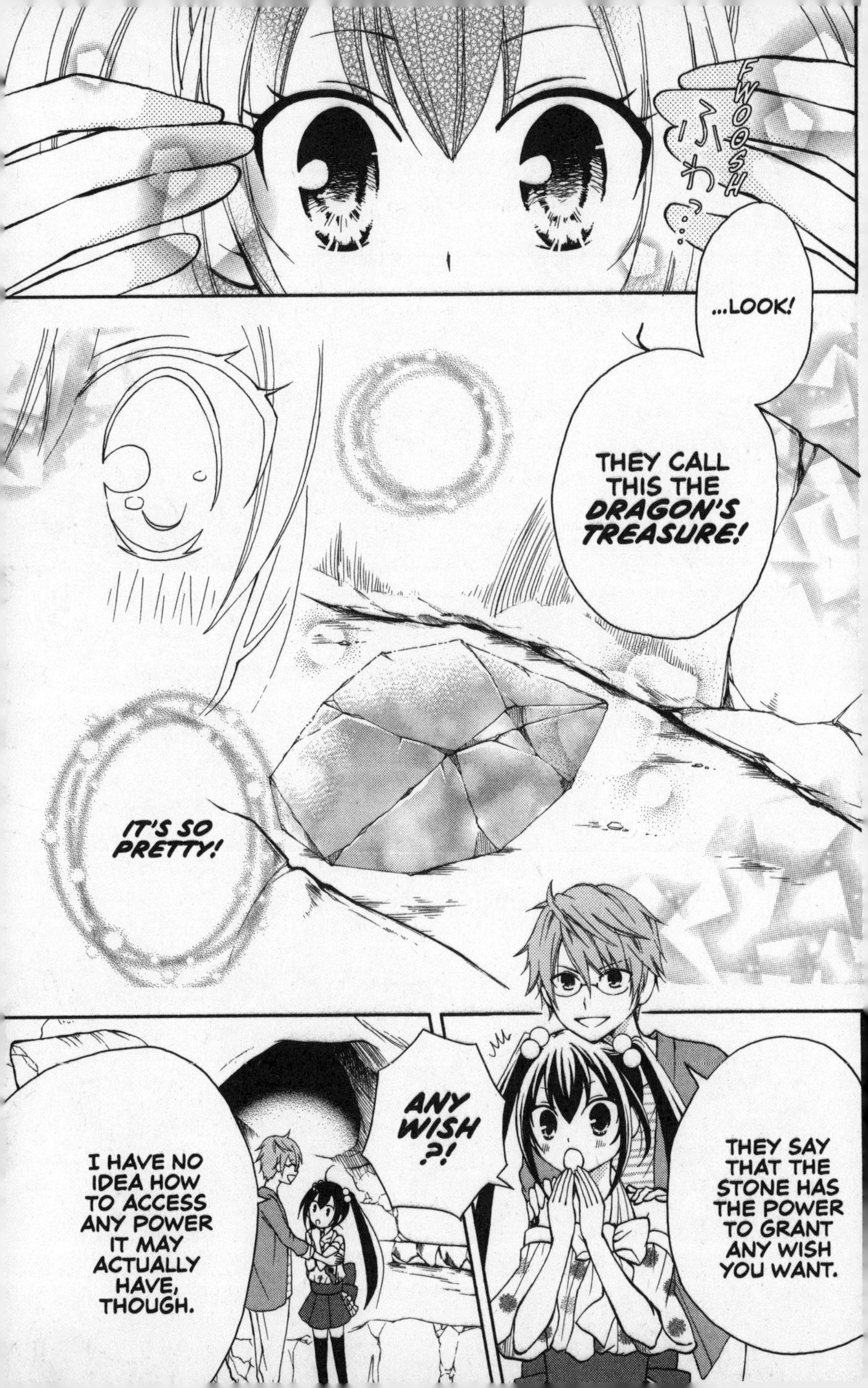
FWOOSH
ふわ…
...LOOK!
THEY CALL THIS THE DRAGON'S TREASURE!
IT'S SO PRETTY!
THEY SAY THAT THE STONE HAS THE POWER TO GRANT ANY WISH YOU WANT.
ANY WISH?!
I HAVE NO IDEA HOW TO ACCESS ANY POWER IT MAY ACTUALLY HAVE, THOUGH.

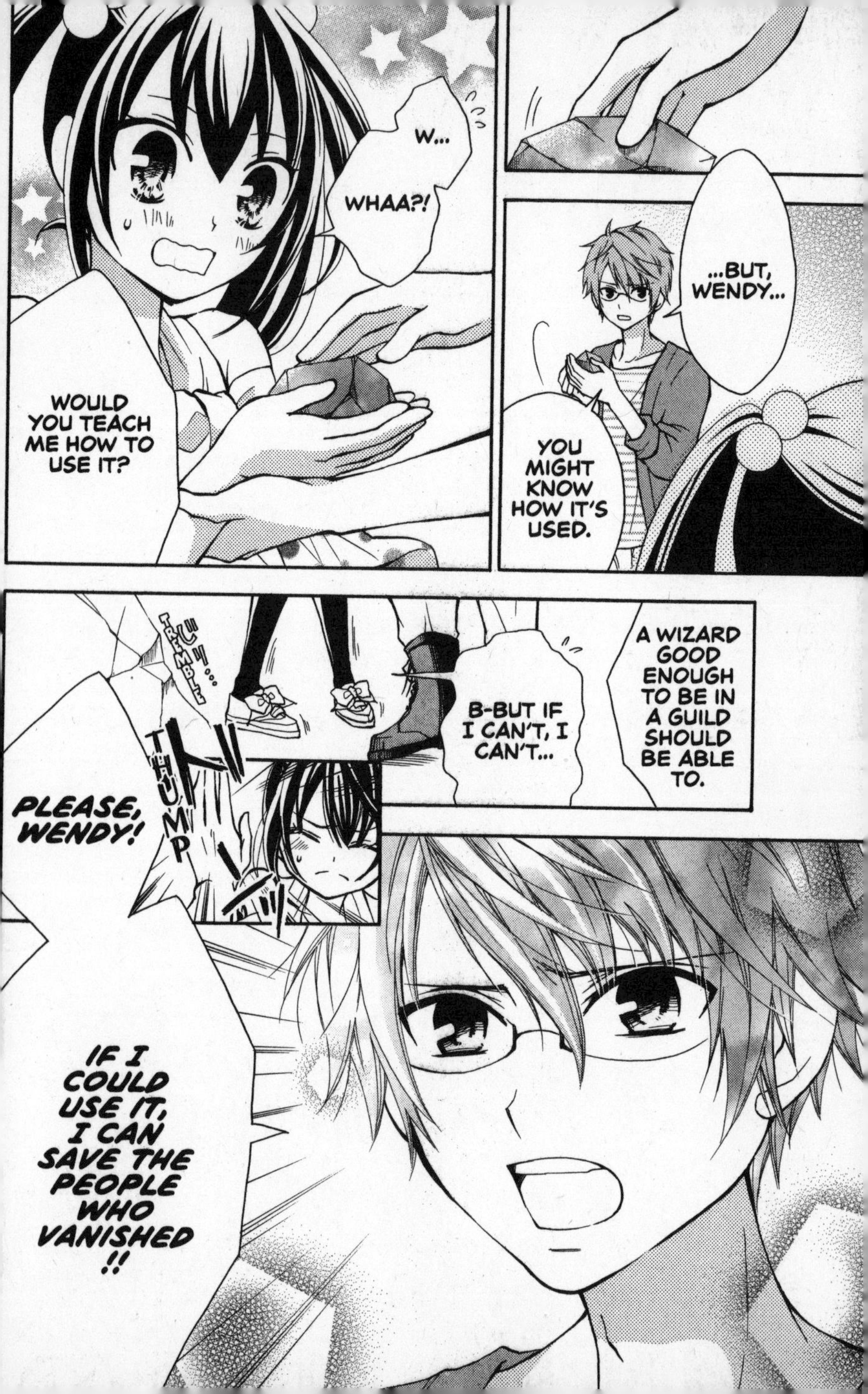
...BUT, WENDY...
YOU MIGHT KNOW HOW IT'S USED.
W...
WHAA?!
WOULD YOU TEACH ME HOW TO USE IT?
A WIZARD GOOD ENOUGH TO BE IN A GUILD SHOULD BE ABLE TO.
B-BUT IF I CAN'T, I CAN'T...
TREMBLE
THUMP
PLEASE, WENDY!
IF I COULD USE IT, I CAN SAVE THE PEOPLE WHO VANISHED!!

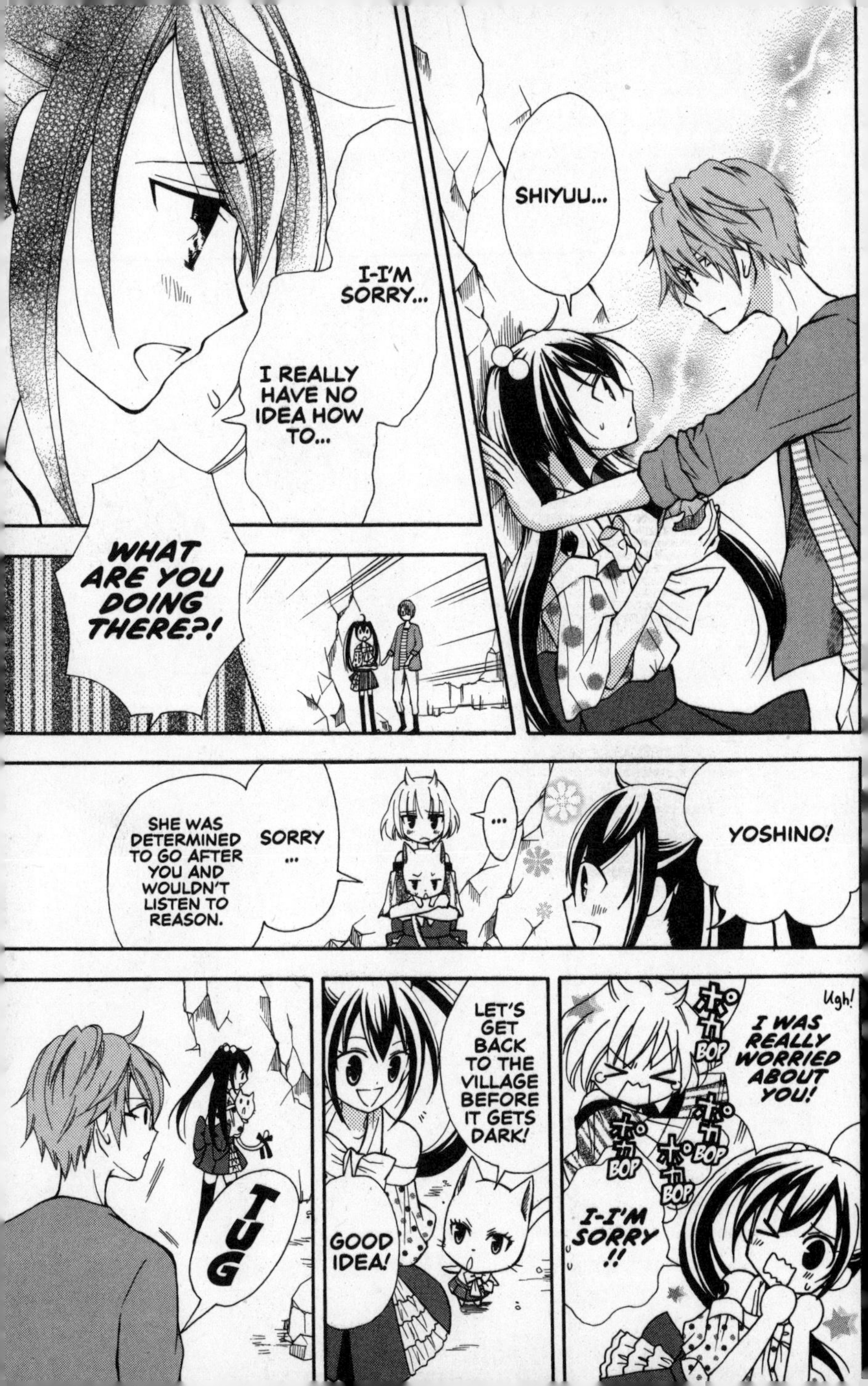
SHIYUU...
I-I'M SORRY...
I REALLY HAVE NO IDEA HOW TO...
WHAT ARE YOU DOING THERE?!
YOSHINO!
...
SORRY ...
SHE WAS DETERMINED TO GO AFTER YOU AND WOULDN'T LISTEN TO REASON.
Ugh!
ポカ BOP
I WAS REALLY WORRIED ABOUT YOU!
ポカ BOP
ポカ BOP
ポカ BOP
I-I'M SORRY!!
LET'S GET BACK TO THE VILLAGE BEFORE IT GETS DARK!
GOOD IDEA!
TUG

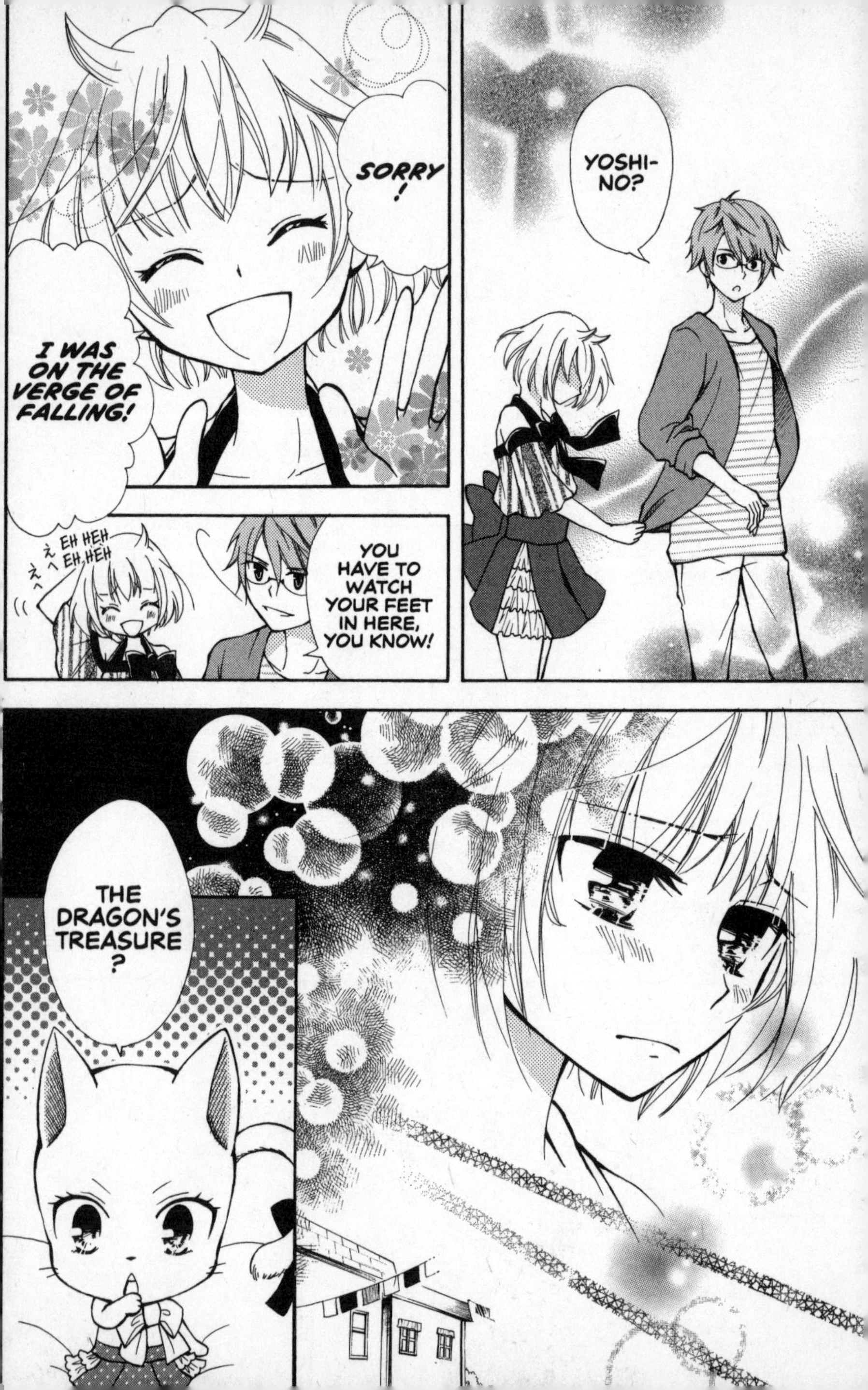
YOSHI-NO?
SORRY!
I WAS ON THE VERGE OF FALLING!
YOU HAVE TO WATCH YOUR FEET IN HERE, YOU KNOW!
EH HEH EH HEH
えへ えへ
THE DRAGON'S TREASURE?

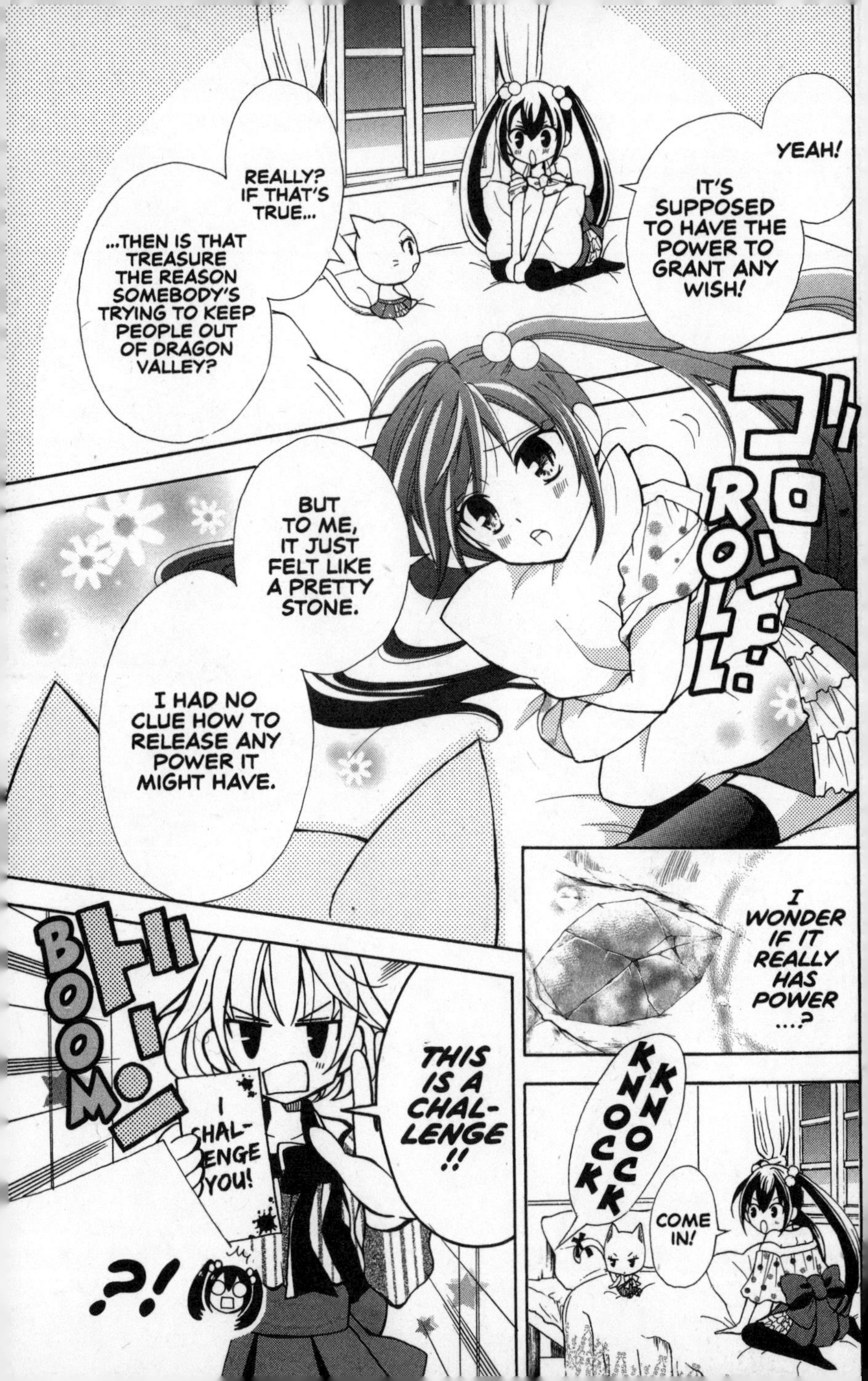
YEAH!
IT'S SUPPOSED TO HAVE THE POWER TO GRANT ANY WISH!
REALLY? IF THAT'S TRUE...
...THEN IS THAT TREASURE THE REASON SOMEBODY'S TRYING TO KEEP PEOPLE OUT OF DRAGON VALLEY?
ROLL...
BUT TO ME, IT JUST FELT LIKE A PRETTY STONE.
I HAD NO CLUE HOW TO RELEASE ANY POWER IT MIGHT HAVE.
I WONDER IF IT REALLY HAS POWER ...?
KNOCK KNOCK
COME IN!
THIS IS A CHAL-LENGE!!
I CHAL-LENGE YOU!
BOOM!
?!

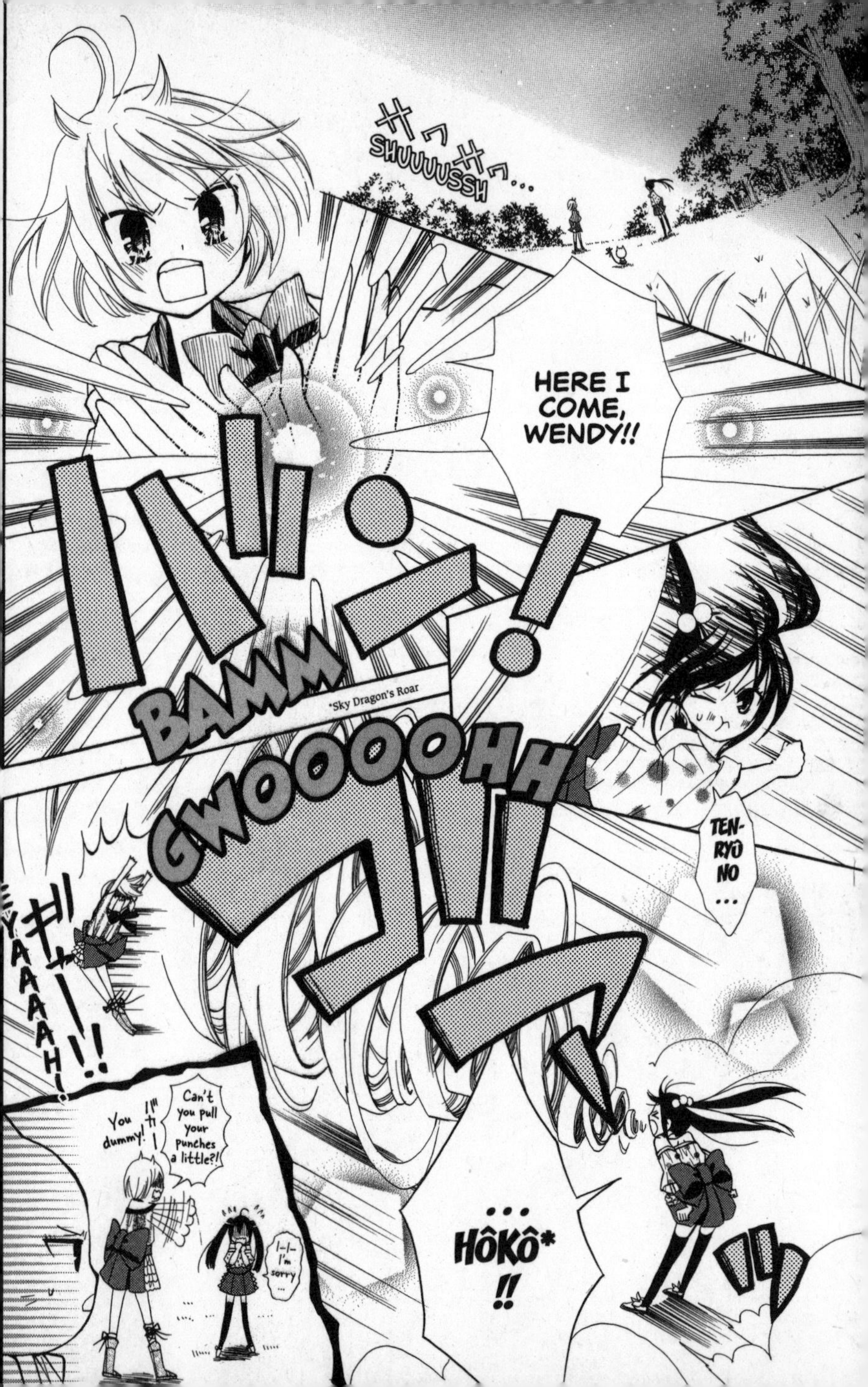
SHUUUUSSH
HERE I COME, WENDY!!
TEN-RYÛ NO ...
... HÔKÔ* !!
BAMM
GWOOOOHH
EYAAAAAH!!
Can't you pull your punches a little?!
You dummy!
I-I-I'm sorry ...
*Sky Dragon's Roar

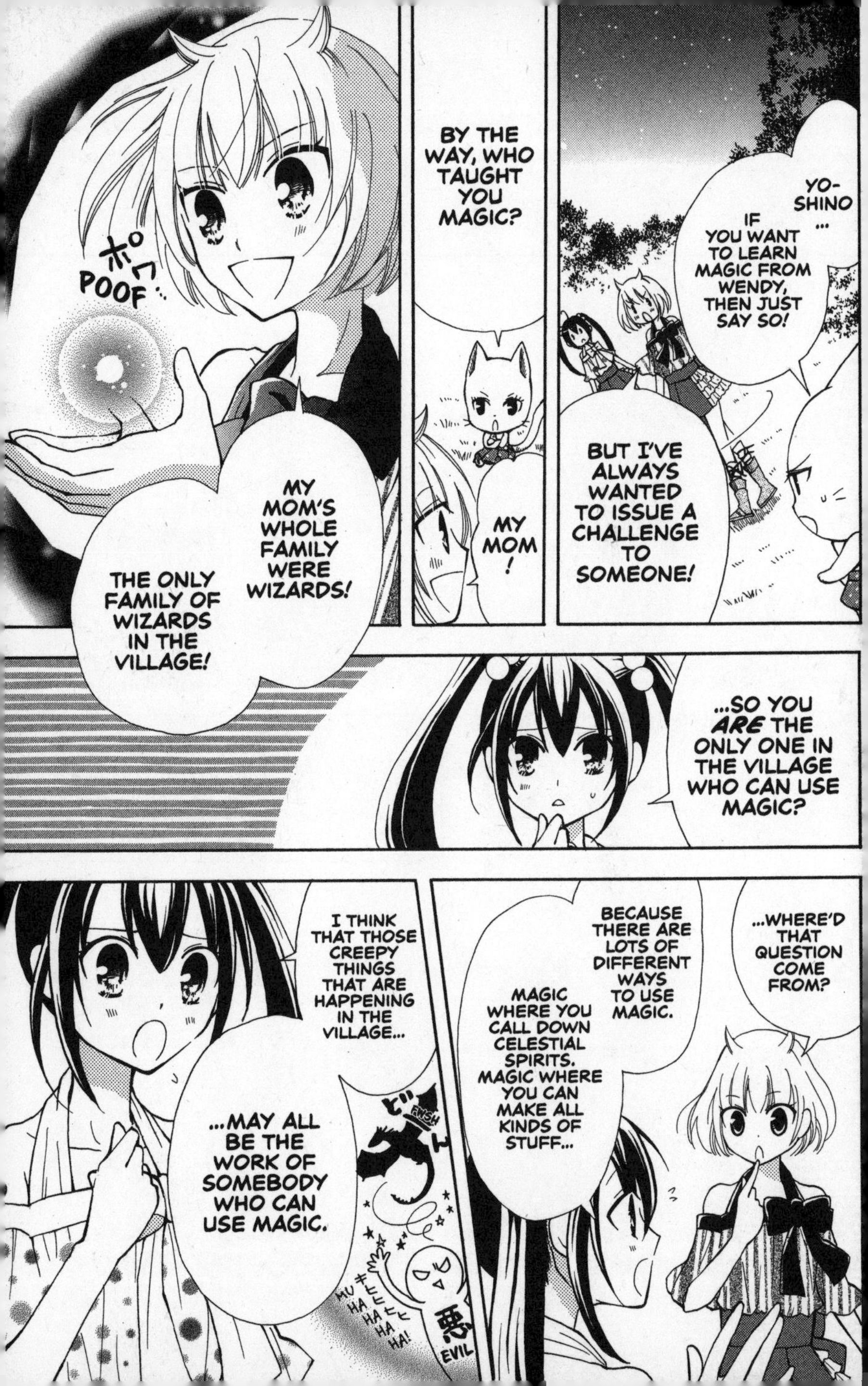
YO-SHINO...
IF YOU WANT TO LEARN MAGIC FROM WENDY, THEN JUST SAY SO!
BUT I'VE ALWAYS WANTED TO ISSUE A CHALLENGE TO SOMEONE!
BY THE WAY, WHO TAUGHT YOU MAGIC?
MY MOM!
ポフ POOF
MY MOM'S WHOLE FAMILY WERE WIZARDS!
THE ONLY FAMILY OF WIZARDS IN THE VILLAGE!
...SO YOU *ARE* THE ONLY ONE IN THE VILLAGE WHO CAN USE MAGIC?
...WHERE'D THAT QUESTION COME FROM?
BECAUSE THERE ARE LOTS OF DIFFERENT WAYS TO USE MAGIC.
MAGIC WHERE YOU CALL DOWN CELESTIAL SPIRITS. MAGIC WHERE YOU CAN MAKE ALL KINDS OF STUFF...
I THINK THAT THOSE CREEPY THINGS THAT ARE HAPPENING IN THE VILLAGE...
...MAY ALL BE THE WORK OF SOMEBODY WHO CAN USE MAGIC.
FWSH
MUHAHAHAHA!
悪 EVIL

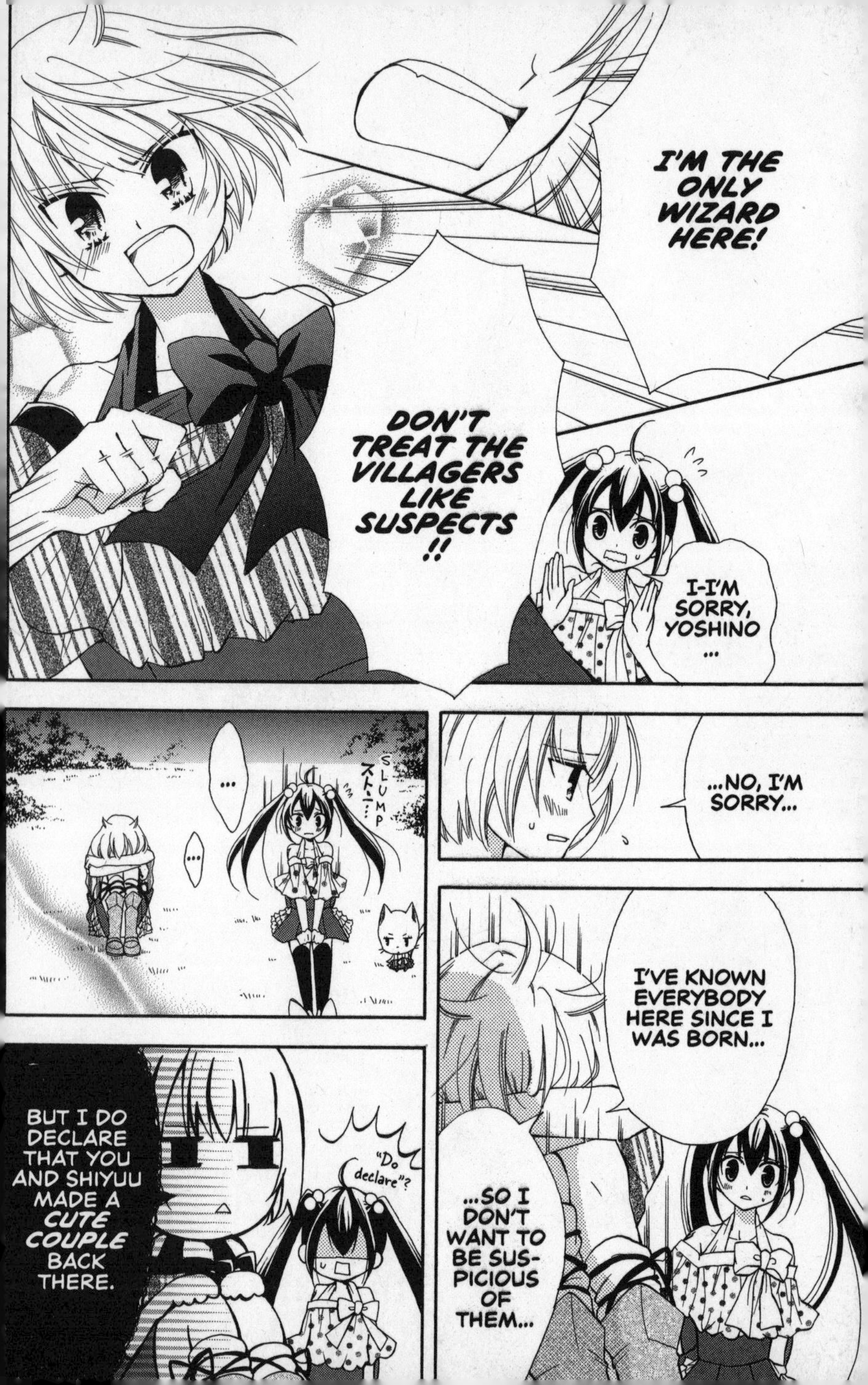
I'M THE ONLY WIZARD HERE!
DON'T TREAT THE VILLAGERS LIKE SUSPECTS!!
I-I'M SORRY, YOSHINO...
...NO, I'M SORRY...
...
...
SLUMP
ストーー...
I'VE KNOWN EVERYBODY HERE SINCE I WAS BORN...
...SO I DON'T WANT TO BE SUS-PICIOUS OF THEM...
BUT I DO DECLARE THAT YOU AND SHIYUU MADE A *CUTE COUPLE* BACK THERE.
"Do declare"?

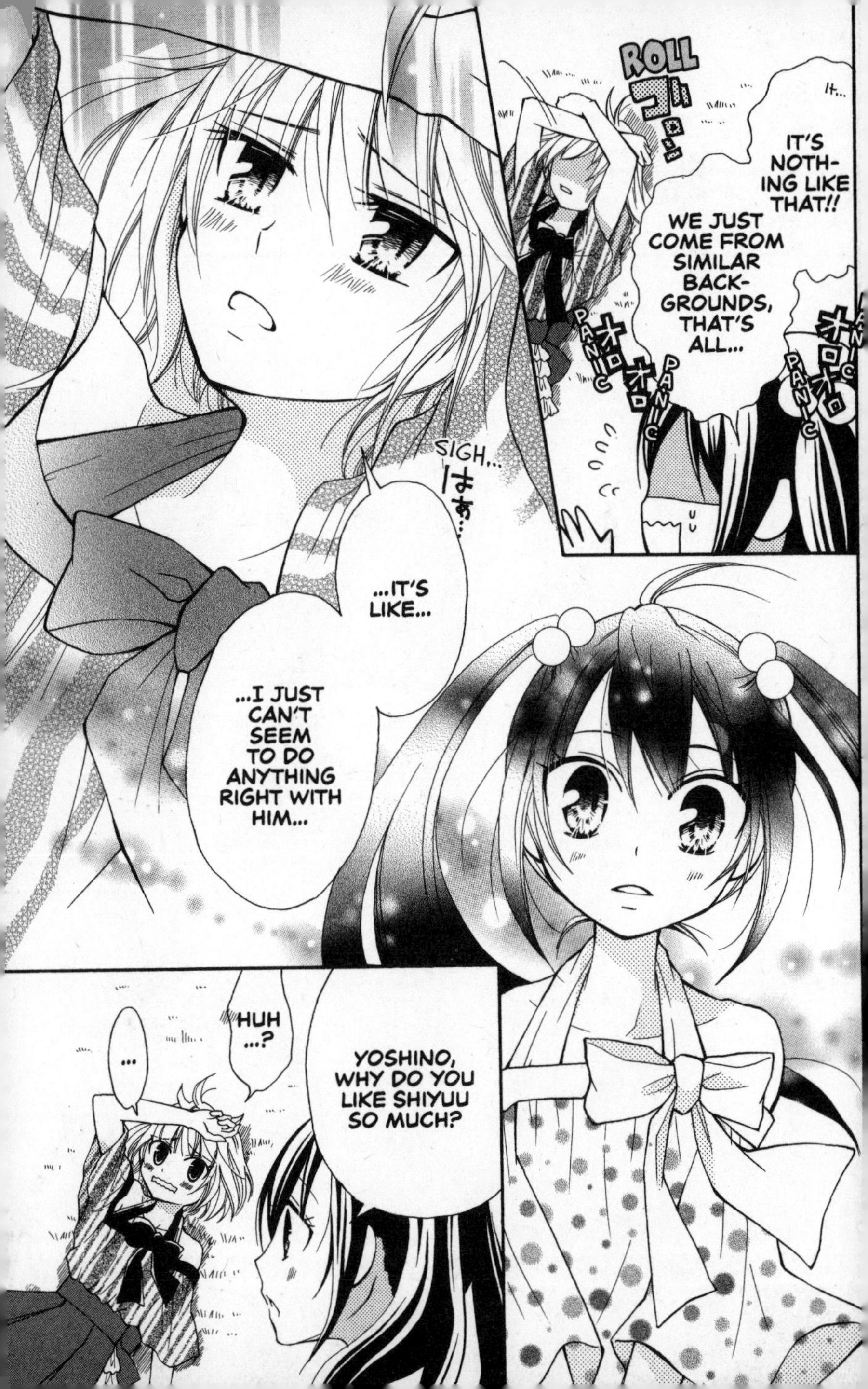
ROLL
ゴロッ
It...
IT'S NOTHING LIKE THAT!!
WE JUST COME FROM SIMILAR BACKGROUNDS, THAT'S ALL...
PANIC
オロ
PANIC
オロ
PANIC
オロ
PANIC
オロ
SIGH...
はぁ…
...IT'S LIKE...
...I JUST CAN'T SEEM TO DO ANYTHING RIGHT WITH HIM...
YOSHINO, WHY DO YOU LIKE SHIYUU SO MUCH?
HUH ...?
...

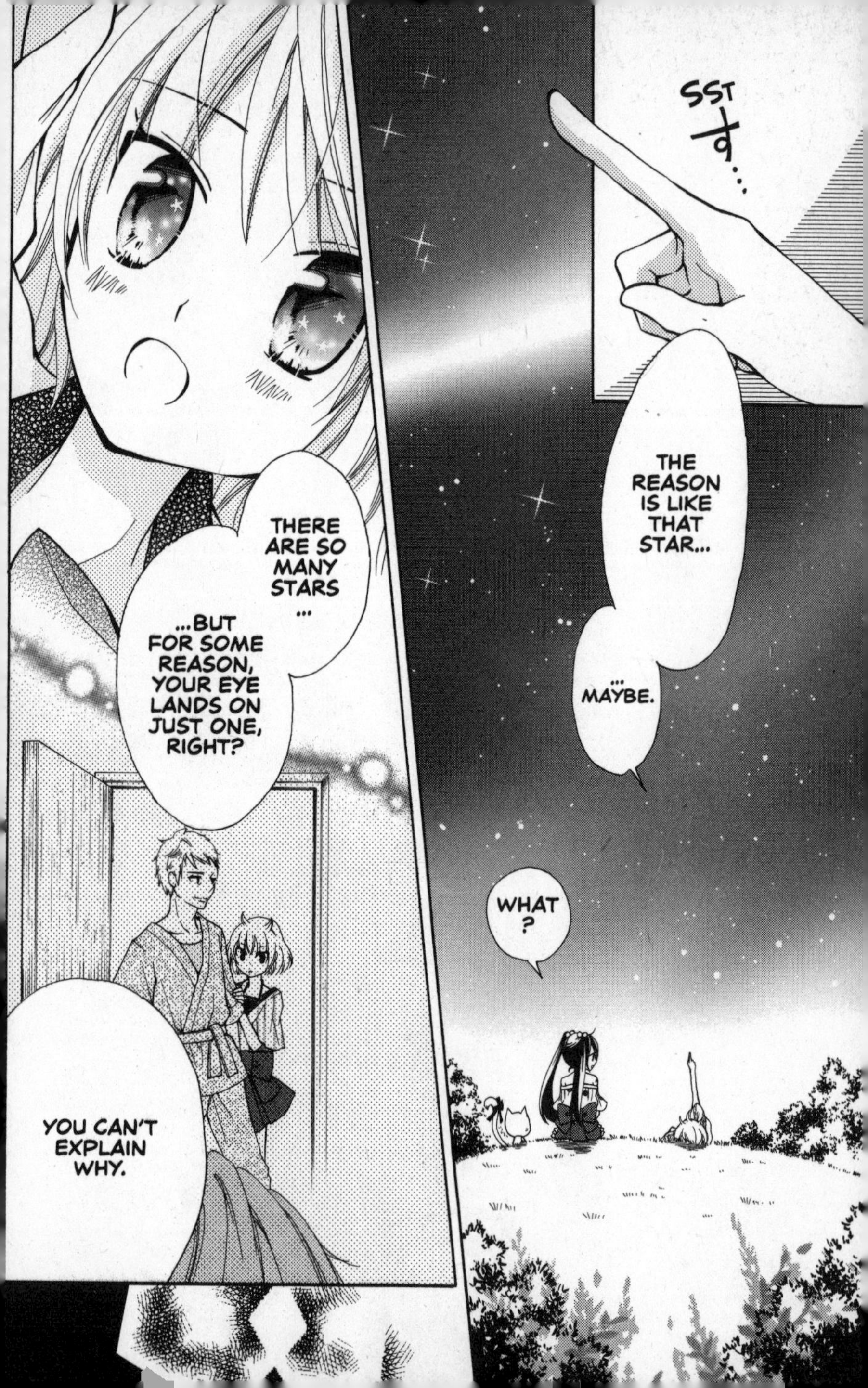
SST す...
THE REASON IS LIKE THAT STAR...
...MAYBE.
WHAT?
THERE ARE SO MANY STARS...
...BUT FOR SOME REASON, YOUR EYE LANDS ON JUST ONE, RIGHT?
YOU CAN'T EXPLAIN WHY.

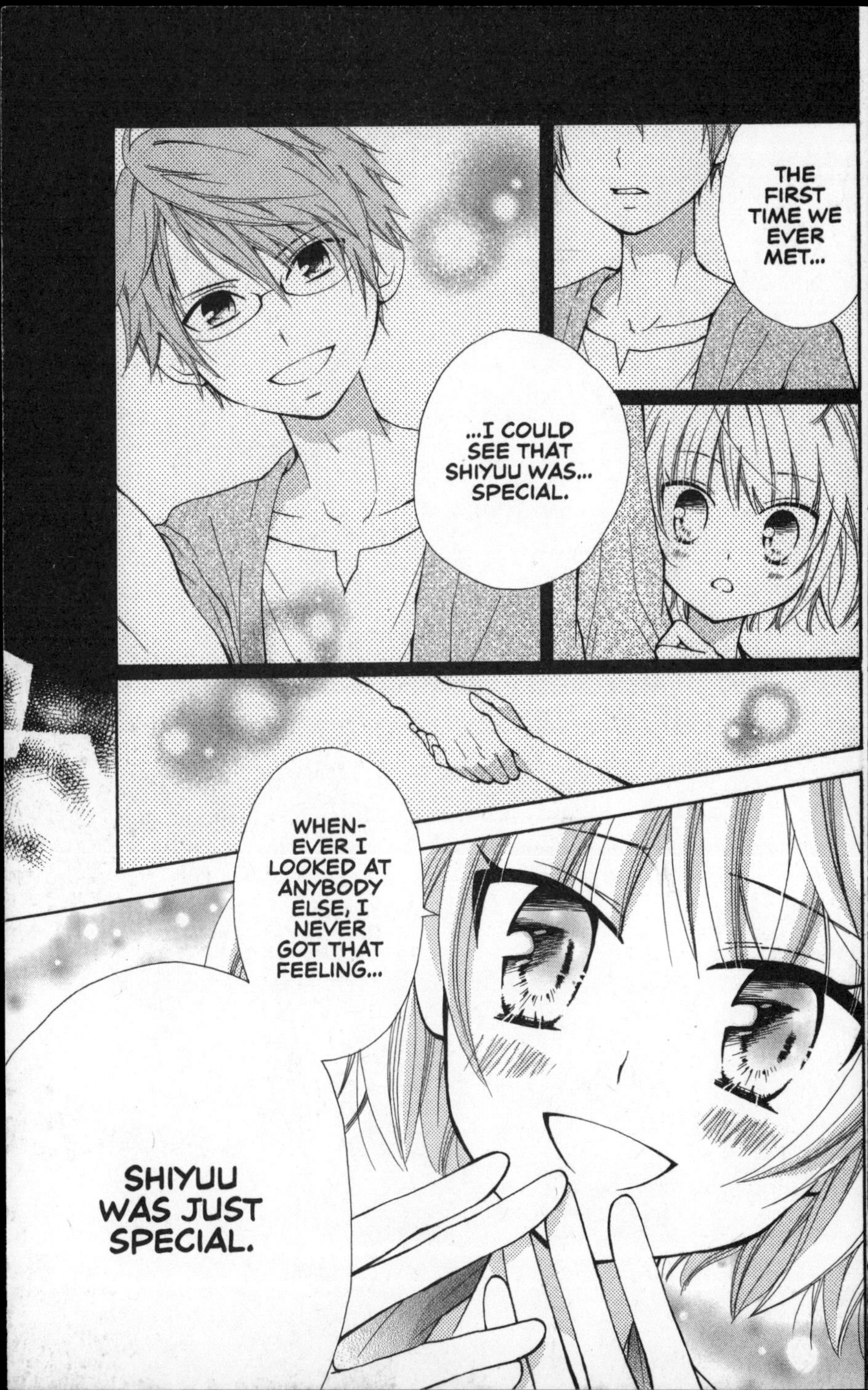
THE FIRST TIME WE EVER MET...
...I COULD SEE THAT SHIYUU WAS... SPECIAL.
WHEN-EVER I LOOKED AT ANYBODY ELSE, I NEVER GOT THAT FEELING...
SHIYUU WAS JUST SPECIAL.

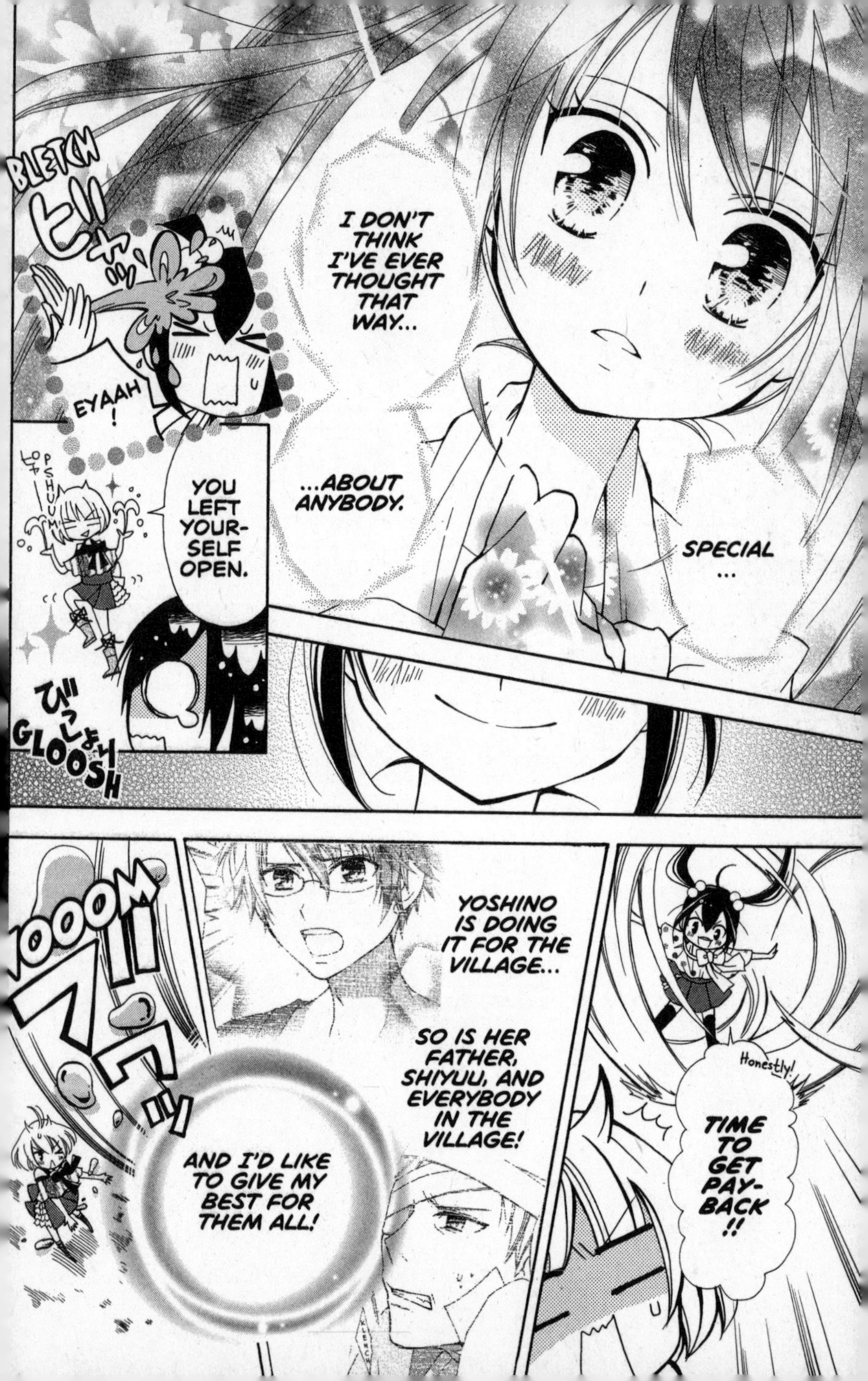
SPECIAL ...
I DON'T THINK I'VE EVER THOUGHT THAT WAY...
...ABOUT ANYBODY.
BLETCH
EYAAH!
PSHUUM
YOU LEFT YOURSELF OPEN.
びっしょり
GLOOSH
Honestly!
TIME TO GET PAY-BACK!!
YOSHINO IS DOING IT FOR THE VILLAGE...
SO IS HER FATHER, SHIYUU, AND EVERYBODY IN THE VILLAGE!
AND I'D LIKE TO GIVE MY BEST FOR THEM ALL!
KLENCH
OOOM

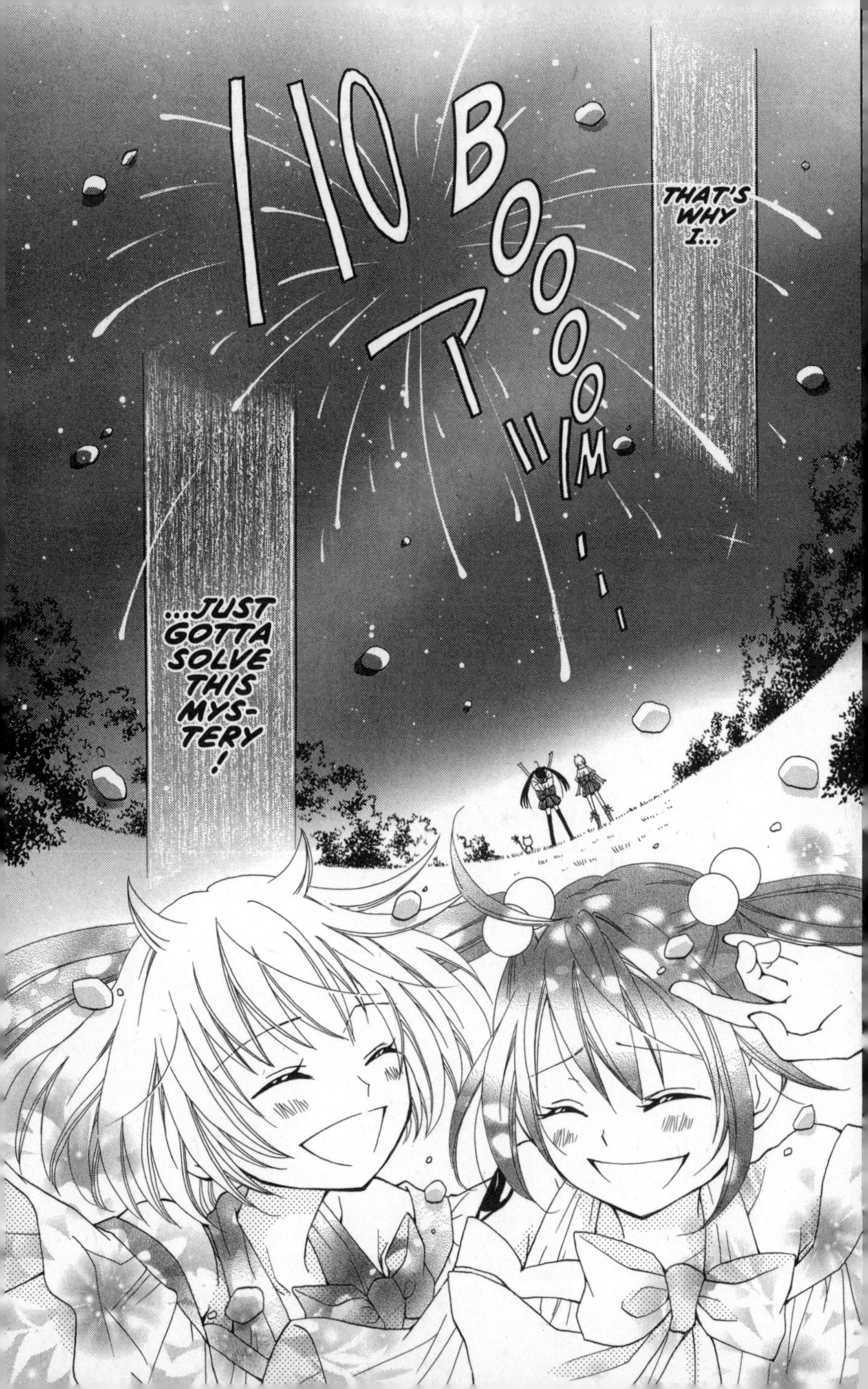
THAT'S WHY I...
BOOOOOM
...JUST GOTTA SOLVE THIS MYS-TERY!

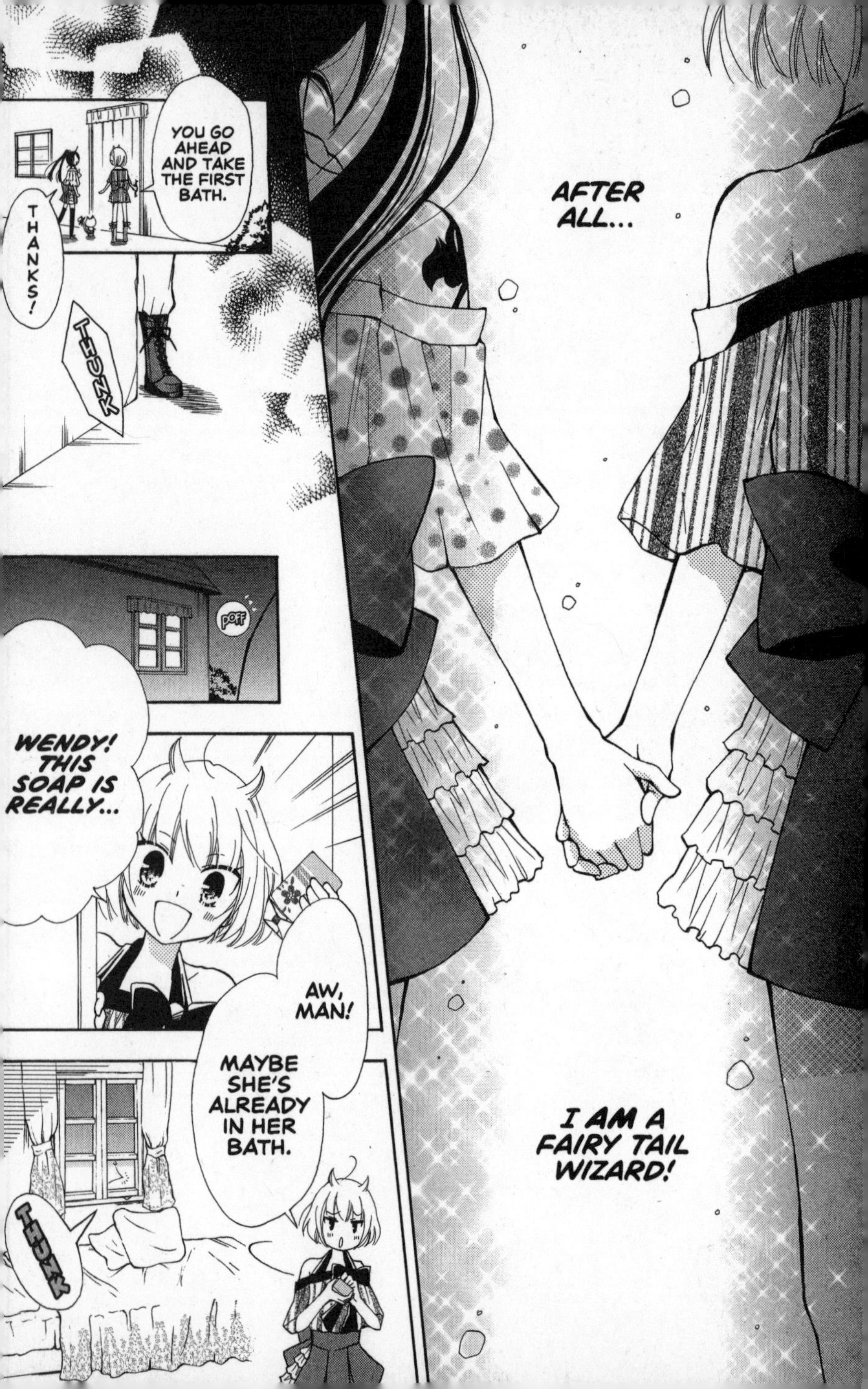
AFTER ALL...
I AM A FAIRY TAIL WIZARD!
YOU GO AHEAD AND TAKE THE FIRST BATH.
THANKS!
THUNK
poff
WENDY! THIS SOAP IS REALLY...
AW, MAN!
MAYBE SHE'S ALREADY IN HER BATH.
THUNK

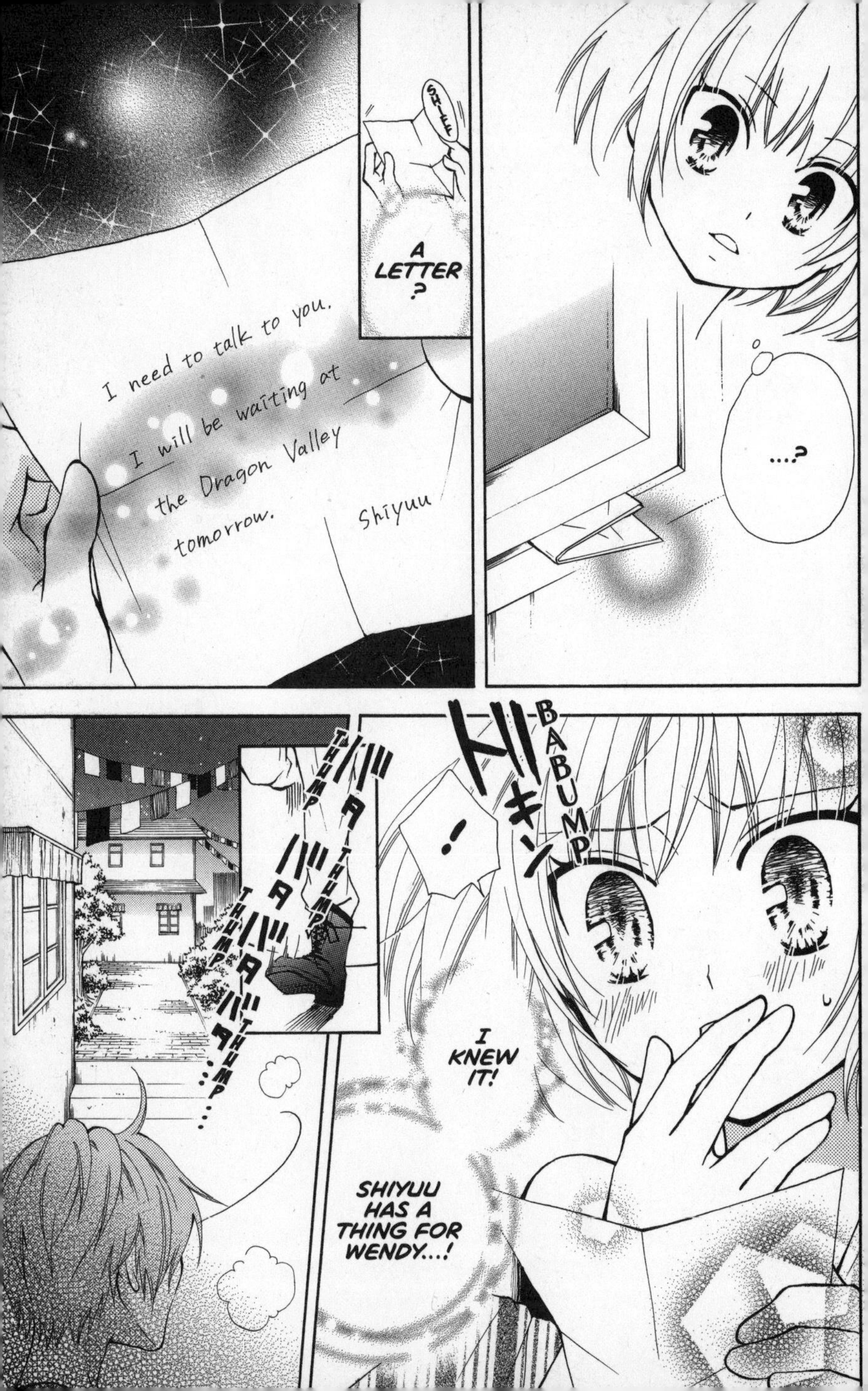
...?
SHIFF
A LETTER?
I need to talk to you.
I will be waiting at the Dragon Valley tomorrow.
Shiyuu
BABUMP
ドキン
!
I KNEW IT!
SHIYUU HAS A THING FOR WENDY...!
THUMP THUMP THUMP THUMP...

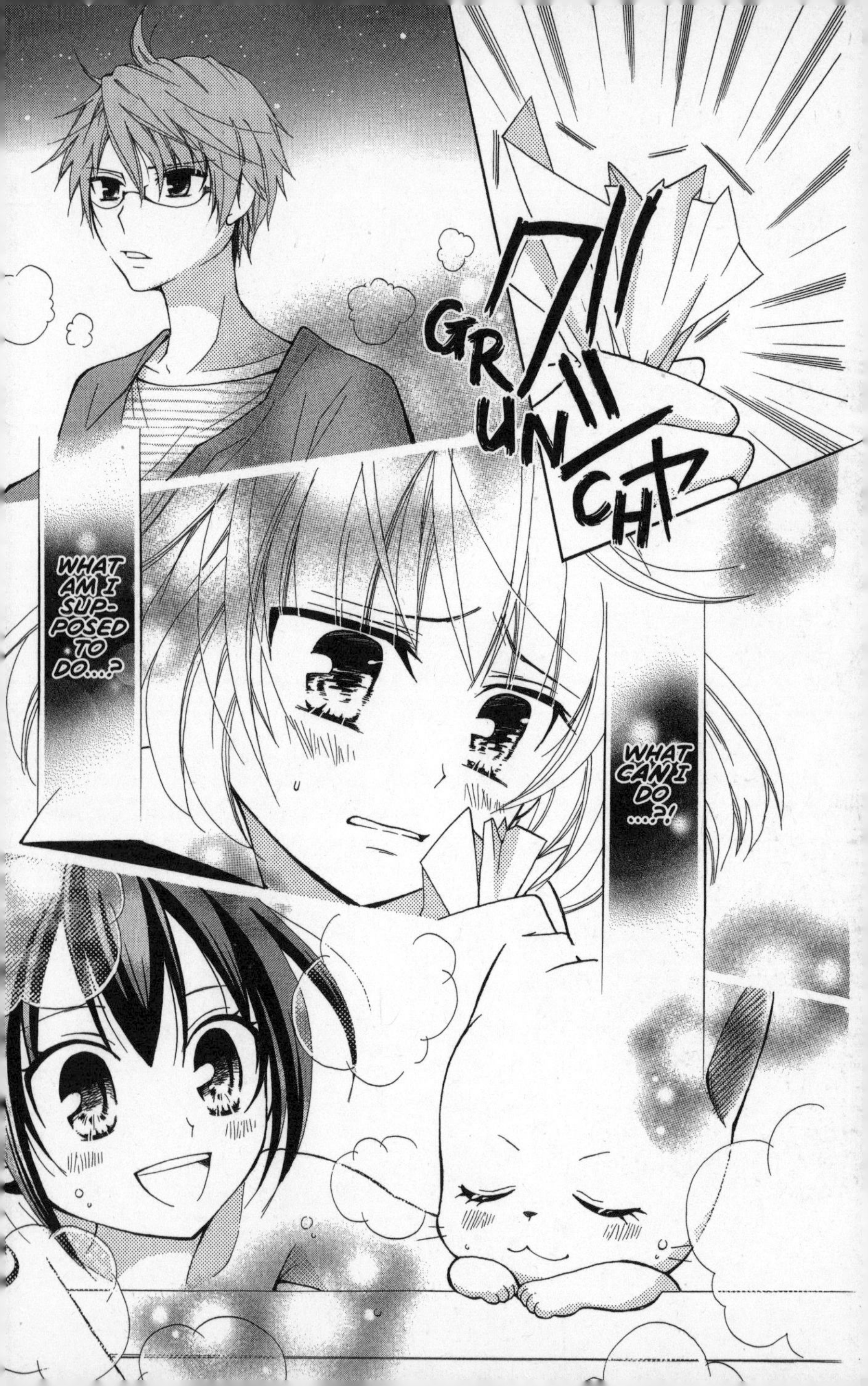
GRUNCH
WHAT CAN I DO ...?!
WHAT AM I SUP-POSED TO DO...?

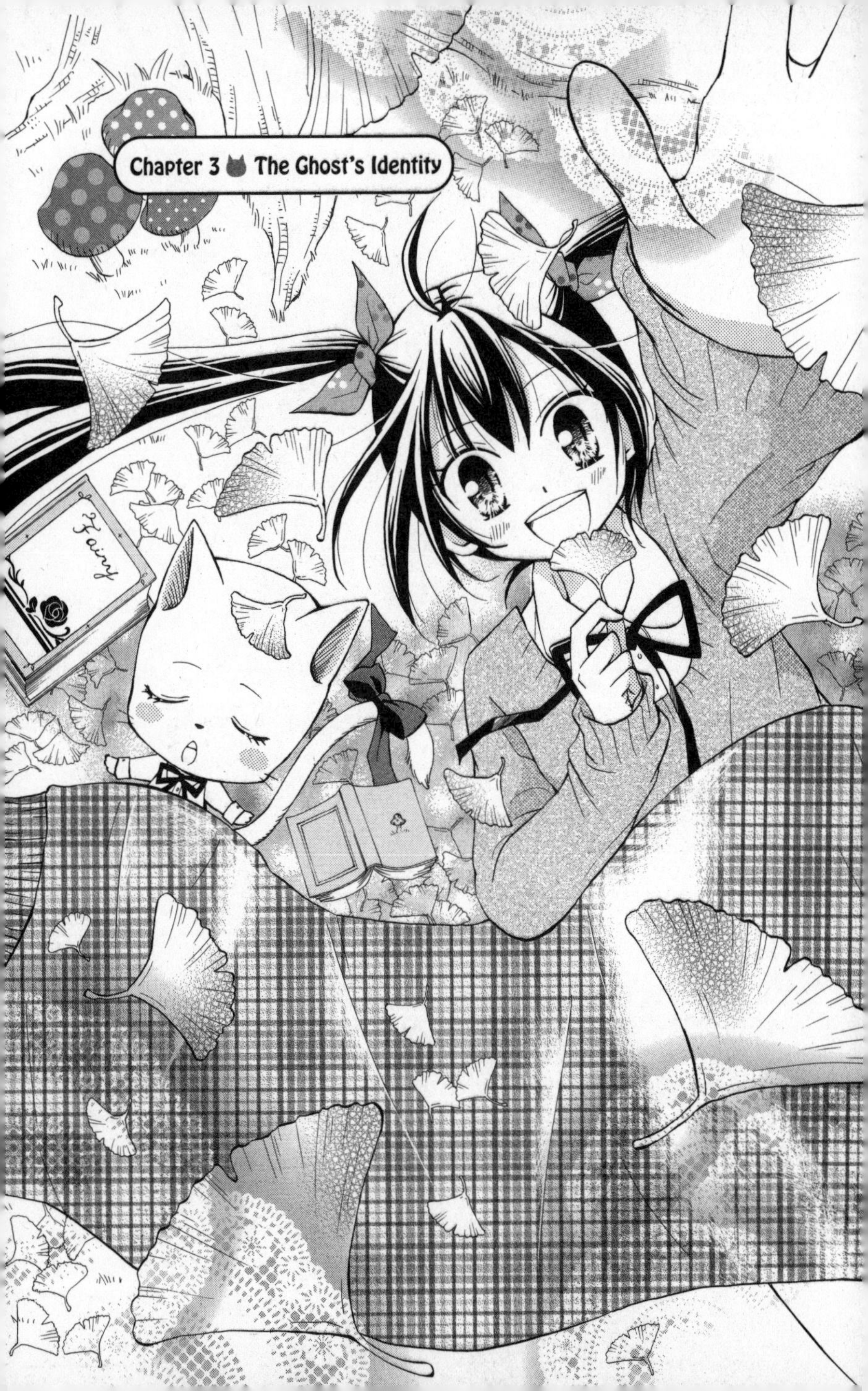
Chapter 3 The Ghost's Identity
Fairy

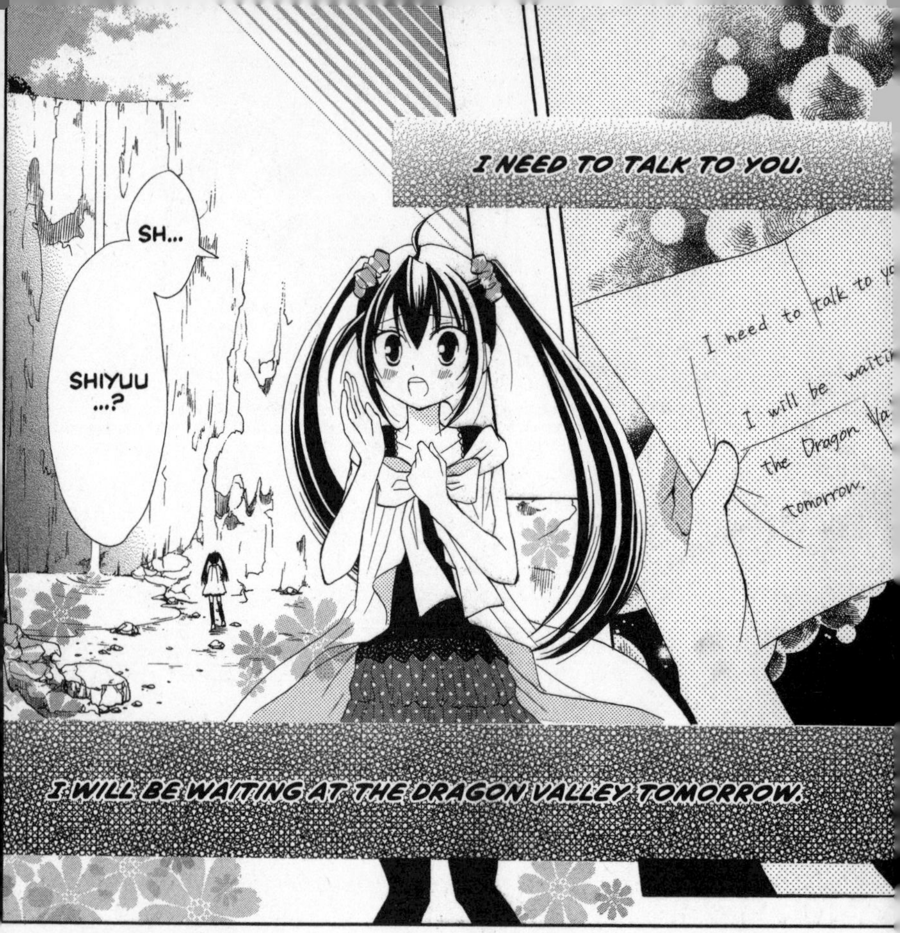
I NEED TO TALK TO YOU.
I need to talk to
I will be
the Dragon
tomorrow.
SH...
SHIYUU ...?
I WILL BE WAITING AT THE DRAGON VALLEY TOMORROW.

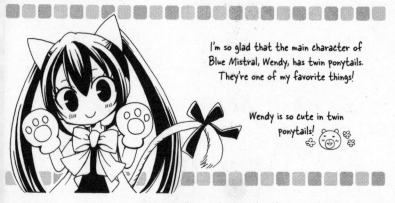

I'm so glad that the main character of Blue Mistral, Wendy, has twin ponytails. They're one of my favorite things!

Wendy is so cute in twin ponytails!

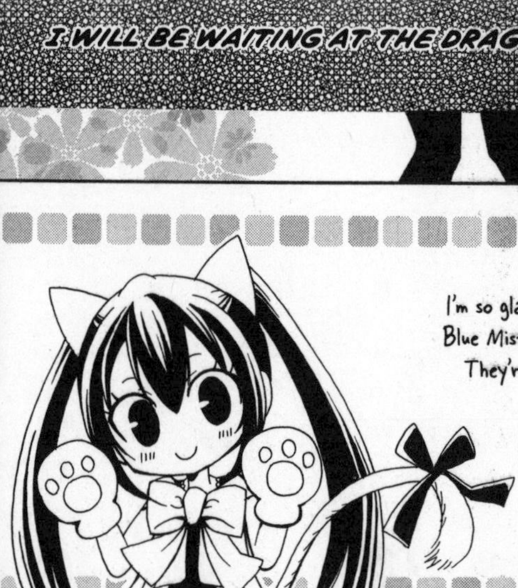

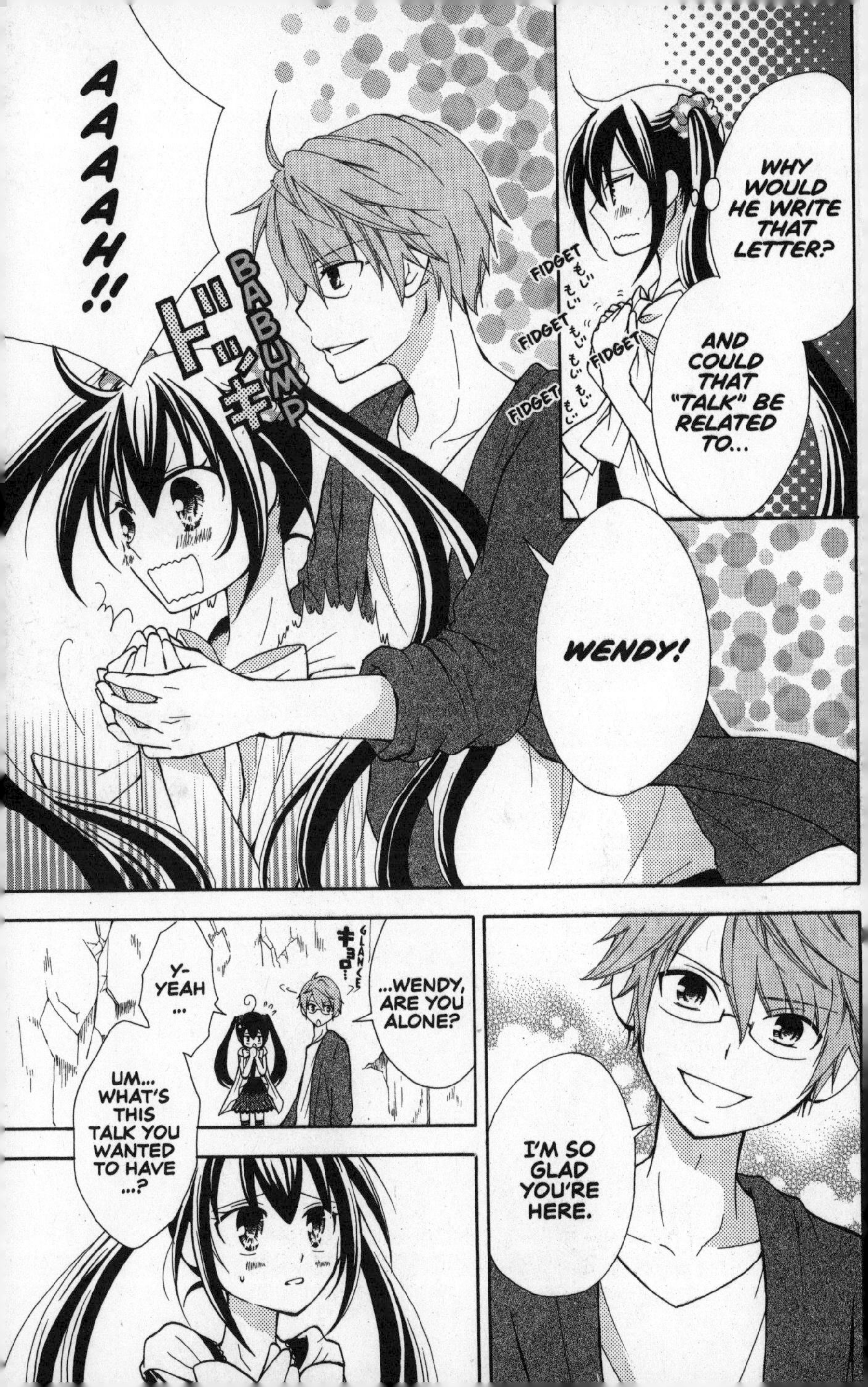
WHY WOULD HE WRITE THAT LETTER?
FIDGET もじ もじ
FIDGET もじ もじ
FIDGET もじ もじ
FIDGET もじ もじ
AND COULD THAT "TALK" BE RELATED TO...
WENDY!
BABUMP
ドッキ
AAAAAH!!
I'M SO GLAD YOU'RE HERE.
...WENDY, ARE YOU ALONE?
GLANCE
キョロ...
Y-YEAH ...
UM... WHAT'S THIS TALK YOU WANTED TO HAVE ...?

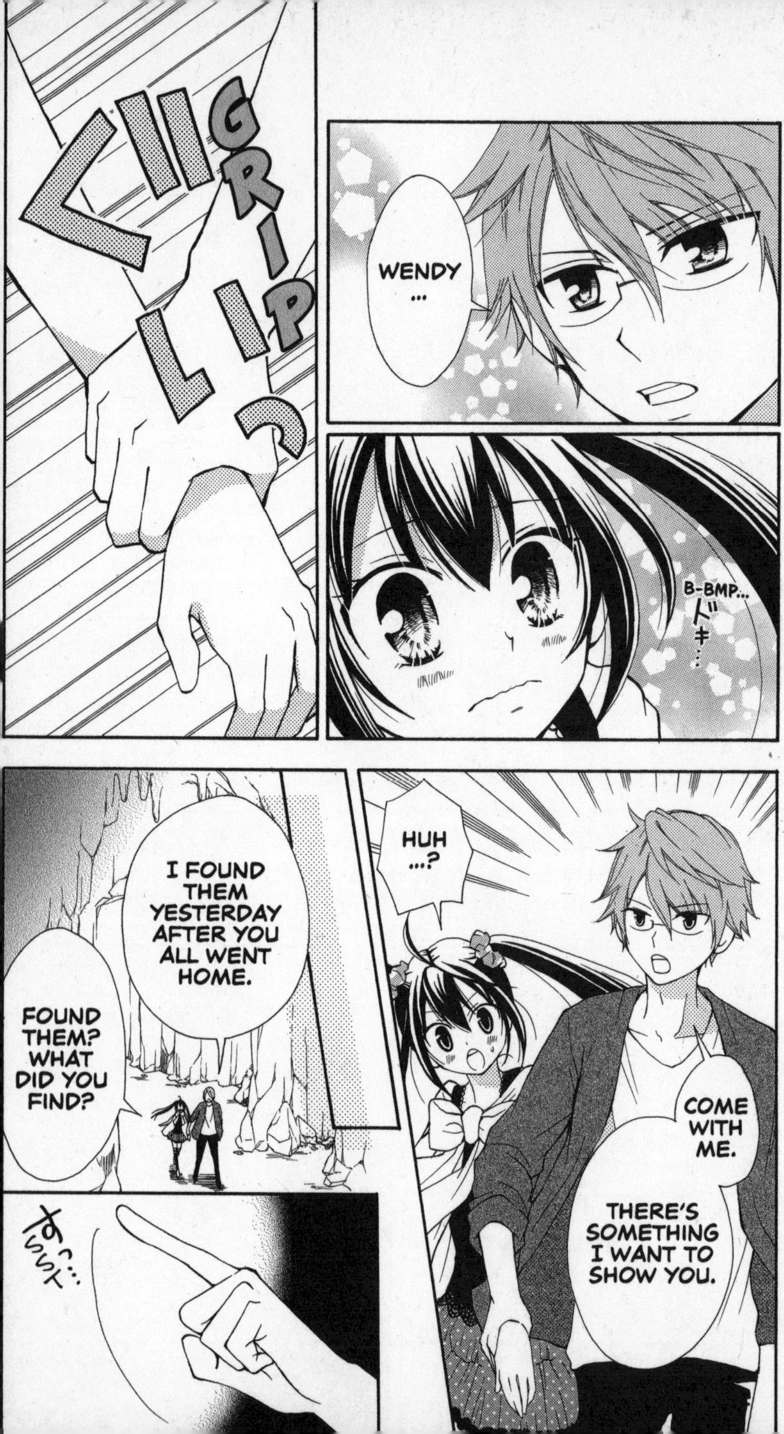
WENDY ...
B-BMP...
ドキ...
GRIP
HUH ...?
COME WITH ME.
THERE'S SOMETHING I WANT TO SHOW YOU.
I FOUND THEM YESTERDAY AFTER YOU ALL WENT HOME.
FOUND THEM? WHAT DID YOU FIND?
すっ...
SST

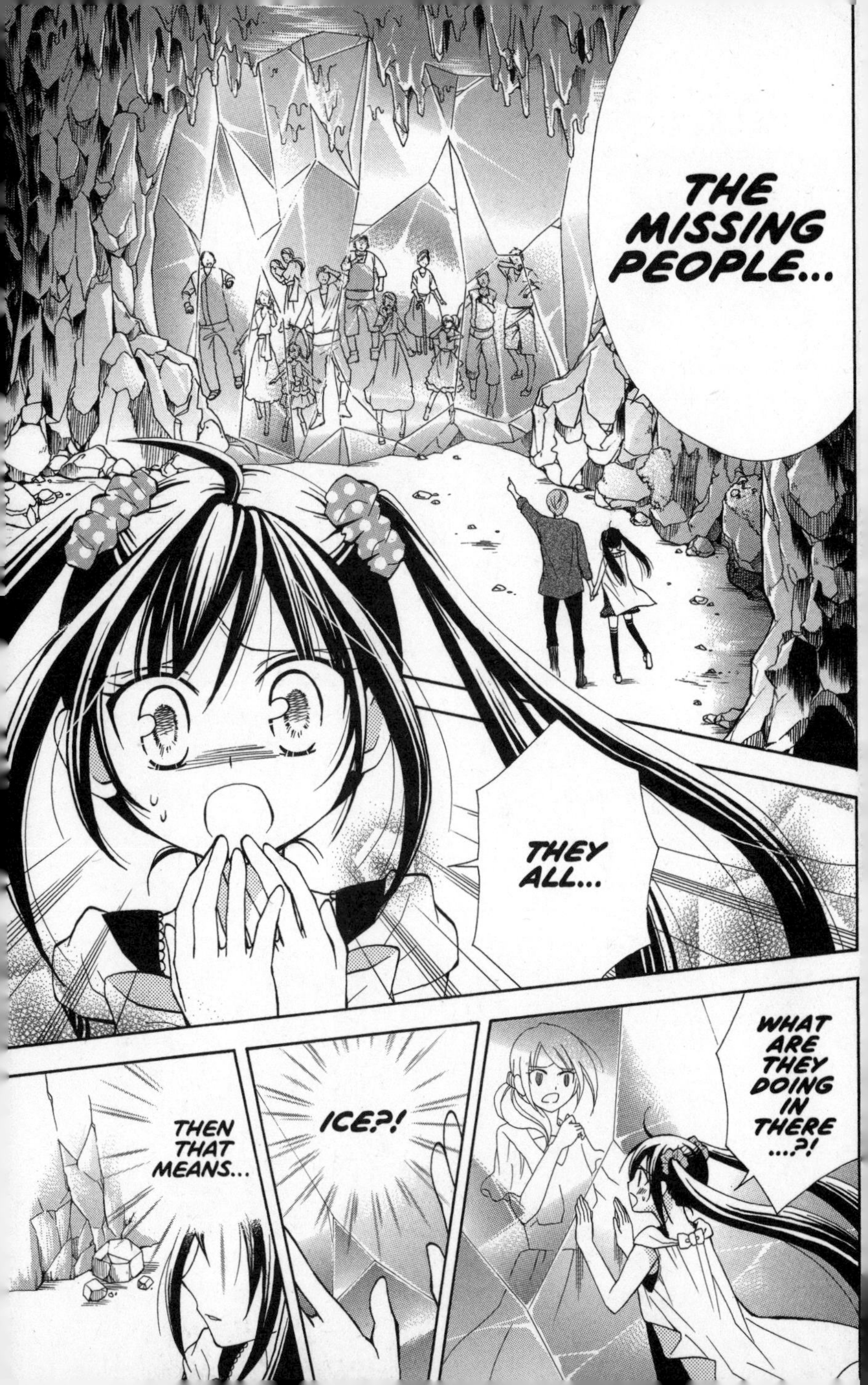
THE MISSING PEOPLE...
THEY ALL...
WHAT ARE THEY DOING IN THERE ...?!
ICE?!
THEN THAT MEANS...

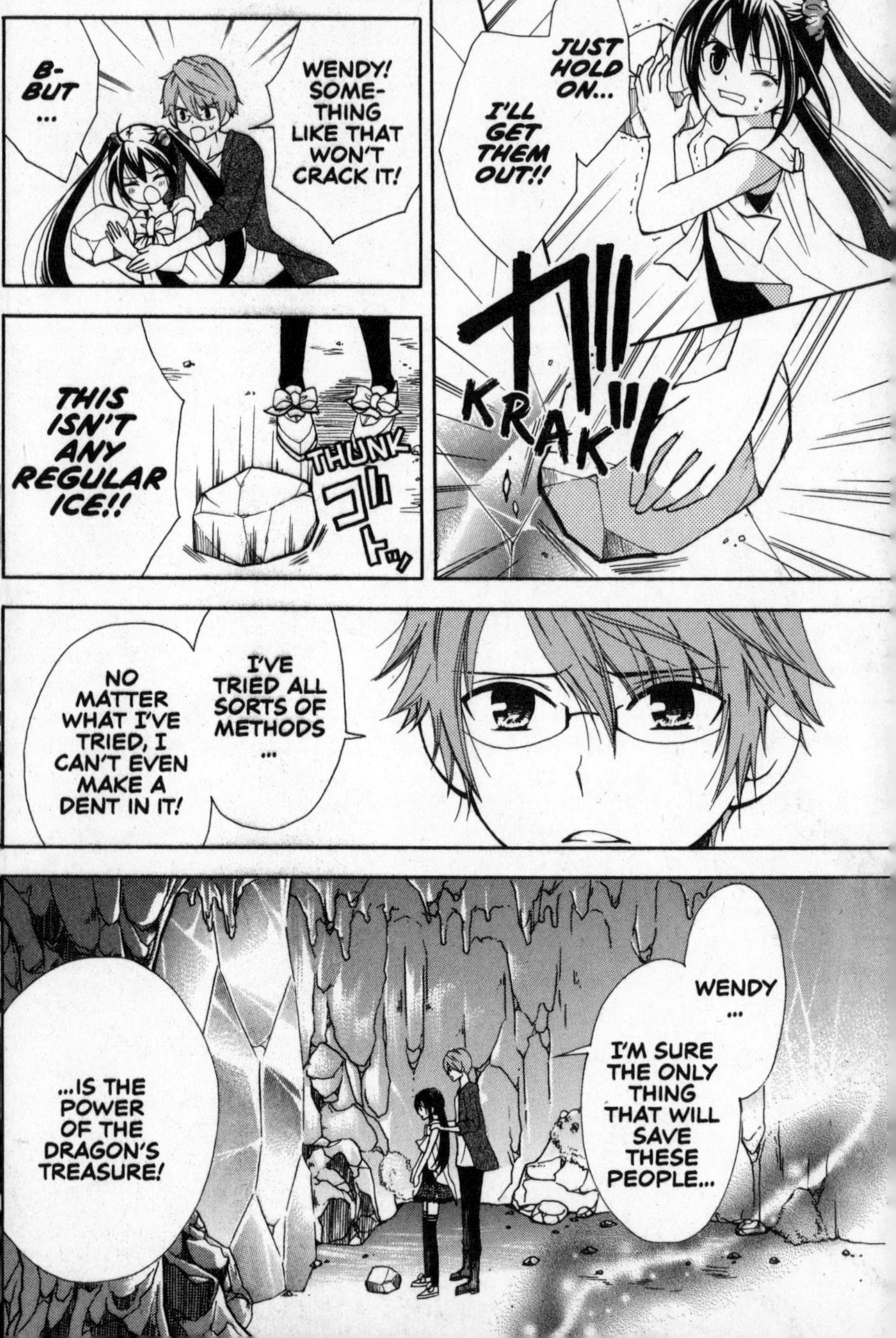
JUST HOLD ON...
I'LL GET THEM OUT!!
KRAK
WENDY! SOME-THING LIKE THAT WON'T CRACK IT!
B-BUT...
THUNK
THIS ISN'T ANY REGULAR ICE!!
I'VE TRIED ALL SORTS OF METHODS...
NO MATTER WHAT I'VE TRIED, I CAN'T EVEN MAKE A DENT IN IT!
WENDY...
I'M SURE THE ONLY THING THAT WILL SAVE THESE PEOPLE...
...IS THE POWER OF THE DRAGON'S TREASURE!

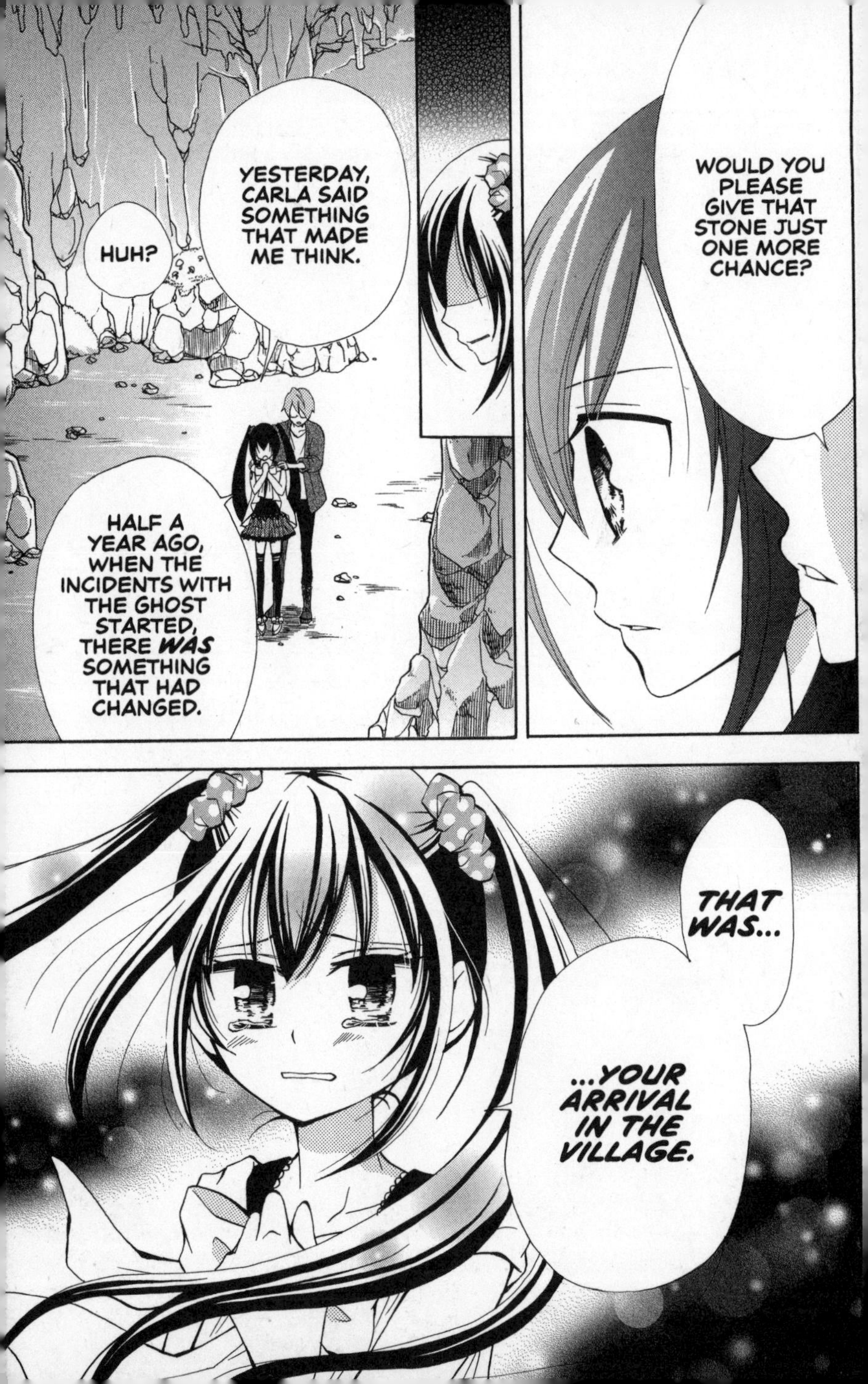
WOULD YOU PLEASE GIVE THAT STONE JUST ONE MORE CHANCE?
YESTERDAY, CARLA SAID SOMETHING THAT MADE ME THINK.
HUH?
HALF A YEAR AGO, WHEN THE INCIDENTS WITH THE GHOST STARTED, THERE *WAS* SOMETHING THAT HAD CHANGED.
THAT WAS...
...YOUR ARRIVAL IN THE VILLAGE.

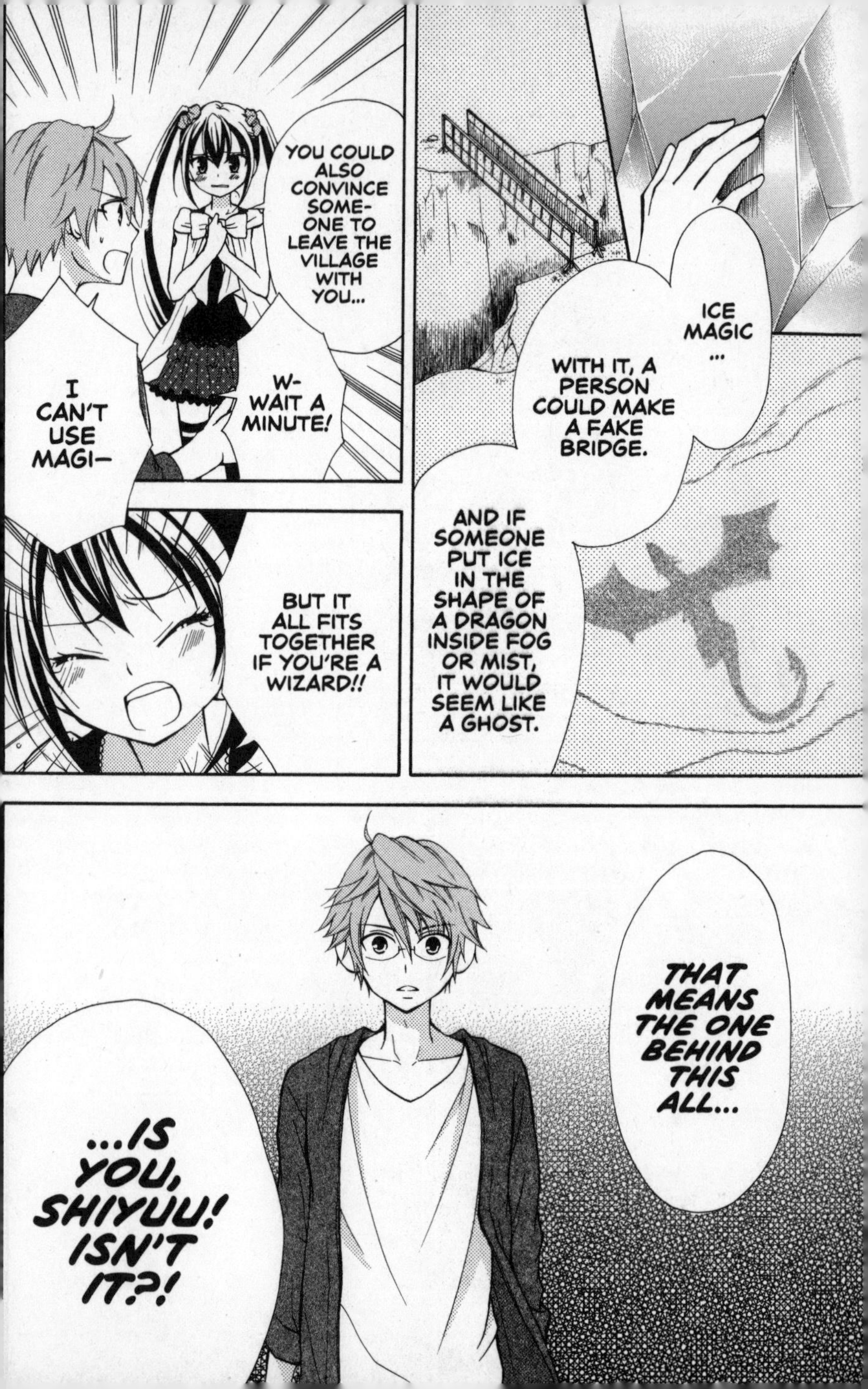
ICE MAGIC ...
WITH IT, A PERSON COULD MAKE A FAKE BRIDGE.
AND IF SOMEONE PUT ICE IN THE SHAPE OF A DRAGON INSIDE FOG OR MIST, IT WOULD SEEM LIKE A GHOST.
YOU COULD ALSO CONVINCE SOME-ONE TO LEAVE THE VILLAGE WITH YOU...
W- WAIT A MINUTE!
I CAN'T USE MAGI—
BUT IT ALL FITS TOGETHER IF YOU'RE A WIZARD!!
THAT MEANS THE ONE BEHIND THIS ALL...
...IS YOU, SHIYUU! ISN'T IT?!

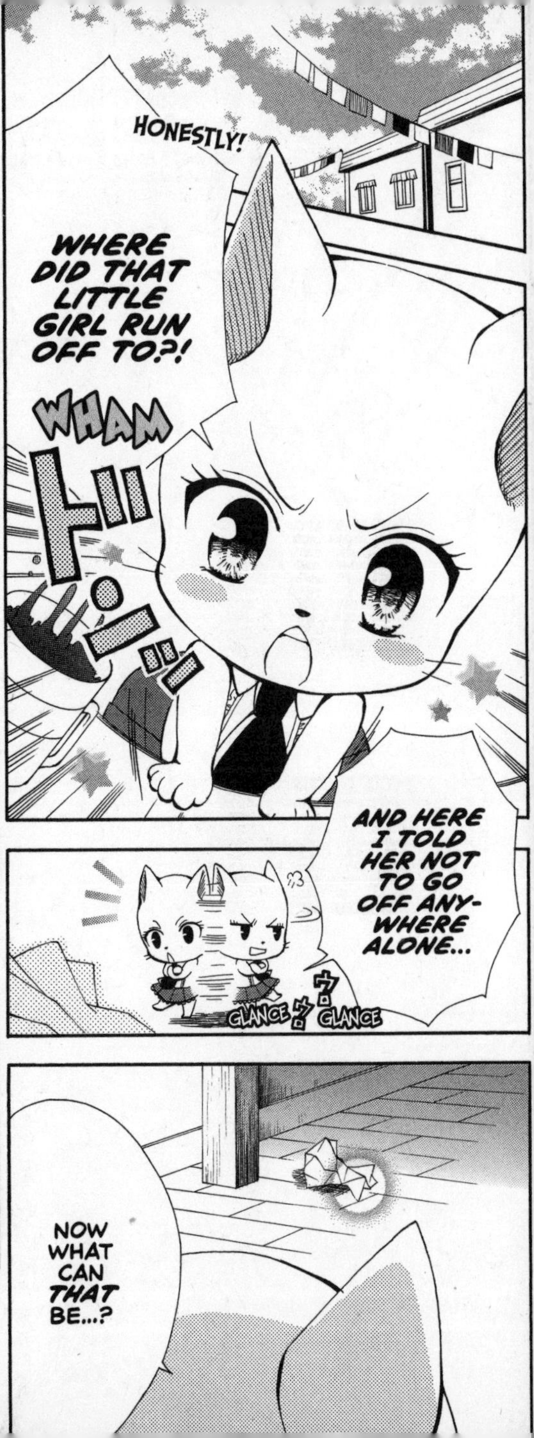
HONESTLY!
WHERE DID THAT LITTLE GIRL RUN OFF TO?!
WHAM
AND HERE I TOLD HER NOT TO GO OFF ANY-WHERE ALONE...
GLANCE GLANCE
NOW WHAT CAN THAT BE...?

BONUS MANGA 2

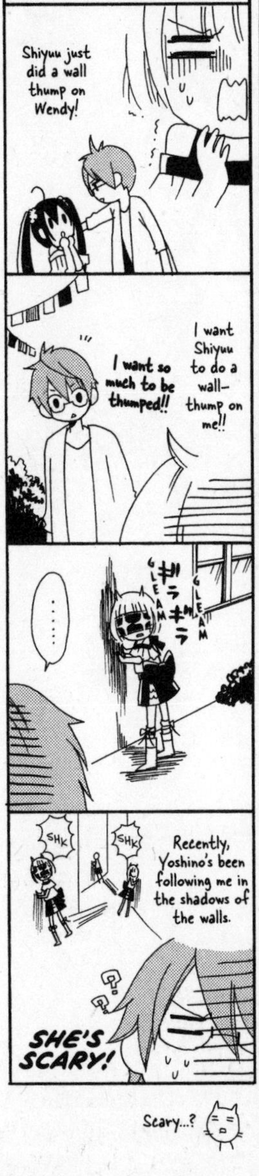
Shiyuu just did a wall thump on Wendy!
I want Shiyuu to do a wall-thump on me!!
I want so much to be thumped!!
......
GLEAM GLEAM
SHK
SHK
Recently, Yoshino's been following me in the shadows of the walls.
SHE'S SCARY!
Scary...?

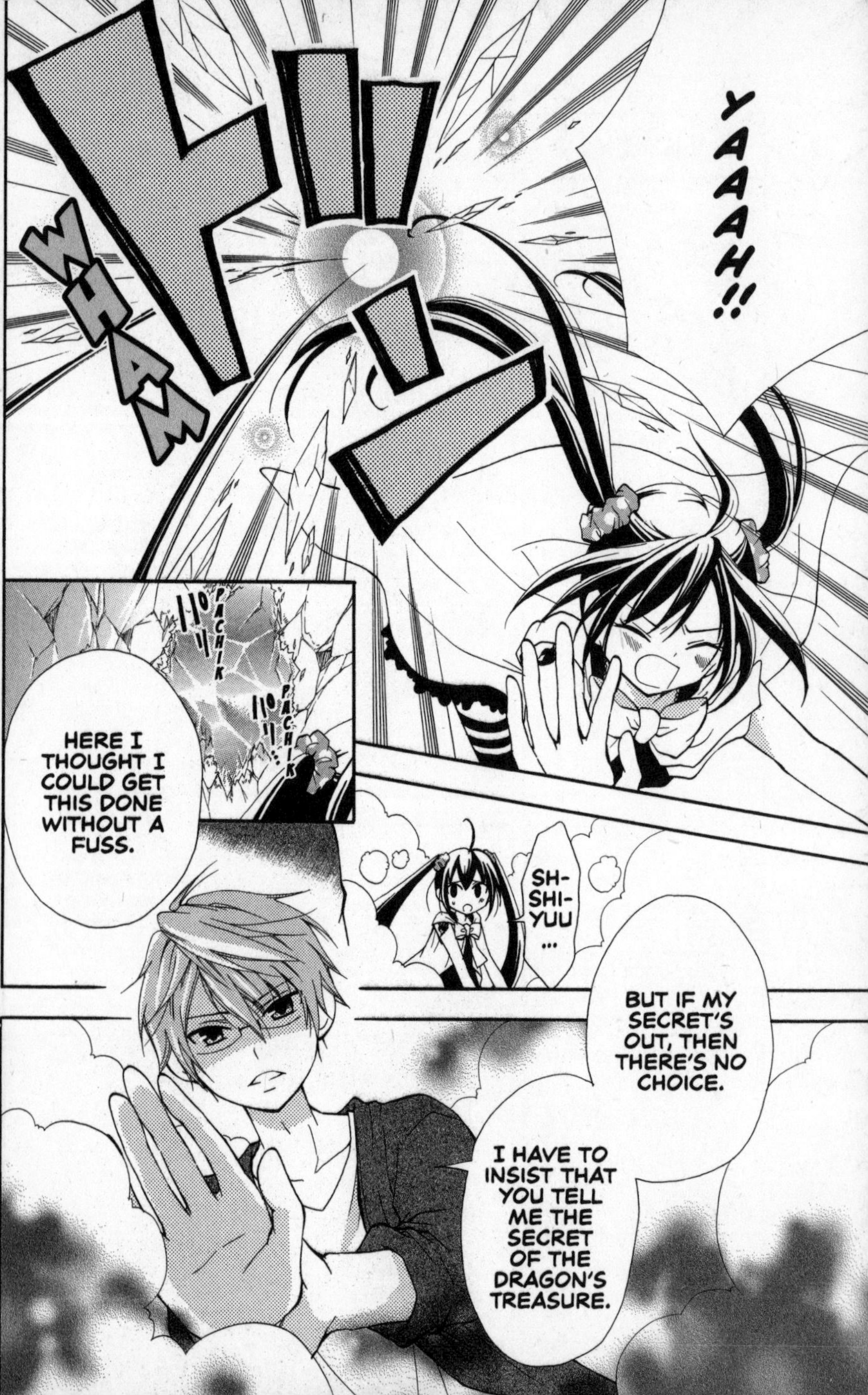
YAAAAH!!
WHAM
PACHIK
PACHIK...
SH-SHI-YUU...
HERE I THOUGHT I COULD GET THIS DONE WITHOUT A FUSS.
BUT IF MY SECRET'S OUT, THEN THERE'S NO CHOICE.
I HAVE TO INSIST THAT YOU TELL ME THE SECRET OF THE DRAGON'S TREASURE.

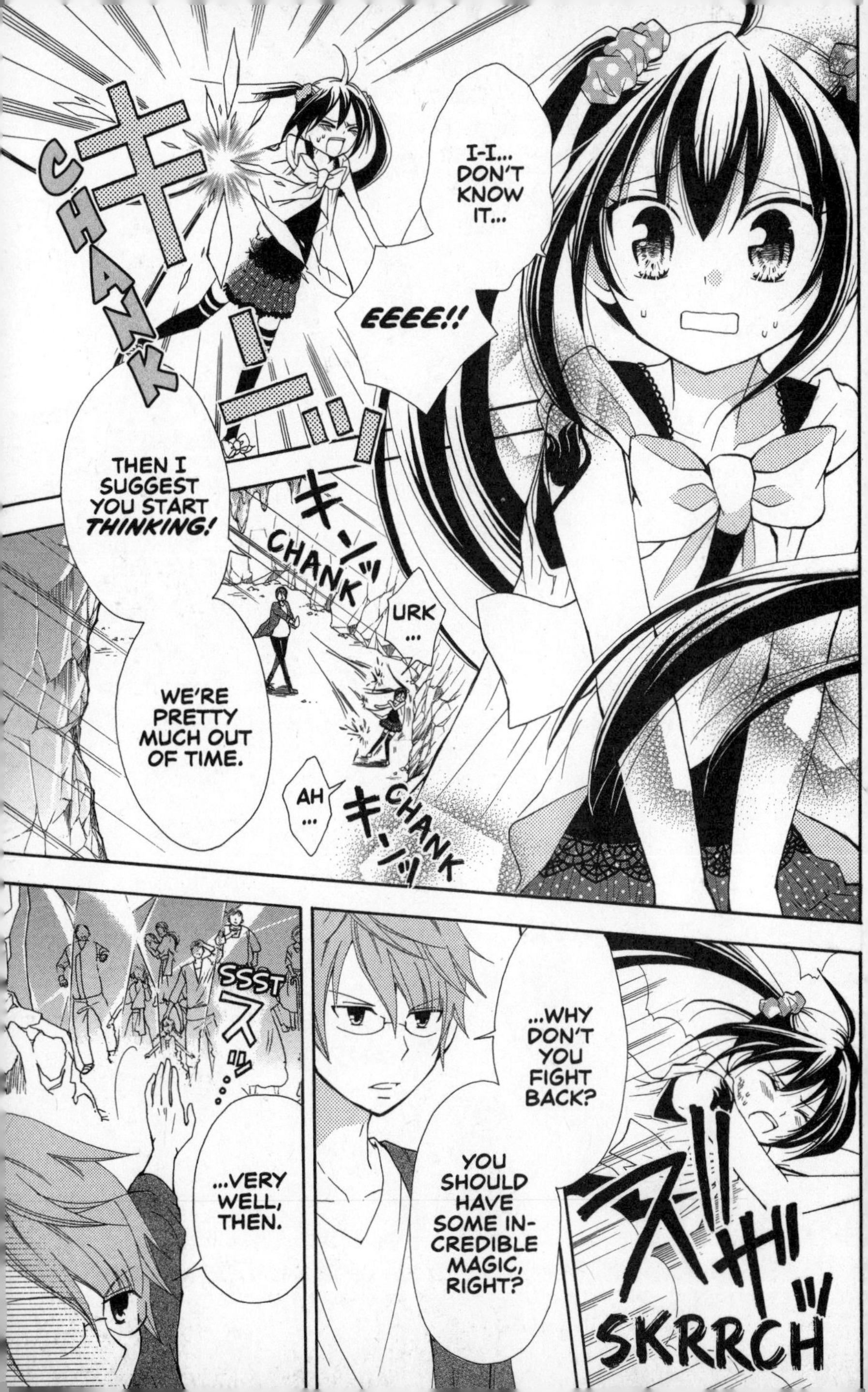
I-I... DON'T KNOW IT...
EEEE!!
CHANK
THEN I SUGGEST YOU START *THINKING!*
CHANK
URK ...
WE'RE PRETTY MUCH OUT OF TIME.
AH ...
CHANK
SKRRCH
...WHY DON'T YOU FIGHT BACK?
YOU SHOULD HAVE SOME IN-CREDIBLE MAGIC, RIGHT?
SSST
...VERY WELL, THEN.

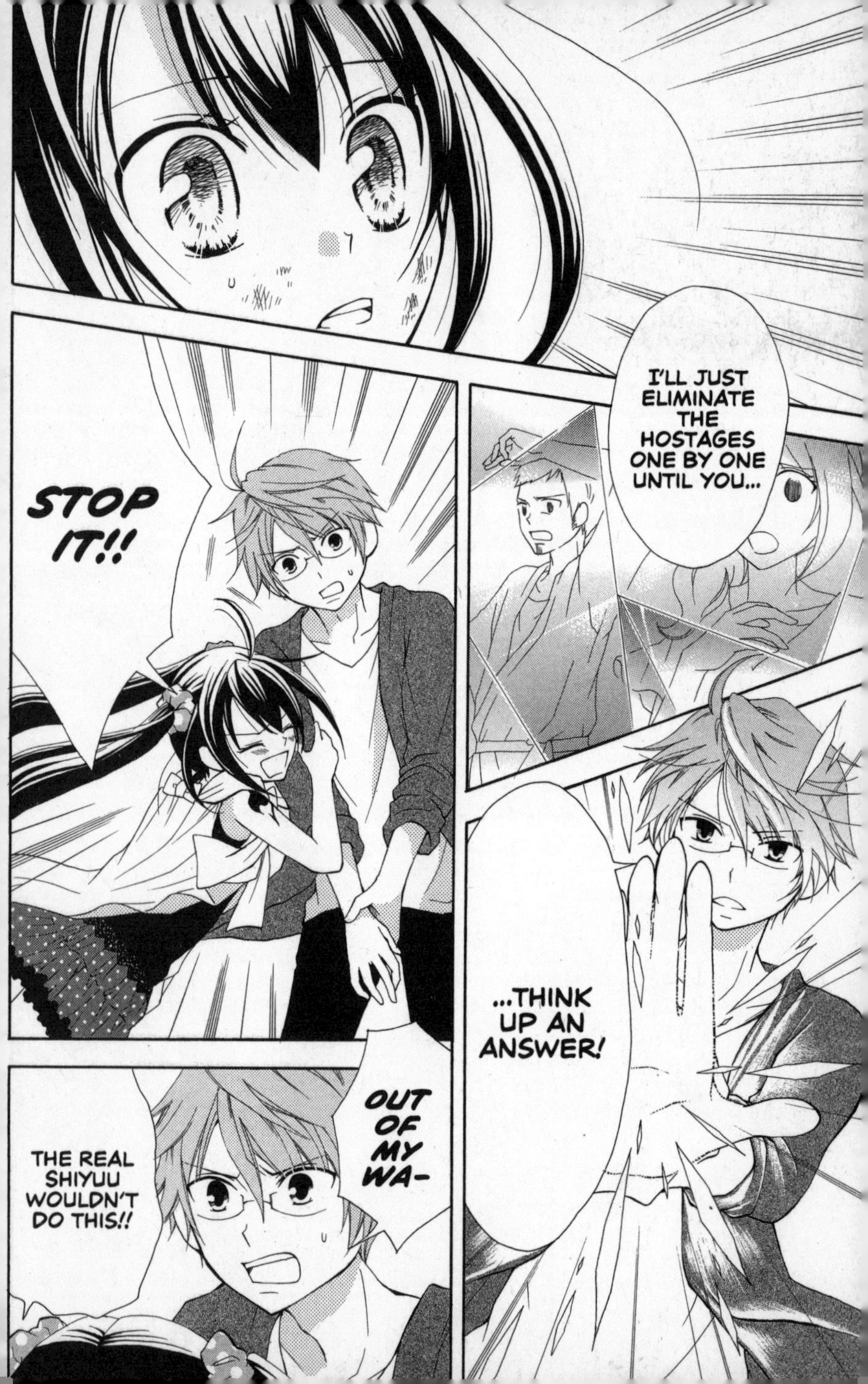
I'LL JUST ELIMINATE THE HOSTAGES ONE BY ONE UNTIL YOU...
...THINK UP AN ANSWER!
STOP IT!!
OUT OF MY WA-
THE REAL SHIYUU WOULDN'T DO THIS!!

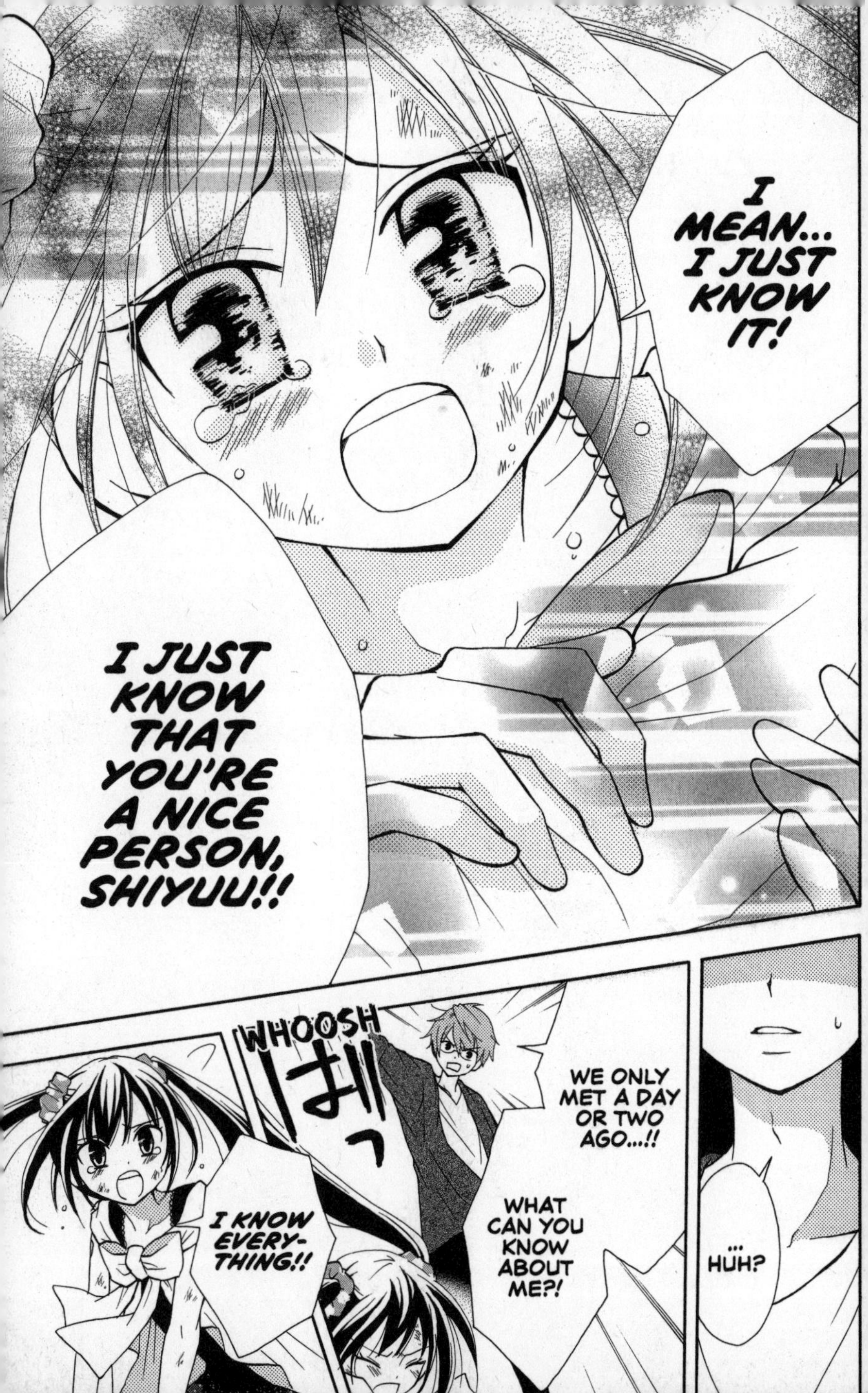
I MEAN... I JUST KNOW IT!
I JUST KNOW THAT YOU'RE A NICE PERSON, SHIYUU!!
... HUH?
WE ONLY MET A DAY OR TWO AGO...!!
WHOOSH
WHAT CAN YOU KNOW ABOUT ME?!
I KNOW EVERY-THING!!

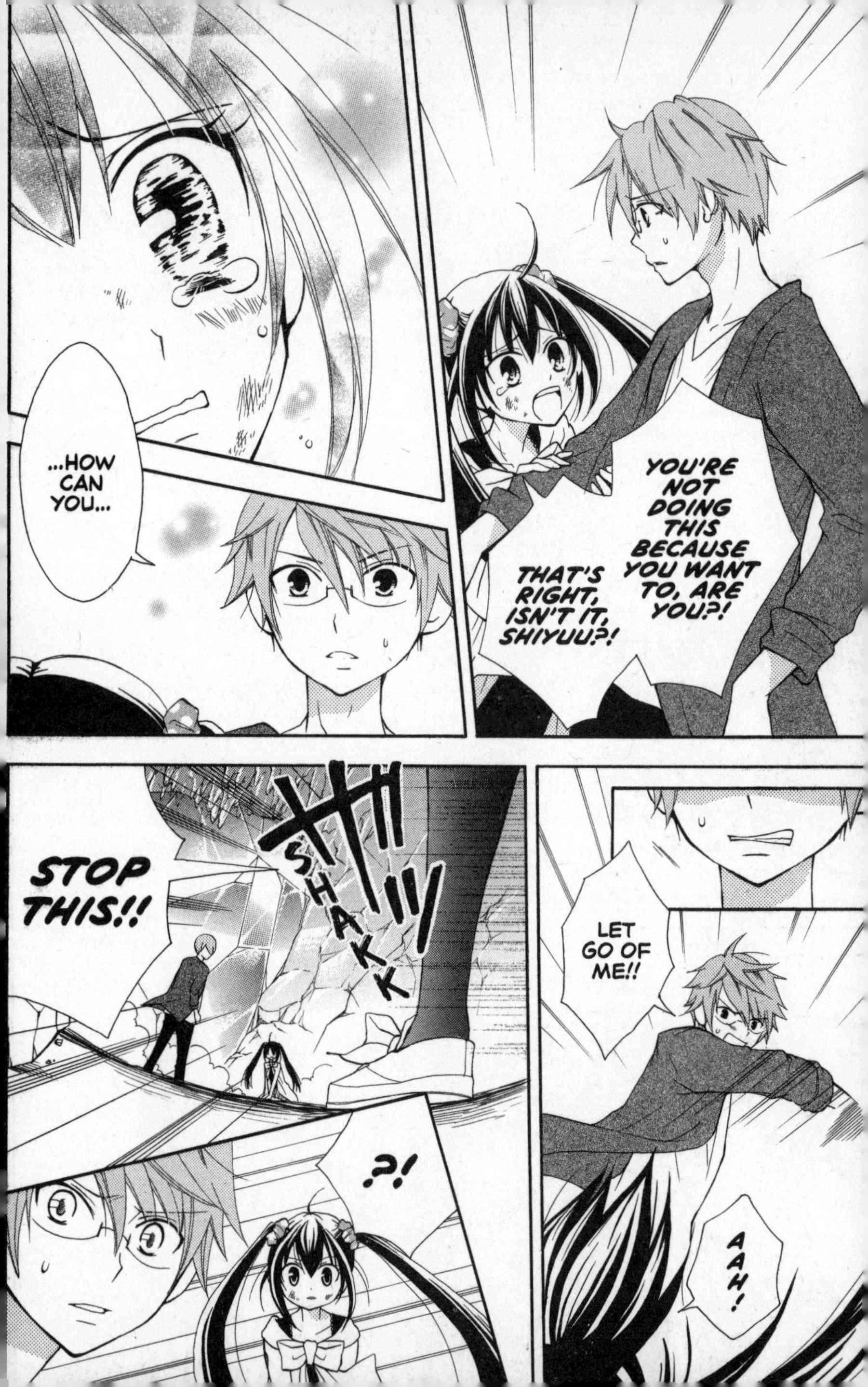
YOU'RE NOT DOING THIS BECAUSE YOU WANT TO, ARE YOU?!
THAT'S RIGHT, ISN'T IT, SHIYUU?!
...HOW CAN YOU...
LET GO OF ME!!
AAH!
STOP THIS!!
SHAKK
?!

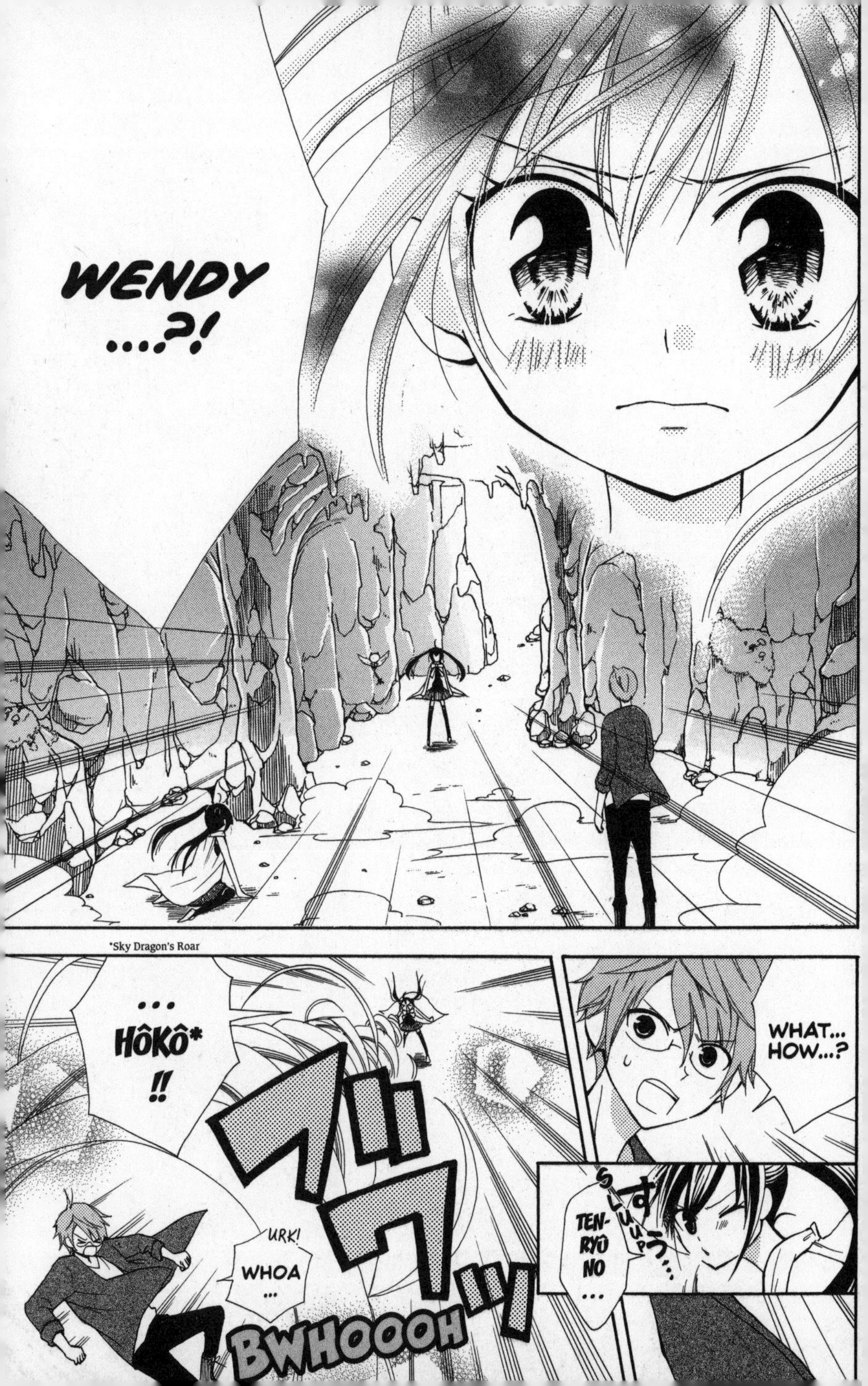
WENDY ...?!
WHAT... HOW...?
TENRYÛ NO ...
SLUUUP
すう…
... HÔKÔ* !!
BWHOOOH
URK!
WHOA ...

*Sky Dragon's Roar

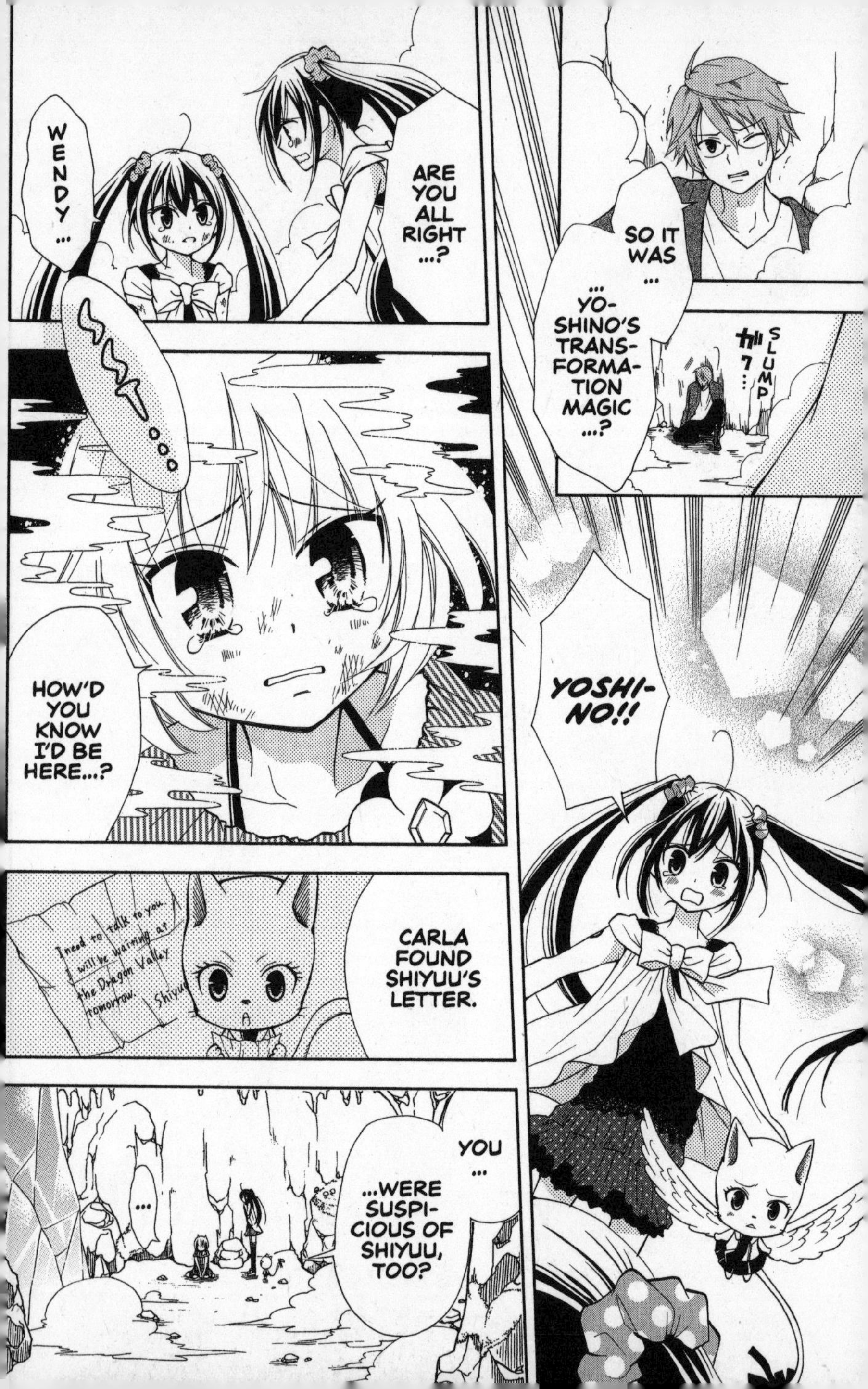
SO IT WAS ... ... YO-SHINO'S TRANS-FORMA-TION MAGIC ...?
ガク…
SLUMP
YOSHI-NO!!
ARE YOU ALL RIGHT ...?
WENDY ...
...
HOW'D YOU KNOW I'D BE HERE...?
CARLA FOUND SHIYUU'S LETTER.
I need to talk to you. I will be waiting at the Dragon Valley tomorrow. Shiyu
YOU ...
...WERE SUSPI-CIOUS OF SHIYUU, TOO?
...

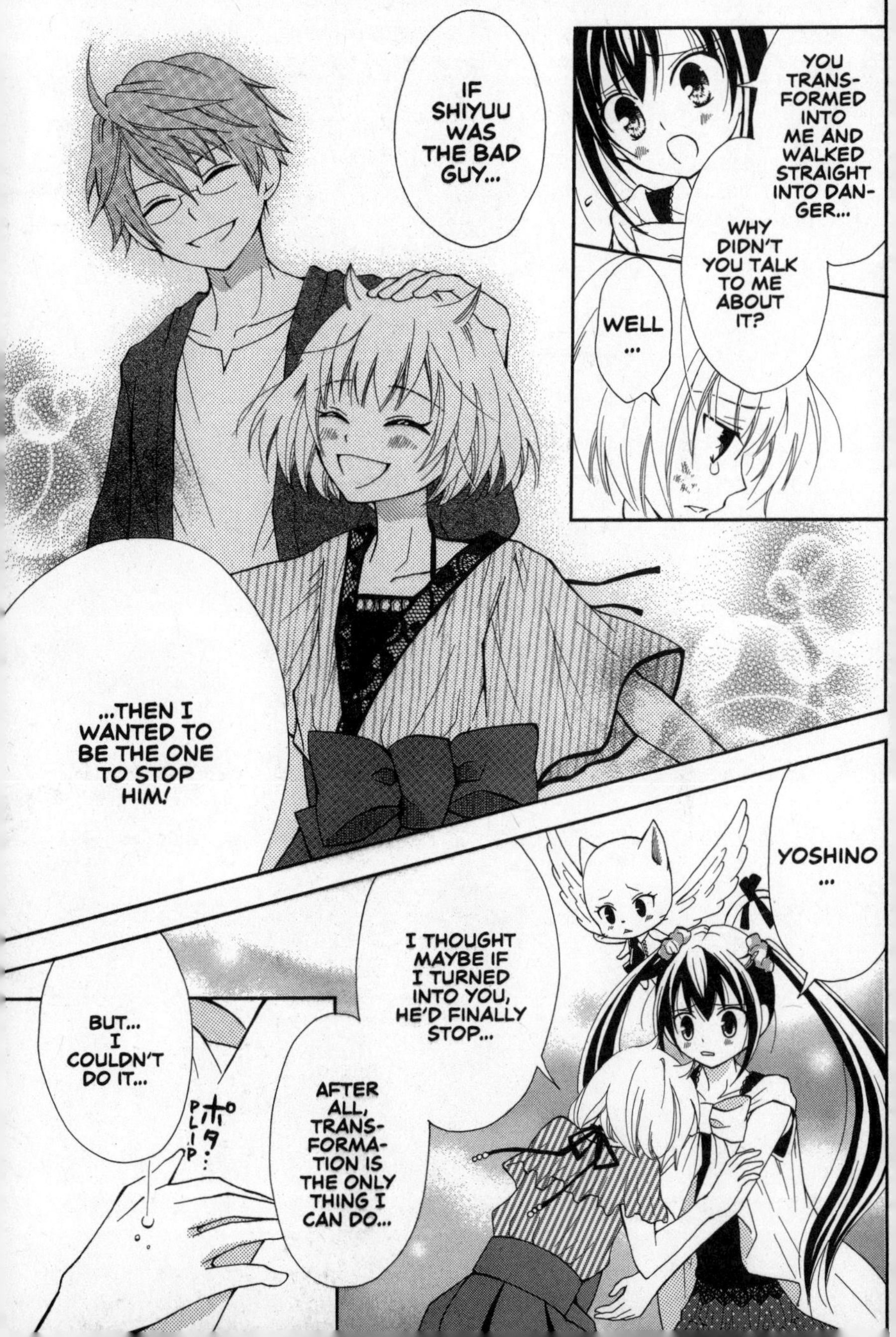
YOU TRANSFORMED INTO ME AND WALKED STRAIGHT INTO DANGER...
WHY DIDN'T YOU TALK TO ME ABOUT IT?
WELL...
IF SHIYUU WAS THE BAD GUY...
...THEN I WANTED TO BE THE ONE TO STOP HIM!
YOSHINO...
I THOUGHT MAYBE IF I TURNED INTO YOU, HE'D FINALLY STOP...
AFTER ALL, TRANSFORMATION IS THE ONLY THING I CAN DO...
BUT... I COULDN'T DO IT...
PLIP

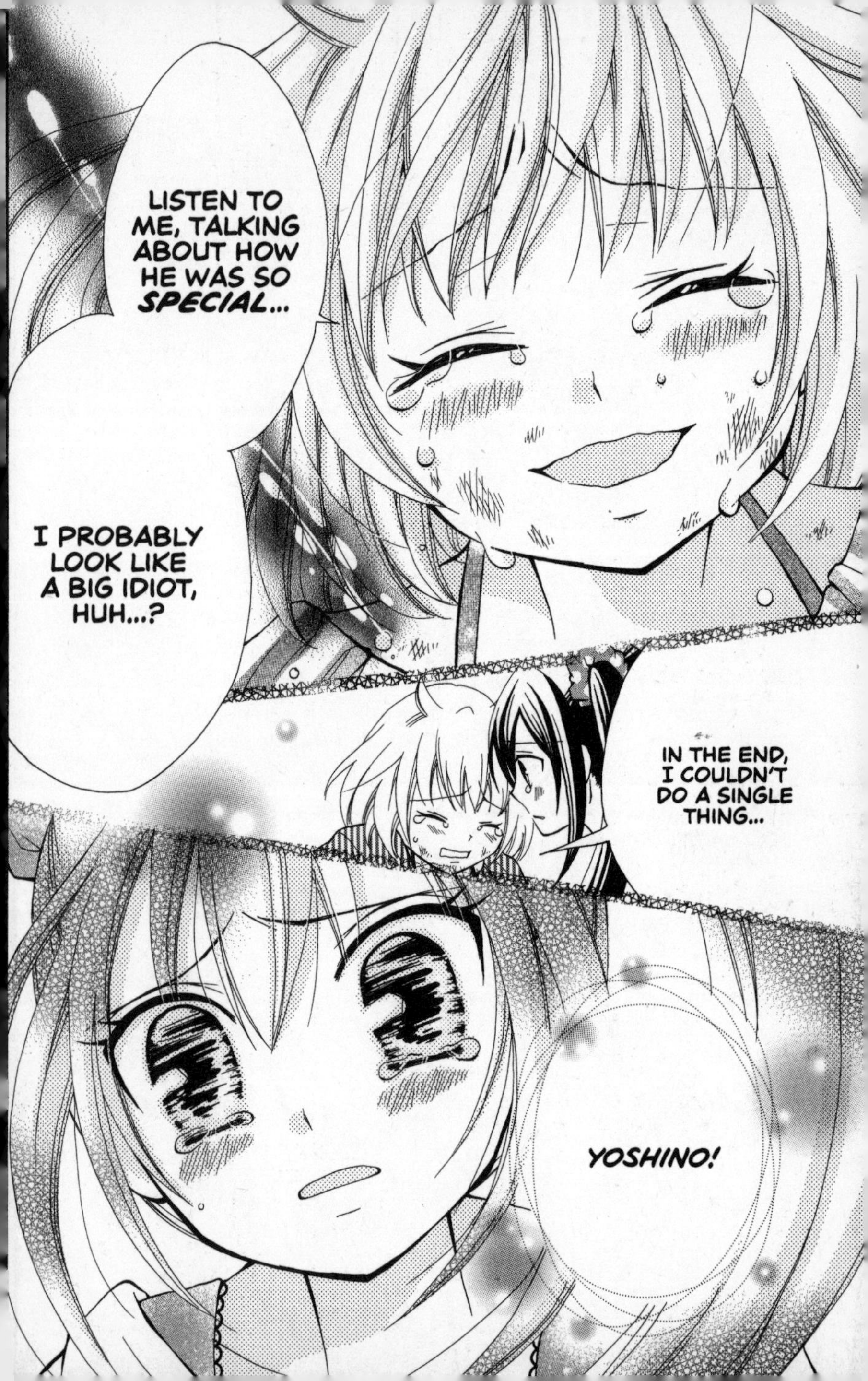
LISTEN TO ME, TALKING ABOUT HOW HE WAS SO *SPECIAL*...
I PROBABLY LOOK LIKE A BIG IDIOT, HUH...?
IN THE END, I COULDN'T DO A SINGLE THING...
YOSHINO!

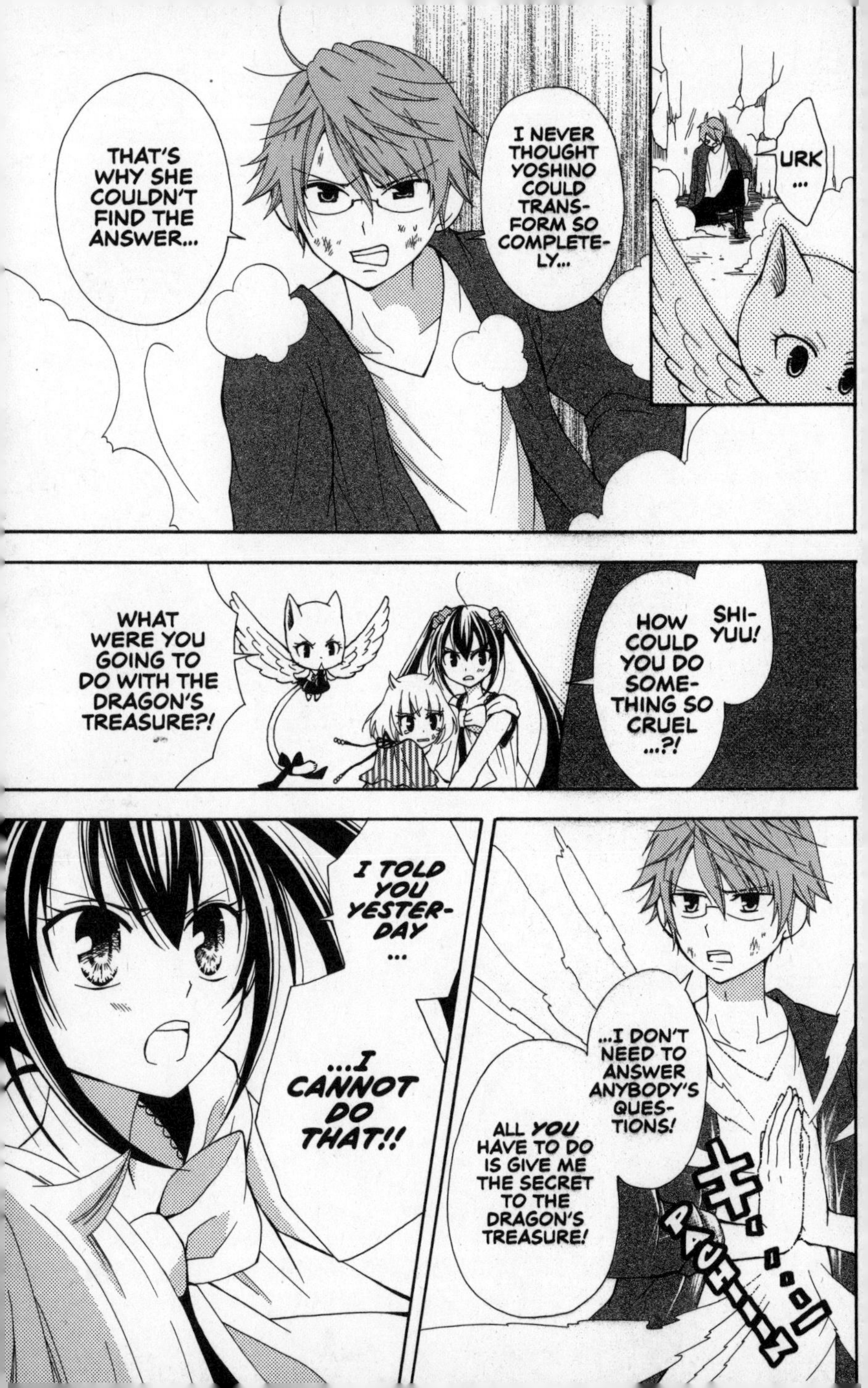
URK...
I NEVER THOUGHT YOSHINO COULD TRANSFORM SO COMPLETELY...
THAT'S WHY SHE COULDN'T FIND THE ANSWER...
SHIYUU!
HOW COULD YOU DO SOMETHING SO CRUEL...?!
WHAT WERE YOU GOING TO DO WITH THE DRAGON'S TREASURE?!
...I DON'T NEED TO ANSWER ANYBODY'S QUESTIONS!
ALL *YOU* HAVE TO DO IS GIVE ME THE SECRET TO THE DRAGON'S TREASURE!
PACHIIIN
I TOLD YOU YESTERDAY...
...I CANNOT DO THAT!!

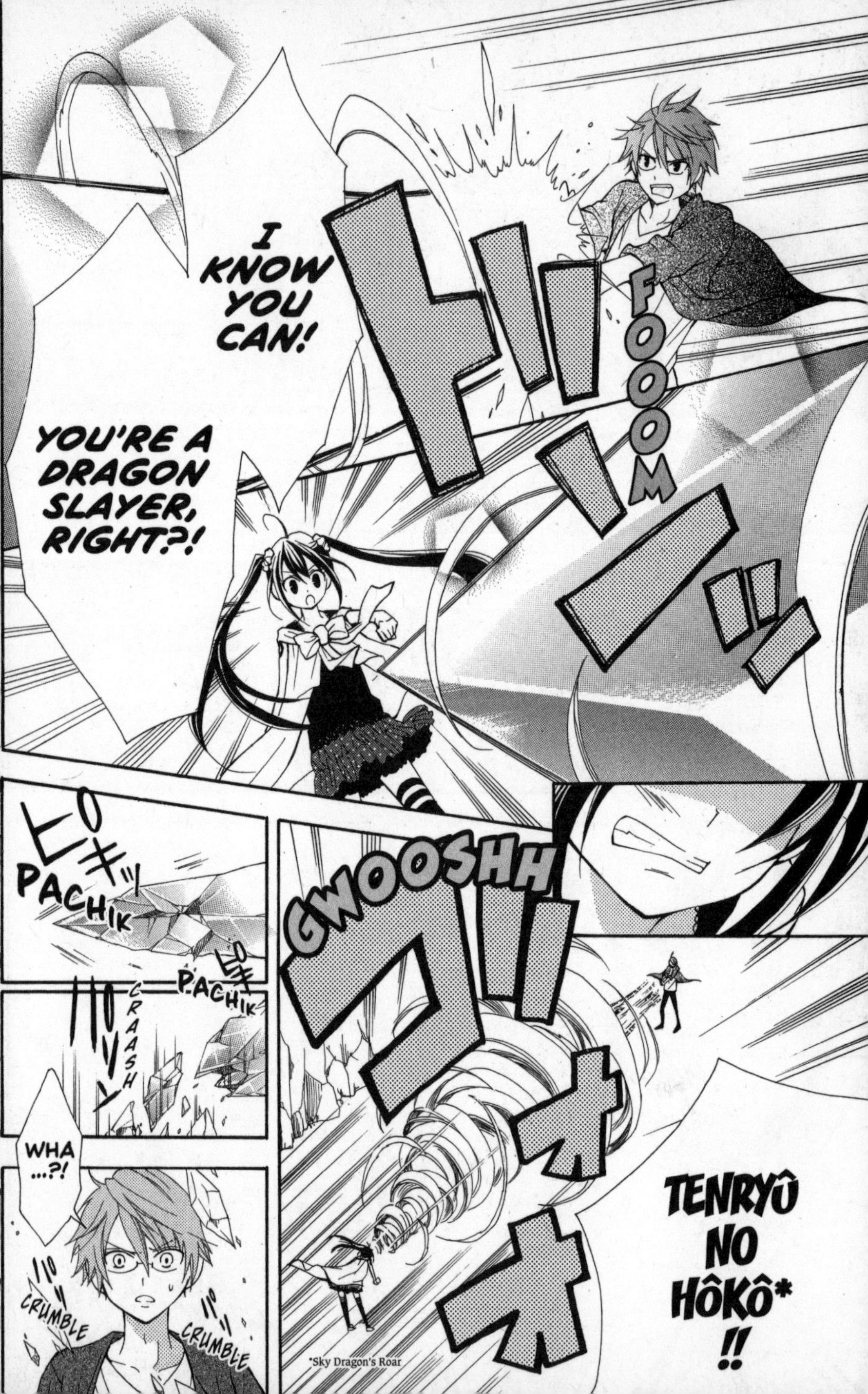
FOOOM
I KNOW YOU CAN!
YOU'RE A DRAGON SLAYER, RIGHT?!
GWOOSHH
TENRYÛ NO HÔKÔ*!!
PACHIK
PACHIK
CRAASH
WHA ...?!
CRUMBLE
CRUMBLE
*Sky Dragon's Roar

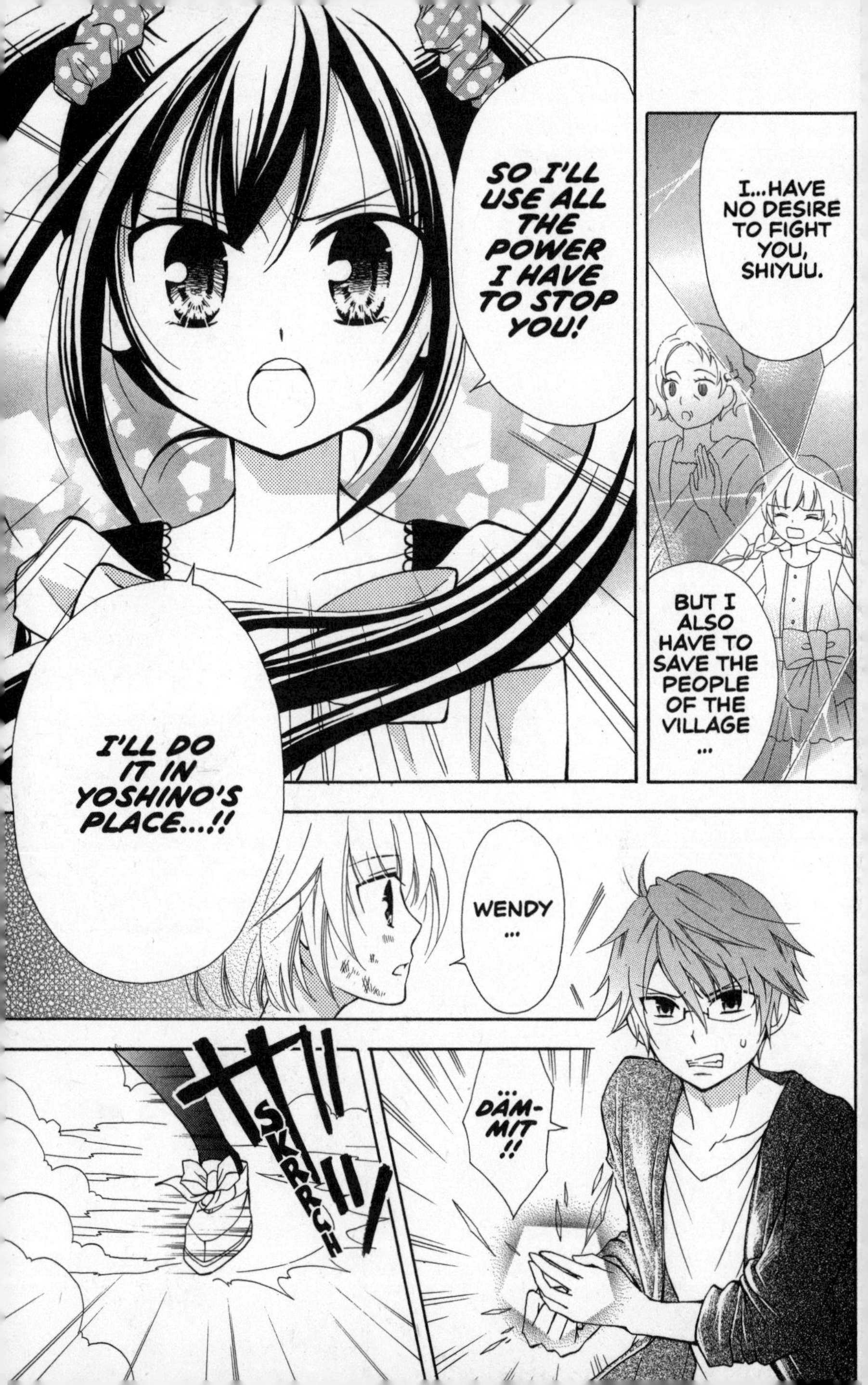
I...HAVE NO DESIRE TO FIGHT YOU, SHIYUU.
BUT I ALSO HAVE TO SAVE THE PEOPLE OF THE VILLAGE...
SO I'LL USE ALL THE POWER I HAVE TO STOP YOU!
I'LL DO IT IN YOSHINO'S PLACE...!!
WENDY...
...DÄMMIT!!
SKRRCH

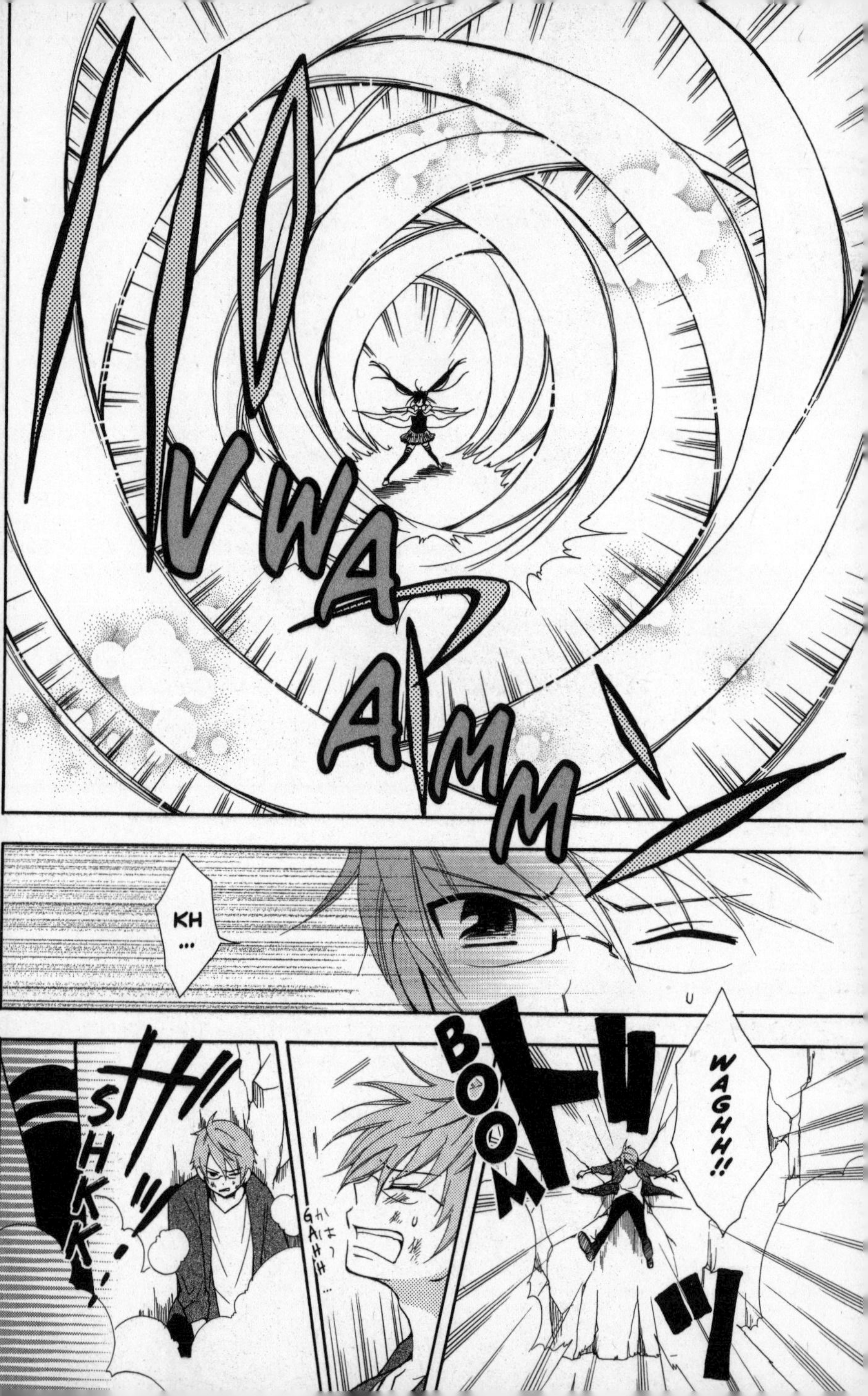
VWAAMM
KH...
WAGHH!!
BOOM
GAHH...
SHKK

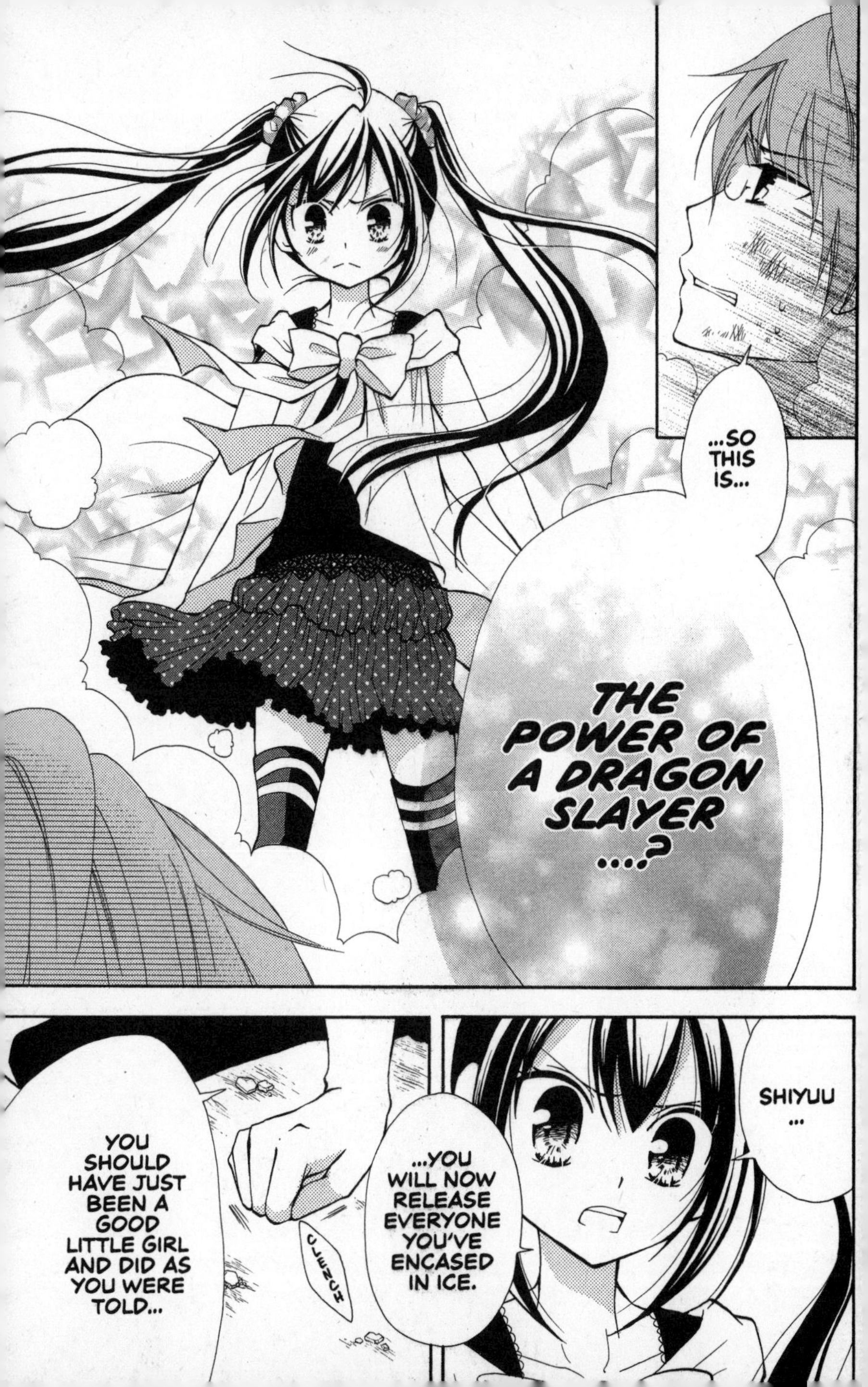
...SO THIS IS...
THE POWER OF A DRAGON SLAYER ...?
SHIYUU ...
...YOU WILL NOW RELEASE EVERYONE YOU'VE ENCASED IN ICE.
CLENCH
YOU SHOULD HAVE JUST BEEN A GOOD LITTLE GIRL AND DID AS YOU WERE TOLD...

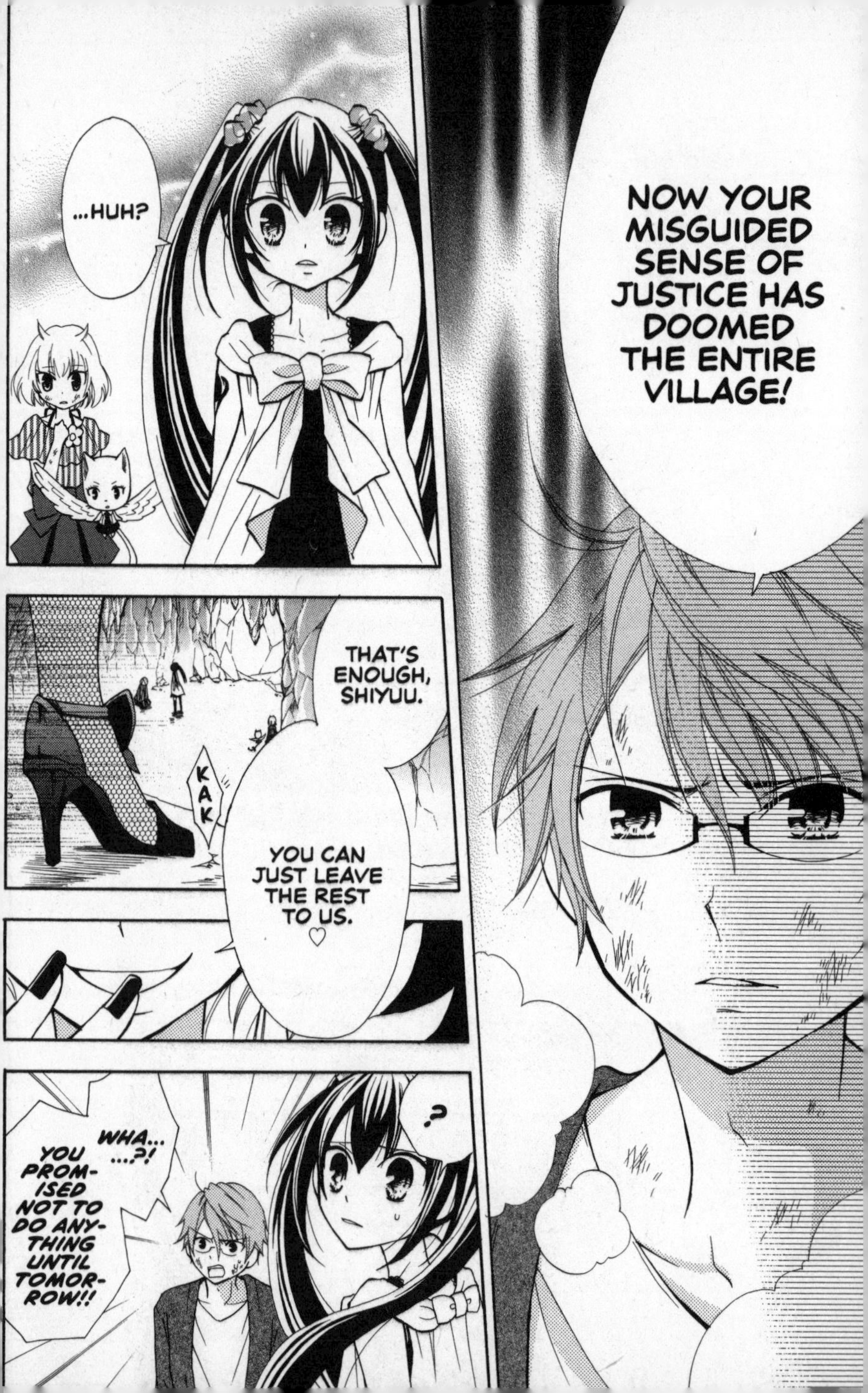
NOW YOUR MISGUIDED SENSE OF JUSTICE HAS DOOMED THE ENTIRE VILLAGE!
...HUH?
THAT'S ENOUGH, SHIYUU.
KAK
YOU CAN JUST LEAVE THE REST TO US. ♡
?
WHA... ...?!
YOU PROMISED NOT TO DO ANYTHING UNTIL TOMORROW!!

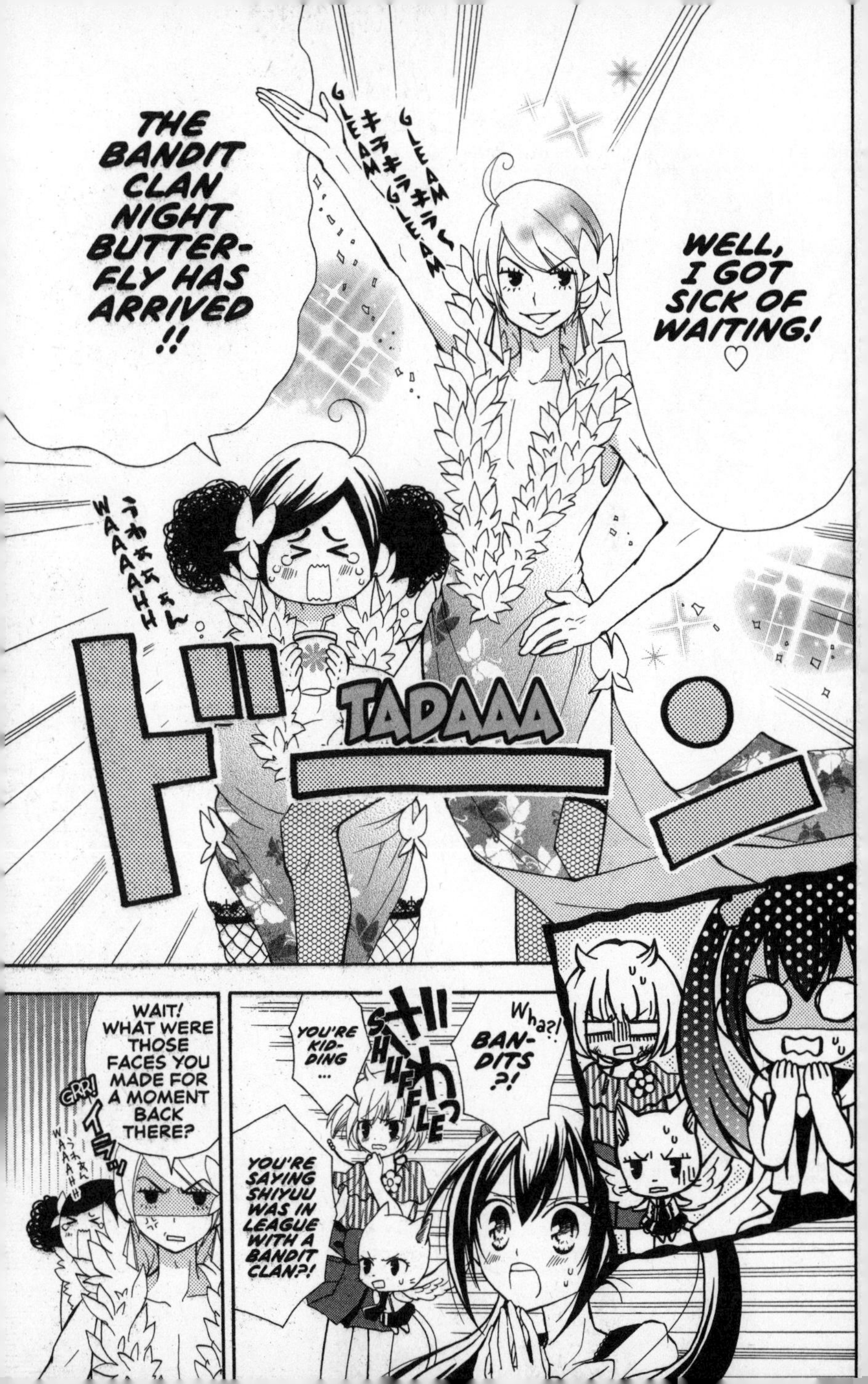
WELL, I GOT SICK OF WAITING! ♡
GLEAM GLEAM
GLEAM GLEAM
THE BANDIT CLAN NIGHT BUTTERFLY HAS ARRIVED!!
WAAAAAHH
TADAAA
Wha?!
BANDITS?!
YOU'RE KIDDING...
SHUFFLE
YOU'RE SAYING SHIYUU WAS IN LEAGUE WITH A BANDIT CLAN?!
WAIT! WHAT WERE THOSE FACES YOU MADE FOR A MOMENT BACK THERE?
GRR!
WAAAHH

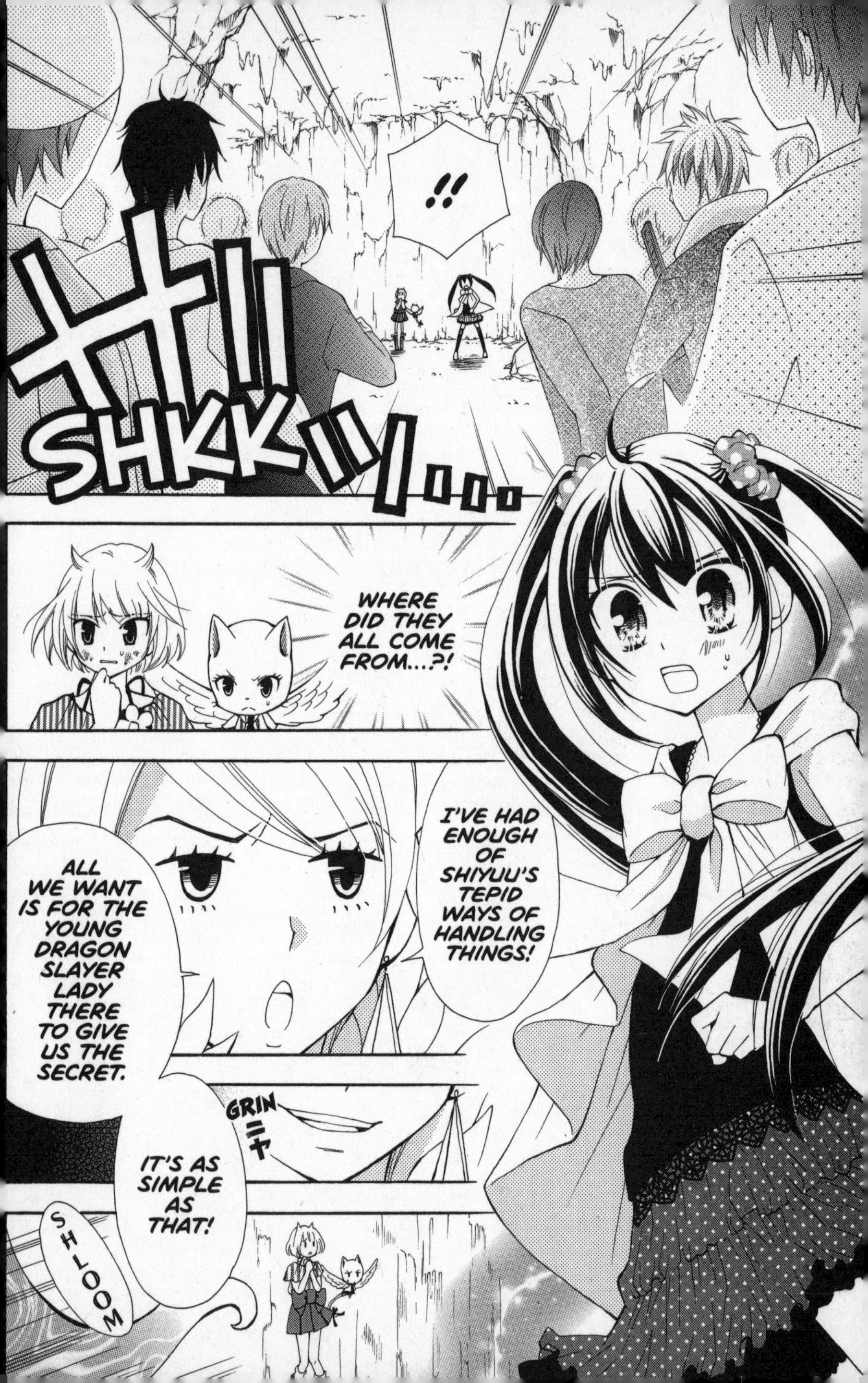
!!
SHKK...
WHERE DID THEY ALL COME FROM...?!
I'VE HAD ENOUGH OF SHIYUU'S TEPID WAYS OF HANDLING THINGS!
ALL WE WANT IS FOR THE YOUNG DRAGON SLAYER LADY THERE TO GIVE US THE SECRET.
GRIN ニヤ
IT'S AS SIMPLE AS THAT!
SHLOOM

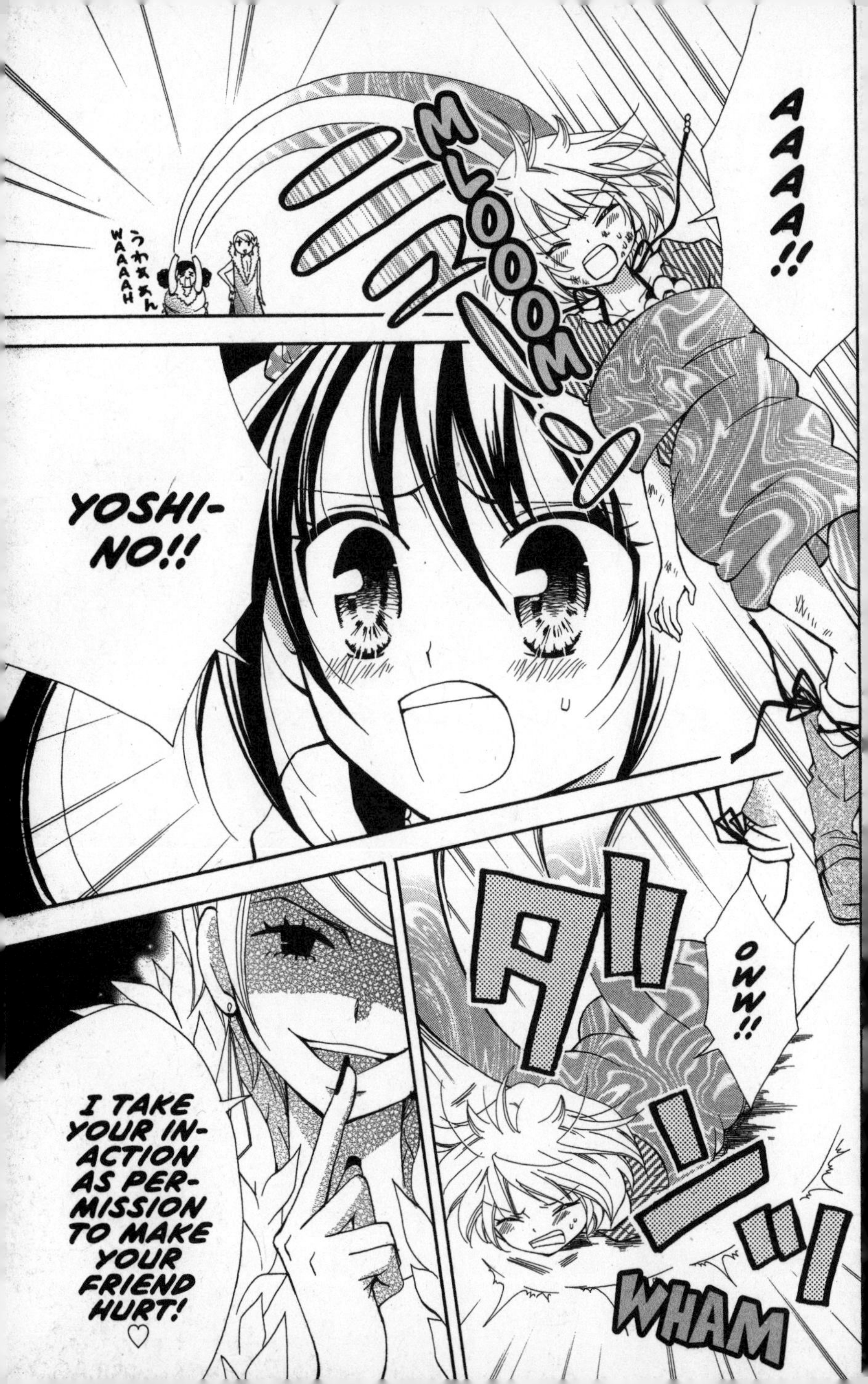
AAAAA!!
MWOOOM!
うわああん
WAAAAH
YOSHI-
NO!!
OWW!!
WHAM
I TAKE YOUR IN-ACTION AS PER-MISSION TO MAKE YOUR FRIEND HURT! ♡

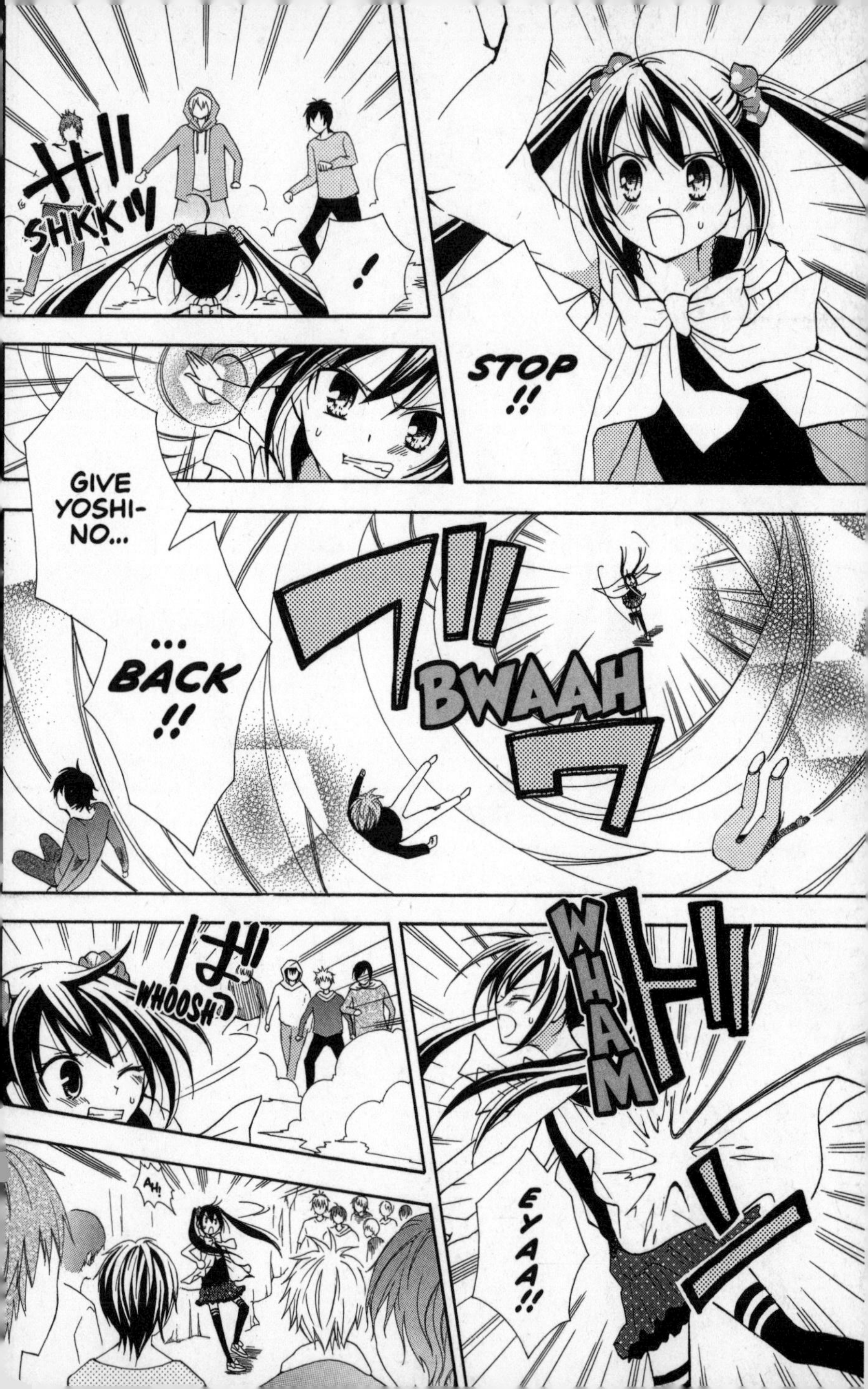
STOP!!
SHKK!!
!
GIVE YOSHINO...
...BACK!!
BWAAH
WHAM
EYAAA!!
WHOOSH
AH!

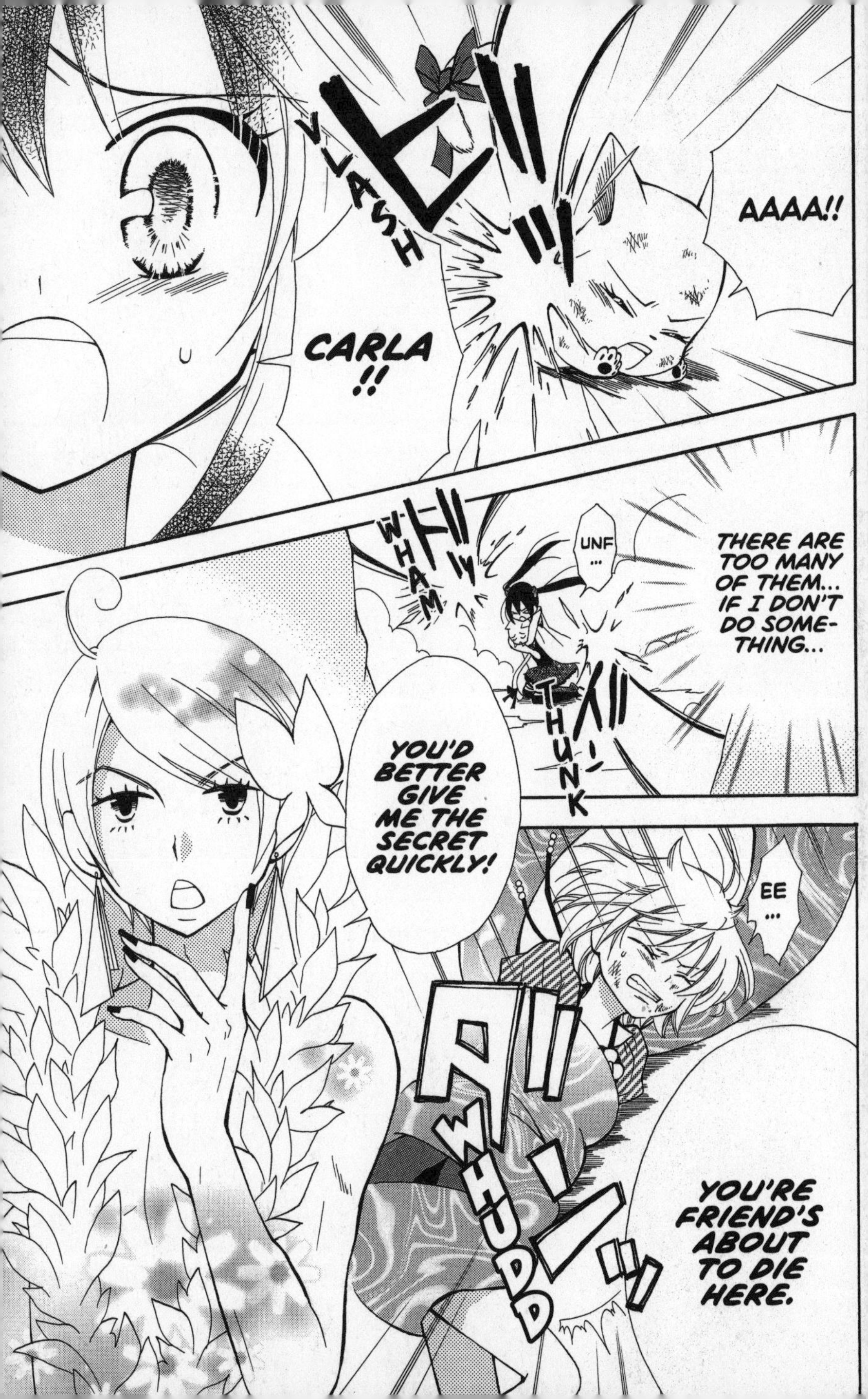
AAAA!!
VLASH
CARLA !!
THERE ARE TOO MANY OF THEM... IF I DON'T DO SOME-THING...
UNF ...
WHAM
THUNK
EE ...
YOU'RE FRIEND'S ABOUT TO DIE HERE.
WHUDD
YOU'D BETTER GIVE ME THE SECRET QUICKLY!

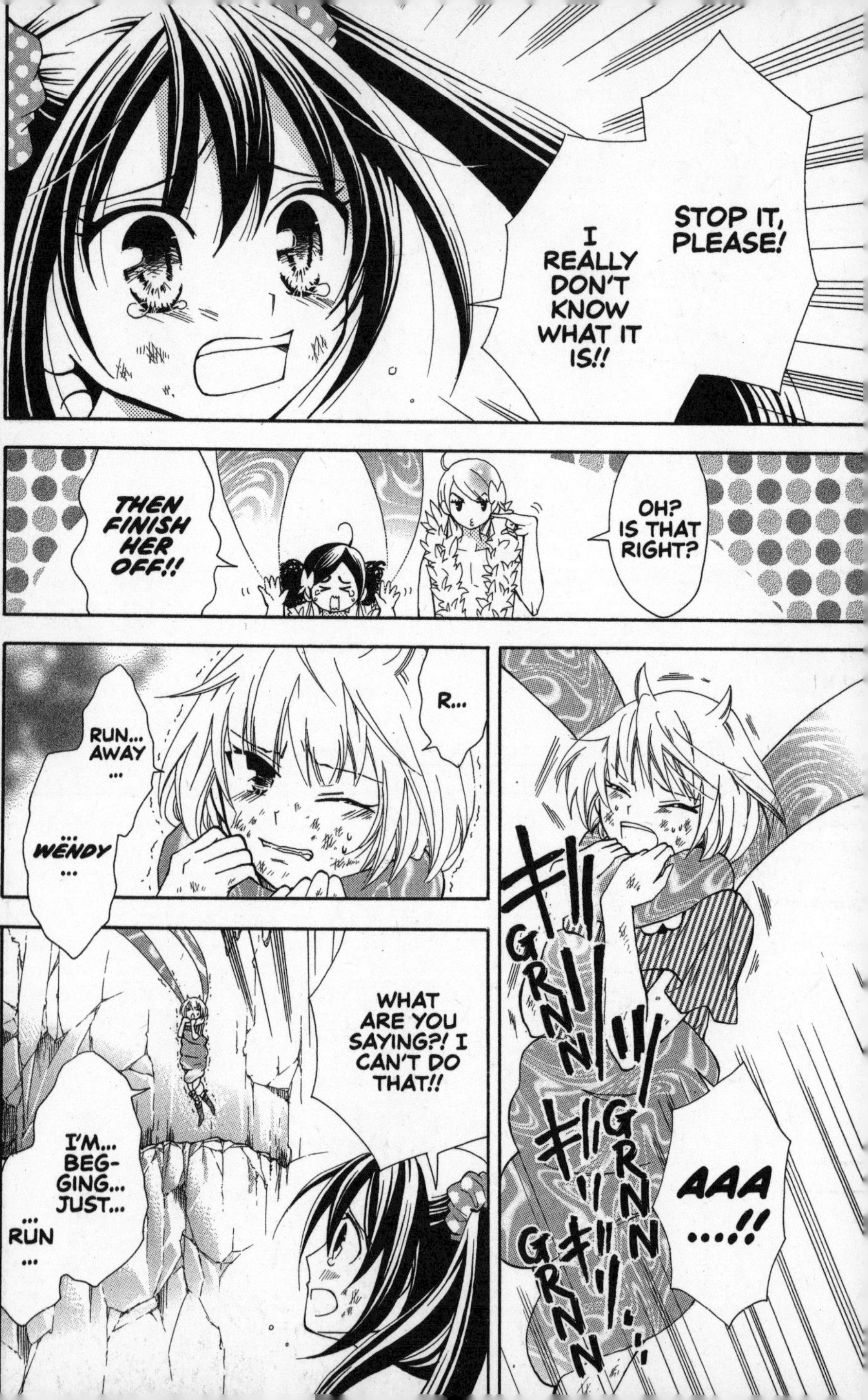
STOP IT, PLEASE!
I REALLY DON'T KNOW WHAT IT IS!!
OH? IS THAT RIGHT?
THEN FINISH HER OFF!!
GRNN GRNN GRNN
AAA ...!!
R...
RUN... AWAY ...
...WENDY ...
WHAT ARE YOU SAYING?! I CAN'T DO THAT!!
I'M... BEG-GING... JUST... ...RUN ...

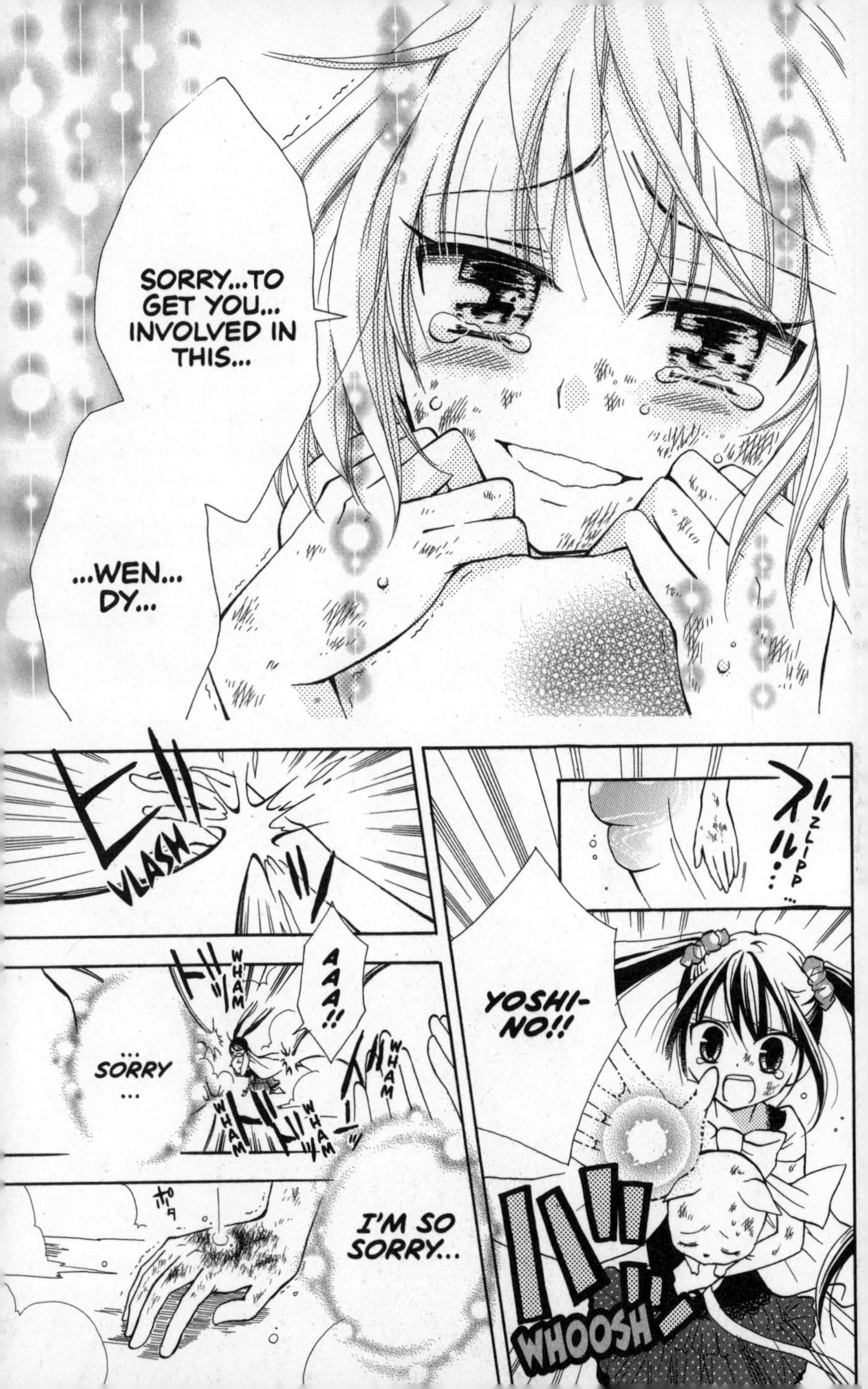
SORRY...TO GET YOU... INVOLVED IN THIS...
...WEN... DY...
ZLIPP...
YOSHI-NO!!
WHOOSH
VLASH
AAA!!
WHAM
WHAM
WHAM
WHAM
...SORRY...
I'M SO SORRY...

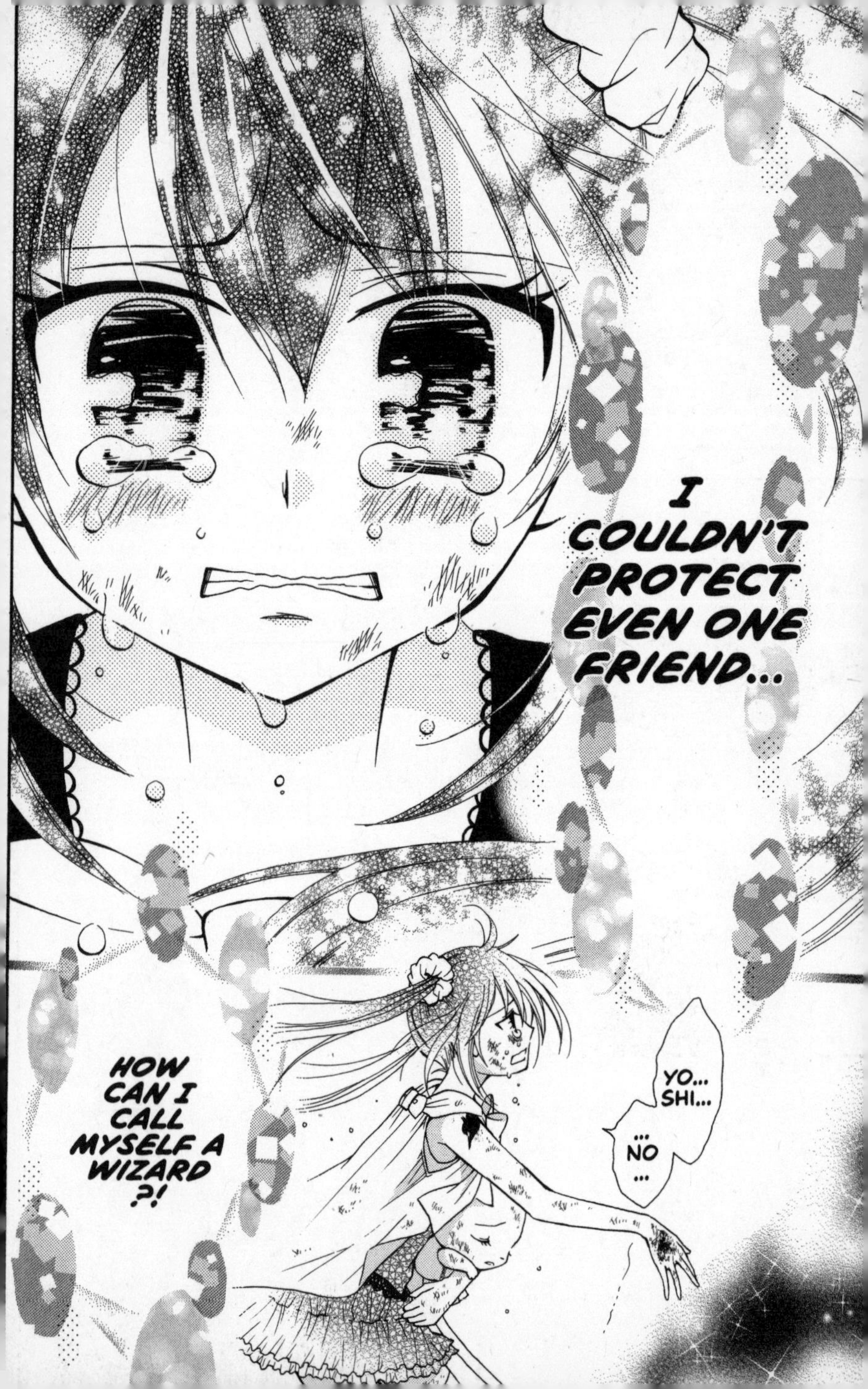
I COULDN'T PROTECT EVEN ONE FRIEND...
HOW CAN I CALL MYSELF A WIZARD ?!
YO... SHI...
... NO ...

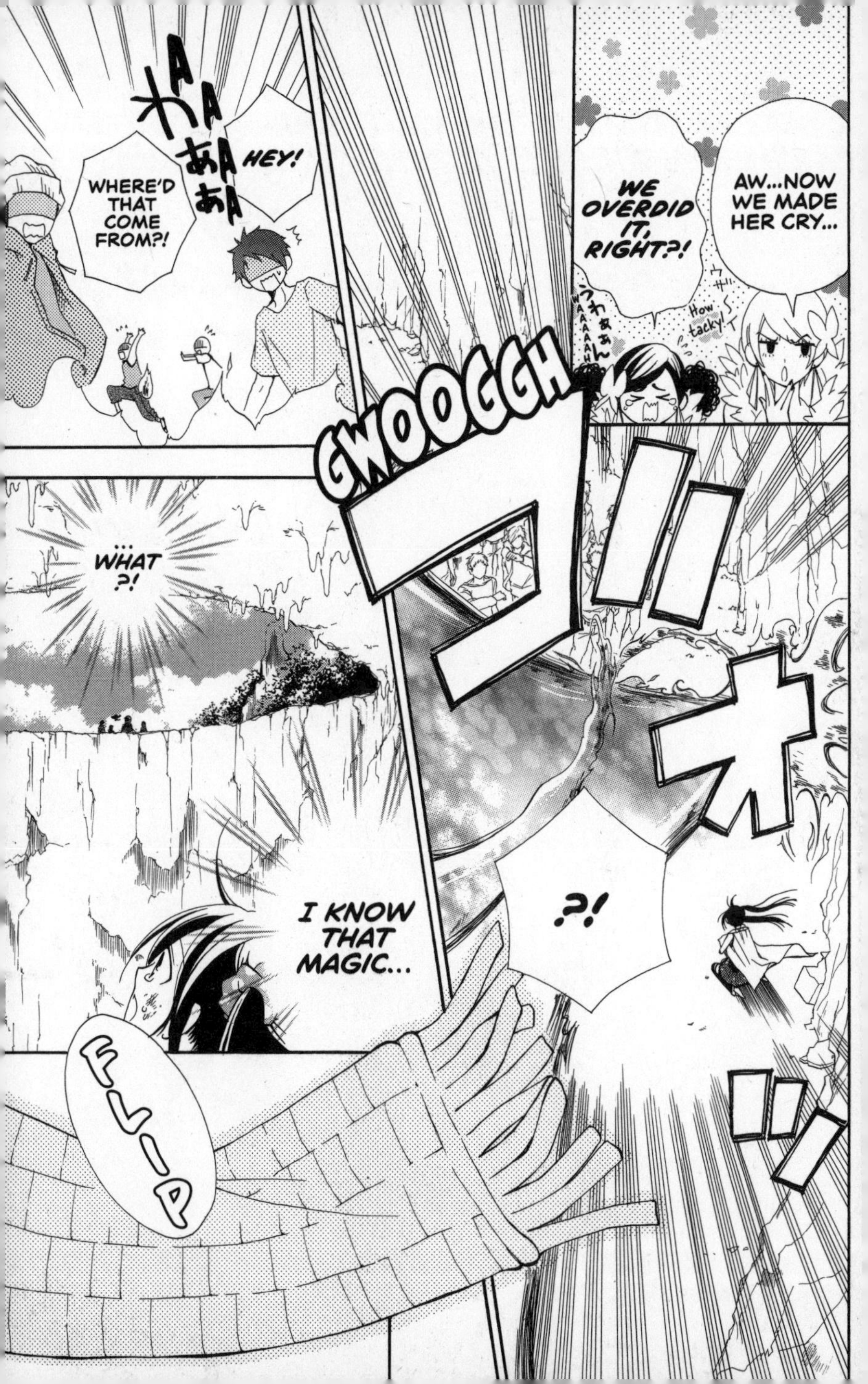
AW...NOW WE MADE HER CRY...
WE OVERDID IT, RIGHT?!
WAAAAAH
How tacky!
GWOOGGH
HEY!
WHERE'D THAT COME FROM?!
AAAA
?!
...WHAT?!
I KNOW THAT MAGIC...
FLIP

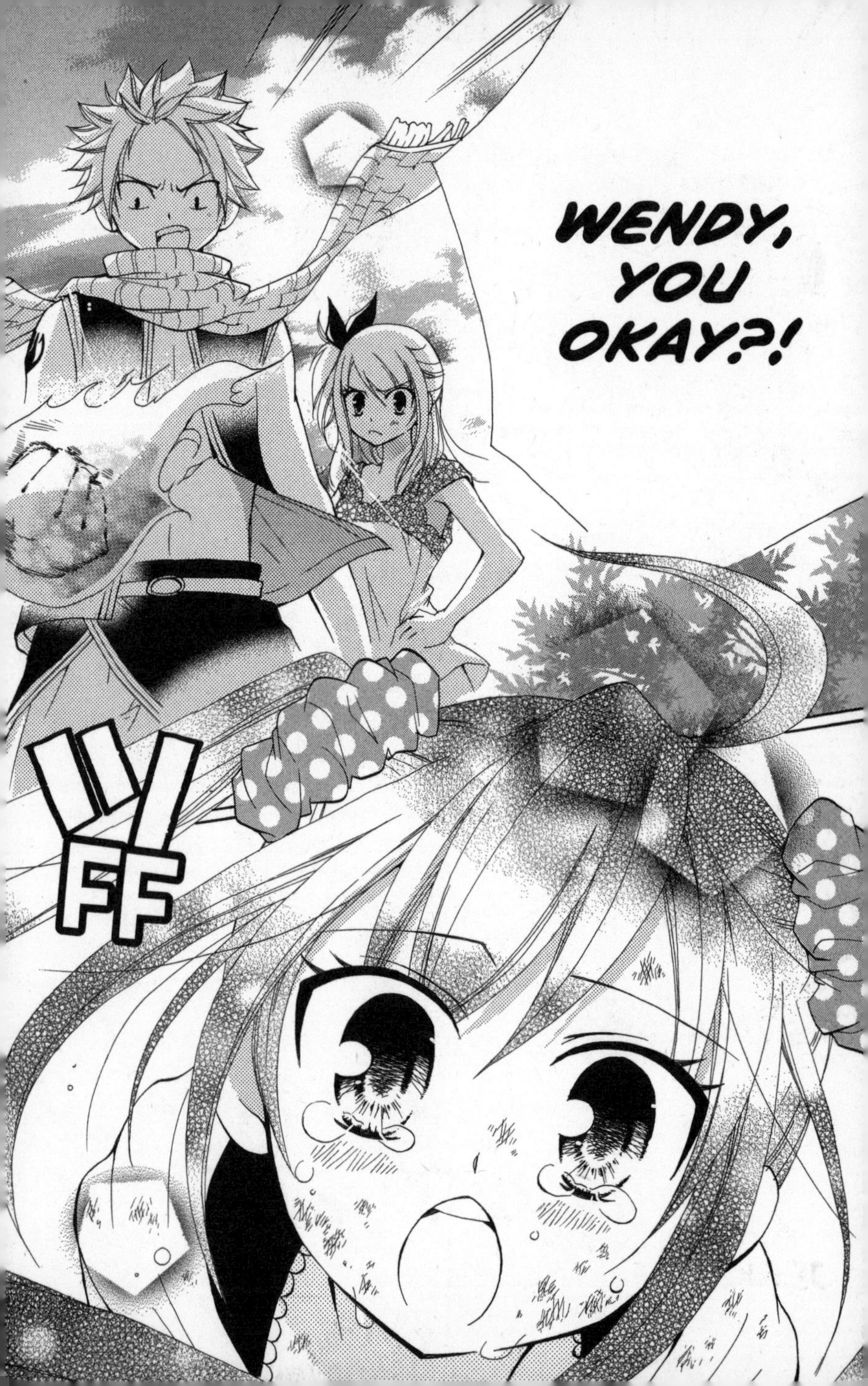
WENDY, YOU OKAY?!

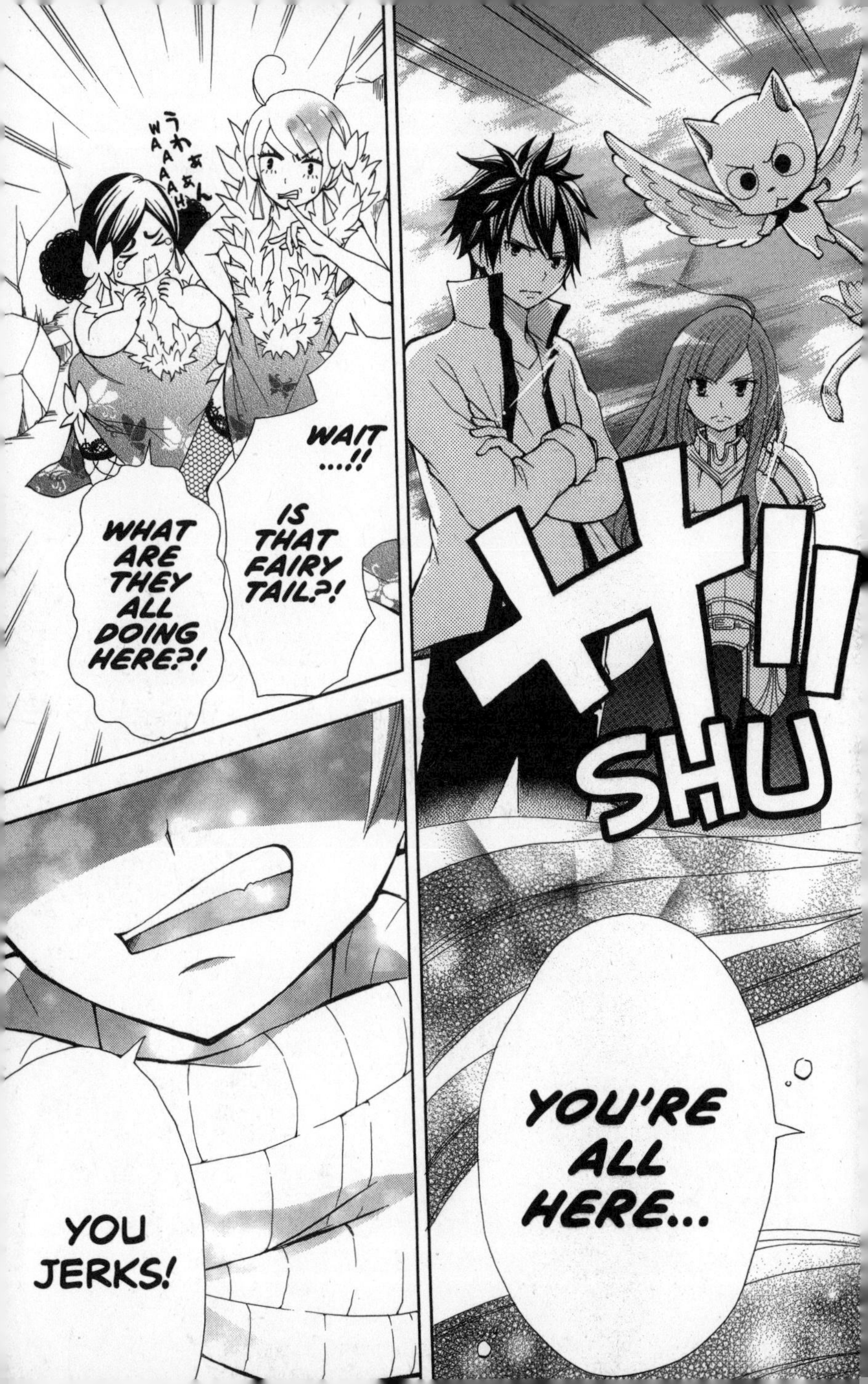
SHU
うわあぁん
WAAAAAH
WAIT ...!!
IS THAT FAIRY TAIL?!
WHAT ARE THEY ALL DOING HERE?!
YOU'RE ALL HERE...
YOU JERKS!

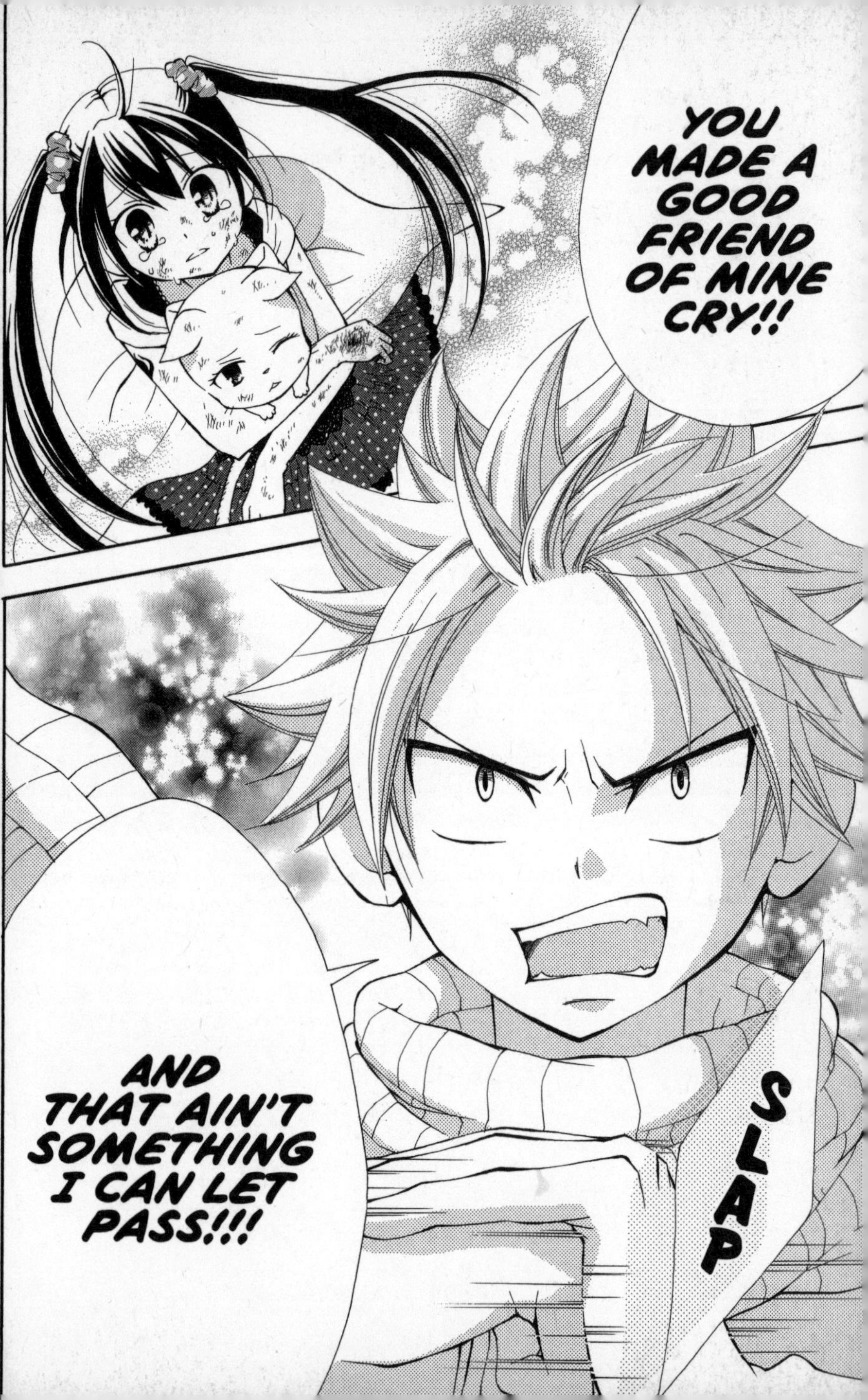
YOU MADE A GOOD FRIEND OF MINE CRY!!
SLAP
AND THAT AIN'T SOMETHING I CAN LET PASS!!!

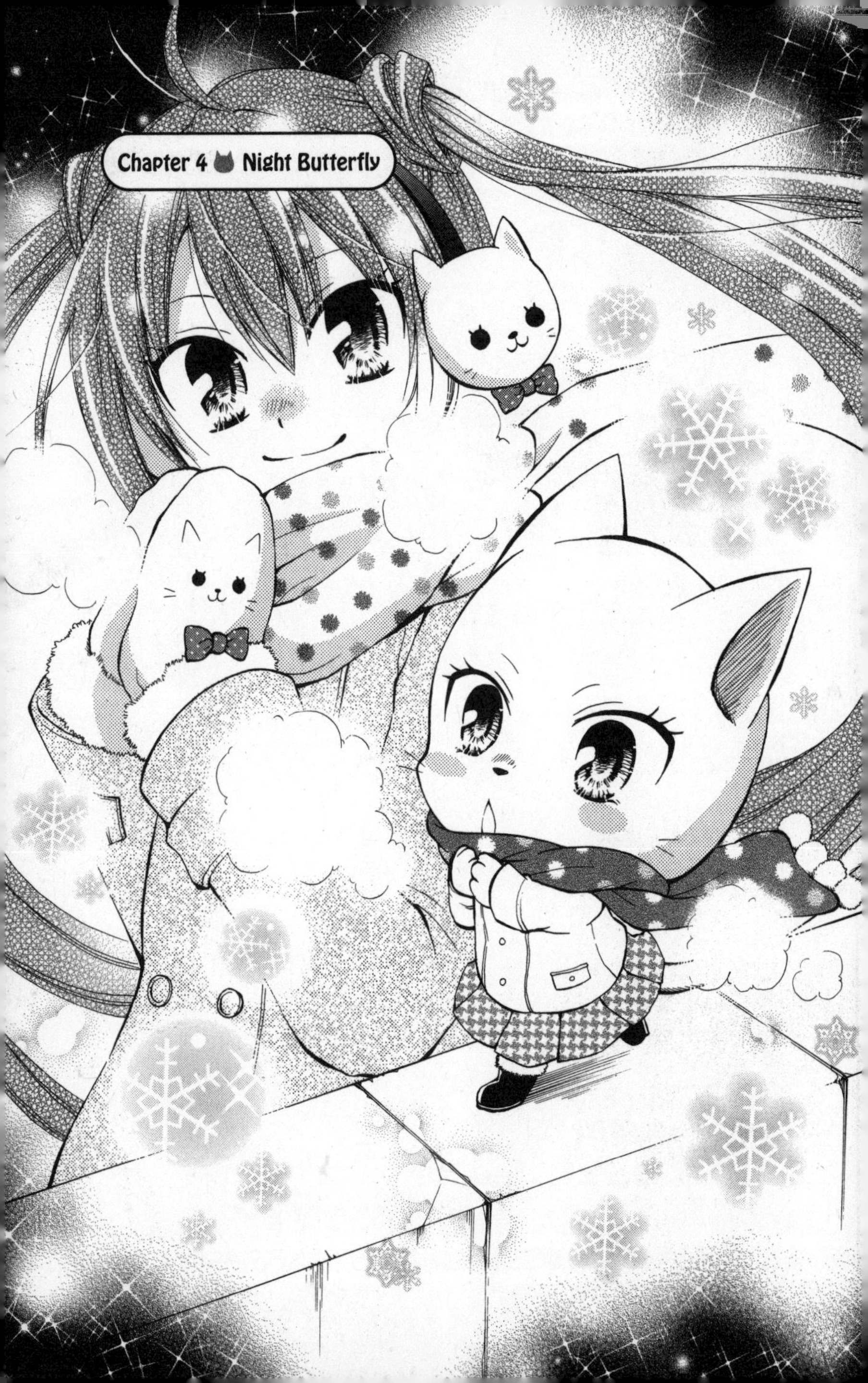
Chapter 4 Night Butterfly

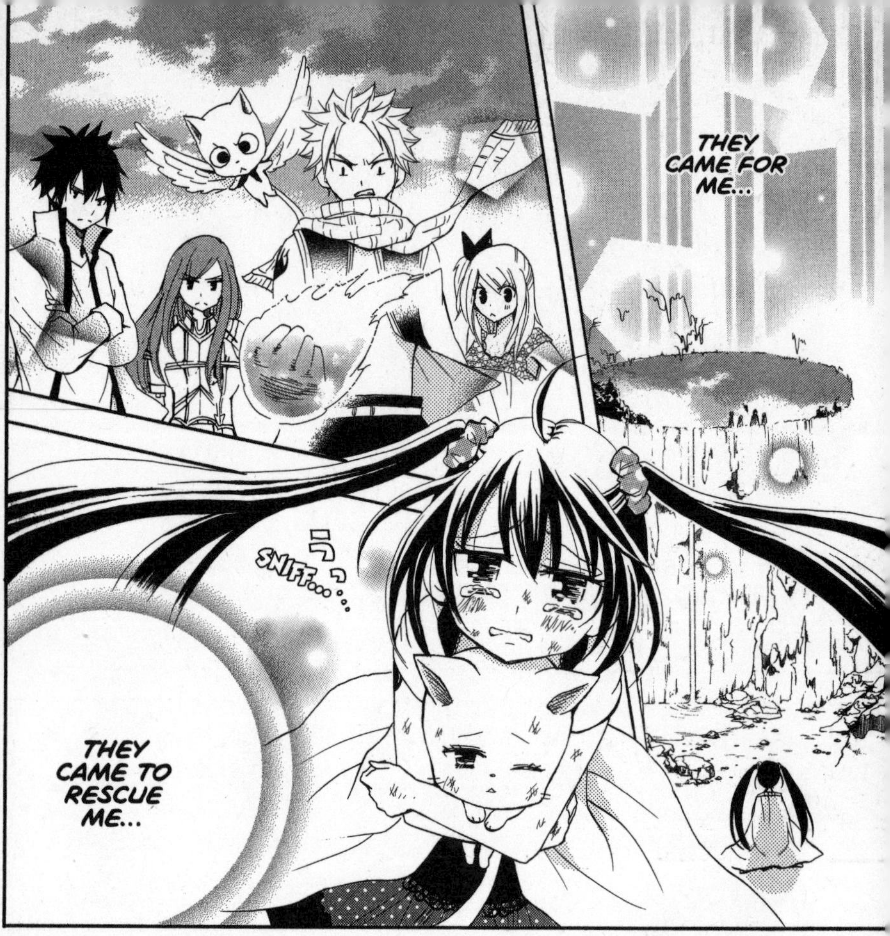
THEY CAME FOR ME...
SNIFF...
THEY CAME TO RESCUE ME...

I patterned the main characters of Nanalu village after a favorite of mine, indigenous Japanese dogs!

Yoshino → Shiba

Shiyuu → Kishu

Kishu...Kishiyu...Ki Shiyu...Ki Shiyuu...

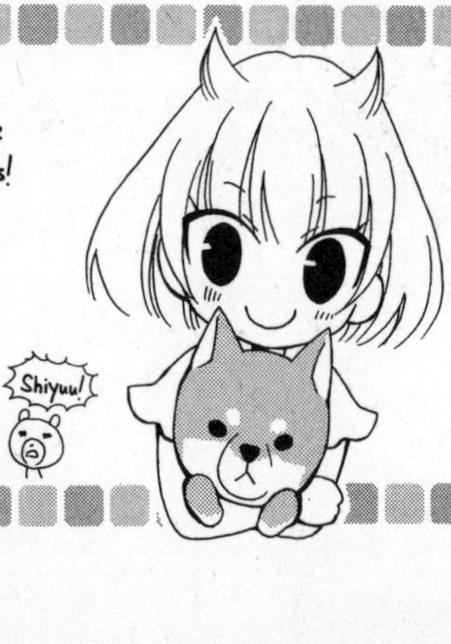
Shiyuu!
Ah!

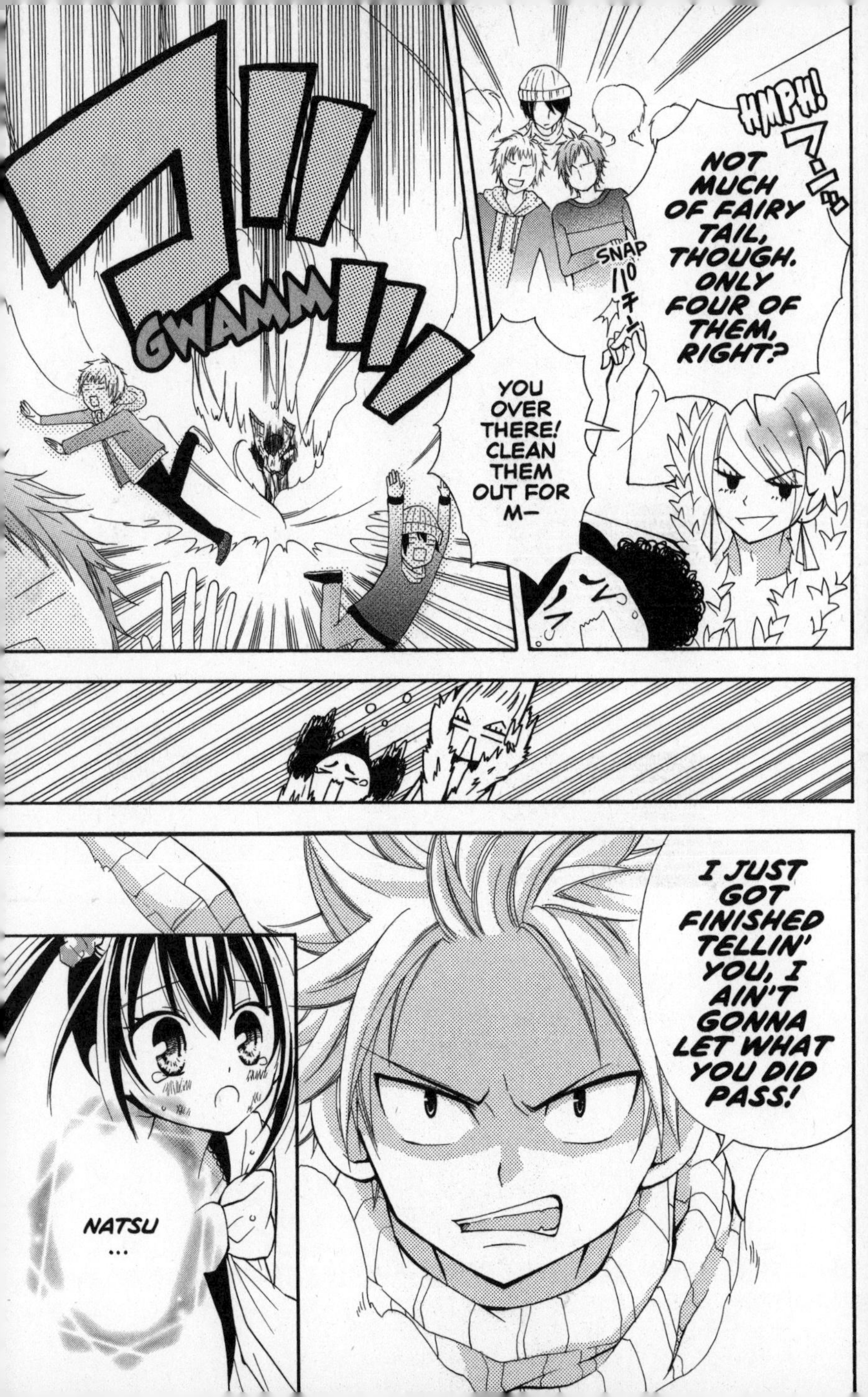
HMPH!
NOT MUCH OF FAIRY TAIL, THOUGH. ONLY FOUR OF THEM, RIGHT?
SNAP
YOU OVER THERE! CLEAN THEM OUT FOR M—
GWAMM
I JUST GOT FINISHED TELLIN' YOU, I AIN'T GONNA LET WHAT YOU DID PASS!
NATSU ...

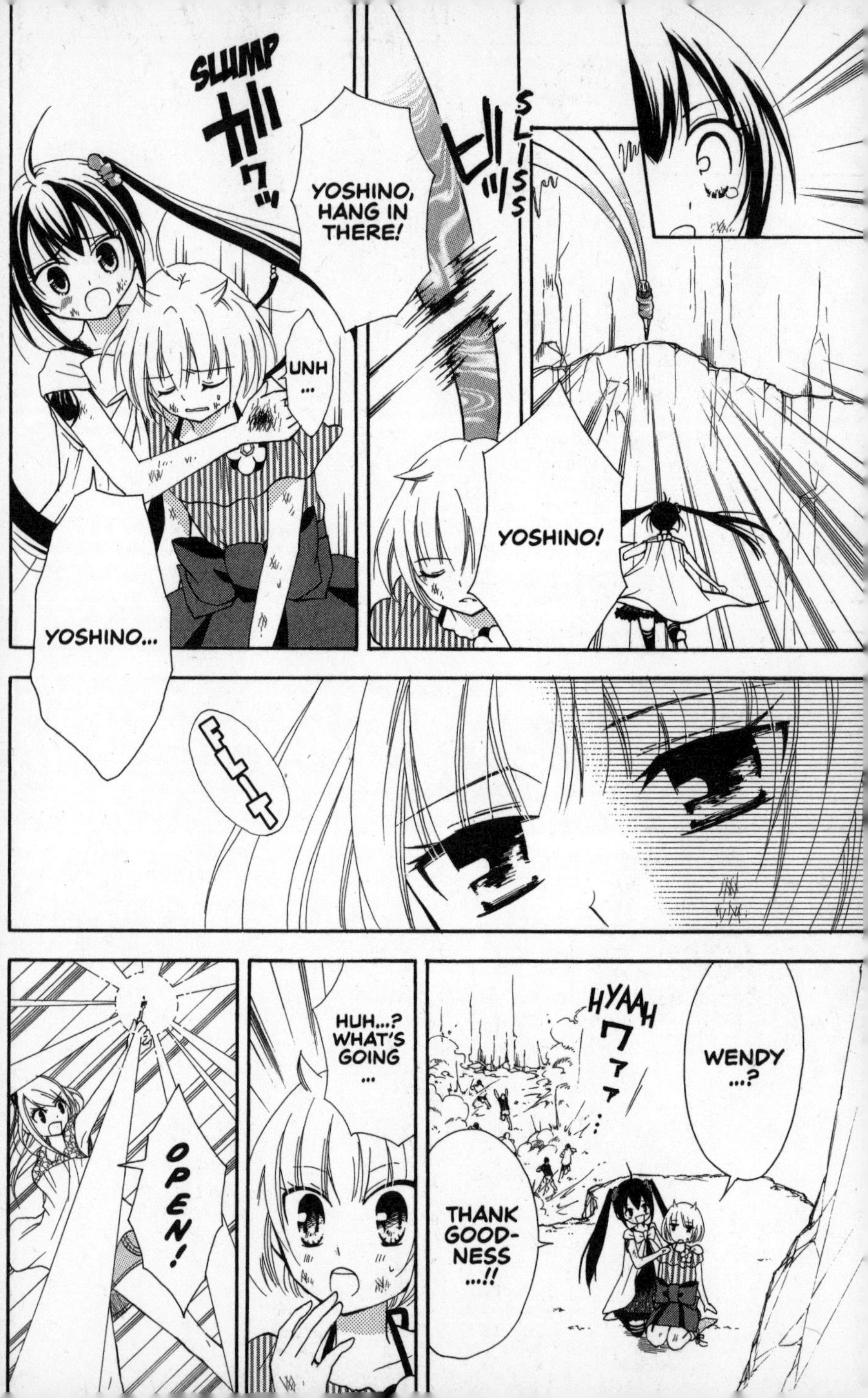
YOSHINO!
SLISS
ビリッ
SLUMP
YOSHINO, HANG IN THERE!
UNH...
YOSHINO...
FLIT
HYAAH
ワァァ
WENDY...?
THANK GOODNESS...!!
HUH...? WHAT'S GOING...
OPEN!

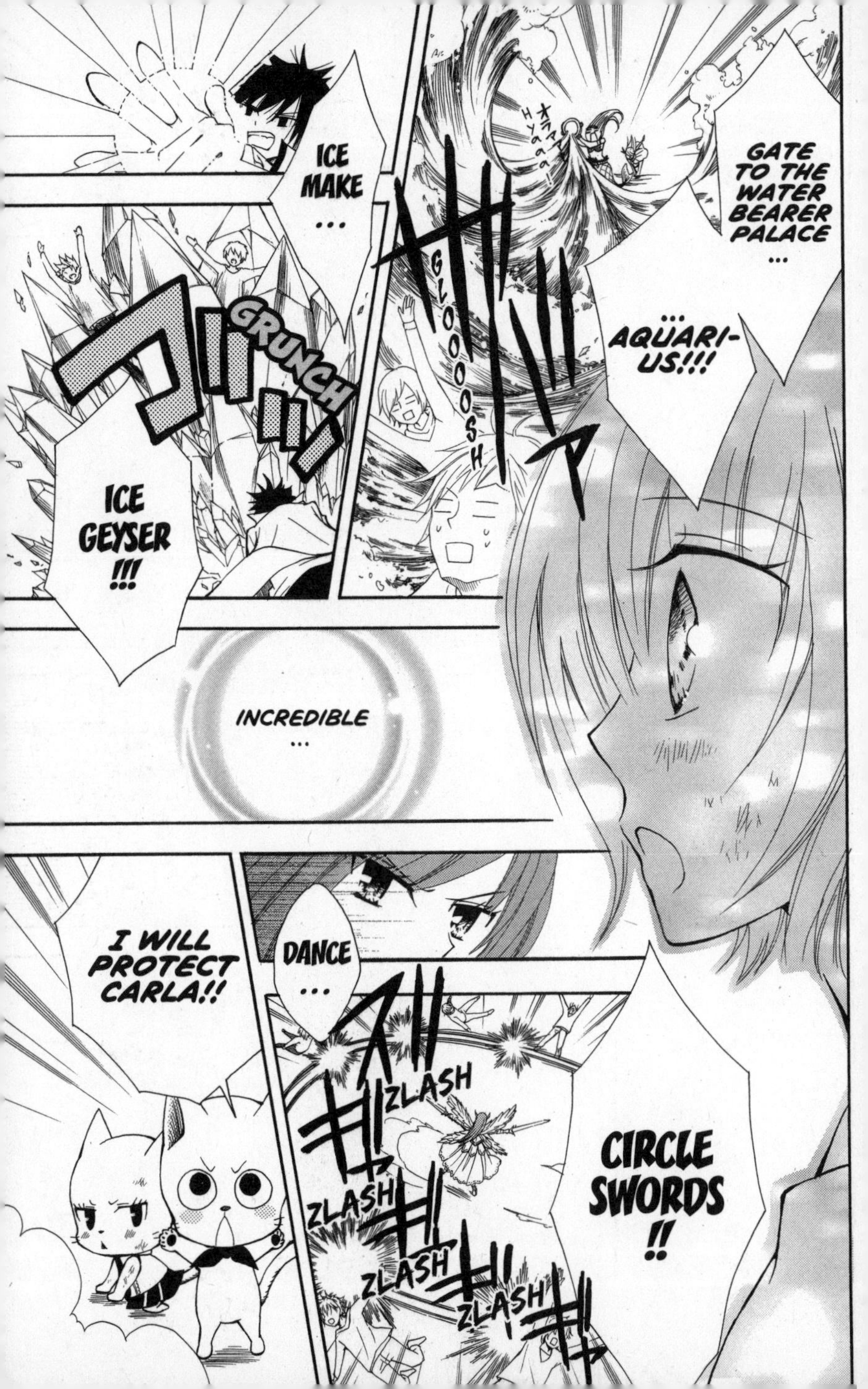
GATE TO THE WATER BEARER PALACE ...
... AQUARI-US!!!
GLOOOOOSH
ICE MAKE ...
ICE GEYSER !!!
GRUNCH
INCREDIBLE ...
DANCE ...
CIRCLE SWORDS !!
ZLASH
ZLASH
ZLASH
ZLASH
I WILL PROTECT CARLA!!

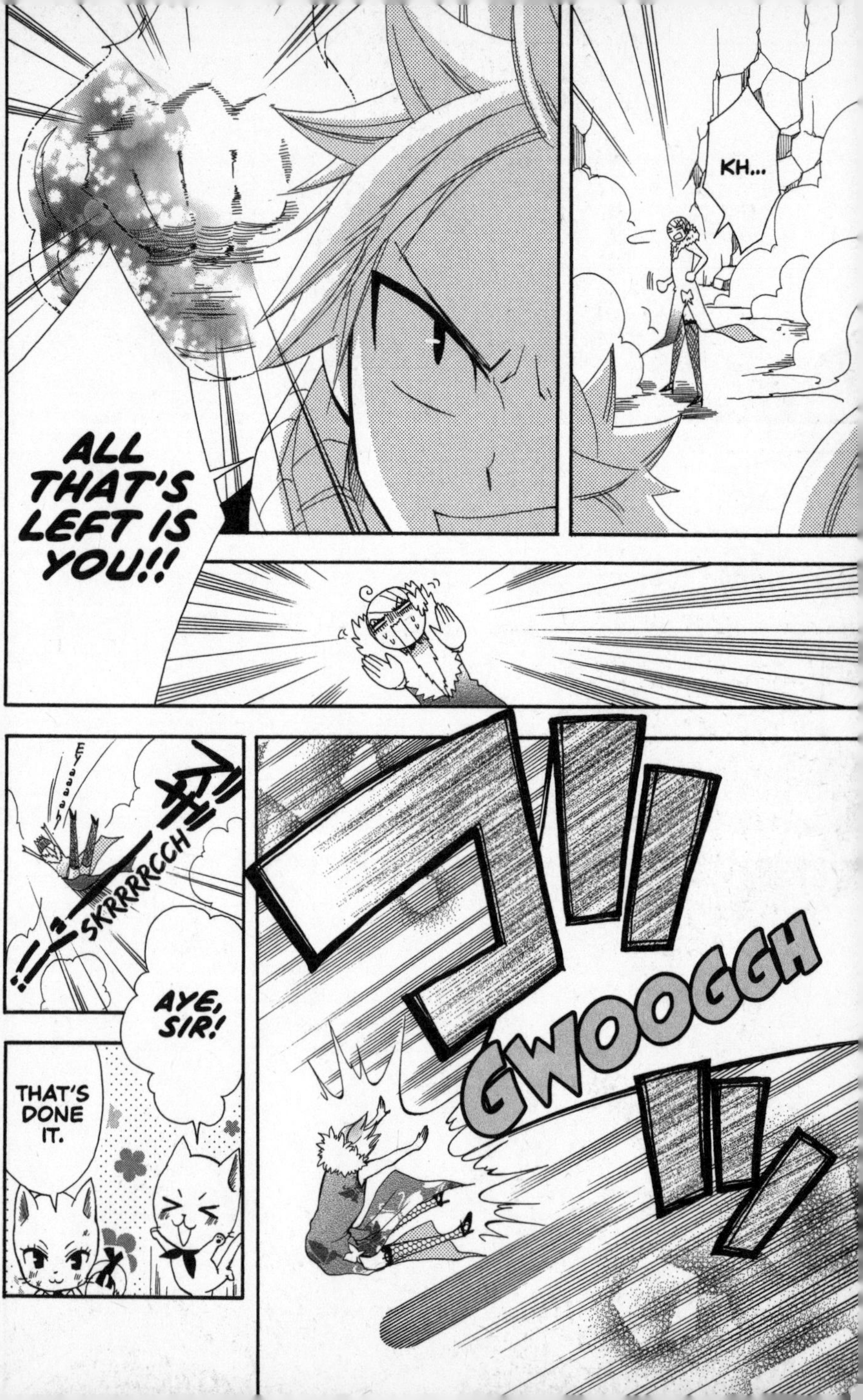
KH...
ALL THAT'S LEFT IS YOU!!
GWOOGGH
SKRRRRCCH
AYE, SIR!
THAT'S DONE IT.

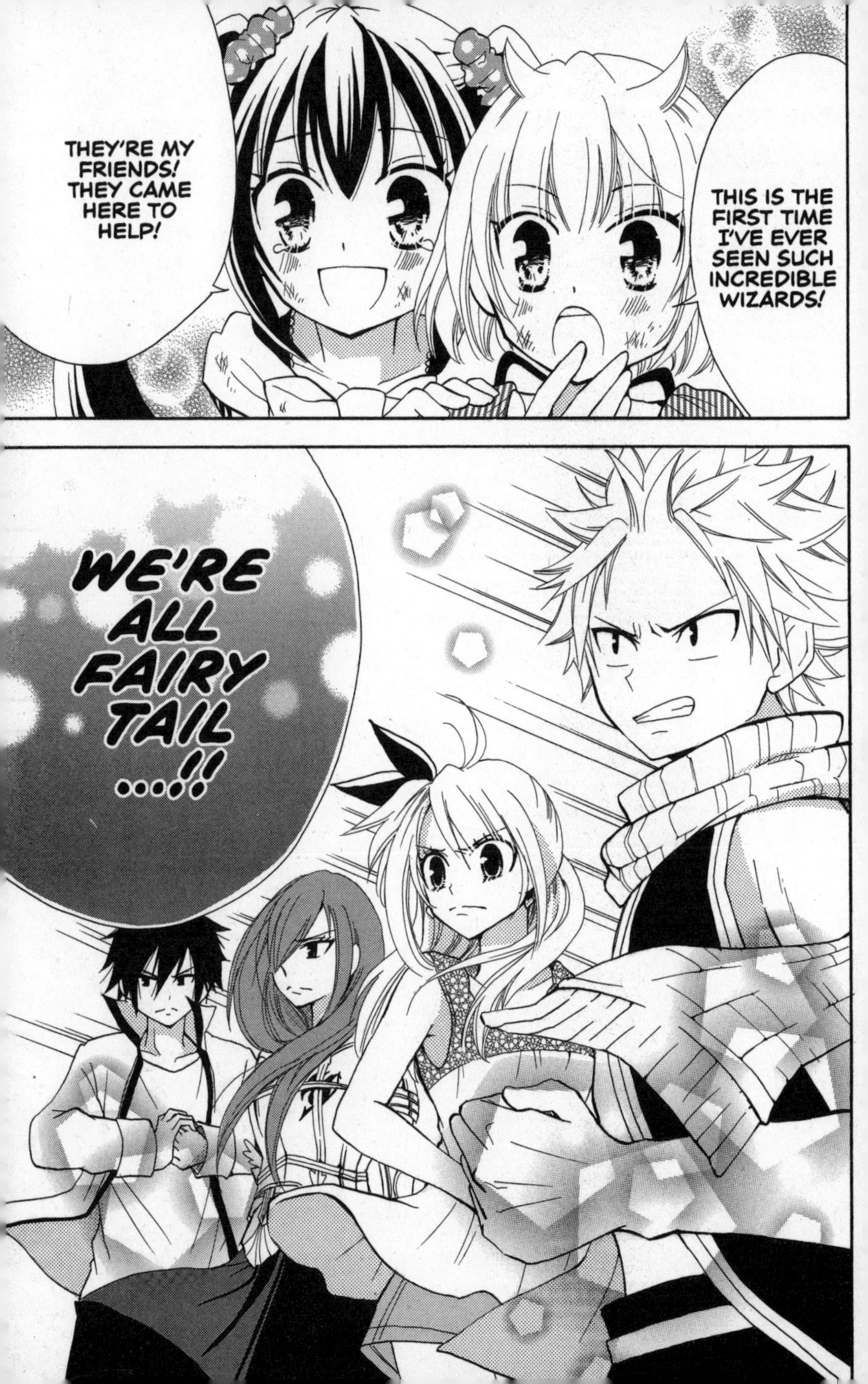
THIS IS THE FIRST TIME I'VE EVER SEEN SUCH INCREDIBLE WIZARDS!
THEY'RE MY FRIENDS! THEY CAME HERE TO HELP!
WE'RE ALL FAIRY TAIL ...!!

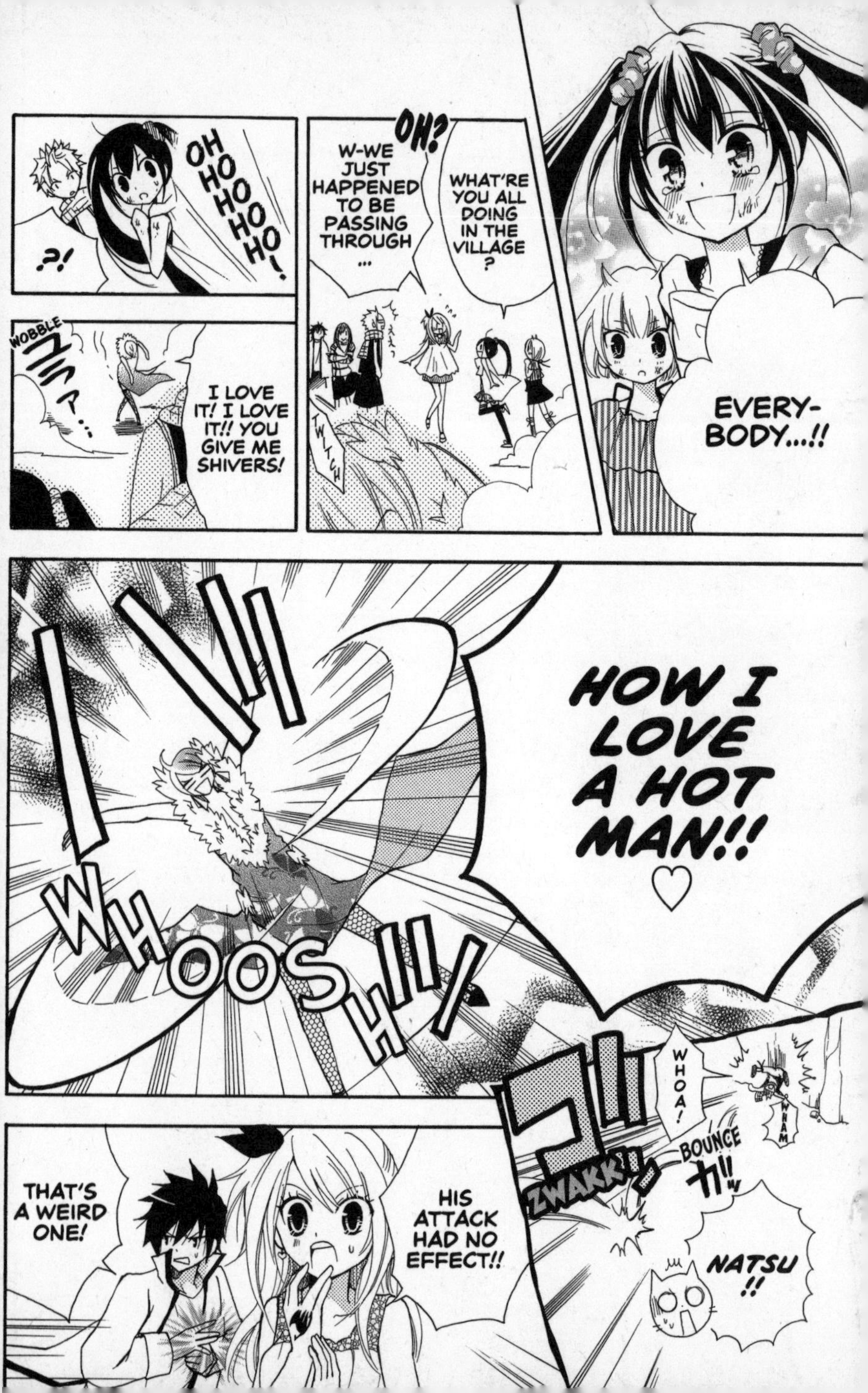
EVERY-BODY...!!
OH?
WHAT'RE YOU ALL DOING IN THE VILLAGE?
W-WE JUST HAPPENED TO BE PASSING THROUGH...
TWITCH
OH HO HO HO HO HO!
?!
WOBBLE
I LOVE IT! I LOVE IT!! YOU GIVE ME SHIVERS!
HOW I LOVE A HOT MAN!! ♡
WHOOSH
WHOA!
WHAM
BOUNCE
ZWAKK!!
NATSU!!
HIS ATTACK HAD NO EFFECT!!
THAT'S A WEIRD ONE!

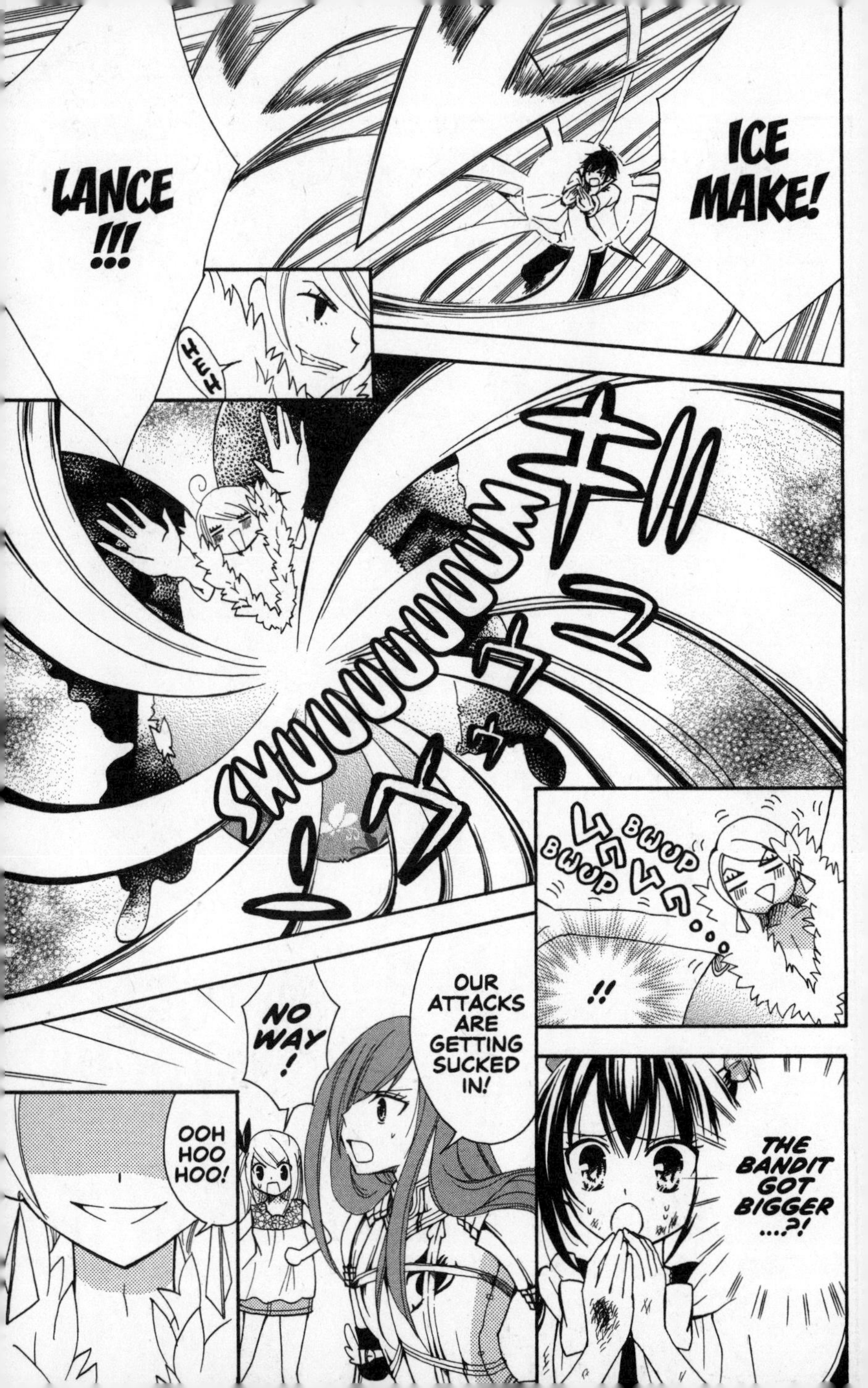
ICE MAKE!
LANCE!!!
HEH
SHUUUUUUUM
BWUP BWUP
!!
THE BANDIT GOT BIGGER ...?!
OUR ATTACKS ARE GETTING SUCKED IN!
NO WAY!
OOH HOO HOO!

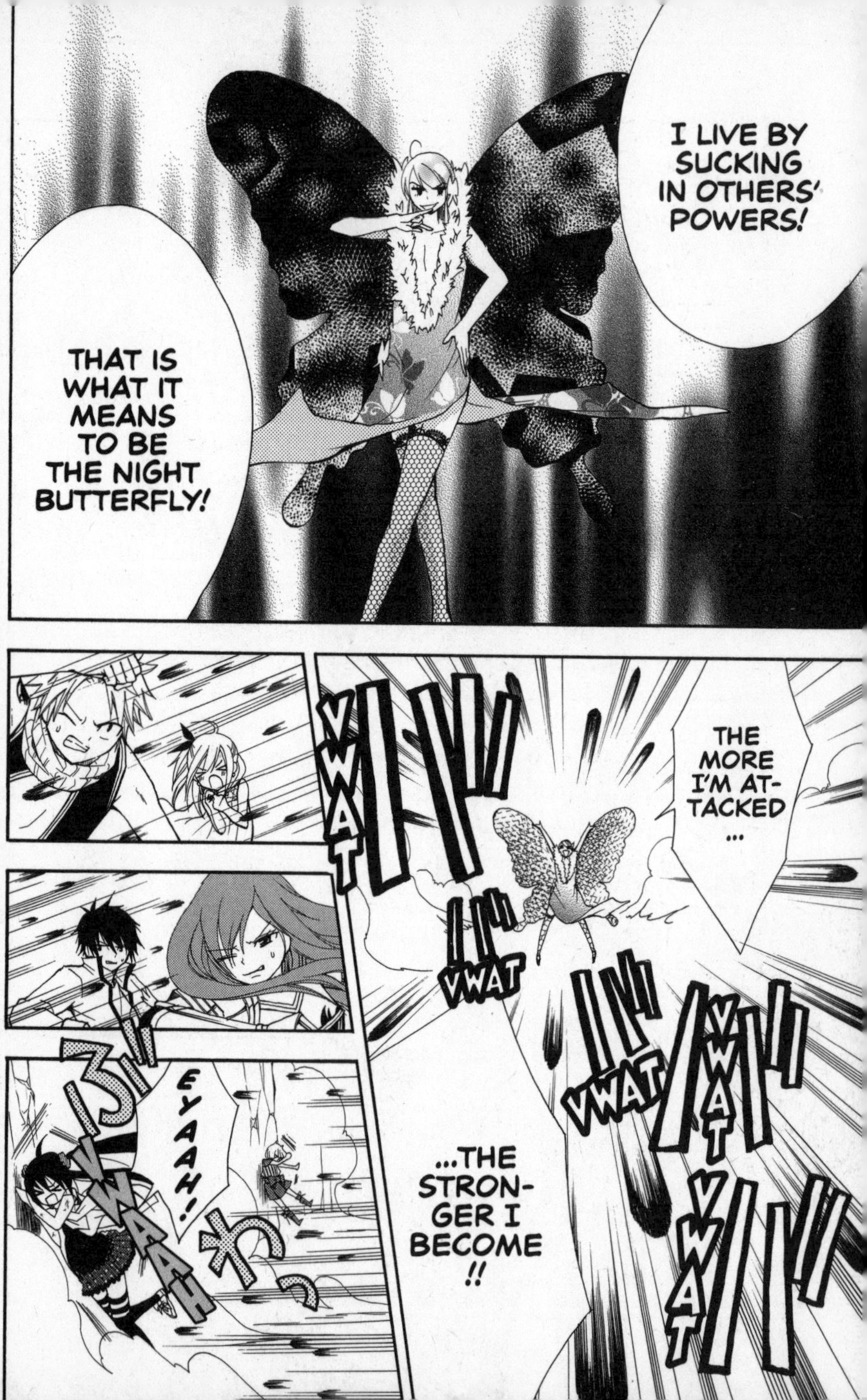
I LIVE BY SUCKING IN OTHERS' POWERS!
THAT IS WHAT IT MEANS TO BE THE NIGHT BUTTERFLY!
THE MORE I'M AT-TACKED ...
...THE STRONGER I BECOME !!
VWAT
VWAT
VWAT
VWAT
VWAT
VWAT
EYAAAH!
VWAAAH

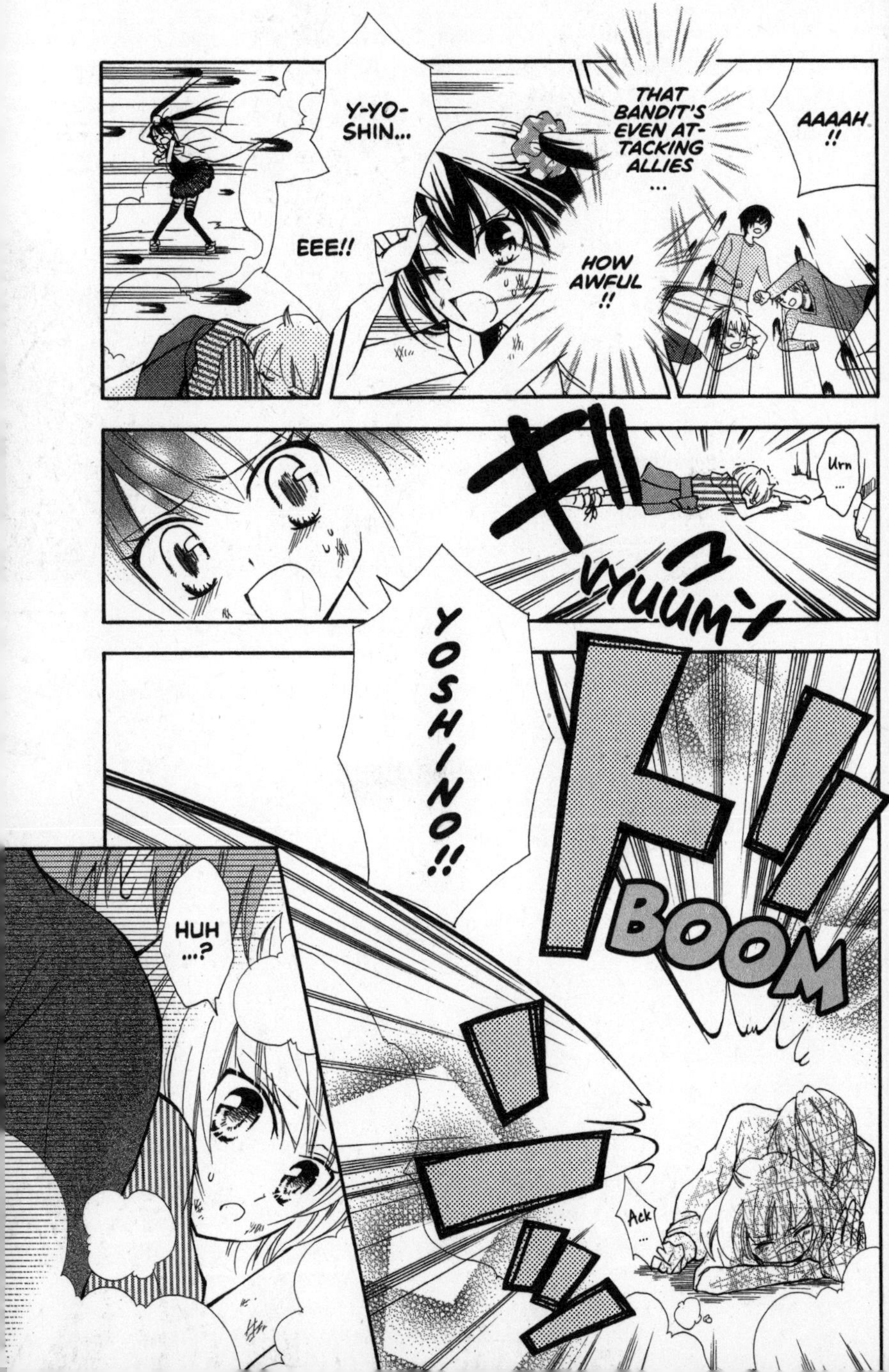
AAAAH!!
THAT BANDIT'S EVEN AT-TACKING ALLIES...
HOW AWFUL!!
Y-YO-SHIN...
EEE!!
Urn...
VYUUUM
YOSHINO!!
BOOM
Ack...
HUH...?

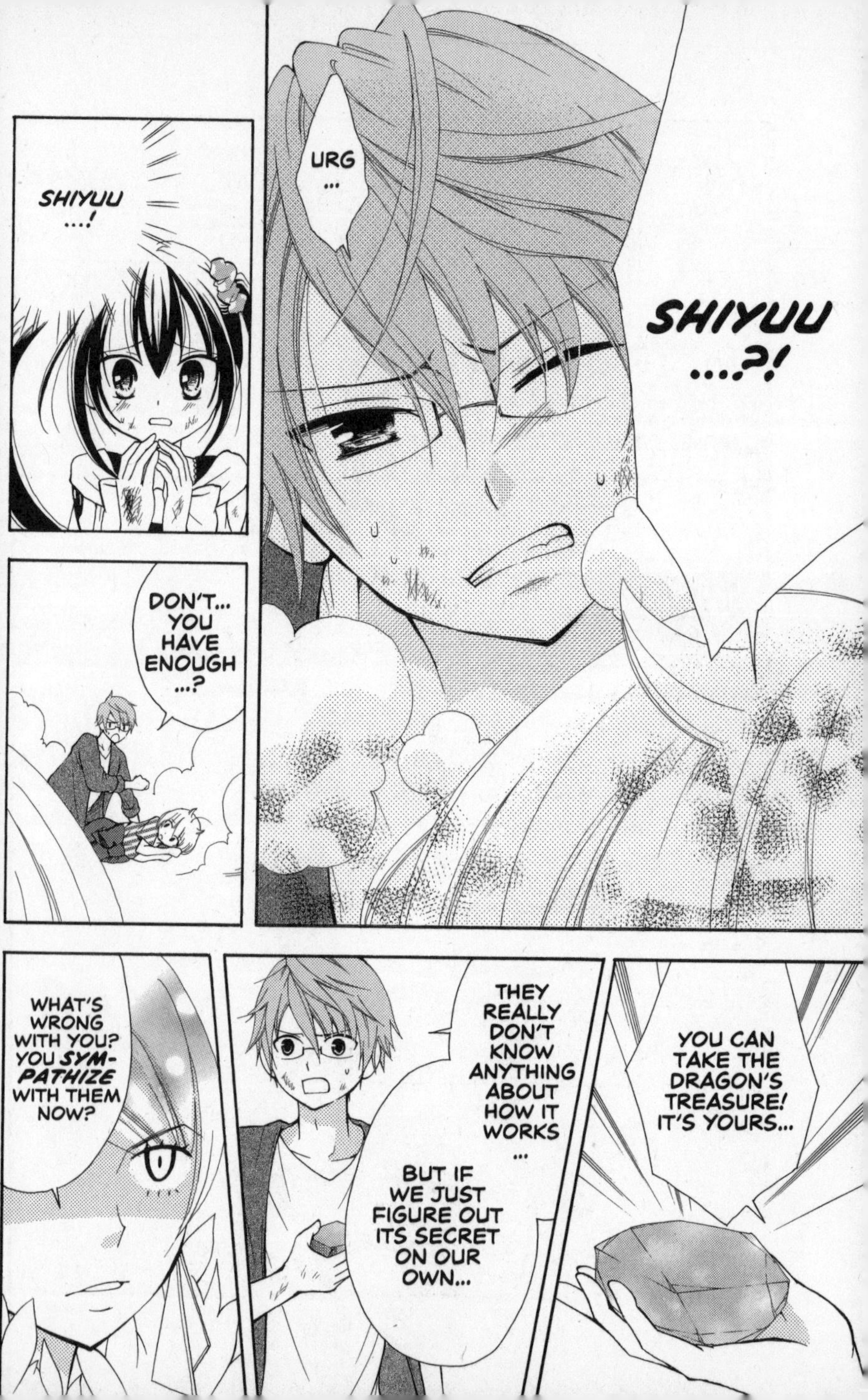
URG ...
SHIYUU ...?!
SHIYUU ...!
DON'T... YOU HAVE ENOUGH ...?
YOU CAN TAKE THE DRAGON'S TREASURE! IT'S YOURS...
THEY REALLY DON'T KNOW ANYTHING ABOUT HOW IT WORKS ...
BUT IF WE JUST FIGURE OUT ITS SECRET ON OUR OWN...
WHAT'S WRONG WITH YOU? YOU *SYMPATHIZE* WITH THEM NOW?

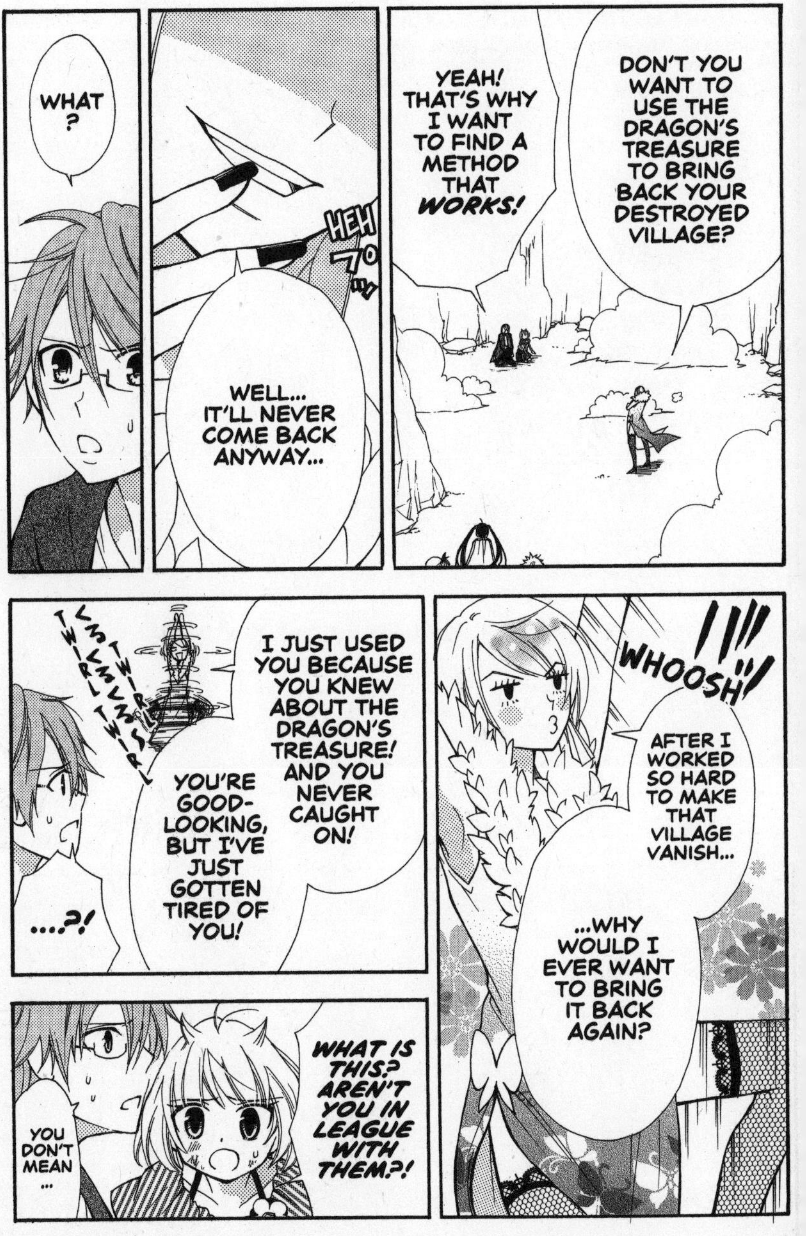
DON'T YOU WANT TO USE THE DRAGON'S TREASURE TO BRING BACK YOUR DESTROYED VILLAGE?
YEAH! THAT'S WHY I WANT TO FIND A METHOD THAT *WORKS!*
HEH
WELL... IT'LL NEVER COME BACK ANYWAY...
WHAT?
WHOOSH
AFTER I WORKED SO HARD TO MAKE THAT VILLAGE VANISH...
...WHY WOULD I EVER WANT TO BRING IT BACK AGAIN?
I JUST USED YOU BECAUSE YOU KNEW ABOUT THE DRAGON'S TREASURE! AND YOU NEVER CAUGHT ON!
YOU'RE GOOD-LOOKING, BUT I'VE JUST GOTTEN TIRED OF YOU!
TWIRL TWIRL TWIRL
...?!
WHAT IS THIS? AREN'T YOU IN LEAGUE WITH THEM?!
YOU DON'T MEAN ...

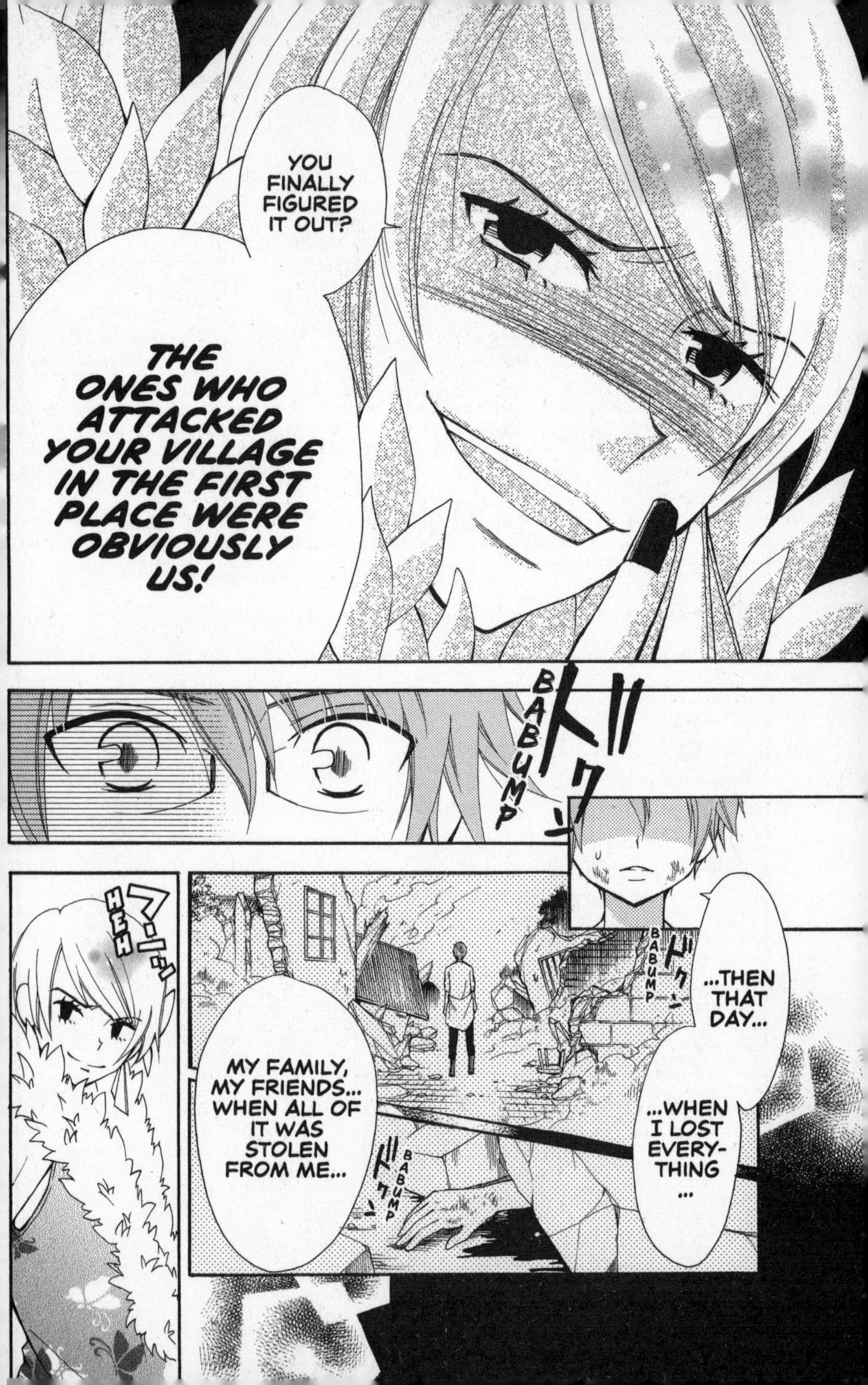

YOU FINALLY FIGURED IT OUT?
THE ONES WHO ATTACKED YOUR VILLAGE IN THE FIRST PLACE WERE OBVIOUSLY US!
BABUMP
BABUMP
...THEN THAT DAY...
...WHEN I LOST EVERYTHING...
MY FAMILY, MY FRIENDS... WHEN ALL OF IT WAS STOLEN FROM ME...
BABUMP
HEH

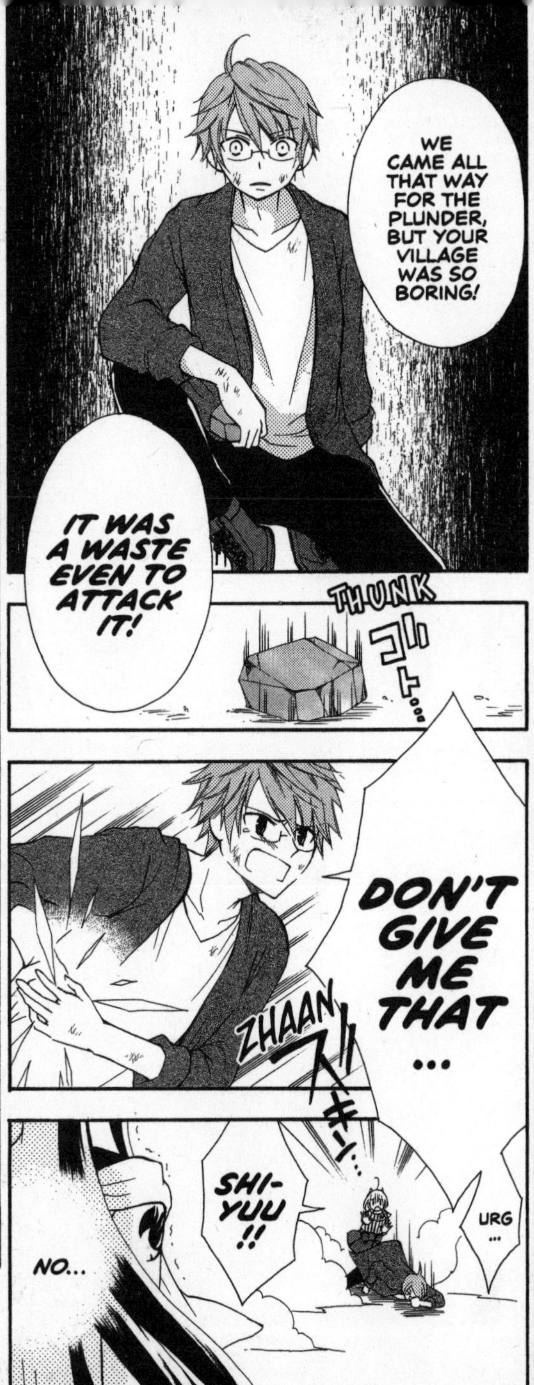
WE CAME ALL THAT WAY FOR THE PLUNDER, BUT YOUR VILLAGE WAS SO BORING!
IT WAS A WASTE EVEN TO ATTACK IT!
THUNK
DON'T GIVE ME THAT...
ZHAAN
URG...
SHI-YUU!!
NO...

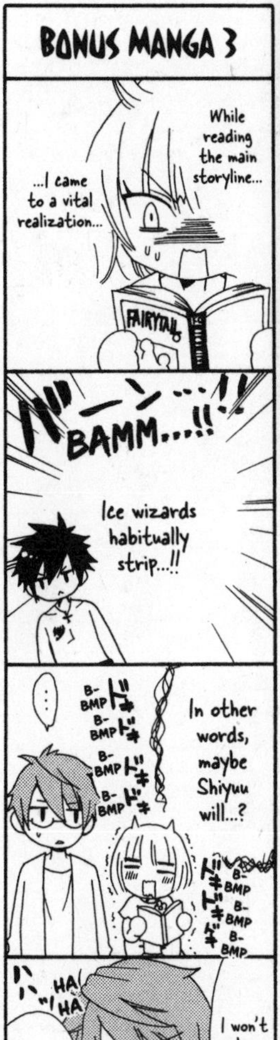
BONUS MANGA 3
While reading the main storyline...
...I came to a vital realization...
FAIRYTAIL
BAMM...!!
Ice wizards habitually strip...!!
In other words, maybe Shiyuu will...?
...
B-BMP
B-BMP
B-BMP
B-BMP
B-BMP
B-BMP
B-BMP
HA HA
I won't be stripping.
After all, this is a kids' manga.
Tsk!

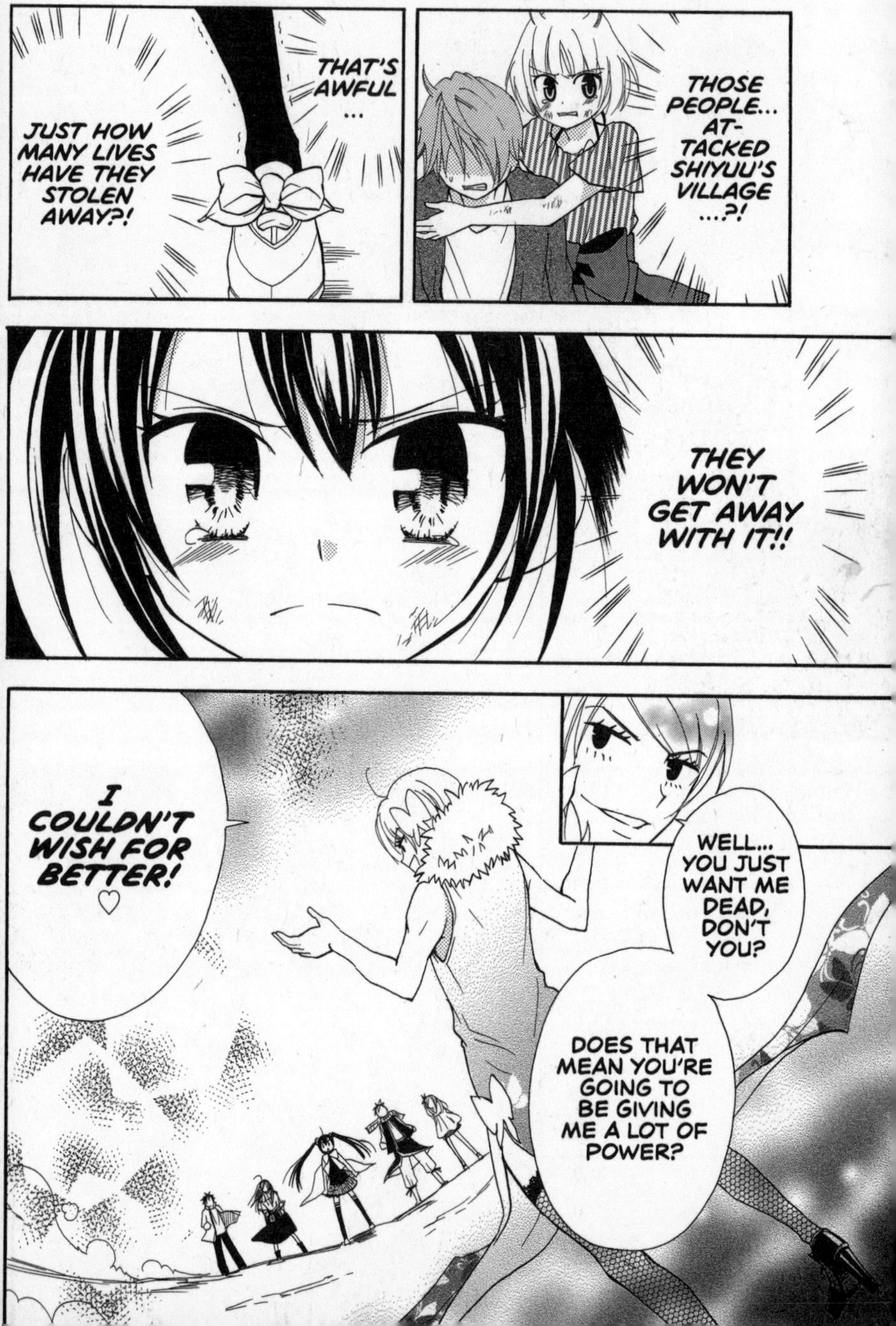
THOSE PEOPLE... AT-TACKED SHIYUU'S VILLAGE ...?!
THAT'S AWFUL ...
JUST HOW MANY LIVES HAVE THEY STOLEN AWAY?!
THEY WON'T GET AWAY WITH IT!!
WELL... YOU JUST WANT ME DEAD, DON'T YOU?
DOES THAT MEAN YOU'RE GOING TO BE GIVING ME A LOT OF POWER?
I COULDN'T WISH FOR BETTER! ♡

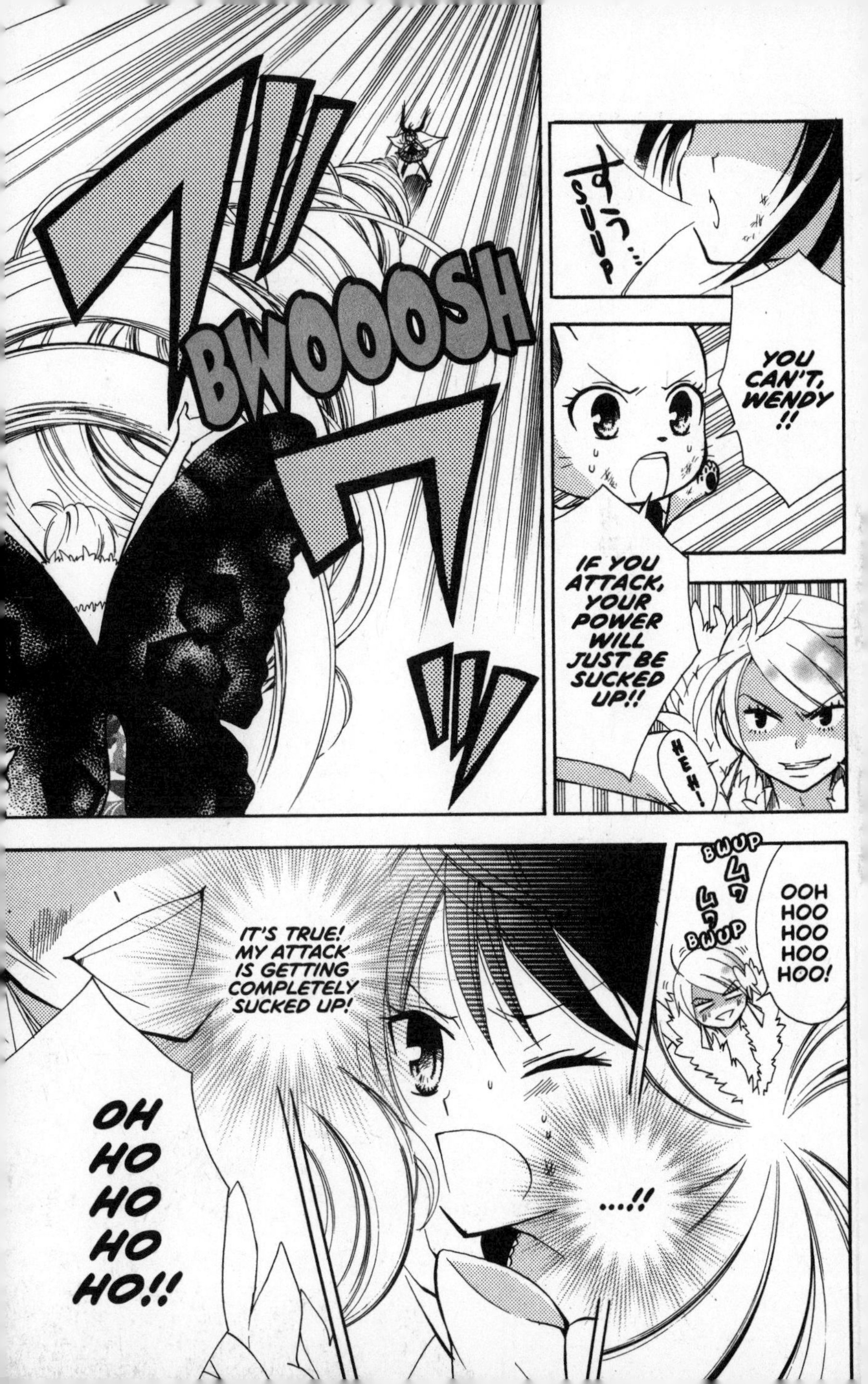

すう…
SUUP
YOU CAN'T, WENDY!!
IF YOU ATTACK, YOUR POWER WILL JUST BE SUCKED UP!!
HEH!
BWOOOSH
BWUP
BWUP
OOH HOO HOO HOO HOO!
IT'S TRUE! MY ATTACK IS GETTING COMPLETELY SUCKED UP!
...!!
OH HO HO HO HO!!

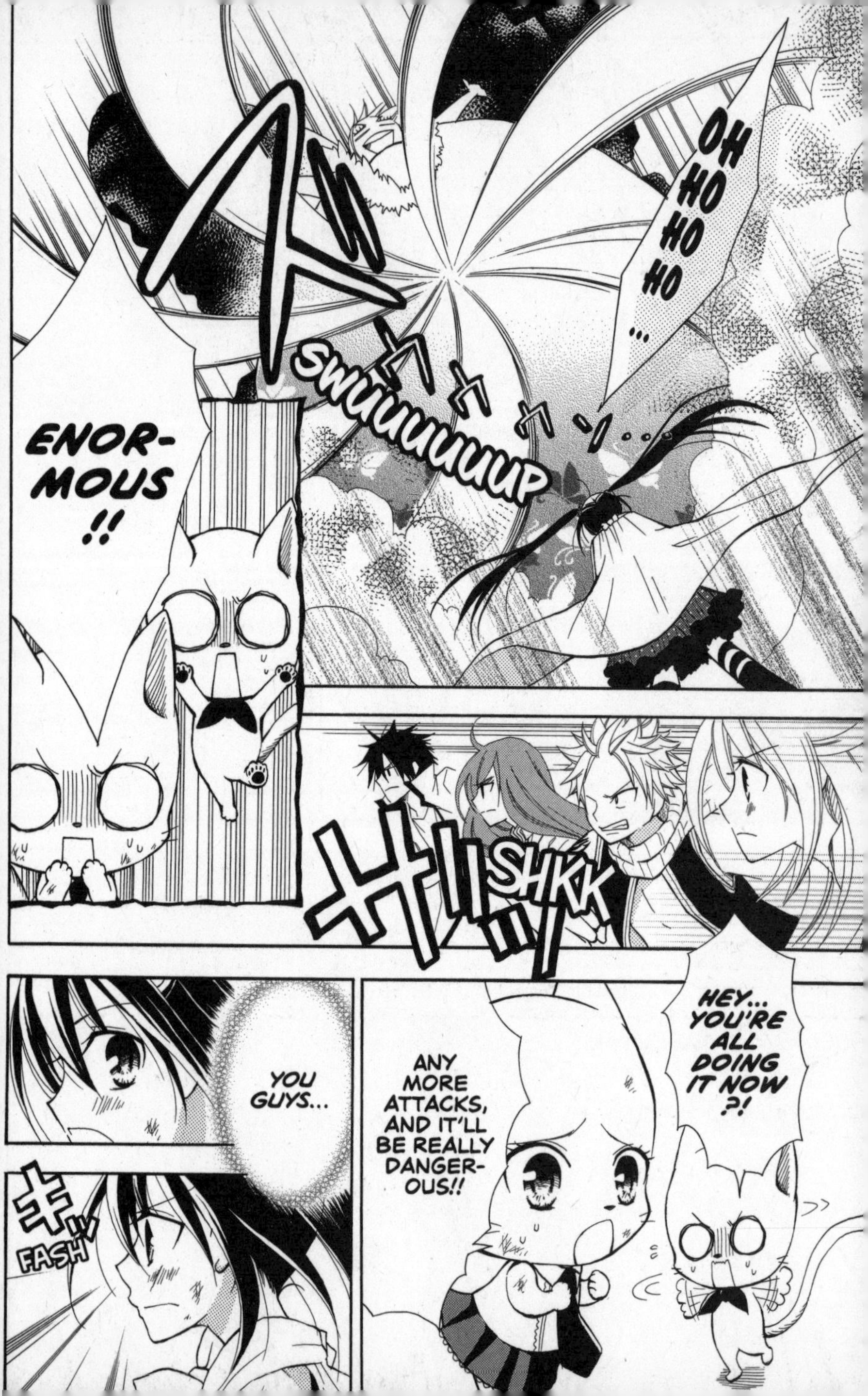
OH HO HO HO HO...
SWUUUUUUUUP
SHKK
ENOR-MOUS!!
HEY... YOU'RE ALL DOING IT NOW?!
ANY MORE ATTACKS, AND IT'LL BE REALLY DANGER-OUS!!
YOU GUYS...
FASH

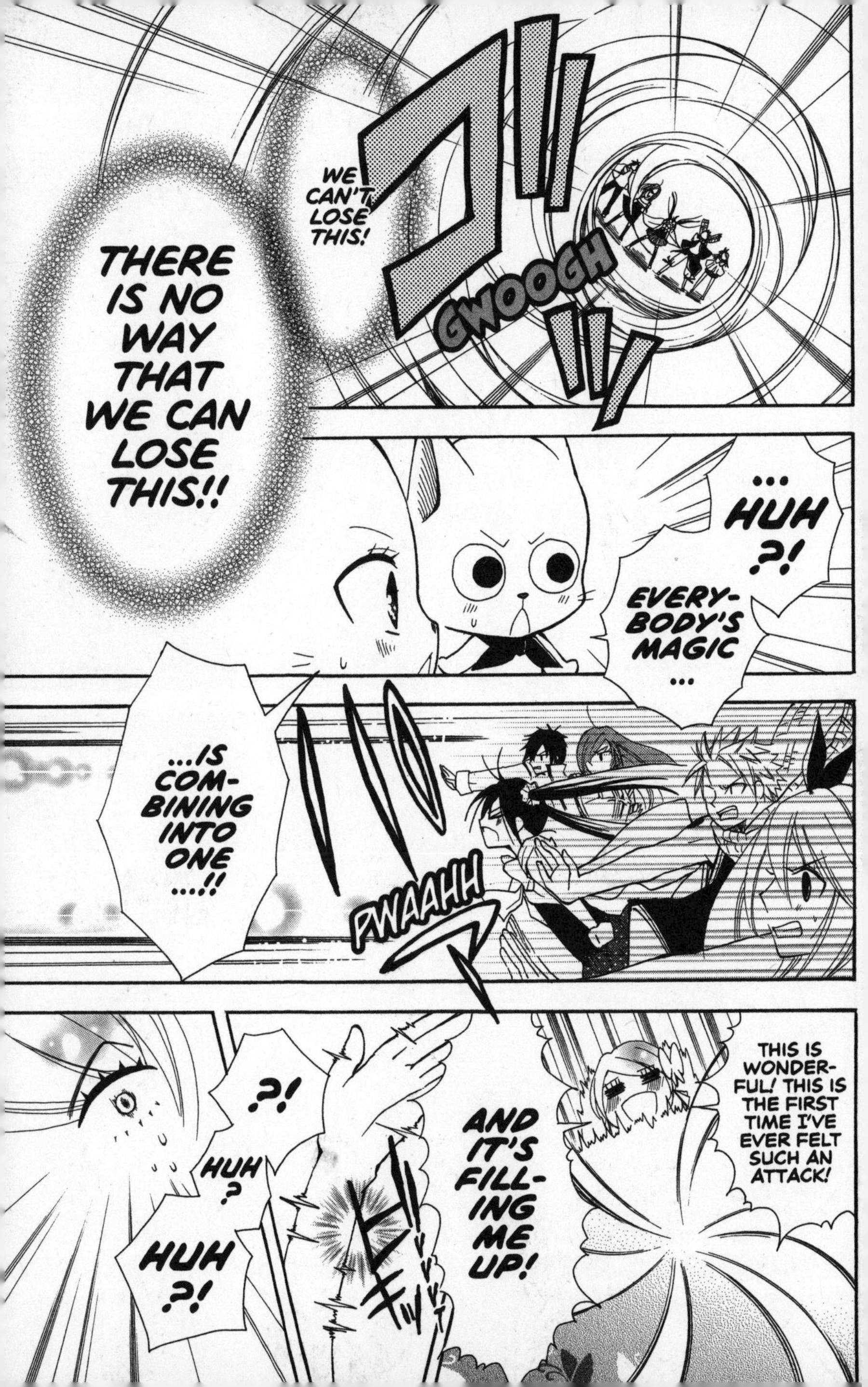
WE CAN'T LOSE THIS!
GWOOGH
THERE IS NO WAY THAT WE CAN LOSE THIS!!
... HUH ?!
EVERY-BODY'S MAGIC ...
...IS COM-BINING INTO ONE ...!!
PWAAHH
THIS IS WONDER-FUL! THIS IS THE FIRST TIME I'VE EVER FELT SUCH AN ATTACK!
AND IT'S FILL-ING ME UP!
?!
HUH ?
HUH ?!

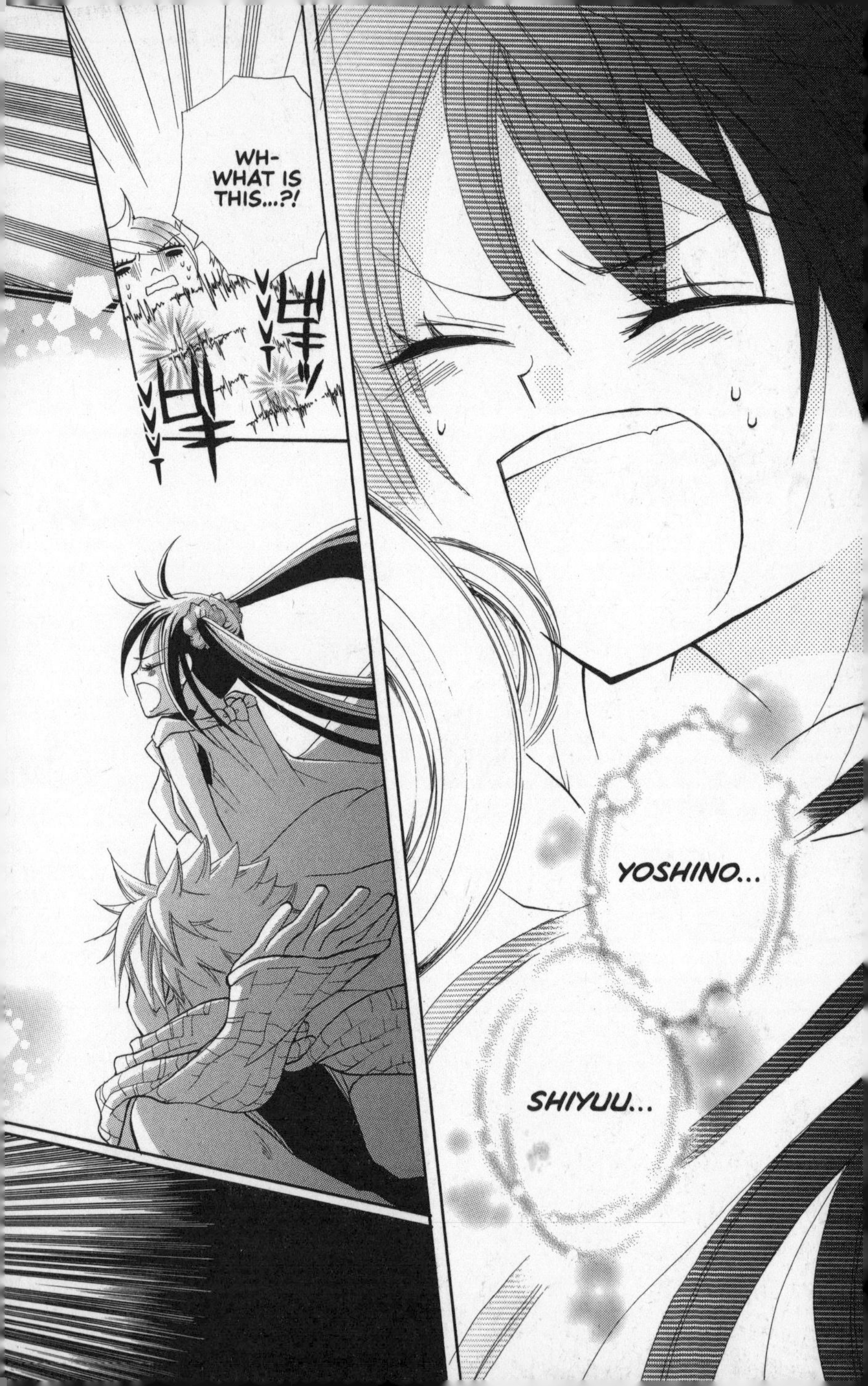
YOSHINO...
SHIYUU...
WH-
WHAT IS
THIS...?!

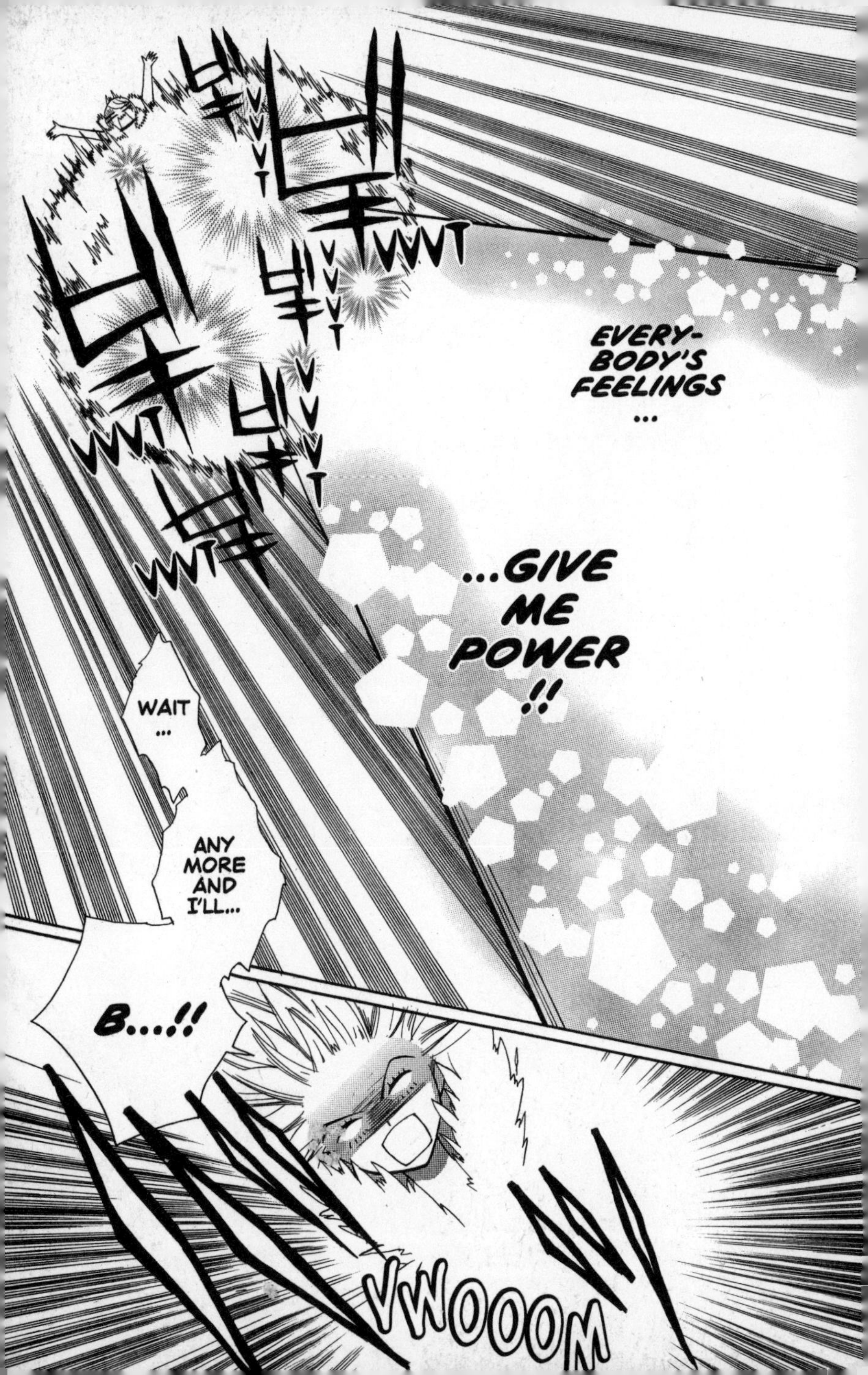
EVERY-BODY'S FEELINGS ...
...GIVE ME POWER !!
VVVT
VVVT
VVVT
VVVT
WAIT ...
ANY MORE AND I'LL...
B...!!
VWOOOM

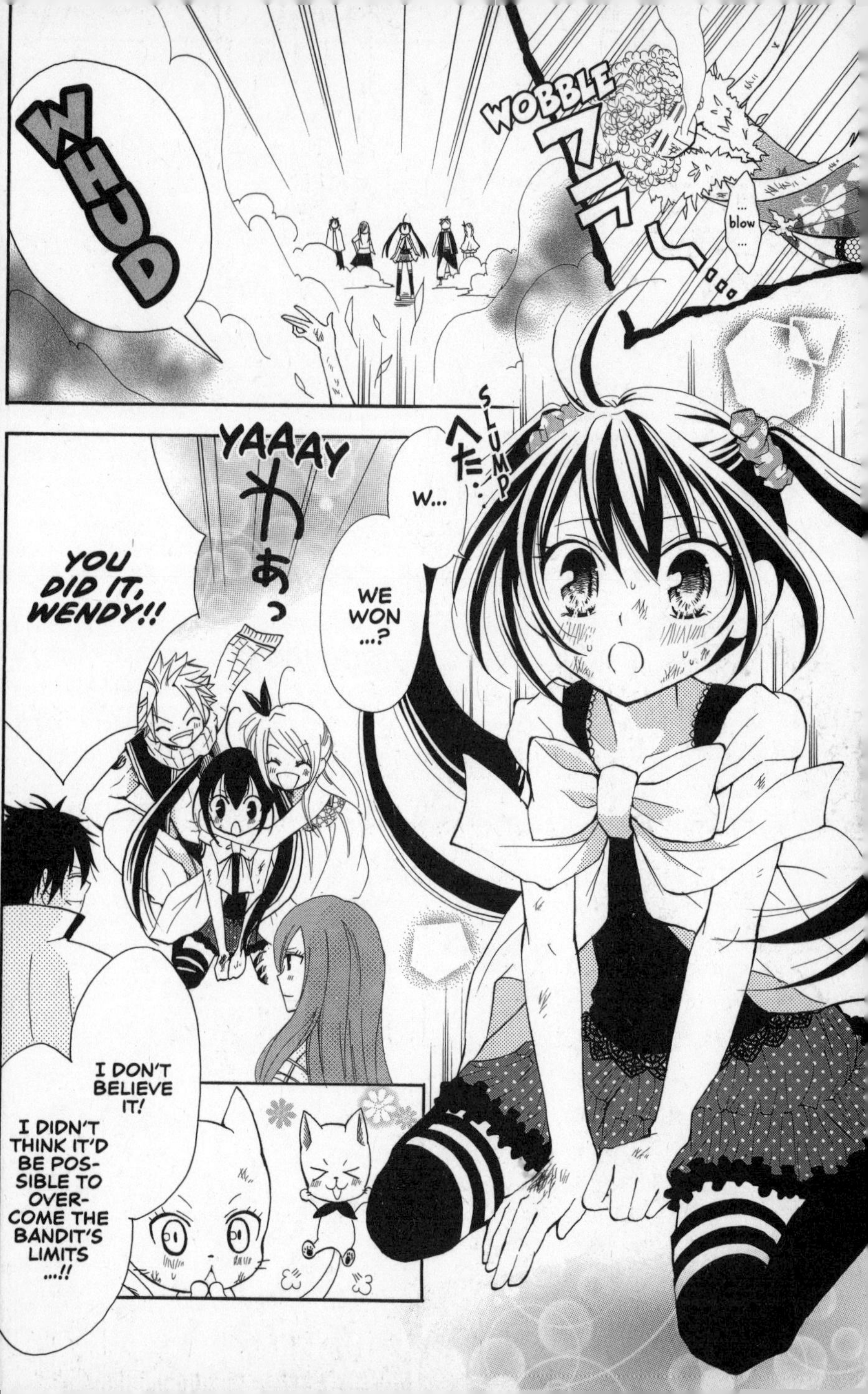

WOBBLE
... blow ...
WHUD
SLUMP
W...
WE WON ...?
YAAAY
YOU DID IT, WENDY!!
I DON'T BELIEVE IT!
I DIDN'T THINK IT'D BE POSSIBLE TO OVERCOME THE BANDIT'S LIMITS ...!!

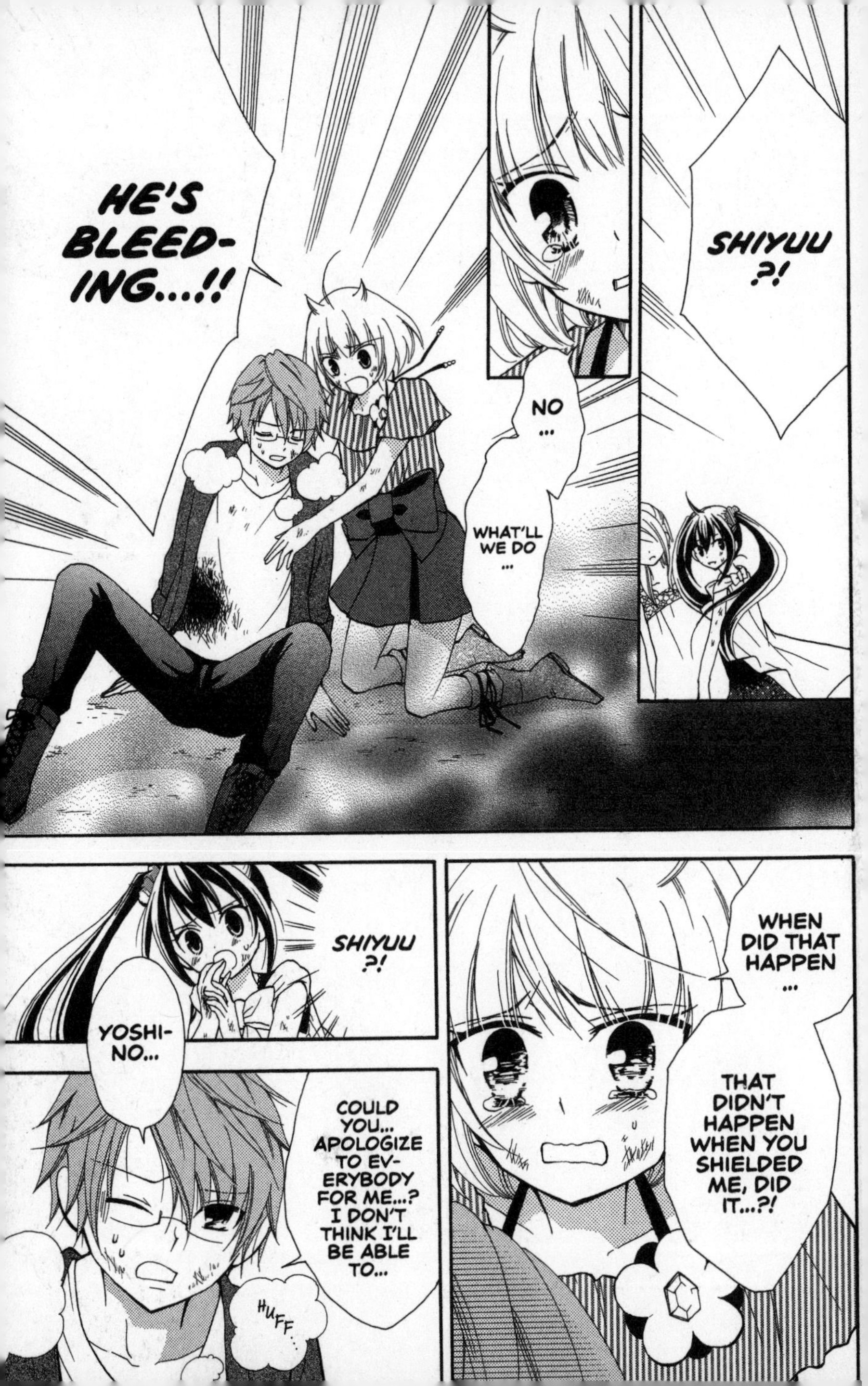
SHIYUU ?!
NO ...
WHAT'LL WE DO ...
HE'S BLEED-ING...!!
WHEN DID THAT HAPPEN ...
THAT DIDN'T HAPPEN WHEN YOU SHIELDED ME, DID IT...?!
SHIYUU ?!
YOSHI-NO...
COULD YOU... APOLOGIZE TO EV-ERYBODY FOR ME...? I DON'T THINK I'LL BE ABLE TO...
HUFF...

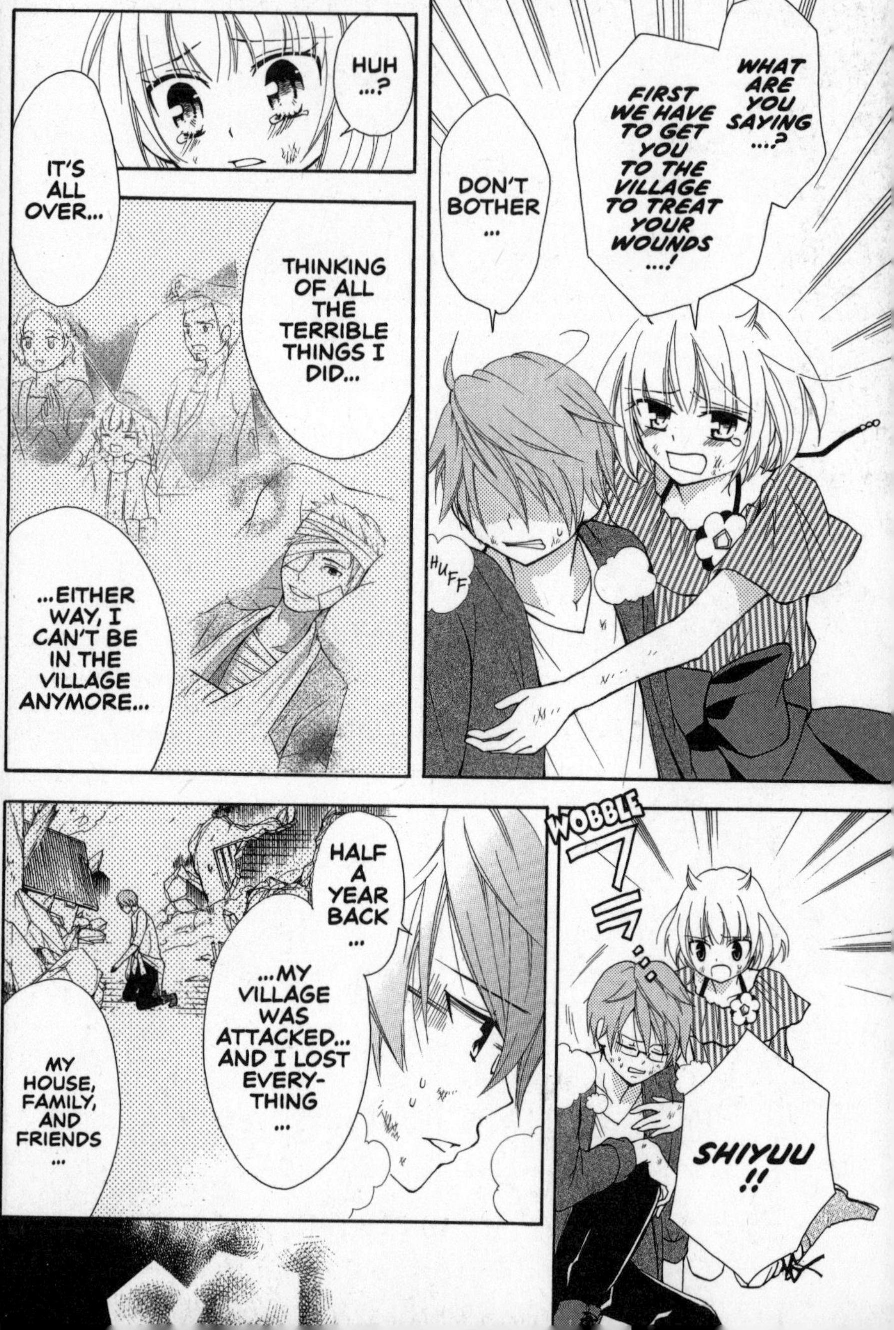
WHAT ARE YOU SAYING ...?
FIRST WE HAVE TO GET YOU TO THE VILLAGE TO TREAT YOUR WOUNDS ...!
DON'T BOTHER ...
HUFF
HUH ...?
IT'S ALL OVER...
THINKING OF ALL THE TERRIBLE THINGS I DID...
...EITHER WAY, I CAN'T BE IN THE VILLAGE ANYMORE...
WOBBLE
SHIYUU !!
HALF A YEAR BACK ...
...MY VILLAGE WAS ATTACKED... AND I LOST EVERY-THING ...
MY HOUSE, FAMILY, AND FRIENDS ...

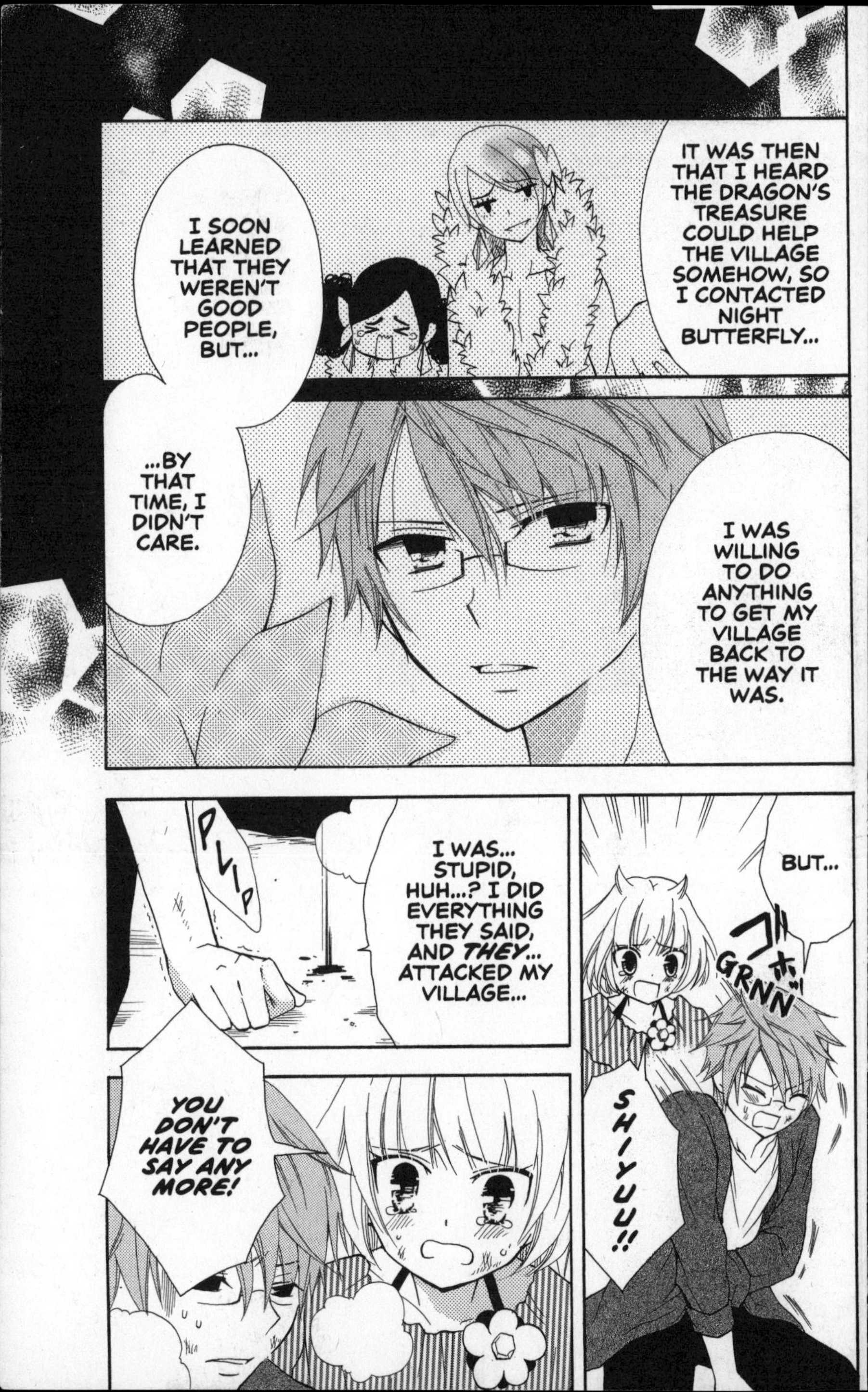
IT WAS THEN THAT I HEARD THE DRAGON'S TREASURE COULD HELP THE VILLAGE SOMEHOW, SO I CONTACTED NIGHT BUTTERFLY...
I SOON LEARNED THAT THEY WEREN'T GOOD PEOPLE, BUT...
...BY THAT TIME, I DIDN'T CARE.
I WAS WILLING TO DO ANYTHING TO GET MY VILLAGE BACK TO THE WAY IT WAS.
BUT...
GRNNN
SHIYUU!!
PLIP
I WAS... STUPID, HUH...? I DID EVERYTHING THEY SAID, AND *THEY*... ATTACKED MY VILLAGE...
YOU DON'T HAVE TO SAY ANY MORE!

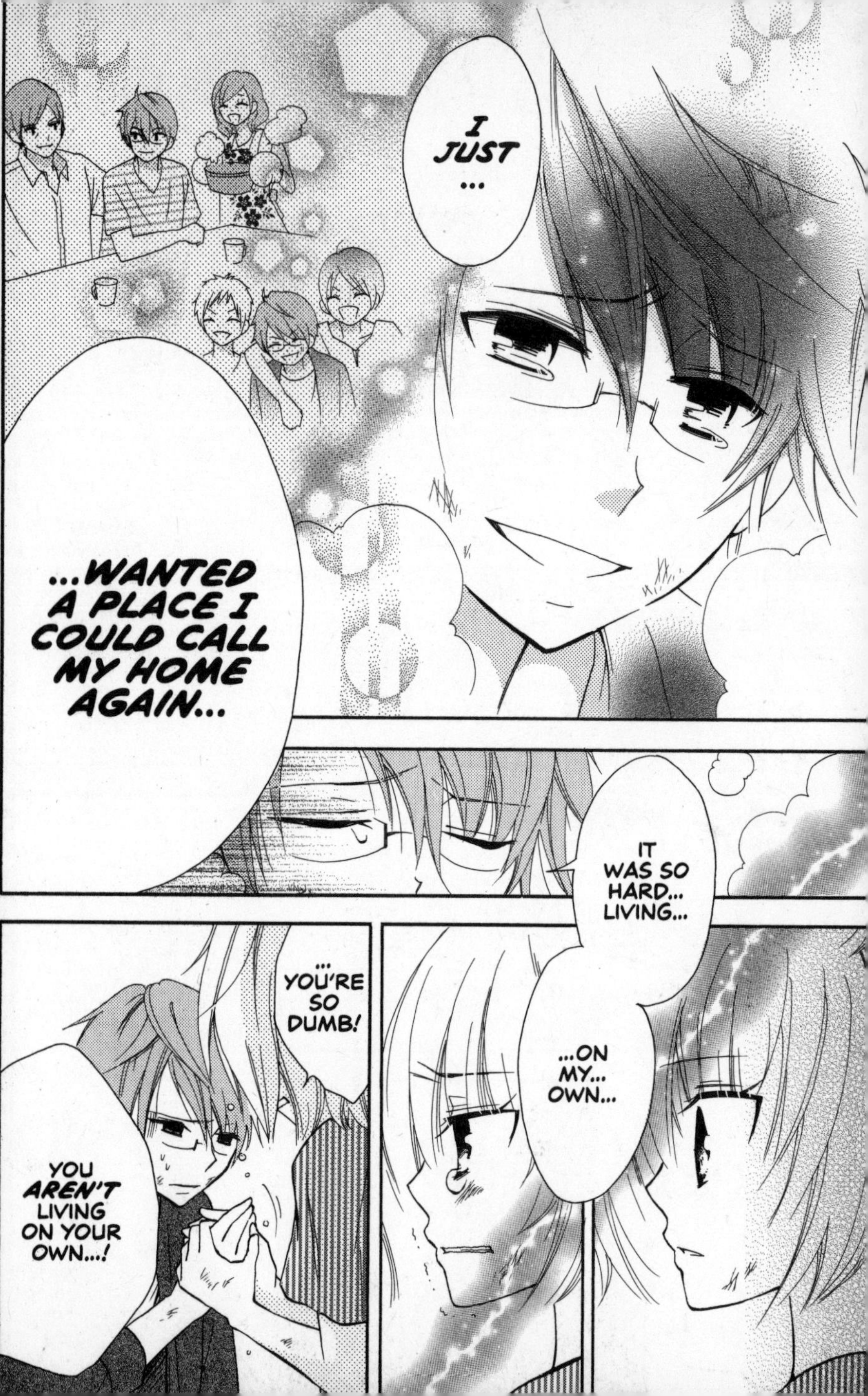
I JUST ...
...WANTED A PLACE I COULD CALL MY HOME AGAIN...
IT WAS SO HARD... LIVING...
...ON MY... OWN...
... YOU'RE SO DUMB!
YOU AREN'T LIVING ON YOUR OWN...!

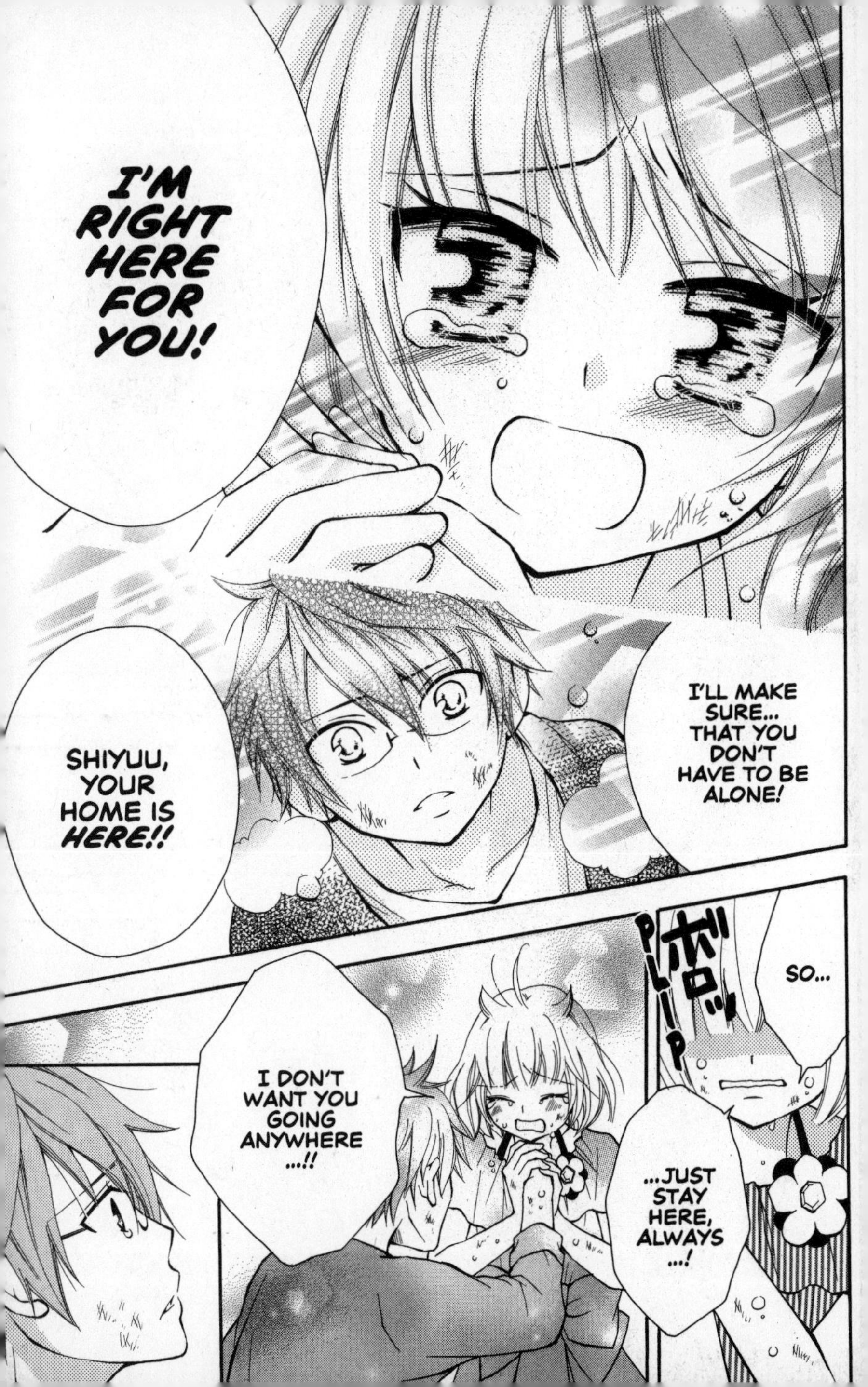
I'M RIGHT HERE FOR YOU!
I'LL MAKE SURE... THAT YOU DON'T HAVE TO BE ALONE!
SHIYUU, YOUR HOME IS *HERE!!*
ポロッ
PLIP
SO...
...JUST STAY HERE, ALWAYS ...!
I DON'T WANT YOU GOING ANYWHERE ...!!

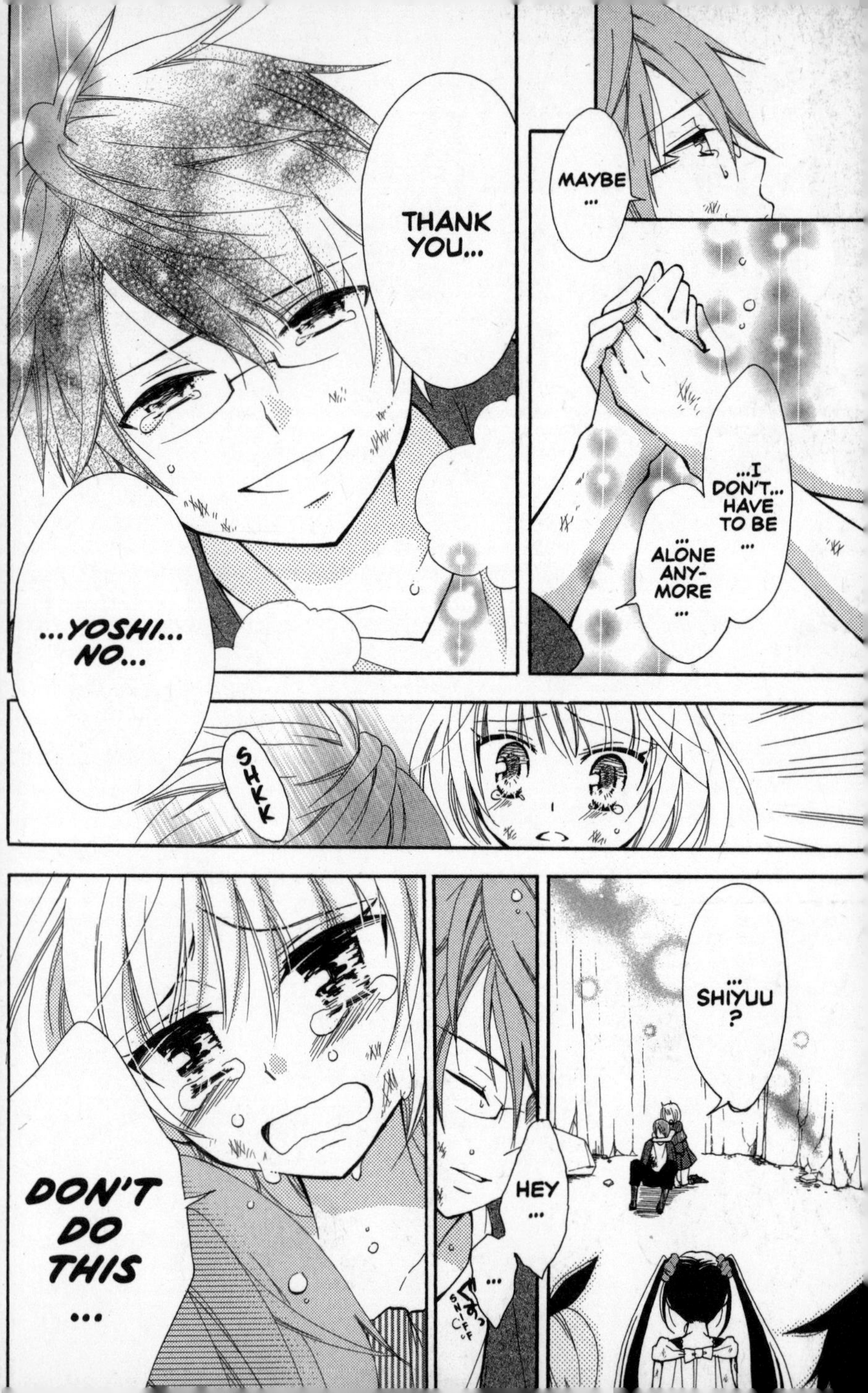
MAYBE ...
...I DON'T... HAVE TO BE ...
... ALONE ANY-MORE ...
THANK YOU...
...YOSHI... NO...
SHKK
... SHIYUU ?
HEY ...
...
SNIFF
DON'T DO THIS ...

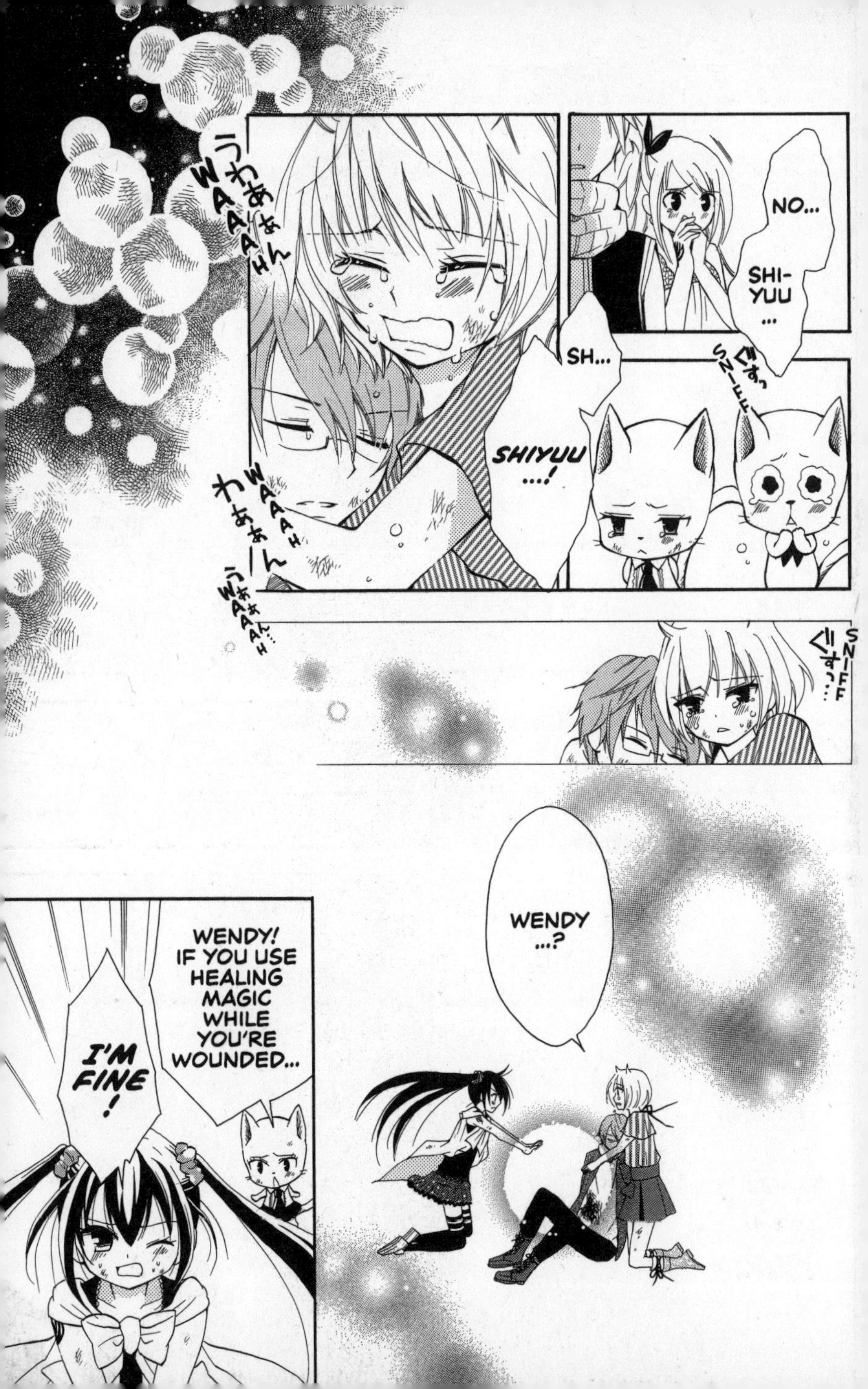
NO...
SHI-YUU ...
SH...
SHIYUU ...!
ぐすっ SNIFF
うわあぁん WAAAAH
わあぁん WAAAAH
うあぁん... WAAAAH...
ぐすっ... SNIFF...
WENDY ...?
WENDY! IF YOU USE HEALING MAGIC WHILE YOU'RE WOUNDED...
I'M FINE!

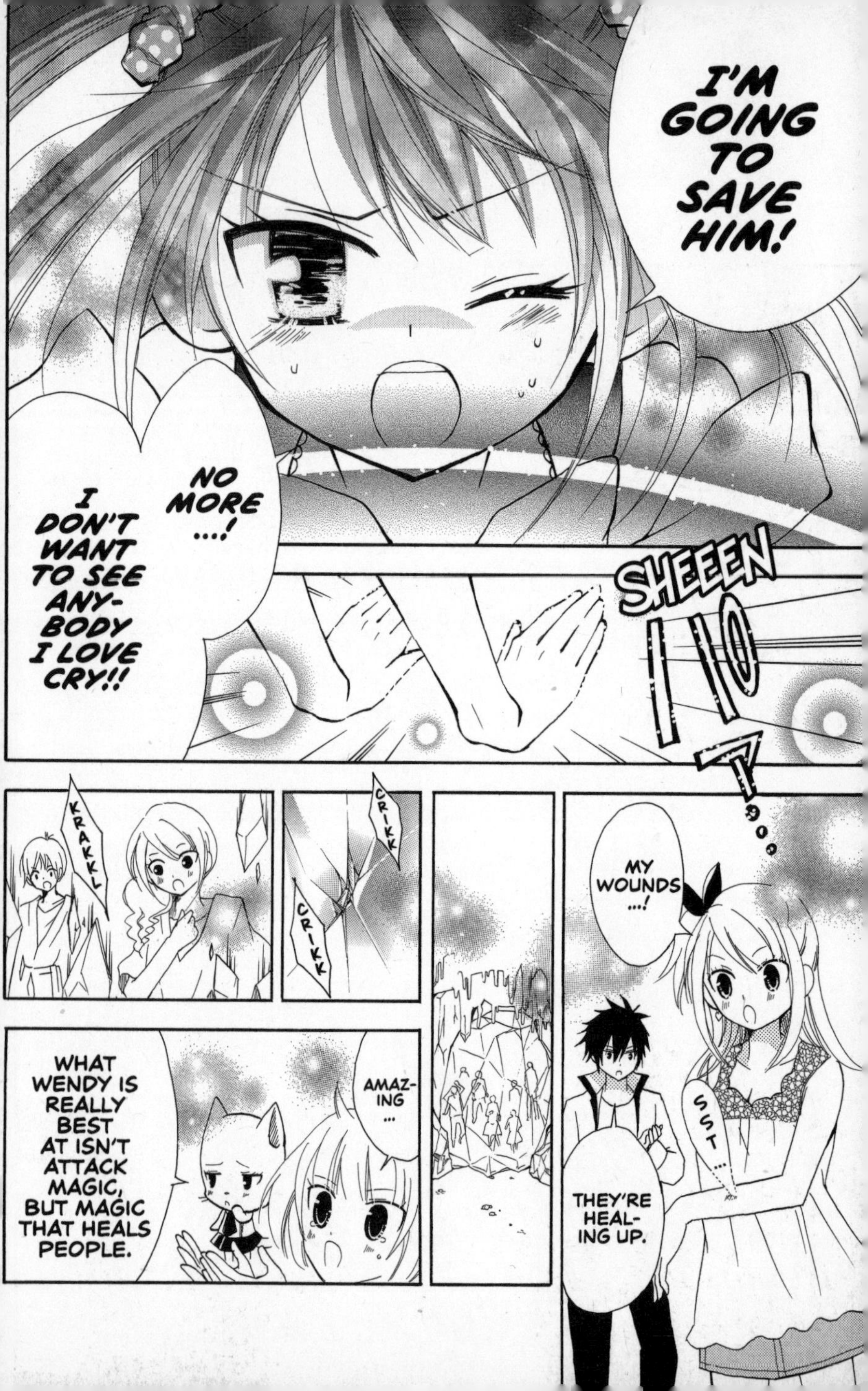
I'M GOING TO SAVE HIM!
NO MORE ...!
I DON'T WANT TO SEE ANY-BODY I LOVE CRY!!
SHEEEN
MY WOUNDS ...!
SST ...
THEY'RE HEAL-ING UP.
CRIKK
CRIKK
KRAKKL
AMAZ-ING ...
WHAT WENDY IS REALLY BEST AT ISN'T ATTACK MAGIC, BUT MAGIC THAT HEALS PEOPLE.

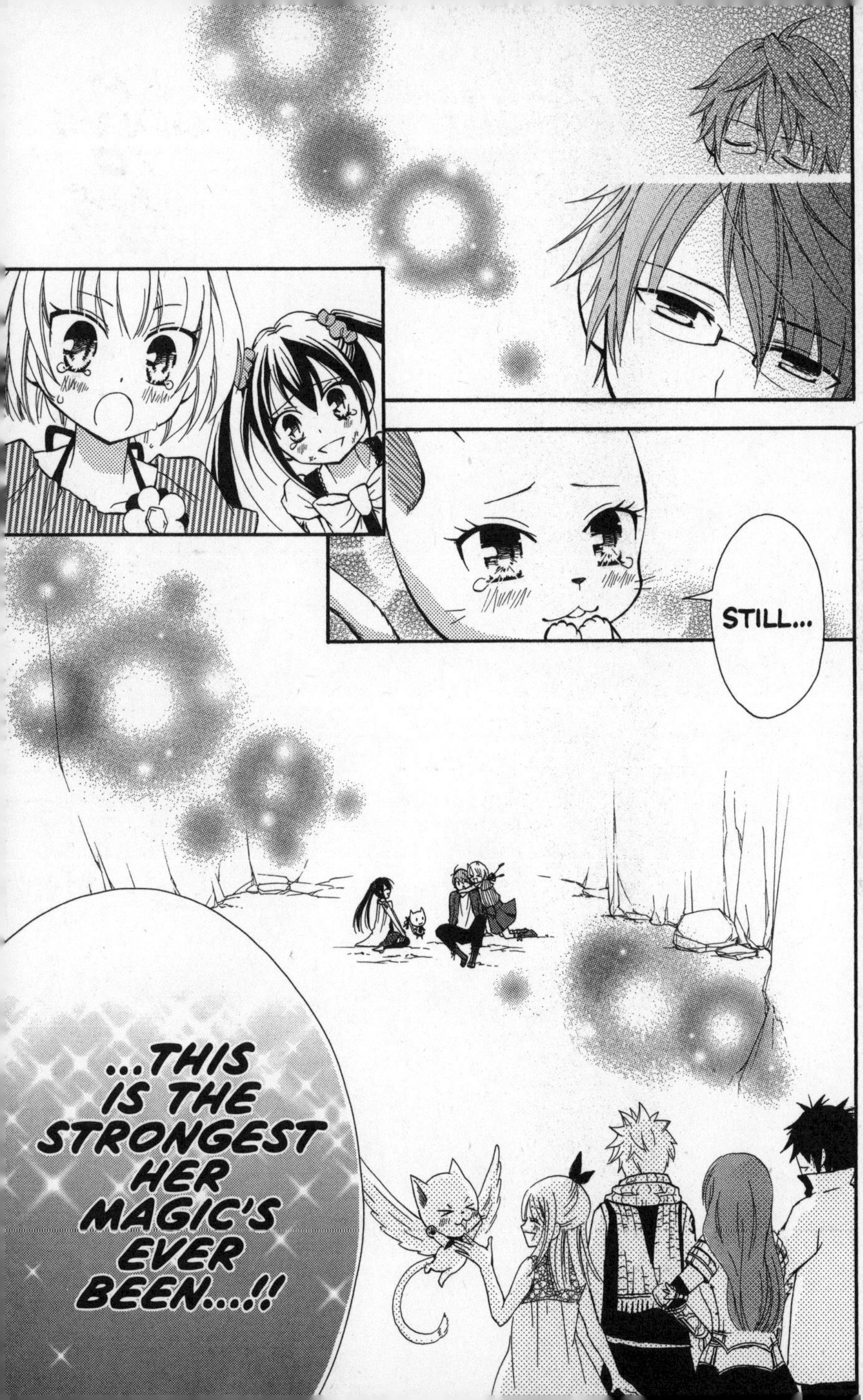
STILL...
...THIS IS THE STRONGEST HER MAGIC'S EVER BEEN...!!

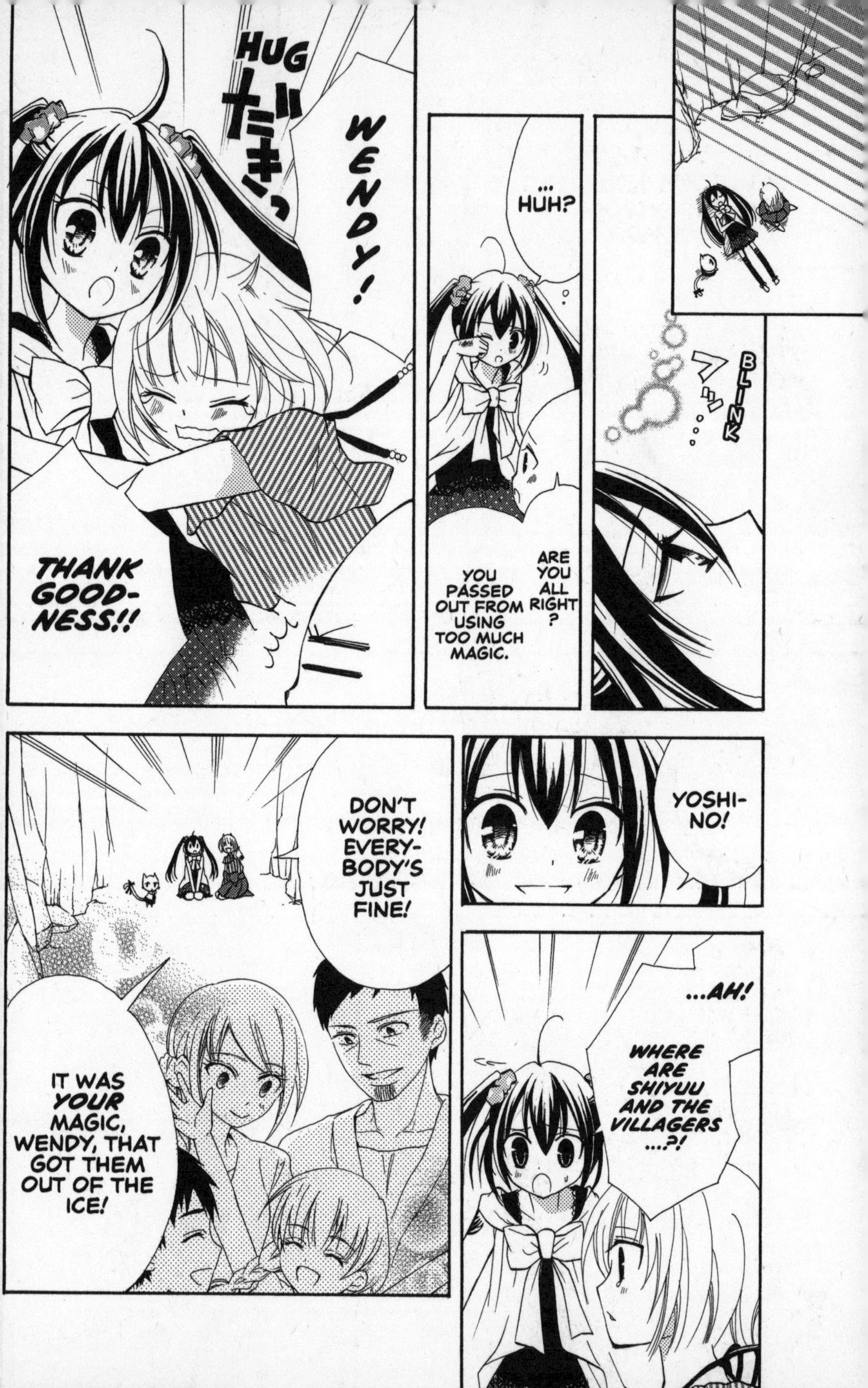
BLINK
...HUH?
ARE YOU ALL RIGHT?
YOU PASSED OUT FROM USING TOO MUCH MAGIC.
HUG
WENDY!
THANK GOODNESS!!
YOSHI-NO!
...AH!
WHERE ARE SHIYUU AND THE VILLAGERS ...?!
DON'T WORRY! EVERYBODY'S JUST FINE!
IT WAS YOUR MAGIC, WENDY, THAT GOT THEM OUT OF THE ICE!

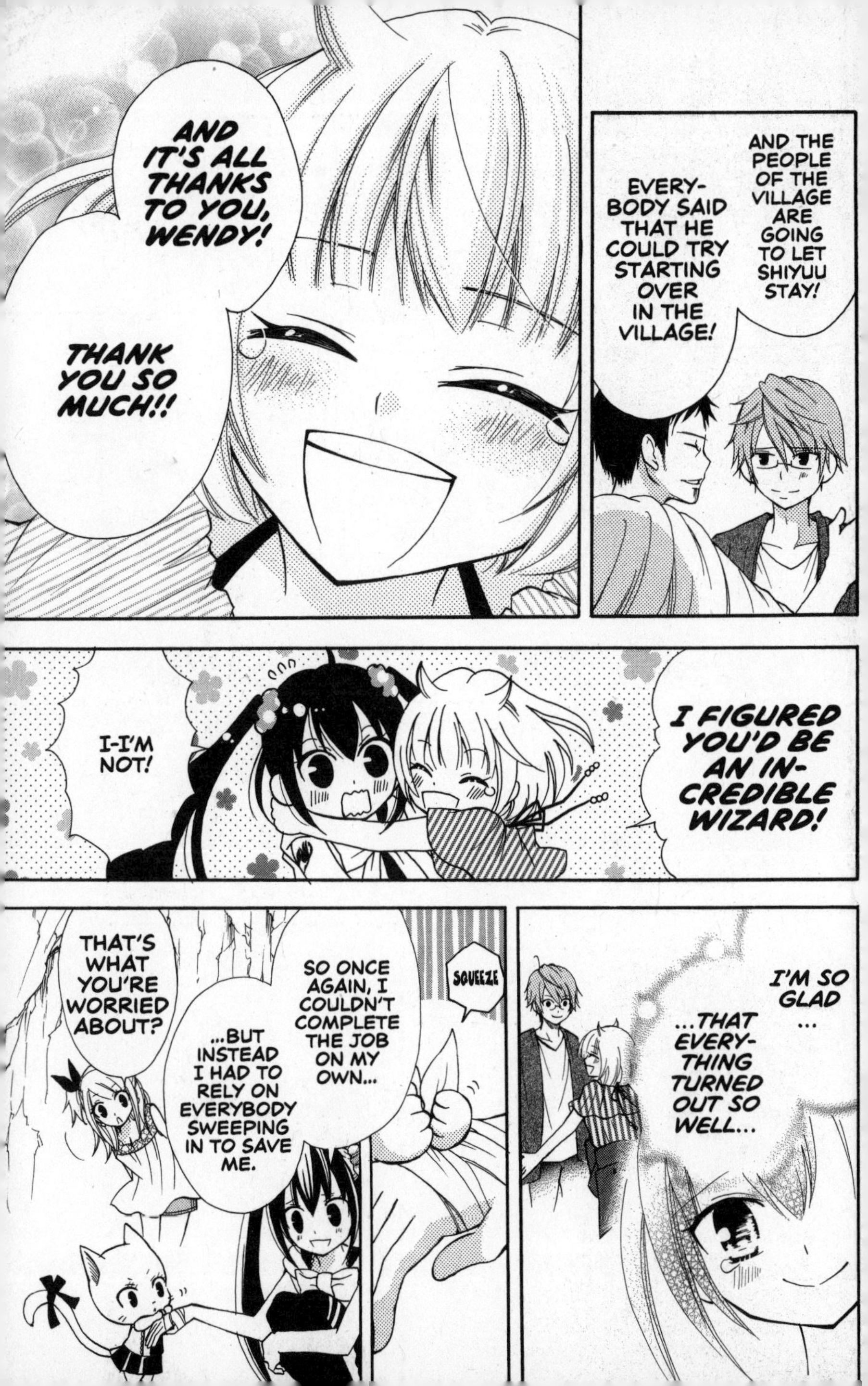
AND THE PEOPLE OF THE VILLAGE ARE GOING TO LET SHIYUU STAY!
EVERY-BODY SAID THAT HE COULD TRY STARTING OVER IN THE VILLAGE!
AND IT'S ALL THANKS TO YOU, WENDY!
THANK YOU SO MUCH!!
I FIGURED YOU'D BE AN IN-CREDIBLE WIZARD!
I-I'M NOT!
I'M SO GLAD ...
...THAT EVERY-THING TURNED OUT SO WELL...
SQUEEZE
SO ONCE AGAIN, I COULDN'T COMPLETE THE JOB ON MY OWN...
...BUT INSTEAD I HAD TO RELY ON EVERYBODY SWEEPING IN TO SAVE ME.
THAT'S WHAT YOU'RE WORRIED ABOUT?

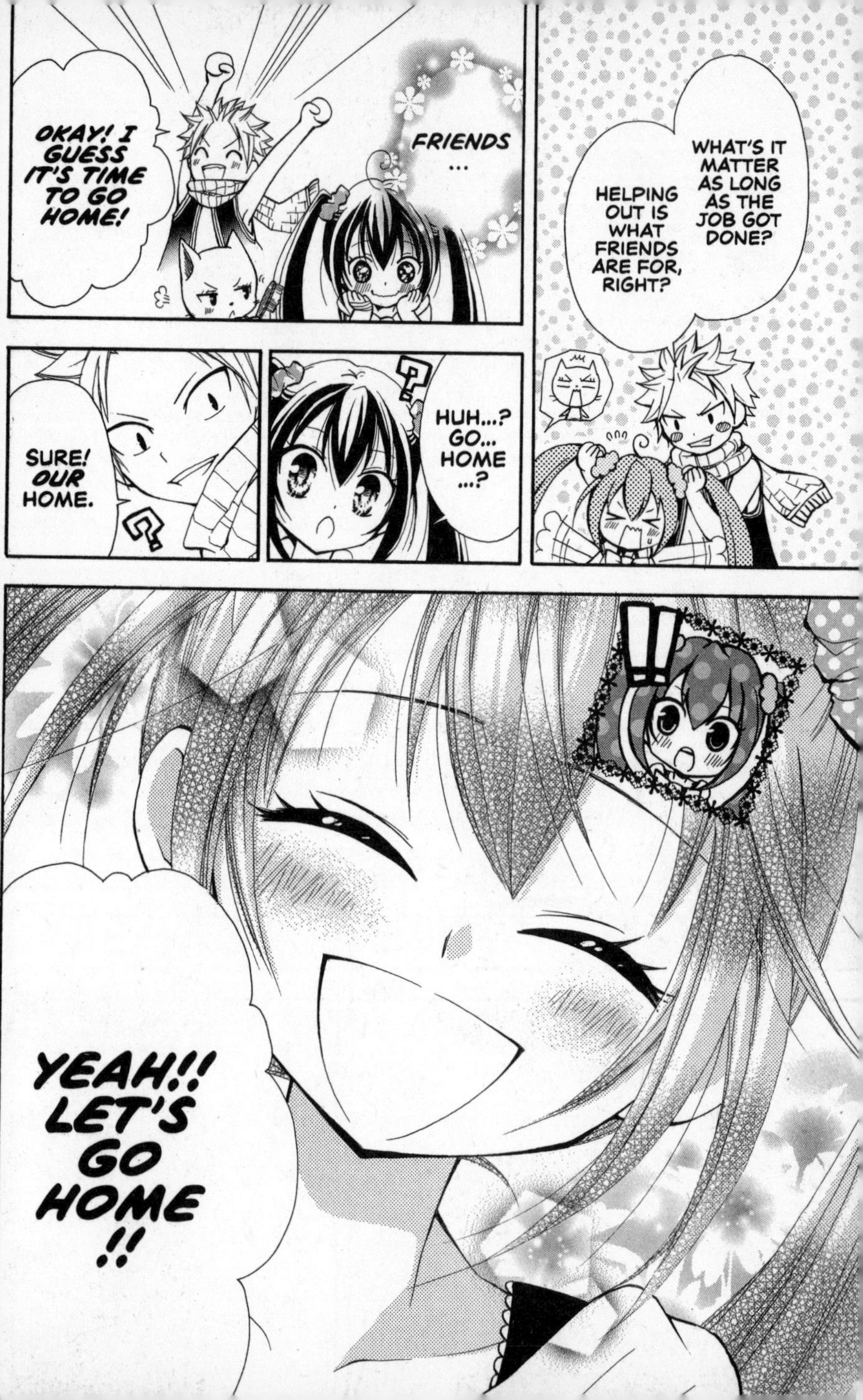
WHAT'S IT MATTER AS LONG AS THE JOB GOT DONE?
HELPING OUT IS WHAT FRIENDS ARE FOR, RIGHT?
FRIENDS ...
OKAY! I GUESS IT'S TIME TO GO HOME!
HUH...? GO... HOME ...?
SURE! OUR HOME.
YEAH!! LET'S GO HOME !!

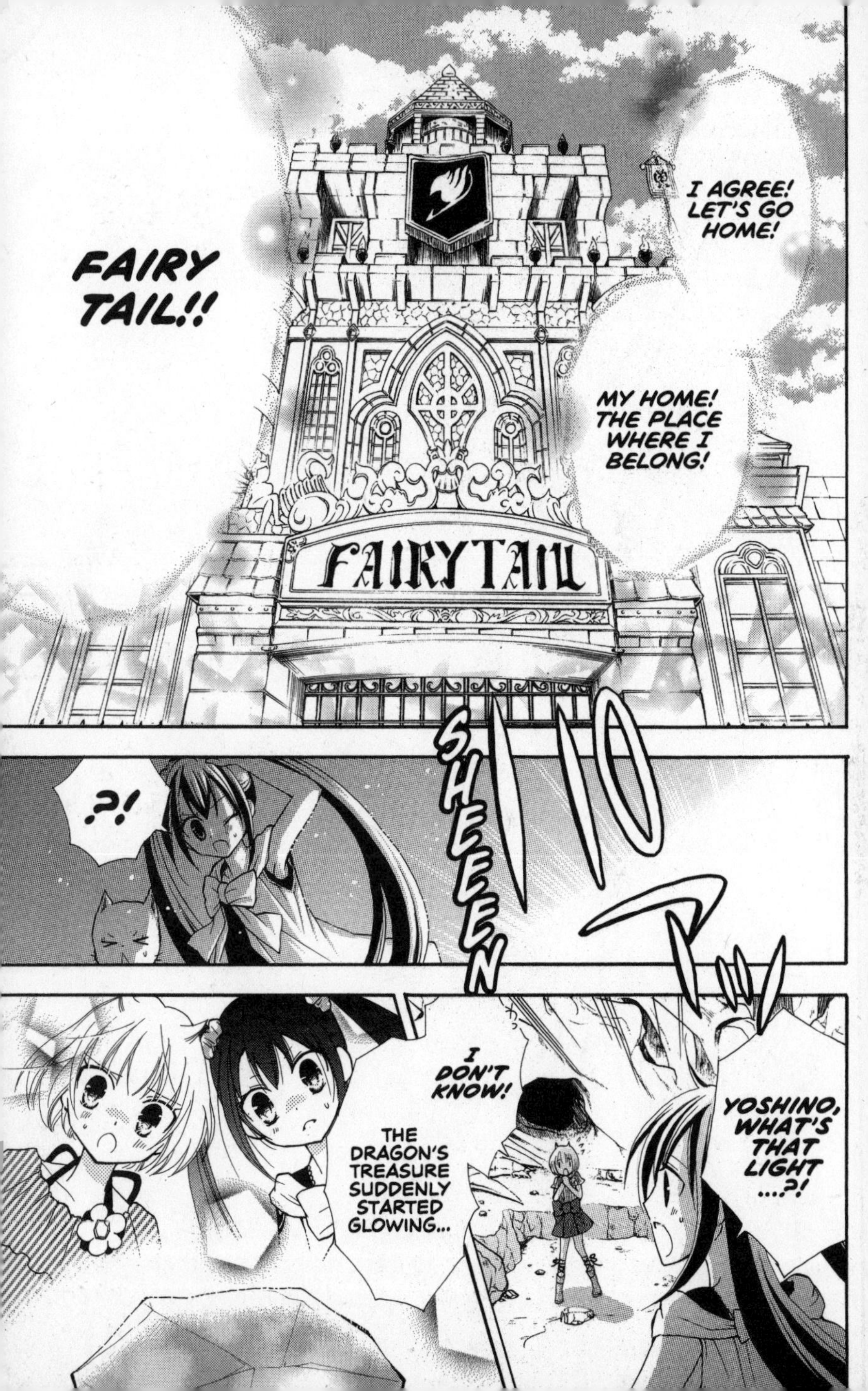
I AGREE! LET'S GO HOME!
MY HOME! THE PLACE WHERE I BELONG!
FAIRYTAIL
FAIRY TAIL!!
SHEEEEN
?!
YOSHINO, WHAT'S THAT LIGHT ...?!
I DON'T KNOW!
THE DRAGON'S TREASURE SUDDENLY STARTED GLOWING...

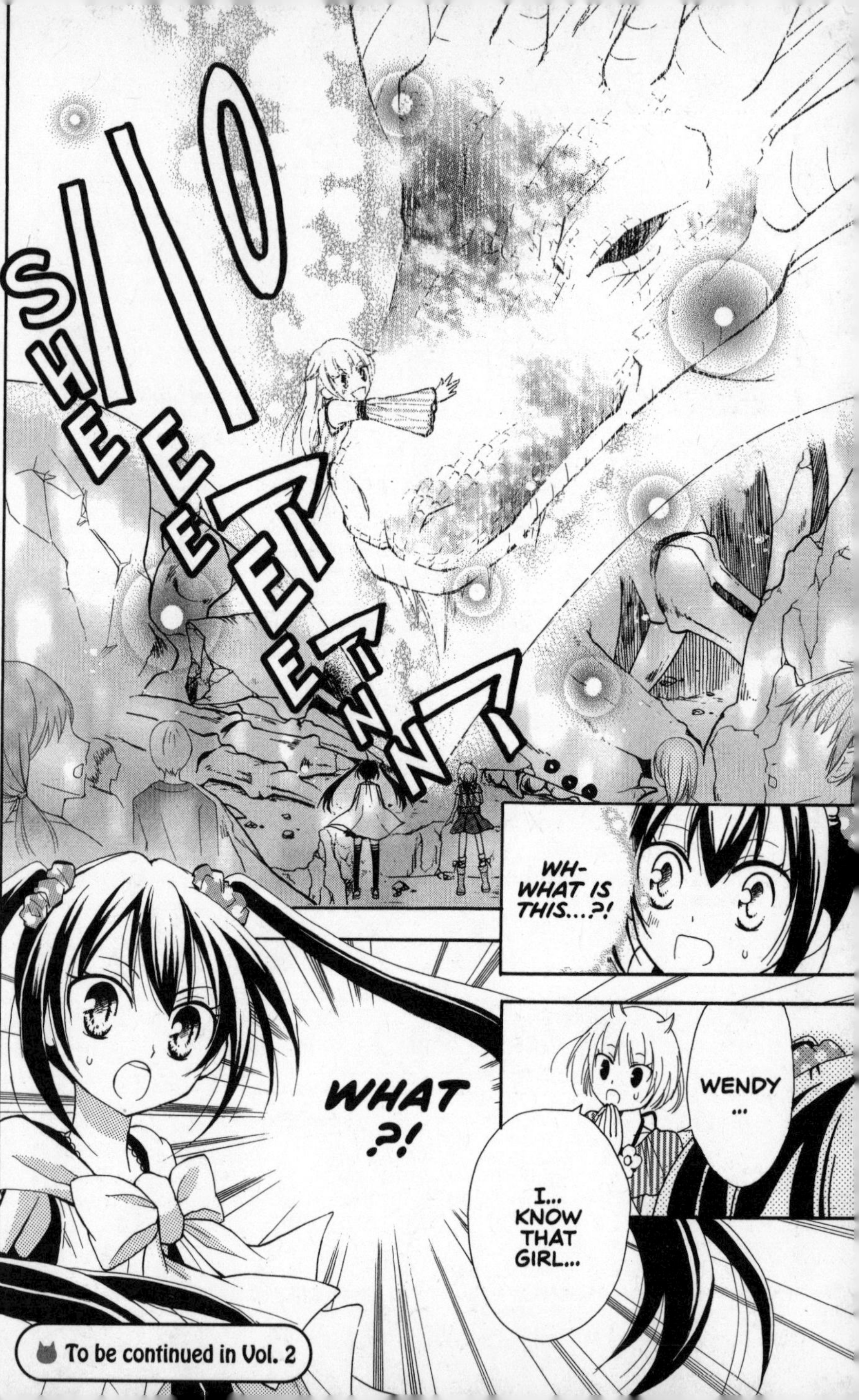
SHEEEEEEN...
WH-WHAT IS THIS...?!
WENDY...
I... KNOW THAT GIRL...
WHAT?!
To be continued in Vol. 2

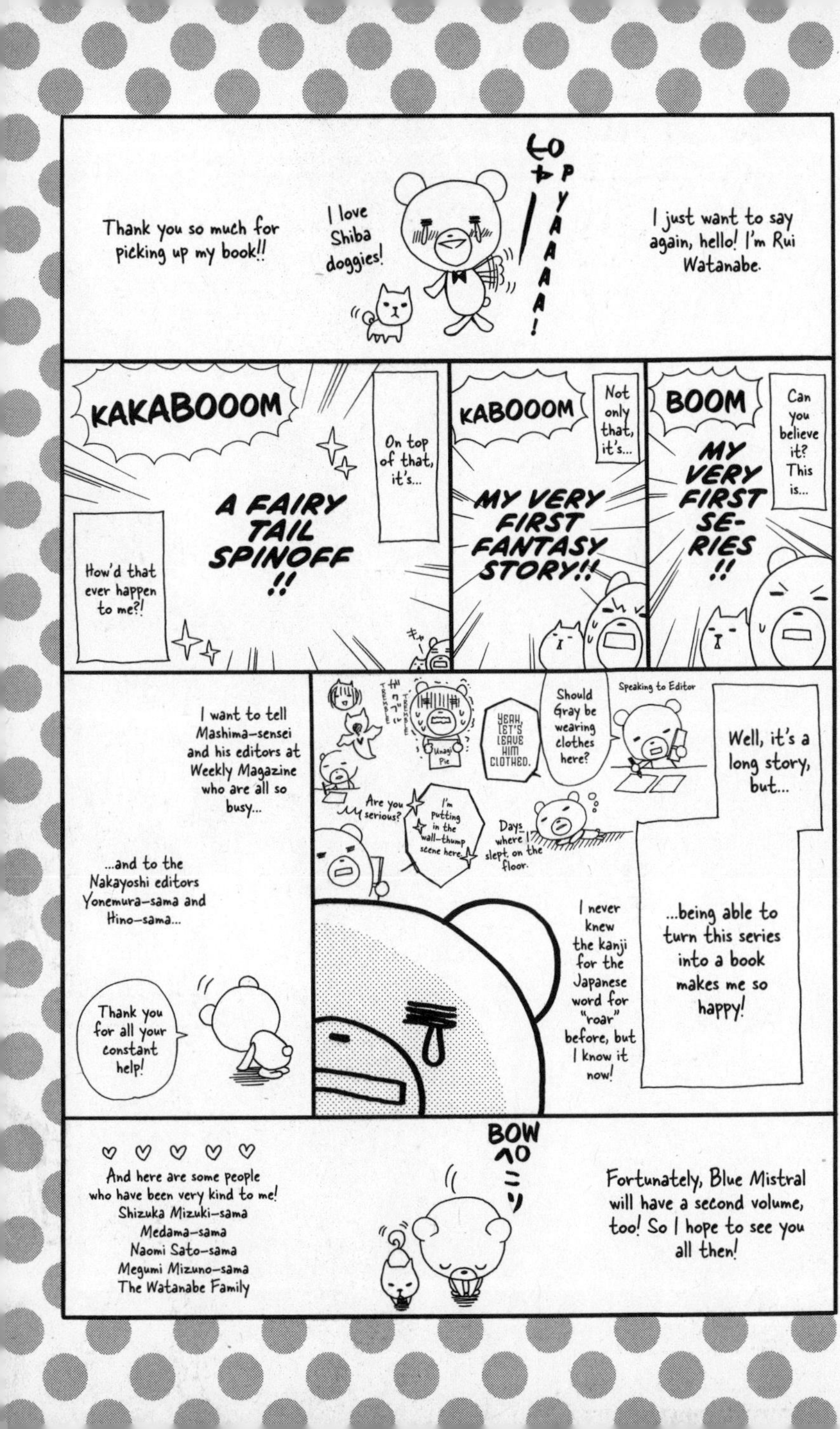

I just want to say again, hello! I'm Rui Watanabe.
PYAAAAA!
I love Shiba doggies!
Thank you so much for picking up my book!!
Can you believe it? This is...
BOOM
MY VERY FIRST SE-RIES!!
Not only that, it's...
KABOOOM
MY VERY FIRST FANTASY STORY!!
On top of that, it's...
KAKABOOOM
A FAIRY TAIL SPINOFF!!
How'd that ever happen to me?!
Well, it's a long story, but...
Speaking to Editor
Should Gray be wearing clothes here?
YEAH, LET'S LEAVE HIM CLOTHED.
TREMBLE
TREMBLE
Unagi Pie
I'm putting in the wall-thump scene here.
Are you serious?
Days where I slept on the floor.
...being able to turn this series into a book makes me so happy!
I never knew the kanji for the Japanese word for "roar" before, but I know it now!
I want to tell Mashima-sensei and his editors at Weekly Magazine who are all so busy...
...and to the Nakayoshi editors Yonemura-sama and Hino-sama...
Thank you for all your constant help!
Fortunately, Blue Mistral will have a second volume, too! So I hope to see you all then!
BOW
And here are some people who have been very kind to me!
Shizuka Mizuki-sama
Medama-sama
Naomi Sato-sama
Megumi Mizuno-sama
The Watanabe Family

PREVIEW OF NEXT VOL.

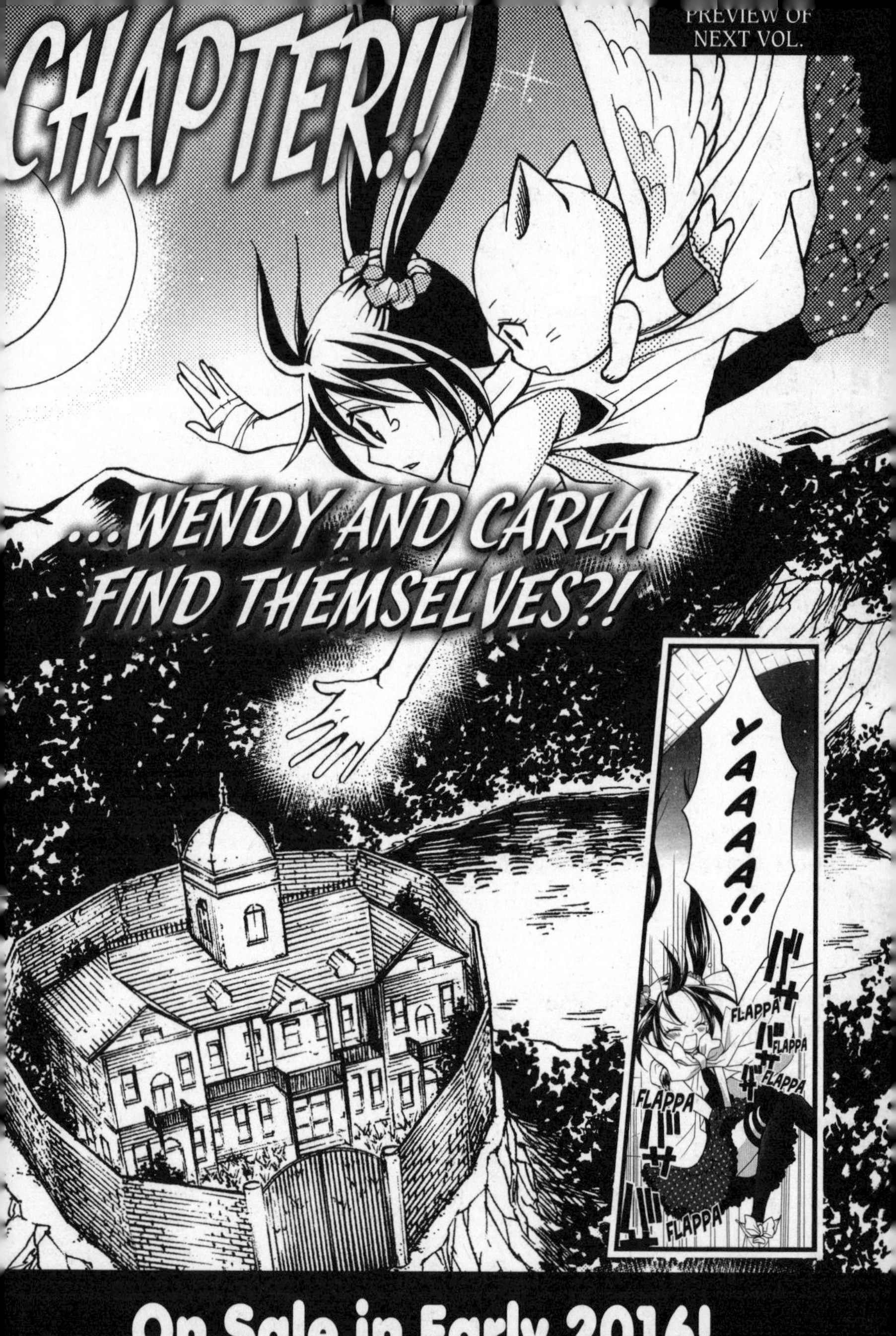
CHAPTER!!
...WENDY AND CARLA FIND THEMSELVES?!
YAAAAA!!
FLAPPA
FLAPPA
FLAPPA
FLAPPA
FLAPPA

On Sale in Early 2016!

PLUNGE INTO A NEW

IN WHAT WORLD DO...

> WHAT IS A MANSION DOING IN THE MIDDLE OF THIS FOREST?!

On the way home to Fairy Tail from Nanalu village, Wendy and Carla get separated from Natsu's group! Lost in the woods, they come across a strange mansion! They say it's a home for cursed beasts, but can that be true...?!

You won't want to turn away from all of Wendy's adventures!

FAIRY TAIL
Blue Mistral 2

HIRO MASHIMA

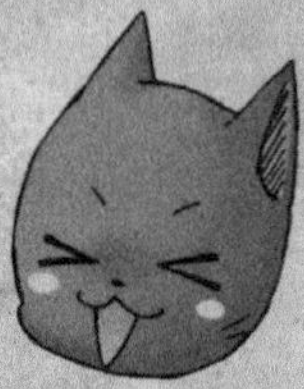

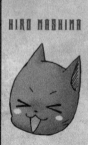

I'm so happy to see Wendy and Carla drawn in such a cute fashion! She has expressions I was hardly ever able to show in the main story, so I'm reading a Wendy even I never knew before, and it's like a breath of fresh air. Also, Yoshino is such a cutie!

RUI WATANABE

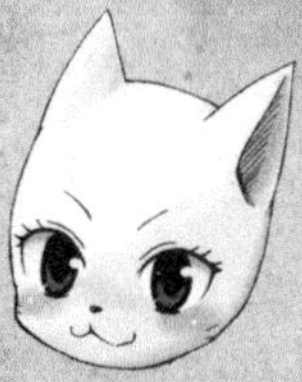

I never dreamed I'd be able to draw a Fairy Tail story! I'm sure if I had told myself this one year ago, I wouldn't have believed it! And every chapter I draw is so much fun! You don't know how happy I am to be a part of a great story such as this!

Original Jacket Design: Hisao Ogawa

Translation Notes:

Japanese is a tricky language for most Westerners, and translation is often more art than science. For your edification and reading pleasure, here are notes on some of the places where we could have gone in a different direction with our translation of the work, or where a Japanese cultural reference is used.

Page 3, Pickled plums

Umeboshi are a pickled fruit that are the most common filling for Japanese rice balls. They are so often called "pickled plums" in English that even this translator thought they were actually plums, but it turns out that *ume* are more closely related to apricots.

Main Characters...

Wendy Marvell

A 12-year-old Dragon Slayer wizard who specializes in a magic that uses air, Sky Magic. When she was very little, she was raised by a dragon. She loves Carla. She hates pickled plums.

Carla

A creature that looks very much like a cat, which was born from an egg that Wendy once found. She loves black tea. She can sprout wings and fly through the sky.

Page 76, Do declare

Well, no, Yoshino didn't say, "do declare" in Japanese, but she did talk a bit out of character in that scene. She had been speaking in a friendly, informal manner to Wendy from their first meeting, but when she gets a bit jealous of Wendy, she suddenly takes on an uncharacteristic, more formal, more distant attitude. I hoped that the uncharacteristic English dialog would draw attention to her attitude change.

Page 82, First bath

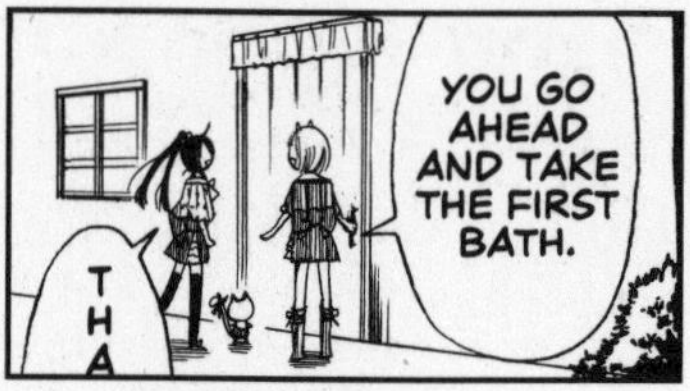
YOU GO AHEAD AND TAKE THE FIRST BATH.
THA

In Japan, most people take their baths at night rather than in the morning (although there is a strong minority who do take a morning shower). In most Japanese houses, they fill the bathtub only once, and only enter to soak in it after they have already washed and rinsed their entire bodies (so the water isn't too dirty before the next person enters). However, in large families, the final bath begins to look a little suspect, so the first bath of the evening is usually a treat reserved for the head of the household or guests. Here, Yoshino is offering Wendy the first bath as a guest.

Page 93, Wall thump

This is a gesture that has been going on for a long time in Japan, but has recently received a name and some Internet recognition. In Japan, it's called *kabe-don. Kabe* means "wall," and *don* is the thumping sound when the hand hits the wall. A *kabe-don* happens when a woman stands with her back to the wall, and the man leans in supporting himself against the wall with one hand. Many people in Japan consider this position romantic.

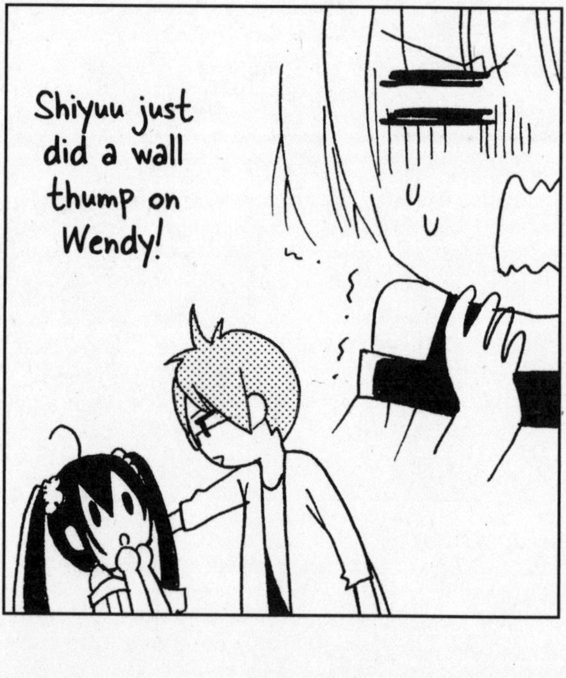
Shiyuu just did a wall thump on Wendy!

Page 157, Unagi Pie

Unagi means "eel," but although eel is pretty delicious over rice, the Japanese don't make pies out of them (that I have ever heard of). Instead, this is a flat wafer of sweetened pie crust that is made by rolling and elongating the dough. What comes out is a flat, cookie-like treat that looks similar to an eel in a sort-of "S" shaped curve. It looks so much like an eel that the snack was named after it. It was very popular some 30 or 40 years ago, when it was thought to give a person a boost of energy late at night.

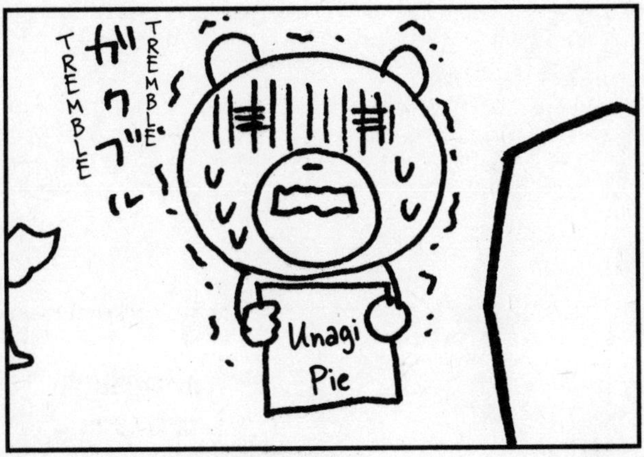
TREMBLE
ガクブル
TREMBLE
Unagi Pie

SHERLOCK BONES

DEDUCTIVE DOG DETECTIVE

When Takeru adopts a new pet, he's in for a surprise—the dog is none other than the reincarnation of Sherlock Holmes. With no one else able to communicate with Holmes, Takeru is roped into becoming Sherdog's assistant, John Watson. Using his sleuthing skills, Holmes uncovers clues to solve the trickiest crimes.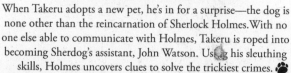

My Little Monster

OPPOSITES ATTRACT...MAYBE?

Haru Yoshida is feared as an unstable and violent "monster." Mizutani Shizuku is a grade-obsessed student with no friends. Fate brings these two together to form the most unlikely pair. Haru firmly believes he's in love with Mizutani and she firmly believes he's insane.

Praise for the anime:

"The show provides a pleasant window on the highs and lows of young love with two young people who are first-timers at the real thing."

-The Fandom Post

"Always it is smarter, more poetic, more touching, just plain better than you think it is going to be."

-Anime News Network

KC KODANSHA COMICS

Mei Tachibana has no friends — and says she doesn't need them!

But everything changes when she accidentally roundhouse kicks the most popular boy in school! However, Yamato Kurosawa isn't angry in the slightest—in fact, he thinks his ordinary life could use an unusual girl like Mei. But winning Mei's trust will be a tough task. How long will she refuse to say, "I love you"?

NO.6

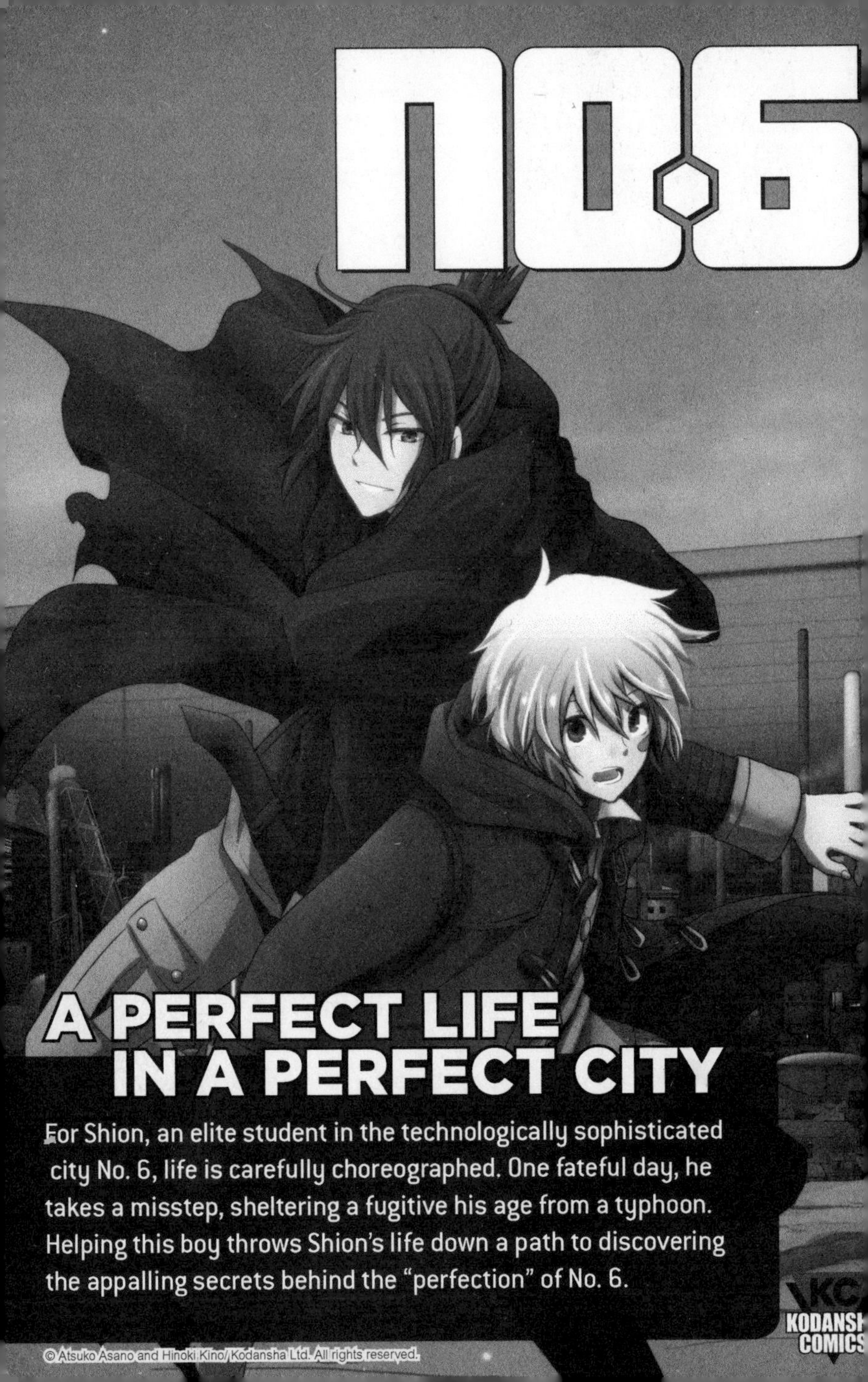

A PERFECT LIFE IN A PERFECT CITY

For Shion, an elite student in the technologically sophisticated city No. 6, life is carefully choreographed. One fateful day, he takes a misstep, sheltering a fugitive his age from a typhoon. Helping this boy throws Shion's life down a path to discovering the appalling secrets behind the "perfection" of No. 6.

KODANSHA COMICS

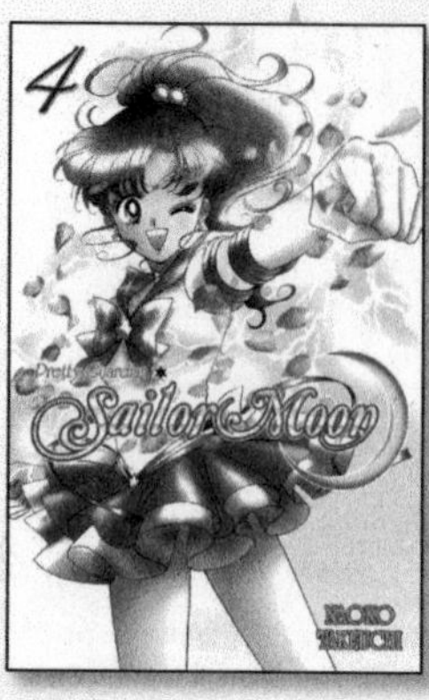
4
Pretty Guardian
Sailor Moon
NAOKO TAKEUCHI

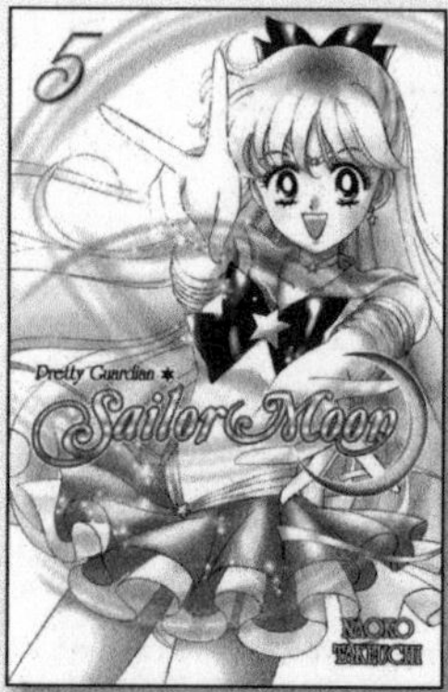
5
Pretty Guardian
Sailor Moon
NAOKO TAKEUCHI

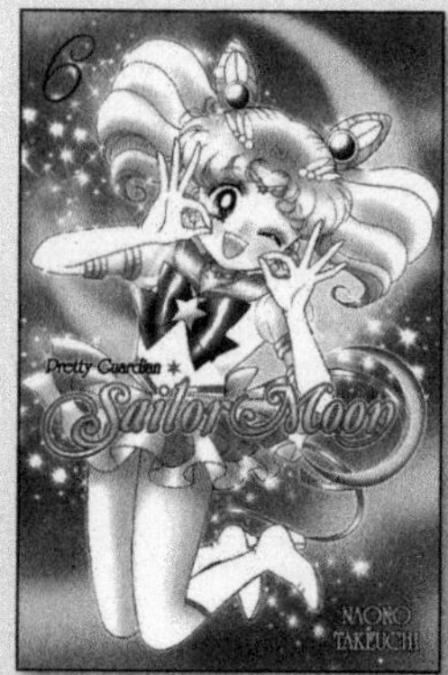
6
Pretty Guardian
Sailor Moon
NAOKO TAKEUCHI

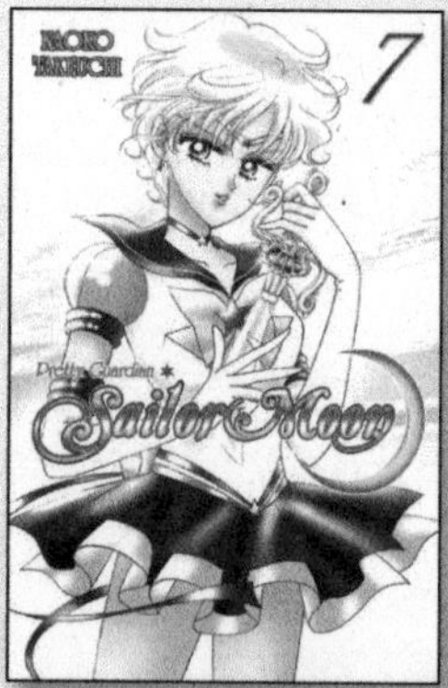
NAOKO TAKEUCHI
7
Pretty Guardian
Sailor Moon

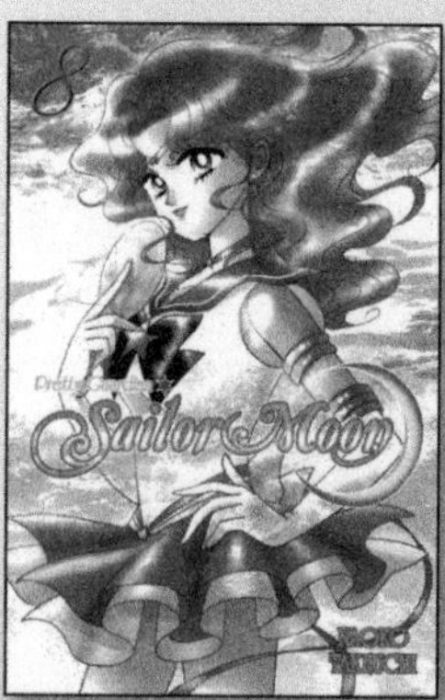
8
Sailor Moon
NAOKO TAKEUCHI

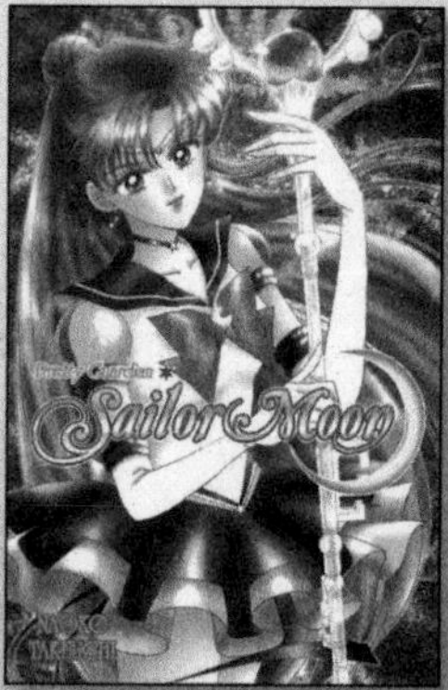
Sailor Moon

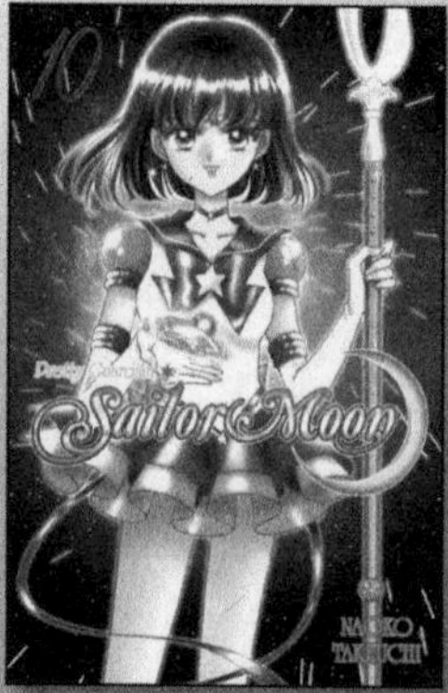
10
Sailor Moon
NAOKO TAKEUCHI

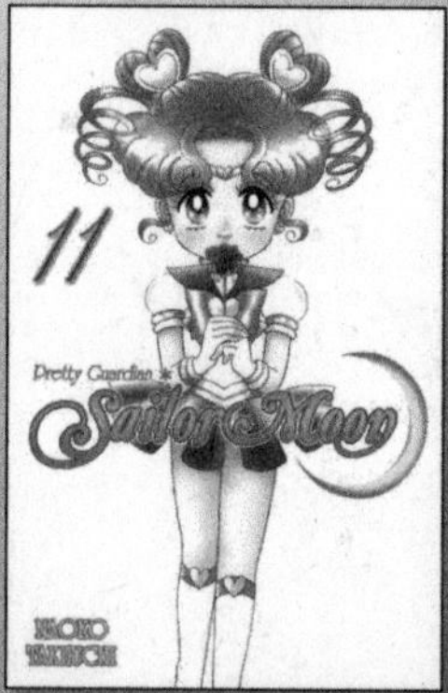
11
Pretty Guardian
Sailor Moon
NAOKO TAKEUCHI

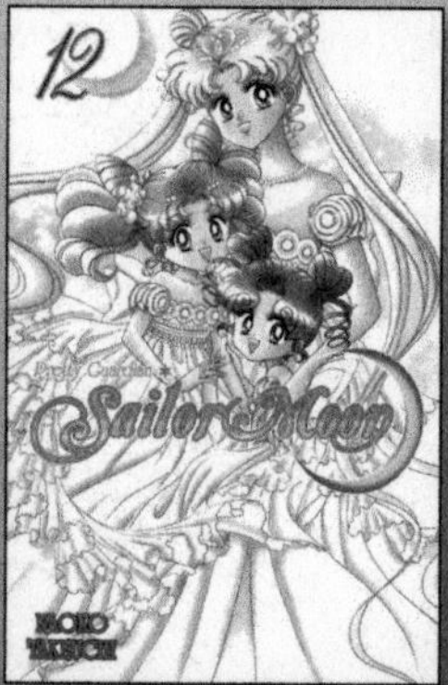
12
Sailor Moon
NAOKO TAKEUCHI

KC
KODANSHA COMICS

The Pretty Guardians are back!

✶

Kodansha Comics is proud to present *Sailor Moon* with all new translations.

For more information, go to **www.kodanshacomics.com**

SANKAREA
undying love

"I ONLY LIKE ZOMBIE GIRLS."

Chihiro has an unusual connection to zombie movies. He doesn't feel bad for the survivors – he wants to comfort the undead girls they slaughter! When his pet passes away, he brews a resurrection potion. He's discovered by local heiress Sanka Rea, and she serves as his first test subject!

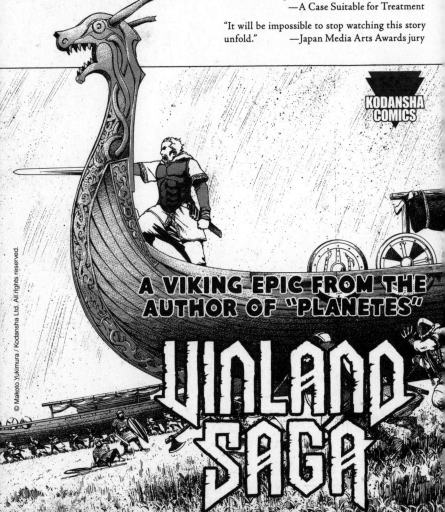

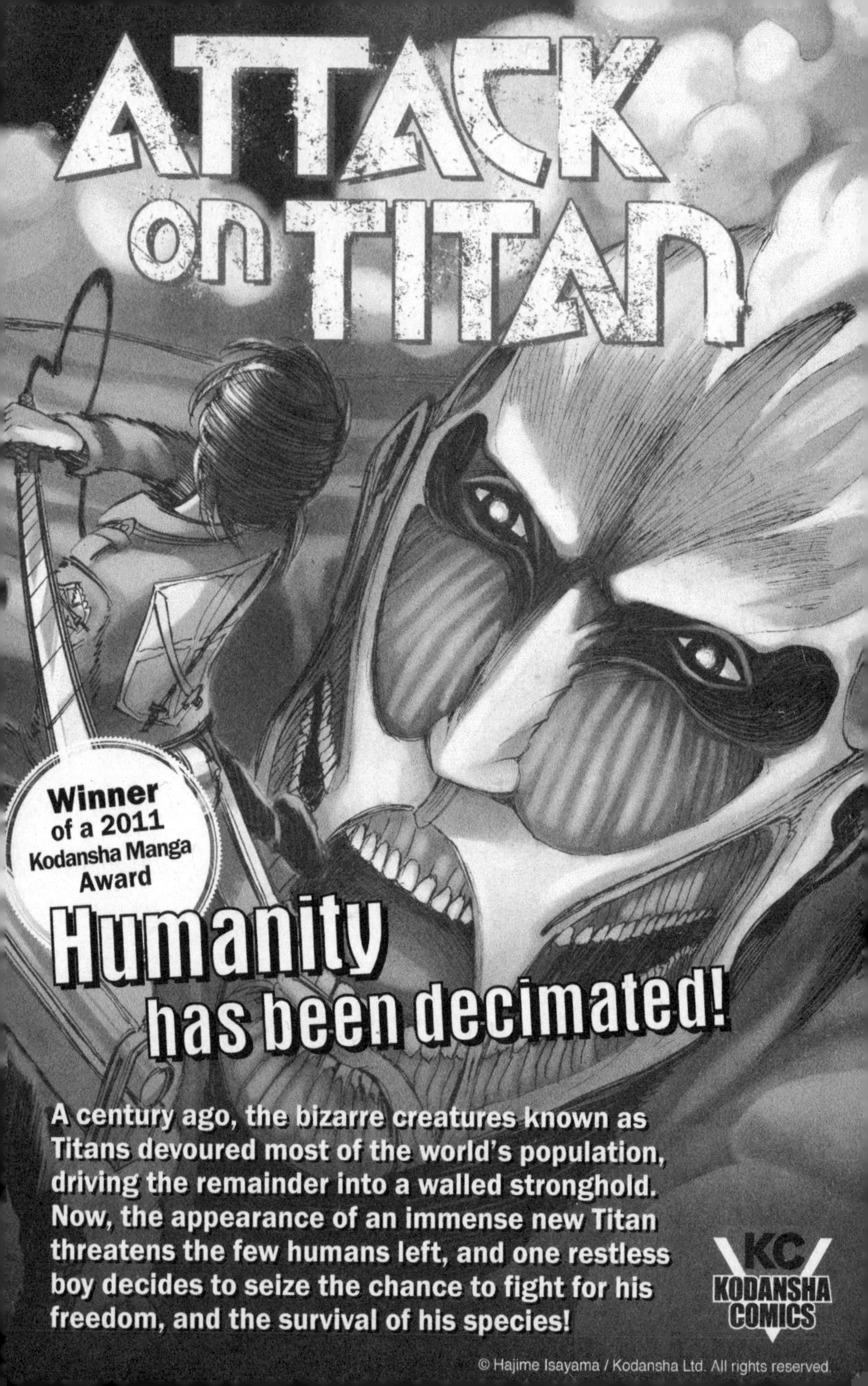
ATTACK on TITAN
Winner of a 2011 Kodansha Manga Award
Humanity has been decimated!
A century ago, the bizarre creatures known as Titans devoured most of the world's population, driving the remainder into a walled stronghold. Now, the appearance of an immense new Titan threatens the few humans left, and one restless boy decides to seize the chance to fight for his freedom, and the survival of his species!
KC KODANSHA COMICS
© Hajime Isayama / Kodansha Ltd. All rights reserved.

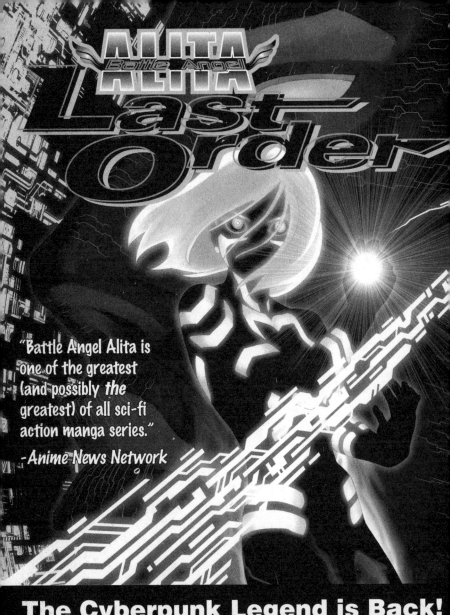

MARDOCK

マルドゥック・スクランブル

SCRAMBLE

**Created by
Tow Ubukata** ✕ **Manga by
Yoshitoki Oima**

"I'd rather be dead."

Rune Balot was a lost girl with
nothing to live for. A man
named Shell took her in and
cared for her...until he tried
to murder her. Standing at
the precipice of death Rune is
saved by Dr. Easter, a private
investigator, who uses an
experimental procedure known
as "Mardock Scramble 09."
The procedure grants Balot
extraordinary abilities. Now,
Rune must decide whether to
use her new powers to help Dr.
Easter bring Shell to justice, or if she even has the will to keep
living a life that's been broken so badly.

Ages: 16+

**KODANSHA
COMICS**

VISIT KODANSHACOMICS.COM TO:

• View release date calendars for upcoming volumes
• Find out the latest about upcoming Kodansha Comics series

A Kodansha Comics Trade Paperback Original.

Fairy Tail Blue Mistral volume 1 copyright © 2015 Hiro Mashima / Rui Watanabe
English translation copyright © 2015 Hiro Mashima / Rui Watanabe

All rights reserved.

Published in the United States by Kodansha Comics, an imprint of Kodansha USA Publishing, LLC, New York.

Publication rights for this English edition arranged through Kodansha Ltd., Tokyo.

First published in Japan in 2015 by Kodansha Ltd., Tokyo
ISBN 978-1-63236-133-2

Printed in the United States of America.

www.kodanshacomics.com

9 8 7 6 5 4 3 2

Translation: William Flanagan
Lettering: AndWorld Design
Editing: Ben Applegate
Kodansha Comics edition cover design by Phil Balsman

TOMARE!

[STOP!]

You're going the wrong way!

Manga is a completely different type of reading experience.

To start at the *beginning,* go to the *end!*

That's right! Authentic manga is read the traditional Japanese way— from right to left, exactly the *opposite* of how American books are read. It's easy to follow: Just go to the other end of the book and read each page—and each panel—from right side to left side, starting at the top right. Now you're experiencing manga as it was meant to be!